Nobel Prize
Winners
in
PHYSICS
1901-1950

A Volume in The Life of Science Library
Number 30

Nobel Prize Winners in PHYSICS

1901-1950

by

Niels H. de V. Heathcote

with a foreword by
Prof. Herbert Dingle

Henry Schuman · New York

Dedicated
To the Memory of
My Father,
The Rev. Herbert Heathcote
(1865-1951)
Who took great interest in
the progress of the work
but did not live to see it
completed.

FOREWORD

THE WORK OF THE NOBEL LAUREATES IN PHYSICS PROVIDES IN A compact form the history of the subject during the last fifty years. That is not to say, of course, that physics advances only by the work of outstanding men. Their achievements would have been impossible without the slow accumulation of data resulting from the labor of physicists, astronomers, mathematicians, chemists and others all over the world, to whom it was not given to see the culmination of their efforts. Every great generalization or discovery is the result of a long course of preparation, and it is also the source of a fresh outburst of activity, so that it stands, as it were, at a focal point to which the past converges and from which the future expands.

This may be illustrated by almost any of the researches described in this volume. The work of Niels Bohr may be cited as an example. The theory of the hydrogen atom which he put forward in 1913 was based on observations of line spectra in the laboratory and in the astronomical observatory, on the mathematical expression for the series of wave-lengths which the spectra revealed, and on Planck's seemingly quite independent theoretical consideration of the distribution of energy in the radiation from a black body. The significance of these researches having been revealed by Bohr, a new field of physical investigation was opened up, and of the succeeding achievements for which the Nobel prize was given a large proportion would have been impossible without the Bohr theory.

A noteworthy feature of the awards is the evidence they give of the fact that physics consists of the investigation (in its own field) of truth in the abstract and not of the satisfaction of material human desires, as some modern philosophers, particularly those of the Marxist school, would have us believe. Very few indeed of the researches described here owed their existence to, or derive their significance from, anything but the attempt to understand the world in which we live. The results obtained, of course, have been applied with overwhelming effect to other human affairs, but that has come later and has added nothing to the esteem in which the work has been held as a contribution to physics. Any philosophy of physics (or, in general, of science) that presupposes physics to be in essence a social product directed towards the better organization of society, is arbitrarily adopting a definition of the word at variance with that sanctioned by history and common usage.

Dr. Heathcote, who has prepared this volume, is excellently fitted to do so. He is himself a qualified physicist, he has made distinguished researches into the history of physics of which his publications give sufficient testimony, and he is an exceptionally competent linguist. He is, by nature and by training, meticulously careful in matters of detail, and the reader may be confident that his account of the many and various researches described here is as accurate as it is humanly possible to make it.

Herbert Dingle

CONTENTS

FIGURES

AUTHOR'S PREFACE

BETWEEN 1901, WHEN RÖNTGEN RECEIVED THE FIRST NOBEL award in physics for his discovery of X rays, and 1950, fifty-three of the world's most distinguished physicists received awards for outstanding discoveries and achievements in physics. The names of some of these are widely known outside scientific circles; those of the majority not at all. It is the purpose of the present volume to introduce each one of them to the general reader, in the order in which the Prizes were awarded, and to describe, as far as possible in non-technical language, the work for which the Prize was given.

Briefly, the plan of the book is this. A short account of the Laureate's life and work is followed by an historical and explanatory introduction to the particular discovery or achievement which gained him the Prize. The actual details of the prize-winning work are given *by the Laureate himself* in extracts from his own published account. In all but a few cases these extracts are taken from the Nobel lecture delivered at the Presentation Ceremony, since these addresses, by reason of their non-technical language, are admirably suited to the purpose. The extracts have been chosen not merely to illustrate certain features of the prize-winning work, but to give as complete a picture of it as possible. Each account concludes with a brief indication of the importance of the work in theory and practice.

Inevitably in a work of this kind great reliance has had to be placed on secondary sources, though original papers have been consulted wherever possible and in all cases where any uncertainty has arisen. Both the biographical sketches and the accounts of the prize-winning work are based in the first instance on the material published in *Les Prix Nobel,* the official reports of the Nobel Foundation. This material has been supplemented in the case of deceased Fellows or Foreign Members of the Royal Society of London by the obituary notices published in the *Proceedings* or in

the later *Obituary Notices;* in the case of others by the obituary
notices and notices of the award published in *Nature*. For the details of Einstein's life I have drawn largely on Philipp Frank's
excellent biography, *Einstein: His Life and Times* (London, 1948);
for those of Dalén's life and work, on the biography by E. Wästberg:
Gustaf Dalén, en stor svensk (Stockholm, 1938); for the general
account of Planck's life and work I have drawn on the obituary
notice by Professor William Wilson published in the *Proceedings*
of the Physical Society of London (December, 1949), though for
the details of both Einstein's and Planck's work I have used their
original papers. Biographical details subsequent to the date of the
award are taken mainly from *Who's Who* and the equivalent publications in America and various European countries; Chamber's
Dictionary of Scientists, by A. V. Howard (London, 1951) has
supplied much up-to-date information. Great help has been obtained throughout from the relevant articles in the *Encyclopaedia
Britannica.*

Of the numerous works consulted in connection with experimental
and theoretical details only those which have been in almost constant use at one stage or another can be mentioned here. Chief among
these are such classics as J. J. Thomson's *Conduction of Electricity
through Gases,* E. Rutherford's *Radioactive Substances and their
Radiations,* O. W. Richardson's *The Emission of Electricity from
Hot Bodies,* W. H. Bragg's *Studies in Radioactivity,* W. H. Bragg
and W. L. Bragg's *X Rays and Crystal Structure,* R. A. Millikan's
Electrons (+ *and* −), J. Perrin's *Les Atomes,* A. Sommerfeld's
Atombau und Spectrallinian; and, for more recent theoretical work,
F. K. Richtmyer and E. H. Kennard's *Introduction to Modern
Physics* (1950), Max Born's *Atomic Physics* (1946), N. Feather's
An Introduction to Nuclear Physics (1948); also, used throughout,
William Wilson's *A Hundred Years of Physics* (1950).

It is with great pleasure that I tender my thanks to the following
publishers, editors and authors for their kindness in giving permission for the inclusion of diagrams or extracts: to the Editors of
the *Physical Review* for permission to quote the extracts from Rabi's
paper given on page 402 and those from Lawrence's paper on page
381; to the proprietors and publishers, Messrs. Taylor and Francis
(London), and the Editors of the *Philosophical Magazine* for per-

mission to quote the extract from Moseley's paper given on page 222; to the Nobel Foundation for permission to use the material published in *Les Prix Nobel* and to quote extracts from the Nobel lectures, subject to the approval of the Laureate concerned; to Messrs. G. Bell & Sons, Ltd., and Sir Lawrence Bragg for permission to include Figs. 12, 13, 14, 15 and 20, taken from *X Rays and Crystal Structure*, by W. H. Bragg and W. L. Bragg; to Messrs. Macmillan & Co., Ltd., and Sir Lawrence Bragg for permission to use Fig. 11, taken from W. H. Bragg's *Studies in Radioactivity;* to Messrs. Edward Arnold & Co. and Dr. Crowther for permission to use Fig. 18, taken from the second edition of J. A. Crowther's *Ions, Electrons, and Ionizing Radiations,* and Figs. 22, 28 and 32, taken from the eighth edition of the same work; to Messrs. Longmans, Green & Co., Ltd. and Professor Tolansky, for permission to include Fig. 46, taken from S. Tolansky's *Introduction to Atomic Physics.*

Formal acknowledgments to the Laureates for permission to include extracts from their Nobel lectures or papers are made at appropriate places in the body of the work, but I should like here to say how warmly I appreciate the kind terms in which that permission was invariably conveyed, and the expressions of interest and good wishes which in so many cases accompanied the permission. I am greatly indebted to Professor Franck, Professor von Laue and Professor Millikan, all of whom gave me helpful information; to Professor Powell, Sir Owen Richardson and Professor Schrödinger, who read the original typescript accounts of their work and made valuable suggestions for their improvement, Professor Schrödinger even going to the trouble to re-write certain sections, for which separate acknowledgments are made in the text; Professor Powell also very kindly provided the frontispiece and its caption; to Professor Hess, for correcting his biographical sketch and for very kindly sending me a copy of his article in the *Fordham University Quarterly;* to Professor Siegbahn, for his great kindness in sending me a copy of the valuable account of the work of the Nobel Laureates in physics which he wrote for the Nobel Foundation publication, *Nobel, The Man and His Prizes* (Stockholm, 1950).

I offer my most grateful thanks to Professor Herbert Dingle, Head of the Department of the History and Philosophy of Science

at University College, London, not only for contributing the Foreword, but also for reading the entire work in typescript and sug-
gesting numerous corrections and amendments; to Professor Leon
Rosenfeld, Professor of Theoretical Physics in the University of
Manchester, for revising and correcting my translation of the
extracts from Heisenberg's Nobel lecture in the light of his special-
ist knowledge of the subject-matter; to Professor E. N. da C.
Andrade, for help in translating an obscure passage in one of the
extracts; to the Royal Society of London, for the loan, at one time
or another, of their entire set of *Les Prix Nobel;* to the Librarians
of the Royal Society for assistance in connection with some of the
biographical sketches; to Mr. Hellmuth Hertz, of the University
of Lund, Sweden, for supplying me with details of his father's
later career and for permission to include the extracts from his
father's Nobel lecture; to my young friend, Mr. Geoffrey N. King,
for the time and care he devoted to the preparation of the forty-six
diagrams; to my wife Caroline for unfailing encouragement, for
reading the proofs, and for help with the translations and in the
preparation of the index.

Finally, I wish to offer my thanks to Mr. Henry Schuman for
showing so much courtesy, patience and understanding in the face
of repeated delays in the completion of the work.

N. H. DE V. H.

University College, London,
May, 1953.

Nobel Prize
Winners
in
PHYSICS
1901-1950

1 9 0 1

WILHELM KONRAD RÖNTGEN
(1845–1923)

"For his discovery of X rays."

BIOGRAPHICAL SKETCH

THE GERMAN PHYSICIST WILHELM KONRAD RÖNTGEN WAS born on March 27, 1845, at Lennep, Prussian Rhine Province. After receiving his early education at Utrecht, Holland, he went to the Polytechnic School at Zurich, Switzerland, where he obtained his doctor's degree in 1869. At this time the professor of physics at the Zurich Polytechnic was August Kundt, German physicist famous for his work on sound. Röntgen became his assistant. When, shortly afterward, Kundt was appointed to the chair of physics at Würzburg, Bavaria, Röntgen followed him there, again as his assistant. In 1872 Kundt was appointed professor of physics at the newly founded University of Strasbourg, and here, in 1874, Röntgen received the appointment of *privatdozent,* an unsalaried lecturer who receives fees from his students. The following year he was made professor of mathematics and physics at the Agricultural Academy of Hohenheim, the most important agricultural college in Germany. In 1876, however, he exchanged this post for one at Strasbourg, this time as professor *extraordinary,* that is, not full, his old friend Kundt still holding the *ordinary* professorship there. In 1879 Röntgen himself received an ordinary professorship in physics, at Giessen University, where he became also director of the Physical Institute. Here he remained until 1885, when he left to take up a similar appointment at Würzburg. In 1900 he became professor of physics at Munich, where he continued until his death on February 10, 1923.

Röntgen's work covered almost every branch of physics. Among his earlier investigations were a determination of the ratio of the specific heats of a gas (1870; 1873); the absorption of infrared rays by moist air (1884); a number of researches on fluids, such as the influence of pressure on viscosity (1884), the compressibility of solutions (1886), capillarity, elasticity, and the influence of pressure on the refractive indices of various liquids. Researches in electricity dealt with pyroelectricity (a phenomenon whereby certain crystals exhibit electric charges when heated or cooled), piezo-electricity (a phenomenon whereby crystals possessing pyroelectric properties exhibit electric charges when subjected to tension or compression, discovered in 1881 by the brothers J. and P. Curie), the optical and electric properties of quartz, and the magnetic rotation of the plane of polarization of light. His most important discovery was that made in 1895, while he was at Würzburg— Röntgen rays, or, as he himself named them, X rays.

DESCRIPTION OF THE PRIZE-WINNING WORK

Röntgen discovered X rays while investigating the passage of electricity through a high vacuum. Since the discharge of electricity through gases at low pressures enters into the work of several of the Nobel prize-winners in physics, it will be well to describe briefly what happens in a discharge tube as the pressure is gradually decreased. If the tube contains air at atmospheric pressure and the terminals are not too far apart, the discharge will take the form of a spark as in the open air; if the air is at reduced pressure, the distance between the terminals may be increased and a spark will still pass. On further decrease of pressure the spark becomes a series of parallel streamers reaching from one terminal to the other. At a still lower pressure these streamers are replaced by a pinkish column, the "positive column," extending from the positive terminal, or anode, nearly the whole length of the tube, but separated from the negative terminal, or cathode, by a dark space first observed by

Faraday; the negative terminal is surrounded by a bluish glow, the "negative glow." This occurs at a pressure of about $1\frac{1}{2}$ cm. of mercury. When the pressure is reduced to about 1 mm. of mercury, the positive column shrinks toward the anode, at the same time breaking up into disklike striations, while the Faraday dark space moves further down the tube toward the anode; the negative glow detaches itself from the cathode, leaving only a film adhering to the cathode; between these two portions of the negative glow there appears a second dark space—named after Sir William Crookes, who investigated the discharge of electricity through very high vacua in the 1870's. As the pressure is still further reduced the Crookes dark space expands until ultimately it fills the whole tube and all luminosity disappears. At the same time the walls of the tube begin to fluoresce. The pressure is then about 0.01 mm. of mercury. The fluorescence increases with further reduction of pressure.

It was this fluorescence that Röntgen was studying when, quite by accident, he made his great discovery. A paper screen coated with barium platinocyanide was lying near the discharge tube. To Röntgen's surprise the platinocyanide began to fluoresce when the tube was operated. The following passages, translated from the German, are taken from the paper of December 1895 in which Röntgen communicated the results of his subsequent investigations to the Physico-medical Society at Würzburg:

ON A NEW KIND OF RAYS

"1. If the discharge from a fairly large Ruhmkorff coil is passed through a sufficiently exhausted vacuum tube such as a Hittorf tube or a Lenard's or a Crookes's, the tube being covered with closely fitting thin black cardboard, then in a completely darkened room a screen coated with barium platinocyanide is seen, when brought near the apparatus, to . . . fluoresce at each discharge, . . . whether the coated side or the other side is turned toward the discharge tube. The fluorescence is still noticeable at . . . two meters from the apparatus.

"It is easy to show that the cause of the fluorescence lies in the discharge apparatus and in no other part of the circuit.

"2. The most striking thing about this phenomenon is that some agent, able to excite a lively fluorescence, passes through a black cardboard cover which is completely opaque to the visible and ultraviolet rays of the sun or of the electric arc. The first point to investigate therefore is whether other bodies also possess this property.

"We soon find that all bodies are transparent to this agent, but to very different degrees. . . . Paper is very transparent: I still saw the fluorescence clearly behind a bound book consisting of about a thousand pages. . . . The fluorescence was also visible behind a double pack of playing cards, a single card held between the tube and the screen being almost invisible to the eye. Similarly, a single sheet of tinfoil is hardly visible, and it is only after several layers have been placed one on another that their shadow can be clearly seen on the screen. Thick blocks of wood are also transparent; pine boards 2 or 3 cm. thick absorb but very little. A strip of aluminum about 15 mm. thick weakened the effect quite considerably, but was not able to do away with the fluorescence altogether. A piece of vulcanite several centimeters thick still let the rays through; for the sake of brevity I shall use the term 'rays,' and sometimes, to distinguish them from other rays, the term 'X rays.' Glass plates of equal thickness behave quite differently according as they contain lead or not; the former are much less transparent than the latter. If the hand is held between the discharge tube and the screen, the darker shadow of the bones is seen surrounded by the faint shadow of the hand itself. . . . A rectangular piece of wood of square cross section (20 by 20 mm.), one side of which has been painted with white lead paint, behaves quite differently according to the way it is held between the tube and the screen: when the X rays pass through parallel to the painted side there is practically no effect, but when the rays have to pass through the paint the block throws a dark shadow. The salts of metals, solid or in solution, can be arranged in a similar series to the metals themselves with regard to their transparency.

· · · · ·

"10. . . . Lenard, in the beautiful experiments in which he passed Hittorf's cathode rays through a thin aluminum sheet, came to the conclusion that these rays are processes in the ether, and that

they are scattered and diffused by all bodies. We can say the same
thing of our rays.

. . . . .

"11. Another very noticeable difference in the behavior of the
cathode rays and X rays lies in the fact that, in spite of many attempts, I have not succeeded in obtaining any deflection of the X rays
by means of a magnet, even in the case of very strong magnetic fields.

"Up to the present it has, however, been a characteristic feature of
the cathode rays that they are deflected in a magnetic field. It is true
that Hertz and Lenard found that . . . cathode rays . . . 'differed from one another in their power of exciting phosphorescence,
in their absorbability, and in the degree to which they are deflected
by a magnet,' but a considerable deflection was observed in all cases
examined by them. . . .

"12. Experiments . . . make it certain that the X rays . . . [origi-
nate] at that point in the wall of the discharge tube which fluoresces
most strongly, and that they then spread out in all directions; that
they originate therefore at the spot where . . . the cathode rays
strike the glass wall. If the cathode rays are deflected inside the discharge tube by means of a magnet, . . . the X rays now start from
. . . where the cathode rays strike the wall. . . .

"For this reason, too, the X rays, which it is impossible to deflect,
cannot be cathode rays simply transmitted or reflected by the glass
wall without change. The greater density of the gas outside the tube
cannot, according to Lenard, account for the great difference in the
deflection.

"I have therefore come to the conclusion that X rays are not identical with cathode rays, but that they are excited by the cathode rays
at the glass wall of the discharge tube.

. . . . .

"14. The justification for applying the name 'rays' to the agent
proceeding from the walls of the discharge tube I derive in part
from the quite regular shadows seen when more or less transparent
bodies are placed between the tube and the fluorescent screen (or
photographic plate)."

At the time of making his announcement Röntgen was still investigating the properties of X rays. He had already found that the rays affected a photographic plate, and used this property to check the observations made with the fluorescent screen. In March 1896 he described his investigations into another important property of the rays, namely, that X rays can discharge electrified bodies. He traced this effect to air which had been exposed to the action of the rays; this he did by shielding a charged body in a tube from the direct effect of the rays, finding that an electroscope connected to the body showed no loss of charge as long as the air in the tube remained at rest; when, however, air which had been exposed to X rays was drawn past the body, the electroscope showed an immediate loss of charge. Röntgen was unable to arrive at any conclusion as to the mechanism by which the air acquired this property beyond the fact that the X rays were in some way responsible.

CONSEQUENCES IN THEORY AND PRACTICE

To him then, in addition to the actual discovery of the rays, are due the three standard methods of investigation in use at the present day: the fluorescent screen, the photographic plate, and one which was later to develop into the ionization chamber method.

The possibilities of the rays for medical diagnosis were immediately recognized, Röntgen himself being the first to photograph the bones in the human body; their use in the treatment of certain diseases was to come later. For physics, the discovery opened up an entirely new field of research and led to other discoveries of a most fundamental nature. It is singularly fitting that the first Nobel award in physics should have gone to the man whose discovery has played so important a part in the development of modern physics—how important will be appreciated from the number of Nobel laureates in physics whose work hinged on Röntgen's initial discovery.

1 9 0 2

HENDRIK ANTOON LORENTZ
(1853–1928)

PIETER ZEEMAN
(1865–1943)

"For their investigations concerning the influence of magnetism upon the phenomena of radiation."

BIOGRAPHICAL SKETCHES

LORENTZ

HENDRIK ANTOON LORENTZ WAS BORN ON JULY 18, 1853, AT Arnhem, Holland. He attended a primary school in Arnhem, and the newly established high school there. At seventeen he entered Leiden University, where he studied theoretical physics. Two years later he returned to Arnhem as a teacher in a public evening school. He continued his studies and in 1875 received his doctor's degree from Leiden University. His thesis dealt with the theory of the reflection and refraction of light and was of such outstanding merit that in 1878, at the early age of twenty-five, he was appointed professor of theoretical physics at Leiden, a post which he held until 1923. In 1912 he became director of the Teyler Laboratory at Haarlem, still, however, retaining the professorship at Leiden. He died at Haarlem on February 4, 1928.

Lorentz' achievements received wide recognition. The Royal Society of London elected him a Foreign Member in 1905 and awarded him the Rumford Medal in 1908, the Copley Medal in 1918. Many universities conferred honorary degrees on him. In 1900 the twenty-fifth anniversary of his doctorate was celebrated in Leiden, in the presence of leading scientists from many countries. In 1926 the fiftieth anniversary of the same event was commemorated by the creation of a Lorentz Foundation for the promotion of theoretical physics and of international intercourse among young physicists.

Equally fluent in Dutch, English, French, and German, Lorentz, in his later years, frequently visited foreign countries to deliver addresses and attend international scientific gatherings.

In addition to his scientific work, Lorentz had two great interests: the national project for draining the Zuider Zee, and the fostering of international scientific relations, especially, after the First World War, between its belligerents.

ZEEMAN

PIETER ZEEMAN was born on May 25, 1865, at Zonnemaire, Netherlands. After receiving a high-school education, he entered Leiden University in 1885. Here he studied physics under Kamerlingh Onnes (*q.v.* 1913), professor of experimental physics, and H. A. Lorentz, professor of theoretical physics. In 1890 he was appointed assistant in the physics department, one of his duties being to prepare the lecture experiments normally given by the professor of experimental physics; Kamerlingh Onnes, however, being occupied with his low-temperature researches, left much of this work to the professor of theoretical physics, with the result that Zeeman became largely Lorentz' assistant, and his interest, like Lorentz' own, turned to the problems of light. When, in 1893, he obtained his doctor's degree, it was for a thesis dealing with the reflection of light by the polished pole of a magnet, a shortened form of an essay which had already won him a prize offered by the Haarlem Academy of Science. In 1893 he worked for a term under E. Cohn at Strasbourg. On his return to Holland he was appointed *privatdozent* at Leiden University. On January 1, 1897, he was appointed lecturer in physics at Amsterdam University, becoming professor of physics there in 1900, a post which he held until his retirement in 1935. He died on October 9, 1943.

Zeeman was elected a Foreign Member of the Royal Society of London in 1921 and received the Rumford Medal in 1922. His own country created him Knight of the Order of the Netherlands Lion and Commander of the Order of Orange-Nassau.

DESCRIPTION OF THE PRIZE-WINNING WORK

The greater part of Lorentz' work dealt with light and the problems to which it gives rise. In 1880 he published the results of investigations into the change produced in the refractive index when the density of the refracting substance alters as a result of change in pressure or temperature. The same formula was published almost simultaneously by L. Lorenz of Copenhagen, so that this formula has become known as the "Lorentz-Lorenz formula"; it agrees well with experimental results, even when a change of state from liquid to gas is involved, so that it is possible to predict with fair accuracy the refractive index of a substance in the gaseous state when that of the liquid state is known. Lorentz deduced his formula from the electromagnetic theory of light, and it was through the development of this theory that he rendered his greatest service to science.

Newton's corpuscular theory of light gave way, in the early years of the nineteenth century, to the wave theory, according to which light consists of transverse waves in the ether. James Clerk Maxwell built up, between the years 1855 and 1864, an elaborate and highly mathematical structure known as the electromagnetic theory of light, in which the electric and magnetic properties of the medium, the ether, play a fundamental part; Maxwell's theory received strong support when, in 1887, Heinrich Hertz produced and detected invisible electric waves in space and showed that they possessed many of the properties of visible light. However, Maxwell's theory failed in several important respects, one of which concerned the mechanism of reflection and refraction; this was dealt with by Lorentz in his doctoral thesis. Another matter which found no place in Maxwell's theory was the process of electrolysis, in which solutions of certain substances show evidence, under the action of an electric current, of consisting of particles known as "ions" which carry quantities of electricity, all multiples of a certain minute minimum quantity. What

Lorentz did was to take Maxwell's equations and, while in the main preserving their external form, so to modify their content that the imperfections in Maxwell's theory were removed.

The essential element in Lorentz' theory which distinguished it from Maxwell's lay in attributing to electricity the property of atomicity: electricity itself consists of minute entities, or *electrons,* as they soon came to be called, the word "electron" having been introduced by G. Johnstone Stoney in 1891 to denote the charge on a hydrogen ion; an electric current is simply the flow of these electrons along the conductor. An even more important part of the theory lay in making these electrons the basis of an electrical theory of matter, the emission of light by a luminous body being due to vibrations of electrons within the atoms.

If, as Lorentz supposed, the emission of light is due to the vibrations of charged particles, then, since the movement of a charged body is always accompanied by a magnetic field, these vibrations should be modified when the source of light is placed in a strong magnetic field, the external magnetic field either reinforcing or weakening that due to the vibrating particle and so either increasing or decreasing the frequency of the vibration. It was Lorentz' pupil Zeeman who succeeded in demonstrating this effect in the laboratory, while he was *privatdozent* at Leiden. The discovery of what he called the "magnetic splitting of the spectral lines" was communicated by Zeeman to the Academy of Science at Amsterdam on October 31, 1896. We cannot give a better account of Zeeman's work than that given by Lorentz in his Nobel lecture of December 11, 1902. Speaking in German, Lorentz said:

"As is well known to you, Faraday made the discovery that magnetic forces can influence the propagation of light: he showed that under suitable conditions the vibrations of a polarized ray of light are rotated by such forces. Many years later Kerr found that such a ray of light also undergoes similar changes when it is simply reflected from the polished pole of a magnet. It was, however, reserved for Zeeman's skill to show that a magnetic field influences not only the propagation and reflection, but also the events occurring at the origin of the ray of light, i.e., that the rays emitted by a source of light acquire other qualities when this source is placed in the space between magnetic north and south poles. The change shows itself in the splitting up of the spectral lines, and is best seen when we use light sources whose spectrum consists of single bright lines, namely, a colored flame, an electric spark, or a Geissler tube. Imagine, for the sake of illustration, that my hands are the two poles, only much closer together than I am at present holding them, and that the light source is between these poles in the space directly in front of me. When the spectrum of the light proceeding toward a point directly in front of me is examined, instead of the single line seen under ordinary circumstances, a threefold line or triplet is seen whose components lie very close together. Since to each place in the spectrum there corresponds a definite frequency of the light, we can say that the source is now sending out rays of three distinct frequencies under the influence of the magnetic field, instead of rays of a single frequency. If the spectrum consists of more than one line, each of them will be split up into a triplet. . . . some spectral lines break up into more than three components."

Lorentz goes on to give an account of his own theory:

"The theory of which I have to give an account presents the material world as composed of three distinct entities . . . (1) ordinary tangible or ponderable matter, (2) electrons, (3) the ether. . . .

. . . . .

"We return now to the propagation of light in ponderable bodies. We concluded that the vibrating particles must be electrically charged; the name 'electron' . . . is therefore apt. It was possible to investigate, with the help of the well-known electromagnetic laws, the exact manner in which the vibrations occurred and what effect they had on the events in the ether. The result consisted of formulas for the velocity of propagation and the refractive index as depending (1) on the frequency (i.e., on the color of the light) and (2) on the nature and number of the electrons.

"You won't mind if I do not quote the rather complicated equations and only say something of their meaning. First, as regards the dependence of the refractive index on the frequency, and so on the color dispersion: The prismatic spectrum and the rainbow afford us evidence that to the electrons in glass and water there belongs a definite mass, as a result of which they do not respond to the vibrations of light of different colors equally readily. Secondly, by taking into account the influence of the larger or smaller number of electrons in a definite space, we obtain an equation which makes it possible to specify approximately the change in the refractive index due to an increase or decrease in the density of the body. . . .

.   .   .   .   .

"At the time that Professor Zeeman made his discovery, the electron theory was, in its essentials, in a position to explain the new phenomenon. Anyone who has once peopled the whole world with electrons and lets them vibrate in harmony with the incident light will not balk at making them, in their backward and forward motion within the particles of the luminous body, the cause of the emission of light. A vibrating electron forms, as it were, a minute Hertzian oscillator; it acts on the surrounding ether in much the same way that the up-and-down motion of the hand produces the familiar waves in a cord fixed at the other end. As to the force causing the changes in vibration as a result of the magnetic field, this is no other than the force whose existence was first noted by Oersted when he discovered the effect of a current on a magnetic needle.

"The explanation of the triplets I shall leave to Professor Zeeman, contenting myself with the remark that it is the negative electrons that oscillate backward and forward, and that it is possible to deduce the ratio between the numerical values of the charge and mass of these particles from the separation of the components into which the spectral lines are split. The result is in pleasing agreement with that found in other fields of research. Equal or comparable values for this same ratio have been obtained for the negative particles constituting the cathode rays."

The following extracts are taken from Zeeman's Nobel lecture, which he delivered in May 1903, having been prevented by illness from attending the presentation ceremony held the previous December. Speaking in German, he said:

"[In] analyzing the light from a luminous gas into its finer details, the simple glass prisms of Newton and Fraunhofer fail us and

the physicist has recourse to . . . [a] Rowland concave grating,
. . . [a] polished metal mirror on which a very large number of
grooves, say 50,000 in a width of 10 cm., have been engraved. . . .
A compound bundle of light rays is no longer reflected in the ordinary manner from the ruled surface, but each individual kind of
light goes its own way.

. . . . .

"When we examine the familiar sodium flame with a Rowland
grating we see a spectrum which consists principally of two separate
sharp yellow lines, . . . about 1 mm. from each other. We conclude that the sodium radiation consists of two kinds of light, whose
periods differ by an extremely small amount (1/1000). We focus
our attention exclusively on one of these lines.

"[At] the Physical Institute of the University of Leiden [in]
August 1896 I was exposing a sodium flame to strong magnetic
forces and for this purpose placed it between the poles of a powerful
electromagnet. The radiation from the flame was examined with the
Rowland grating, being viewed in a direction at right angles to the
lines of force; each of the lines, which without the influence of
the magnetic field appeared quite sharp, was seen to have broadened.
This showed that the flame was emitting not only the original vibrations, but also others with somewhat greater periods and still others
with somewhat smaller. The change was exceedingly small, amount-
ing, in an easily produced magnetic field, to the thirtieth part of the
distance between the two sodium lines.

. . . . .

"Doubting our result, we examined the light source in the direction of the magnetic force, for this purpose drilling holes in the pole
pieces of the magnet; . . . in this direction too our result was confirmed. We also examined the inverse phenomenon, the absorption
of light by sodium vapor. The following questions suggested themselves. Do different substances behave differently? What happens
when the magnetic force is increased to the maximum value obtainable? How do the different spectral lines of the same substance behave? Before ever these questions were answered, theory stepped in.
I had in fact succeeded in providing experimental proof of conse-

quences which followed from the theory of optical and electrical phenomena put forward by . . . Lorentz.

"According to this theory there are present in all bodies small electrically charged particles, *electrons,* and all electrical and optical phenomena depend on the number and motion of these electrons; it is their oscillations that produce waves of light. If we restrict ourselves, on Lorentz' theory, to a single spectral line, it is sufficient to assume that each atom (or molecule) contains a single moving electron.

"If such an electron is disturbed from its equilibrium position, a force proportional to the displacement brings it back to its position of rest. . . . All the oscillatory motions of such an electron can be resolved into rectilinear vibrations in the direction of the magnetic lines of force, together with two circular periodic motions in opposite directions in a plane at right angles to the magnetic field. In the absence of the magnetic field, the period of all these vibrations is the same; but as soon as the electron is exposed to the action of a magnetic field its motion undergoes a change. According to the well-known laws of electrodynamics, an electron moving in a magnetic field is acted upon by a force at right angles both to the direction of motion of the electron and also to the direction of the field, the magnitude of the force being easily determined. The rectilinear motion suffers no change as a result of the magnetic field, the period remaining the same; the two circular motions, however, are subjected to new forces which, acting parallel to the radius, are either added to or subtracted from the original central force. In the former case the period is diminished, in the latter increased.

"It is now easy to specify what effect electrons moving in this way must have on the light.

"We consider first what happens in a direction at right angles to the lines of force. To the three electron movements there correspond three electrical oscillations, that is, according to the electromagnetic theory of light, three light vibrations of different periods. The source will therefore now emit light of *three* colors instead of the original light of *one* color. Hence three separate lines are observed in place of the one unpolarized line when the source is placed in a magnetic field."

CONSEQUENCES IN THEORY AND PRACTICE

Lorentz' electron theory has exerted a profound influence on the subsequent development of theoretical physics. The imposing structure which Maxwell built on the foundations laid by Faraday received its finishing touches at the hands of Lorentz. At the same time Lorentz stands on the border line between the "classical" and the "new" physics: it is his theory which, in its essentials, has dominated physical thought throughout the period of growing insight into the innermost workings of nature. Zeeman's discovery provided the first direct evidence in its support; later discoveries have but added further support. On the theoretical side modifications have proved necessary, but the formula derived by Lorentz remains intact.

1 9 0 3

ANTOINE HENRI BECQUEREL
(1852–1908)

"For the discovery of spontaneous radioactivity."

PIERRE CURIE
(1859–1906)

MARIE SKLODOWSKA CURIE
(1867–1934)

"For their work on the radiation phenomena discovered by Becquerel."

BIOGRAPHICAL SKETCH

A. H. BECQUEREL

ANTOINE HENRI BECQUEREL WAS BORN IN PARIS ON DECEMBER 15, 1852. His grandfather, Antoine César Becquerel (1788-1878), who did valuable work in electrical science, chiefly electrochemistry, was professor of physics at the Muséum d'Histoire Naturelle, Paris. His father, Edmond Becquerel (1820-1891), was in turn pupil, assistant, and successor to his own father at the Muséum, later becoming professor of applied physics at the Conservatoire des Arts

18

et Métiers, Paris; his researches dealt mainly with light, particularly the phosphorescence shown by sulphides and by compounds of uranium. Henri Becquerel entered the École Polytechnique, Paris, in 1872; in 1874 he went to the École des Pontes-et-Chaussées, where he was graduated as *ingénieur* in 1877, being promoted to *ingénieur de première classe* in 1885 and *ingénieur en chef* in 1894. In 1888 he received the degree of D-ès-Sc. In 1878 he became assistant at the Muséum, where, in 1892, he was appointed to the chair of applied physics. In 1895 he was also appointed professor of physics at the École Polytechnique, where he had actually been a lecturer since 1876. In addition to these duties he deputized for his father in the chair of applied physics at the Conservatoire des Arts et Métiers. He died at Le Croisic in Brittany on August 25, 1908.

Henri Becquerel was a member of numerous scientific societies, including the Royal Society of London, the Berlin Academy and the French Academy of Sciences. He was made an Officer of the Legion of Honor in 1900.

DESCRIPTION OF THE PRIZE-WINNING WORK

Becquerel's work dealt mainly with optics. His doctoral dissertation was on the absorption of light, but he had previously published papers on the rotation of the plane of polarization by a magnetic field (in ordinary light the vibrations take place in continually changing directions; when the vibrations are confined to one plane, that is, always in the same direction, the light is said to be *polarized*). Faraday had discovered this effect in 1845 and had observed it in solids and liquids, but not in gases; Becquerel showed that a gas also possesses this so-called magnetogyric power. He also investigated phosphorescence, the property possessed by certain substances of emitting light in the dark for some time after they have been exposed to light. Becquerel invented an ingenious phosphoroscope, by means of which the duration of the effect after the direct light has been cut off can be measured. He made use of the phenomenon of phosphorescence to investigate infrared spectra, and discovered the infrared emission spectra of incandescent metallic vapors.

All this work was, however, overshadowed by the discovery, made in 1896, of the rays emitted by uranium, a phenomenon to which he gave the name radioactivity. This discovery arose, in part at least, from his interest in phosphorescence. The X rays discovered by Röntgen the previous year have the property of exciting fluorescence in suitably prepared screens, fluorescence being similar to phosphorescence except that it does not persist after the source of light has been removed. Becquerel examined various fluorescent and phosphorescent substances, wrapped in black paper and placed beneath a photographic plate, to see whether they might give rise to radiation similar to that discovered by Röntgen, but without effect. Some time previously he had examined the phosphorescent effect of salts of uranium, certain of which give a phosphorescent light lasting a small fraction of a second when exposed to ultraviolet light in the phosphoroscope. When a crystal of one of these salts, wrapped in black paper, was placed beneath a photographic plate and left for several hours, a distinct photographic effect was found on developing the plate. At first it was thought that the effect was due to phosphorescence, but Becquerel showed that this was not the case: he prepared the crystals direct from solution without their being exposed to light, and obtained the same result. Further, he showed that it was immaterial whether a phosphorescent or a nonphosphorescent salt was used: this penetrating type of radiation was emitted by all salts of uranium and by the metal itself, so that it seemed to be a specific property of uranium. Becquerel also showed that the rays from uranium, like Röntgen rays, possessed the property of discharging an electrified body: when an electroscope was exposed to the radiation, the leaves collapsed rapidly.

Becquerel announced his discovery to the Academy of Sciences at Paris on February 24, 1896. In his Nobel lecture, given at Stockholm on December 11, 1903, he gave an account of his own work and traced the subsequent development of radioactivity up to that date. The following extract is from that lecture, which was delivered in French.

"At the beginning of 1896, on the very day that we learned in Paris of Röntgen's experiment and of the extraordinary properties of the rays emitted by the phosphorescent wall of a Crookes' tube, it occurred to me to investigate whether every phosphorescent substance emitted similar rays. This idea was not supported by experiment, but in the research I came across an unexpected phenomenon.

"Among phosphorescent substances salts of uranium especially invited investigation by reason of their unusual constitution, suggested by the harmonic series of bands forming their absorption and phosphorescence spectra. Thin flakes of the double sulphate of uranium and potassium were therefore placed, wrapped in black paper or protected by a sheet of aluminum, on photographic plates and left for several hours exposed to the light. On developing the plates, I realized that the uranium salt had emitted rays which reproduced the silhouettes of the crystalline flakes through the black paper and the various screens of metal or thin glass placed on the plates.

"Under these circumstances the phenomenon might be attributed to a transformation of solar energy, of the type met with in phosphorescence, but I at once realized that the emission was independent of any known mode of excitation, luminous, electrical, or thermal. It was, then, a spontaneous phenomenon of a new type.

. . . . .

"As the uranium salts used had been prepared some considerable time before, the only possible conclusion was that the intensity of the phenomenon was independent of the time and consequently that the emission was constant. All later experiments have shown that the activity of uranium does not appreciably diminish with time.

"These first results were immediately followed by the discovery that the radiation from uranium discharged electrified bodies at a distance. This provided a second method for the study of the new rays. The photographic method was mainly qualitative; the electrical method supplied numerical data, and the first measurements provided evidence that the radiation is constant with time.

"Both methods served to show that all uranium salts . . . emitted radiation of the same nature; that this property was an atomic property associated with the element *uranium* and that metallic uranium was about three and a half times as active as the salt used in the first experiments.

"An electrified sphere of uranium, which discharged spontaneously in the air under the influence of its own radiation, retained its charge in a complete vacuum. The exchange of electric charges which takes place between electrified bodies under the influence of the new rays is the result of a special conductivity imparted to the surrounding gases, a conductivity which persists for some moments after the radiation has ceased to act.

"These fundamental properties of the radiation emitted by uranium were verified later by a number of observers, among whom I shall mention only Rutherford, who has completely correlated the conductive properties of gases traversed by the uranium radiation with ionization arising from other causes."

After Becquerel's discovery the next great step was taken by the two who shared with him the Nobel Prize for 1903, Pierre and Marie Curie.

BIOGRAPHICAL SKETCHES

P. AND M. CURIE

PIERRE CURIE was born in Paris on May 15, 1859. He received his early education at home; then at the Faculté des Sciences at the Paris Sorbonne. From 1878 to 1882 he was an assistant teacher in the physical laboratory of the Faculté. In 1882 he received an appointment at the École de Physique et de Chemie Industrielles in Paris, becoming professor of physics there in 1895. In 1900 he returned to the Faculté des Sciences at the Sorbonne as assistant professor and in 1904 became professor, a chair at the Faculté being specially created for him. He was killed in a street accident in Paris on April 19, 1906.

Among the research workers at the Faculté was a Polish girl, Marie Sklodowska. Born at Warsaw on November 7, 1867, she left her native land in 1891 to study at the Sorbonne Faculté des Sciences, where she obtained the L-ès-Sc in physics in 1893 and L-ès-Sc in mathematics in 1894. In 1895, while working at the Sorbonne for her doctor's degree, she met Pierre Curie, just appointed professor of physics at the École de Physique et de Chemie Industrielles; they were married the same year. After her marriage Mme. Curie continued her research work, but now at the École, completing her investigations into the magnetic properties of steel in 1897, an investigation which was subsidized by the Société d'Encouragement pour l'Industrie Nationale; the results were published in 1898. In 1900 she was appointed professor of physics at the women's college at Sèvres, near Paris. She obtained her doctor's degree in 1903 and the following year returned to the Sorbonne as *chef des travaux pratiques* in the Faculté des Sciences. On her husband's tragic death in 1906 she succeeded him as professor at the Faculté. She died on July 4, 1934.

Mme. Curie has the distinction of being the only person to be cited twice in a Nobel award: not only was her name linked with that of her husband in the physics award for 1903, but she received the undivided chemistry award for 1911 for her discovery of radium and polonium and her investigations into the chemistry of radium.

At the time of her death Mme. Curie was head of the Radium Institute in Paris, where the design and organization of the Curie Laboratory was largely due to her.

DESCRIPTION OF THE PRIZE-WINNING WORK

One of Pierre Curie's early researches, carried out at the Sorbonne in collaboration with his brother Jacques, was a study of the phenomenon of piezoelectricity (p. 4 above) which the brothers had discovered; the results of the investigation were published in 1881 under their joint names. While at the École de Physique et de Chemie Industrielles he made a detailed examination of the magnetic properties of bodies at different temperatures and discovered that for ferromagnetic substances (iron, nickel, cobalt, and certain alloys, all of which are strongly magnetic) there is a certain critical temperature, now known as the *Curie point,* above which the substance loses its magnetic properties when heated. These latter studies formed the thesis for which he received his doctorate at the Faculté des Sciences in 1895.

On the announcement of Becquerel's discovery the Curies, who were now working together at the École, turned their attention to the new subject of radioactivity. It was possible that other substances besides uranium might show a similar activity; Mme. Curie sought for such an effect in a number of substances and finally found that thorium and its compounds behaved in the same way as uranium. The method used in these investigations was to bring the substance under examination near the charged plate of an electroscope: if the substance was radioactive, the gold leaves of the electroscope rapidly collapsed because of the escape of their charge by way of the surrounding air, now rendered conducting.

Mme. Curie then proceeded to examine a large number of minerals containing uranium or thorium or a mixture of both, in particular the uranium ore *pitchblende;* this showed an activity about four times that of uranium metal, from which Mme. Curie concluded that it must contain an unknown element of greater activity than either uranium or thorium. She and her husband then set to work to separate the source of this activity from the pitchblende; they were completely successful. First they identified a strongly radioactive substance closely akin in its chemical properties to bismuth, one of the many metals contained in pitchblende; this they called *polonium* in honor of Mme. Curie's native land. Another metal occurring in pitchblende is barium; when this was separated, another active substance closely akin to it in chemical properties separated at the same time; to this they gave the name *radium,* a happy choice of name since radium is outstandingly radioactive. Both these discoveries were made in 1898 and published that year in the *Comptes Rendus* of the French Academy. So far only minute quantities of these new substances had been isolated, but by treating several tons of pitchblende waste they had, by 1902, obtained one-tenth of a gram of pure radium chloride. It was not until 1910, after the death of Pierre Curie, that Mme. Curie succeeded in isolating pure radium metal.

The following extract is a translation of part of the Nobel lecture delivered, in French, by Pierre Curie:

"Becquerel discovered in 1896 the special radiation properties of uranium and its compounds. Uranium emits rays of moderate intensity which affect a photographic plate, pass through black paper and metals, and render the air a conductor of electricity. The radiation does not vary with time and the cause of its production is unknown.

"Mme. Curie in France and Schmidt in Germany have shown that thorium and its compounds possess the same properties. Mme. Curie further showed in 1898 that among all the chemical substances prepared or in use in the laboratory, those containing uranium or thorium were alone capable of emitting Becquerel rays in appreciable quantity. We called such substances *radioactive*.

"Radioactivity appeared then as an atomic property of uranium and thorium, a body being more radioactive in proportion to its richness in either of these elements.

"Mme. Curie made an examination of the minerals containing uranium or thorium; in agreement with the preceding views, these minerals are all radioactive. But measurements showed that certain of them were more active than they should have been for the amount of uranium or thorium they contained. She therefore conjectured that these substances contained radioactive chemical elements still unknown. We, Mme. Curie and I, sought for these new hypothetical substances in a uranium mineral, *pitchblende*. In making the chemical analysis of this mineral and in testing the radioactivity of each constituent separated in the treatment, we first of all found a strongly radioactive elementary substance akin to bismuth in its chemical properties—this we named *polonium;* then, in collaboration with Bémont, we found a second strongly radioactive substance akin to barium, which we named *radium*. Finally, Debierne has since isolated a third radioactive substance belonging to the rare earths, *actinium*.

"These substances are present in pitchblende only as traces, but their radioactivity is about two million times as great as that of uranium. After treating an enormous quantity of material we succeeded in obtaining a quantity of barium salt rich in radium sufficient for us to be able to extract the radium in the state of a pure salt, using a fractionization method."

CONSEQUENCES IN THEORY AND PRACTICE

In 1899 Becquerel, using a radium salt placed at his disposal by the Curies, showed that the radiation could be deflected by a magnetic field and drew attention to its similarity in this respect to cathode rays. Using the method employed by J. J. Thomson (*q.v.* 1906) to measure the speed and charge of the cathode-ray particles, he found a value for the speed approaching that of light (186,000 miles per sec.). On the other hand, he found that the radiation from polonium was much less penetrating than that from radium, a fact which led him to conclude that, in radiation of this type, two kinds of rays were emitted.

In the same year Ernest Rutherford, newly appointed professor of physics at McGill University (and winner, in 1908, of the Nobel Prize in Chemistry), found that the radiation from uranium consisted of two kinds, which he named α rays (alpha rays) and β rays (beta rays), the β rays being much more penetrating than the α rays, as measured by the thickness of aluminum foil necessary to reduce them to half strength. In 1900 a still more penetrating type, the γ rays (gamma rays), was discovered by Villard in the radiation from radium; he found that this type was not deflected by a magnetic field, a fact which was confirmed by Becquerel the same year; the γ rays appeared to be very similar to X rays; (they are now known to be electromagnetic waves of shorter wave length than X rays). Mme. Curie in 1900 suggested that the α rays might consist of particles ejected by the radioactive substance, in this case polonium (polonium is now known to emit α rays only, which explains why Becquerel found the radiation from this substance less penetrating than that from radium, which emits β rays also); this suggestion was confirmed in 1903 by Rutherford, who also showed that the α particle carried a positive charge. The α particle was later identified with the nucleus of the helium atom; Becquerel's suggestion that the β particles were fast cathode-ray particles (i.e. electrons) was also confirmed.

X rays, cathode rays, the canal rays discovered by Goldstein (p. 49) were all produced by means of a vacuum tube with the expenditure of considerable amounts of electrical energy. The startling thing about Becquerel's discovery was that uranium and the radioactive substances discovered by the Curies emitted particles, or rays, *spontaneously*—highly energetic particles, or rays, shot out from lifeless matter. Whence did they derive their store of energy? The attempts to answer this question have led far toward a solution of the mystery of the atom.

1904

JOHN WILLIAM STRUTT, BARON RAYLEIGH

(1842–1919)

"For his work on the density of gases and his discovery, in this connection, of argon."

BIOGRAPHICAL SKETCH

JOHN WILLIAM STRUTT WAS BORN AT TERLING PLACE, WITHAM, Essex, England, on November 12, 1842. The future Lord Rayleigh's early education was frequently interrupted by ill-health. After short periods at Eton and Harrow, he was prepared for the University by a tutor. He entered Trinity College, Cambridge, in October 1861, and studied there under the mathematician E. J. Routh. He obtained an astronomical scholarship in 1864 and the following year took his degree as Senior Wrangler. In 1866 he obtained a fellowship at Trinity College, which he held until 1871. He was elected a Fellow of the Royal Society of London in 1873, the year in which he succeeded to the barony.

The world-famous Cavendish Laboratory at Cambridge University was opened in 1874, with Clerk Maxwell as its first director. On Maxwell's death in 1879 Lord Rayleigh was appointed his successor. To him fell the task of organizing the laboratory as a center of instruction and research, a task which he accomplished with outstanding success. Rayleigh resigned his appointment at Cambridge in 1884. In 1885 he was appointed one of the secretaries of the Royal Society, and two years later he became professor of natural philosophy at the Royal Institution of Great Britain. In 1905 he was elected President of the Royal Society and in 1908 Chancellor of Cambridge University.

Rayleigh was one of the leaders of the movement which resulted in the establishment of the National Physical Laboratory at Teddington, Middlesex, in 1900; he assisted greatly in raising the laboratory to the unique position it now holds among the prominent scientific institutions in the world. Rayleigh had long been interested in the problems of flying; when, in 1909, Mr. Asquith, the Prime Minister, appointed an advisory Committee on Aeronautics in connection with the establishment of a special department of the National Physical Laboratory, Lord Rayleigh was nominated its president; the reports of the Committee contain several important contributions by him, in particular one which stresses the importance of scale models in the construction of flying machines.

In 1896 he became scientific adviser to Trinity House, an association of English mariners concerned with the interests of the seamen and shipping of England. In this capacity he investigated certain problems connected with fog signals; in 1917 he drew attention to the advantage of substituting wireless signals for foghorns.

In 1902, at the coronation of King Edward VII, Rayleigh was among the first recipients of the Order of Merit. In 1904 he was awarded the Nobel Prize in Physics, the proceeds of which he presented to the University of Cambridge for an extension of the Cavendish Laboratory. In 1905 he was made a member of the Privy Council. Scientific bodies throughout the world conferred on him honorary degrees or membership. He died on June 30, 1919.

Rayleigh's first published work, which appeared in 1869, dealt with electromagnetic phenomena. During the following ten years his researches touched on nearly every branch of physics. In 1870 he published a paper on resonance, the first of a series of papers ultimately embodied in his *Treatise on Sound*, published in 1877. From vibrations transmitted by air Rayleigh passed naturally to vibrations transmitted by the ether; and optics, in particular the scattering of light by very small particles, continued to engage his attention for many years. A number of outstanding problems were attacked by him and solved. For instance, he applied the wave theory of light to the mathematical investigation of the resolving powers of prisms and diffraction gratings: thus he showed that the resolving power of a grating is determined by the total number of lines in the grating multiplied by the order of the spectrum, and not by the closeness of the lines. In one of his earliest papers on optics Rayleigh explained the blue color of the sky; this is due to the scattering of the light from the sun by the particles in the atmosphere, and Rayleigh showed that the amount of scattering is much greater for the violet end of the spectrum than for the red end (actually, that it is proportional to the inverse fourth power of the wave length); at a distance from the sun the sky is seen by scattered light only and so appears blue. In 1887 he published a paper in which he suggested the method of reproducing colors by photography later adopted in principle by Lippmann (*q.v.* 1908).

One of Lord Rayleigh's most important investigations was concerned with the determination of the ohm. The practical unit of electrical resistance, the ohm, is defined as one thousand million absolute units (i.e., units expressed in the centimeter-gram-second system). A Committee of the British Association had, in 1863, determined the dimensions of a column of mercury which would have this resistance at 0° C. Doubts had arisen, however, as to the correctness of this British Association standard. The Committee was reappointed in 1881, with Lord Rayleigh as its leading member. The new determination was made at the Cavendish Laboratory; as a result of most precise experiments it was found that the B.A. unit was slightly less than the true ohm. Subsequent work determined the fundamental standards of resistance and current with an accuracy of a few parts in ten thousand. In 1908 an International Congress of Electricians, under the presidency of Lord Rayleigh, adopted these standards.

DESCRIPTION OF THE PRIZE-WINNING WORK

The great discovery for which Lord Rayleigh received the Nobel Prize, the discovery of the inert gas *argon,* was the unlooked-for outcome of a series of painstaking investigations into the densities of oxygen and nitrogen. In 1815 William Prout had put forward the hypothesis that all atomic weights were exact multiples of that of hydrogen. This hypothesis had always interested Rayleigh. If Prout was correct, the density of oxygen relative to hydrogen ought to be exactly 16, not 15.96, the best value obtained so far.

The story of the discovery is best given in Rayleigh's own words, as he told it in his Nobel lecture:

"The subject of the densities of gases has engaged a large part of my attention for over 20 years. In 1882 in an address to the British Association I suggested that the time had come for a re-determination of these densities, being interested in the question of Prout's law. At that time the best results were those of Regnault, according to whom the density of oxygen was 15.96 times that of hydrogen. The deviation of this number from the integer 16 seemed not to be outside the limits of experimental error.

"In my work, as in the simultaneous work of Cooke, the method of Regnault was followed in that the working globe was counter-poised by a dummy globe (always closed) of the same external volume as itself. Under these conditions we became independent of fluctuations of atmosphere density. The importance of this consideration will be manifest when it is pointed out that in the usual process of weighing against brass or platinum weights, it might make more apparent difference whether the barometer were high or low than whether the working globe were vacuous or charged with hydrogen to atmospheric pressure. Cooke's result, as at first announced, was practically identical with that of Regnault, but in the calculations of both these experimenters a correction of considerable importance had been overlooked. It was assumed that the external volume of the working globe was the same whether vacuous or charged to atmospheric pressure, whereas of course the volume must be greater in the latter case. The introduction of the correction reduced Cooke's result to the same as that which I had in the meantime announced, viz. 15.88. In this case, therefore, the discrepancy from Prout's law was increased, and not diminished, by the new determination.

"Turning my attention to *nitrogen,* I made a series of determinations, using a method of preparation devised originally by Harcourt, and recommended to me by Ramsay. Air bubbled through liquid ammonia is passed through a tube containing copper at a red heat where the oxygen of the air is consumed by the hydrogen of the ammonia, the excess of the ammonia being subsequently removed with sulphuric acid. In this case the copper serves merely to increase the surface and to act as an indicator. As long as it remains bright, we have security that the ammonia has done its work.

"Having obtained a series of concordant observations on gas thus prepared I was at first disposed to consider the work on nitrogen as finished. Afterwards, however, I reflected that the method which I had used was not that of Regnault and that in any case it was desirable to multiply methods, so that I fell back upon the more orthodox procedure according to which, ammonia being dispensed with, air passes directly over red hot copper. Again a series in good agreement with itself resulted, but to my surprise and disgust the densities obtained by the two methods differed by a thousandth part—a difference small in itself but entirely beyond the experimental errors. The ammonia method gave the smaller density, and the question arose whether the difference could be attributed to recognised impurities. Somewhat prolonged inquiry having answered this question in the negative, I was rather at a loss how to proceed. It is a good rule in experimental work to seek to magnify a discrepancy when it first presents itself rather than to follow the natural instinct of trying to get quit of it. What was the difference between the two kinds of nitrogen? The one was wholly derived from air; the other partially, to the extent of about one-fifth part, from ammonia. The most promising course for magnifying the discrepancy appeared to be the substitution of oxygen for air in the ammonia method, so that *all* the nitrogen should in that case be derived from ammonia. Success was at once attained, the nitrogen from the ammonia being now 1/200 part lighter than that from air, a difference upon which it was possible to work with satisfaction. Among the explanations which suggested themselves were the presence of a gas heavier than nitrogen in the air, or (what was at first rather favoured by chemical friends) the existence in the ammonia-prepared gas of nitrogen in a dissociated state. Since such dissociated nitrogen would probably be unstable, the experiment was tried of keeping a sample for eight months, but the density was found to be unaltered.

"On the supposition that the air-derived gas was heavier than the 'chemical' nitrogen on account of the existence in the atmosphere of an unknown ingredient, the next step was the isolation of this ingredient by absorption of nitrogen. This was a task of considerable difficulty; and it was undertaken by Ramsay and myself working at first independently but afterwards in concert. Two methods were available—the first that by which Cavendish had originally established the identity of the principal component of the atmosphere with the nitrogen of nitre and consisting in the oxidation of the nitrogen under the influence of electric sparks with the absorption of the acid compounds by alkali. The other method was to absorb the nitrogen by means of magnesium at full red heat. In both these ways a gas was isolated of amount equal to about one per cent. of the atmosphere by volume and having a density about half as great again as that of nitrogen. From the manner of its preparation it was proved to be non-oxidisable and to refuse absorption by magnesium at a red heat, and further varied attempts to induce chemical combination were without result. On this account the name *argon* [from the Greek ἀργόν, inactive] was given to it."

The discovery was announced in a joint paper by Rayleigh and Ramsay at the British Association meeting at Oxford on January 31, 1895. It was subsequently discovered by Ramsay, as a result of a series of investigations for which he was awarded the Nobel Prize in chemistry for 1904, that small quantities of other inert gases were present with the argon in the air.

Arising out of his work on the densities of gases came an investigation, made by Rayleigh during his last five years at the Royal Institution, into the variation of the volume of a gas with pressure for pressures between 0.01 and 1.5 mm. of mercury. He established that for these low pressures Boyle's law, that the volume is inversely proportional to the pressure when the temperature remains constant, held to a high degree of accuracy.

CONSEQUENCES IN THEORY AND PRACTICE

From the purely physical point of view the most important consequence of Rayleigh's discovery is that it led to the discovery of helium in the earth's crust. Sir Norman Lockyer in 1868 had observed a bright yellow line in the spectrum of the sun's chromosphere which did not correspond to any known terrestrial element. He took this to indicate the presence in the sun of an unknown element to which he gave the name *helium* (Greek ἥλιος, sun). In 1895 Ramsay, in a search for possible argon compounds, found that the mineral cleveite when heated gave off a gas which showed, not the argon spectrum for which he was looking, but the helium spectrum. An examination of the properties of this gas placed it next above hydrogen in the periodic table, with an atomic weight 4.

The fact that helium was found to be present mainly in minerals containing uranium and thorium, both radioactive elements, led Rutherford and Soddy to suggest in 1903 that helium might be a disintegration product of the radioactive elements, a suggestion which received support when Rutherford found the mass of an α particle to be about four times that of a hydrogen atom, so that the α particle might be a helium atom, the mass of which is also four times that of the hydrogen atom. This received experimental confirmation in 1909 when Rutherford and Royds allowed α particles from radium emanation to escape into a high vacuum, when the helium spectrum was observed. Rutherford had already determined the charge on the α particle as being two unit positive charges, a unit charge being that on the hydrogen ion, so that the α particles appeared to be helium atoms carrying two positive charges. Rutherford suggested that the positive charge might be due to the loss of two electrons by the helium atom as the result of disintegration or collision, the α particle thus being the positively charged remainder of the helium atom. When in 1911 he put forward his planetary theory of the structure of the atom, this "remainder" became the nucleus of the atom.

1 9 0 5

PHILIPP LENARD
(1862–1947)

"For his work on cathode rays."

BIOGRAPHICAL SKETCH

PHILIPP LENARD WAS BORN AT POZSONY (PRESSBURG), HUN-
gary, on June 7, 1862. He was taught, in his native town, by Virgil
Klatt, with whom he later collaborated in a research on phosphorescence. After studying physics at the universities of Budapest
and Vienna, he continued his studies at Berlin under Helmholtz
and at Heidelberg under Quincke and Bunsen, obtaining his doctor's degree at Heidelberg in 1886. In 1893 he became *privatdozent*
at Bonn, where he was assistant to Heinrich Hertz. In 1894 he was
appointed professor extraordinary at Breslau and in 1895 at Aachen.
In 1896 he returned to Heidelberg as professor of theoretical
physics, but two years later went to Kiel as professor of experimental
physics. Here he remained until 1907, when he was recalled to
Heidelberg to be Quincke's successor as professor of experimental
physics; he held this post until his retirement in 1931. In 1909
he was also appointed director of the newly founded Radiological
Institute at Heidelberg. He died on May 20, 1947.

Lenard was awarded the Rumford Medal by the Royal Society
of London and the Franklin Medal by the Franklin Institute.

Lenard's first scientific work dealt with mechanics, among other
things the vibrations of falling drops of water. Soon, however,
he became interested in problems connected with ultraviolet light,

publishing in 1889 the results of investigations made at Heidelberg in collaboration with the astronomer Max Wolf on the effect of ultraviolet light on solid bodies; in 1900 he published a paper on its effect on gaseous bodies. In electricity he investigated such problems as the electrification developed in falling water (1892), the photoelectric effect (1902), the electrical conductivity of flames (1902).

His most important researches, next to those on the cathode rays, were those carried out in collaboration with Klatt. They showed that the phosphorescence of calcium sulphide and other phosphors depends on the presence as impurities in these substances of minute quantities of foreign metals such as copper, bismuth, or manganese; that for a certain proportion of the impurity the intensity of the phosphorescence is a maximum, becoming less when the proportion is either increased or decreased. They also investigated the effect of mechanical stress on phosphorescence, finding that the sulphides of the alkaline earths (calcium, strontium, barium) lose the property when subjected to heavy pressure. These investigations were published in 1904; in 1905 Lenard put forward the theory that the incident light, always necessary to produce phosphorescence, causes the emission of electrons from the atoms of the metal present as an impurity, much as in the photoelectric effect; that these electrons gradually return to the atoms, so producing the phosphorescence. This is the explanation still generally accepted, though the mechanism of the process is not yet fully understood.

DESCRIPTION OF THE PRIZE-WINNING WORK

Lenard's interest in the cathode rays was aroused through reading Sir William Crookes's paper of 1879 on "the fourth state of matter," a German translation of which was published in Leipzig the same year. Ten years earlier Hittorf had noted a stream of faint blue light proceeding from the cathode when the pressure in the discharge tube was less than 1 mm. of mercury; he found that an object placed in the path of this stream threw a shadow on the opposite wall of the tube. Goldstein in 1876, thinking the stream consisted of ether waves similar to those of light, gave it the name *Kathodenstrahlen,* cathode rays. Crookes found that these rays were deflected by a magnetic field in a direction relative to the field consistent with their being streams of negatively charged particles, and considered them to be matter in a new or "fourth" state. Sir Arthur Schuster, in 1890, measured the ratio of charge to mass for these hypothetical particles and found a value about five hundred times that of the same ratio for the hydrogen ion in electrolysis. In 1892 Heinrich Hertz discovered that the cathode rays were able to pass through thin gold or aluminum leaf, a discovery which marked the turning point in Lenard's researches on cathode rays, begun four years earlier. Here is Lenard's own account, translated from the German of his Nobel lecture:

"The beginning takes me back 26 years—to Crookes. I had read his lecture on "radiant matter," as he called the cathode rays, and been greatly impressed by it. You are all of course acquainted with his experiments, but I will just remind you of the main points: the highly exhausted glass tube; the negatively electrified plate, the cathode, where the rays start; a cross placed in the path of the rays, with the shadow of the cross thrown by them on the phosphorescent glass wall; the movement of the shadow when a magnet is brought near, a sign that the cathode rays, unlike light rays, are bent in a magnetic field. [See Fig. 1.]

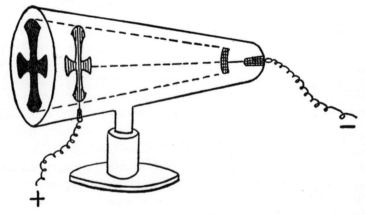

FIG. 1

[Shadow cast by cathode rays.—Crookes's Experiment.]

"During my student years my interest in these matters lay dormant. . . .

"It was not until later, as Quincke's assistant, that I had the opportunity and means to construct a mercury air pump capable of producing very high vacua . . . and with it to carry out experiments on these rays myself. I . . . thought it would be an excellent thing if the rays could be brought out of the tube and into the open air, where it would be possible to experiment with them satisfactorily. For this the wall of the tube would have to be provided with a window through which the rays, but not air, could pass. Now radiant *matter* would certainly have difficulty in passing through air-tight shutters, but it was just possible that Eilhard Wiedemann was right in thinking the cathode rays to be a kind of ultraviolet light. In the end it seemed to me that quartz was the most promising material, since it was the most transparent to all the types of radiation then known. The tube I constructed at that time had an opening opposite the cathode covered with a quartz plate 2.4 mm. thick. It was not, however, a success: I found no effects, either of an electrical nature . . . or of phosphorescence outside the quartz which could not be put down unquestionably to light that had forced its way out of the tube.

"Not until four years later, in 1892, did a new possibility arise. Hertz, whose assistant I then was, had discovered that thin metal leaf was transparent to the cathode rays. He used the quite thin, extremely delicate and porous, gold, silver, and aluminum leaves made for the bookbinding trade, and showed that the cathode rays passed not only through the pores but also actually through the substance, the metal, of the leaves. One day he . . . showed me the phenomenon he had just discovered: uranium glass covered with aluminum leaf was placed inside the discharge tube; when the radiation fell on the leaf from above, the glass beneath it glowed.

. . . . .

"Later I too carried out the experiment. My earlier problem, to get the cathode rays out into the open air, still lured me most of all. I . . . placed several [leaves], one on top of another, in a tube specially prepared for the purpose, gradually increasing the number until I found that 10 or 15 of them were still quite appreciably transparent to the rays. I then procured a piece of aluminum foil of the same thickness as the combined leaves to see whether it would stand the air pressure; I found that it did so if the area was sufficiently small. I now reverted to my old tube, replacing the piece of quartz by a metal plate with a small hole in it, covered the hole with the aluminum foil, sprinkled grains of alkaline earth phosphor on this little aluminum window, excited the discharge tube, and—the grains shone beautifully! They still shone quite brightly when they were fixed in position a little above the aluminum window. So, the cathode rays had not only been brought out from the inside of the discharge tube . . . they showed themselves able to travel quite a distance through air of ordinary density."

Lenard proceeded to make a detailed study of the rays in the open air, using a discharge tube specially designed for this purpose. He first placed a phosphorescent screen in the path of the rays and found that the intensity of the phosphorescence became weaker and weaker as the screen was moved further and further away from the aluminum window, until at a distance of 8 cm. the screen remained quite dark. He next examined the transparency of various substances to the rays and found that the absorbing power depended not at all on the nature of the substance but only on the density, being roughly proportional to the density; thus gold absorbed more than silver, silver more than aluminum, the thickness being the same; but all bodies of the same density cut down the rays by the same amount. He also discovered, though this was later (1903), that the absorbing power diminished as the velocity of the rays increased.

In 1888 Wilhelm Hallwachs, following up an observation made by Hertz the previous year, investigated the influence of the light from an electric arc on electrically charged bodies and discovered that a negatively charged zinc plate rapidly lost its charge when exposed to the light from the arc lamp, whereas there was no loss of charge if the plate was positively charged. He was at a loss to account for the phenomenon, merely surmising that it was in some way due to the action of ultraviolet light. This photoelectric effect, as it is called, immediately caught Lenard's interest—it formed the subject of the investigation carried out in collaboration with Wolf at Heidelberg in 1889. His experiments on the cathode rays had shown him that the air in front of the aluminum window became electrically conducting; this gave him the idea that in the photoelectric effect the ultraviolet light falling on the metal plate gave rise to cathode rays there. He devised an experiment to test this: ultraviolet light was admitted to a vacuum tube, where it fell obliquely on a metal plate; a small disk placed opposite the plate and connected to an electrometer was found to acquire a negative charge; when a magnetic field was applied a second small disk set at right angles to the first acquired the charge instead, the direction of the deflection being the same as for the cathode rays. Lenard also determined the ratio of charge to mass and found it to be in agreement with that for the cathode rays. He was therefore satisfied that the irradiation of the plate with ultraviolet light caused the emission of cathode rays. By giving the disk a small negative charge it was possible to prevent the rays from the irradiated plate from reaching the disk and even to reverse their path and cause them to return to their source; faster rays could be obtained by giving the disk a positive charge. Lenard thus had a means of regulating the velocity of the rays*. His explanation of the mechanism of the photoelectric effect was that the light waves produce a disturbance within the atoms of the metal (Zeeman's discovery had shown that atoms contain negative electricity capable of oscillation), negative *quants* —as Lenard termed them (not to be confused with the *quanta* of the quantum theory)—within the atom vibrating in resonance with the incident light; when the vibration is too strong, the *quant* is shot out of the atom, and so out of the plate, as a cathode ray.

Lenard did not hold with any particle theory of electricity—not at least if by *particle* was meant a particle of matter carrying an electric charge. He held that the cathode rays did not consist of charged particles, but of pure *negative* electricity divorced from matter; also, since *positive* electricity was known only in association with matter, for a body to be positively charged meant that it had lost negative electricity. On the other hand, electricity is not continuous but consists of discrete parts. As early as 1885 Helmholtz had suggested that electricity possessed a discontinuous structure—

---

* Lenard's later application of this method to the study of ionization potentials is described on p. 231.

that it consisted of *Elementarquanten*. In Lenard's view these *Ele-mentarquanten* were simply centers of electric force, whatever name might be given to them: *corpuscles* (J. J. Thomson), *electrions* (Kelvin), or *electrons* (Lorentz and Zeeman); or *quanten* (quants), an abbreviation of Helmholtz' term.

From his experiments with fast cathode rays and the ease with which these rays passed through matter, Lenard concluded that the atom is almost entirely empty space: that the impenetrable "proper volume" of a cubic meter of platinum, for example, would be at most a cubic millimeter. The individual atom consists of a *quant* of electricity, a center of negative electric force within the atom, the field of force more or less defining the cross section of the atom; but so that the atom as a whole may be electrically neutral, there must be an equal quantity of positive electricity which is in some way associated with the *matter* aspect of the atom, since, according to Lenard's views at that time, positive electricity cannot exist apart from matter, whereas negative electricity can and does (e.g., in the cathode stream). To this closely coupled neutral pair he gave the name *dynamid*.

CONSEQUENCES IN THEORY AND PRACTICE

Lenard's picture of the structure of the atom gave way to other, more precise, models, but he was the first to realize that the atom must possess a structure, and to see in it mostly empty space which was yet the seat of forces due to positive and negative electricity. He was also the first to give the accepted explanation of the photoelectric effect, though Sir J. J. Thomson's independent explanation was only slightly later.

1 9 0 6

JOSEPH JOHN THOMSON
(1856–1940)

"For his theoretical and experimental investiga-
tions into the transmission of electricity through
gases."

BIOGRAPHICAL SKETCH

JOSEPH JOHN THOMSON WAS BORN ON DECEMBER 18, 1856, AT Chetham Hall, near Manchester, England. While attending Owens College, Manchester, he came under the influence of Balfour Stewart, professor of physics there, and gave up his intention of becoming an engineer. In 1876 he entered Trinity College, Cambridge, where, with the exception of a few short visits to America, he was to remain for the rest of his long life. Like Lord Rayleigh nearly twenty years earlier, he studied mathematics under Dr. Routh; he was graduated as Second Wrangler in the Mathematical Tripos in 1880. In the same year he was elected a Fellow of Trinity College. On Lord Rayleigh's retirement from the Cavendish professorship at the end of 1884, Thomson, at the early age of twenty-seven, was elected to succeed him; under his able direction the Cavendish Laboratory became a great center of research which attracted workers from far and wide. From 1905 to 1918 he also held the professorship of natural philosophy at the Royal Institution of Great Britain, London. In 1918 the Mastership of Trinity College, Cambridge, fell vacant and Thomson accepted the position, shortly afterward resigning the Cavendish professorship.

41

During the First World War Thomson acted in an advisory capacity to various government departments and was a member of the Board of Inventions and Research. He was elected a Fellow of the Royal Society of London in 1884; in 1916 he became its president and he held the office for the customary five years. He died on August 30, 1940, and was buried in Westminster Abbey.

Thomson was knighted in 1908 and received the Order of Merit in 1912. Among the very great number of dignities conferred on him by British, American, and Continental learned societies and universities were the Royal Medal, the Hughes Medal, and the Copley Medal of the Royal Society of London, the Albert Medal of the Royal Society of Arts, the Hodgkins Medal of the Smithsonian Institution, Washington, D. C., and the Franklin Medal of the Franklin Institute. He was also a member of the Institute of France.

DESCRIPTION OF THE PRIZE-WINNING WORK

After his election to a Fellowship of Trinity College, he settled down to research in mathematical and experimental physics, publishing in 1883 the results of a determination of the ratio of the electromagnetic and electrostatic units carried out under the direction of Lord Rayleigh. Also in 1883 appeared his first paper on the discharge of electricity through gases, a subject which he was to make peculiarly his own. During the next ten years a number of problems in physics occupied his attention; they were concerned mainly with electricity, with increasing emphasis on the discharge through gases; in 1894 he published a paper on the velocity of the cathode rays.

Soon after Röntgen's discovery of X rays in 1895 Thomson discovered that the rays caused gases to become conductors of electricity, so that when a gas between two electrodes maintained at a difference of potential was exposed to the rays, a current passed between the electrodes, even when the potential difference was quite small. Jointly with Rutherford he showed that the function of the rays was to cause the molecules of the gas to break up into positive and negative ions, which then moved under the action of the applied electromotive force toward the oppositely charged electrodes, thus constituting an electric current through the gas. If the electromotive force was small, the ions moved slowly and frequent recombinations into neutral molecules occurred, thus diminishing the current. An increase in the electromotive force led to an increase in the velocity of the ions and so, as a result of the smaller number of recombinations, to an increase in the current, until for a certain value of the electromotive force no recombinations at all occurred and the current became a maximum; Thomson called this maximum current the *saturation current*. It could be increased by increasing the distance between the electrodes.

Thomson's next concern was a more thorough investigation into the nature of the cathode rays. He had always held that these rays consisted of streams of electrically charged particles and in 1881 he had published an important theoretical investigation into the effect of motion on such particles. He found that, whereas a sphere of radius a and mass m, moving with a velocity v, possessed kinetic energy equal to $\frac{1}{2}mv^2$, the same sphere moving with the same velocity possessed, when carrying an electric charge e, kinetic energy equal to $\frac{1}{2}\left(m + \frac{2}{3} \cdot \frac{e^2}{a}\right)v^2$, so that the effective mass of the sphere was increased by $\frac{2}{3} \cdot \frac{e^2}{a}$ as a result of the charge.

At first Thomson thought that the cathode-ray particles were gaseous atoms or molecules, but the amount of the deflection in a magnetic field seemed against this idea. By using a very high vacuum he succeeded in producing a satisfactory deflection of the rays in an electrostatic field—Goldstein in 1876 had observed that the rays were deflected by an electric force—and from these two deflections, the magnetic and the electric, Thomson obtained a value for the ratio of charge to mass for the supposed particles. This turned out to be very large compared with the value of the same ratio for the hydrogen atom in electrolysis, so that if the charge was the same in the two cases, the mass of the cathode-ray particle must be very much less than that of the hydrogen atom, the highest particle known at that time.

So far only the ratio of charge to mass had been determined; the next step was to determine the charge and the mass separately. For this work we shall turn to Thomson's Nobel lecture, including in the extracts his opening description of the cathode-ray phenomenon: *

". . . I wish to give an account of some investigations which have led to the conclusion that the carriers of negative electricity are bodies, which I have called corpuscles, having a mass very much smaller than that of the atom of any known element, and are of the same character from whatever source the negative electricity may be derived.

"The first place in which corpuscles were detected was a highly exhausted tube through which an electric discharge was passing. When an electric discharge is sent through a highly exhausted tube, the sides of the tube glow with a vivid green phosphorescence. That this is due to something proceeding in straight lines from the cathode . . . can be shown in the following way (the experiment is one made many years ago by Sir William Crookes): A Maltese cross made of thin mica is placed between the cathode and the walls of the tube. When the discharge is passed, the green phosphorescence no longer extends all over the end of the tube, as it did when the cross was absent. There is now a well defined cross in the phosphorescence at the end of the tube; the mica cross has thrown a shadow and the shape of the shadow proves that the phosphorescence is due to something travelling from the cathode in straight lines, which is stopped by a thin plate of mica. The green phosphorescence is caused by cathode rays and at one time there was a keen controversy as to the nature of these rays. . . . One [view] was that the rays are negatively electrified bodies shot off from the cathode with great velocity; the other view . . . was that the rays are some kind of ethereal vibration or waves.

"The arguments in favour of the rays being negatively charged particles are primarily that they are deflected by a magnet in just the same way as moving, negatively electrified particles. We know that such particles, when a magnet is placed near them, are acted upon by a force whose direction is at right angles to the magnetic

---

* The following extracts are quoted here by kind permission of Sir G. P. Thomson.

force, and also at right angles to the direction in which the particles are moving.

"Thus, if the particles are moving horizontally from east to west, and the magnetic force is horizontal from north to south, the force acting on the negatively electrified particles will be vertical and downwards.

"When the magnet is placed so that the magnetic force is along the direction in which the particle is moving, the latter will not be affected by the magnet.

"The next step in the proof that the cathode rays are negatively charged particles was to show that when they are caught in a metal vessel they give up to it a charge of negative electricity. This was first done by Perrin. This experiment was made conclusive by placing the catching vessel out of the path of the rays, and bending them into it by means of a magnet, when the vessel became negatively charged.

"If the rays are charged with negative electricity they ought to be deflected by an electrified body as well as by a magnet. In the earlier experiments . . . no such deflection was observed. The reason of this has been shown to be that when cathode rays pass through a gas they make it a conductor of electricity, so that if there is any appreciable quantity of gas in the vessel through which the rays are passing, this gas will become a conductor of electricity and the rays will be surrounded by a conductor which will screen them from the effect of electric force. . . .

"By exhausting the vacuum tube until there was only an exceedingly small quantity of air left in to be made a conductor, I was able to get rid of this effect and to obtain the electric deflection of the cathode rays. This deflection had a direction which indicated a negative charge on the rays.

"Thus cathode rays are deflected by both magnetic and electric forces, just as negatively electrified particles would be.

· · · · ·

"It is not only from . . . cathode rays, that we can obtain corpuscles. When once they had been discovered, it was found that they are of very general occurrence. They are given out by metals when raised to a red heat; indeed any substance when heated gives out corpuscles to some extent. We can detect the emission of them from some substances, such as rubidium and the alloy of sodium and potassium, even when they are cold. . . .

"Corpuscles are also given out by metals and other bodies, but especially by the alkali metals, when these are exposed to light.

"They are being continually given out in large quantities and with very great velocities by radioactive substances such as uranium and radium; they are produced in large quantities when salts are put into flames, and there is good reason to suppose that corpuscles reach us from the sun.

"The corpuscle is thus very widely distributed, but wherever it is found, it preserves its individuality, e/m being always equal to a certain constant value.

"The corpuscle appears to form a part of all kinds of matter under the most divers conditions; it seems natural therefore to re- gard it as one of the bricks of which atoms are built up.

"I shall now return to the proof that the very large value of e/m for the corpuscle, as compared with that for the atom of hydrogen, is due to the smallness of m the mass, and not to the greatness of e the charge. We can do this by actually measuring the value of e, availing ourselves for this purpose of a discovery by C. T. R. Wil- son, that a charged particle acts as a nucleus round which water vapour condenses and forms drops of water.

．　．　．　．　．

"The effect of the charged particles on the formation of a cloud can be shown very distinctly by the following experiment.

"A vessel which is in contact with water is saturated with mois- ture at the temperature of the room. This vessel is in communica- tion with a cylinder in which a large piston slides up and down. The piston to begin with is at the top of its travel; by suddenly exhausting the air from below the piston, the pressure of the air above it will force it down with great rapidity, and the air in the vessel will expand very quickly. When, however, air expands, it gets cool; thus the air in the vessel previously saturated is now

supersaturated. If there is no dust present, no deposition of moisture will take place, unless the air is cooled to such a low temperature that the amount of moisture required to saturate it is only about
$\frac{1}{8}$ of that actually present.

"Now the amount of cooling, and therefore of supersaturation,
depends upon the travel of the piston; the greater the travel the
greater the cooling. Suppose the travel is regulated so that the
supersaturation is less than eightfold and greater than fourfold. We
now free the air from dust by forming cloud after cloud in the dusty
air; as the clouds fall they carry the dust down with them. . . .
We find at last that when we make the expansion no cloud is visible.

"The gas is now made in a conducting state by bringing a little
radium near the vessel; this fills the gas with large quantities of
both positively and negatively electrified particles. On making the
expansion now an exceedingly dense cloud is formed. That this is
due to the electrification in the gas can be shown by the following
experiment:

"Along the inside walls of the vessel we have two vertical insulated plates which can be electrified. If these plates are charged,
they will drag the electrified particles out of the gas as fast as they
are formed, so that in this way we can get rid of, or at any rate
largely reduce, the number of electrified particles in the gas. If the
expansion is now made with the plates charged before bringing up
the radium, there is only a very small cloud formed.

"We can use the drops to find the charge on the particles, for
when we know the travel of the piston, we can deduce the amount
of supersaturation, and hence the amount of water deposited when
the cloud forms. The water is deposited in the form of a number of
small drops all of the same size; thus the number of drops will be
the volume of the water deposited divided by the volume of one of
the drops. Hence, if we find the volume of one of the drops, we can
find the number of drops which are formed round the charged
particles. If the particles are not too numerous, each will have a
drop round it, and we can thus find the number of electrified particles.

"From the rate at which the drops slowly fall we can determine
their size.

. . . . .

"We can in this way find the volume of a drop, and may therefore, as explained above, calculate the number of drops and therefore the number of electrified particles.

"It is a simple matter to find by electrical methods the total quantity of electricity on these particles; and hence, as we know the number of particles, we can deduce at once the charge on each particle.

$$. \quad . \quad . \quad . \quad .$$

"The value of e, found by these methods, is 3.1×10^{-10}* electrostatic units, or 10^{-20} electromagnetic units. This value is the same as that of the charge carried by a hydrogen atom in the electrolysis of dilute solutions. . . .

$$. \quad . \quad . \quad . \quad .$$

"The value of the charge when the electrification is produced by ultra-violet light is the same as when the electrification is produced by radium.

"We have just seen that e, the charge on the corpuscle, is in electromagnetic units equal to 10^{-20}, and we have previously found that e/m, m being the mass of a corpuscle, is equal to 1.7×10^7, hence $m = 6 \times 10^{-28}$ grammes."

The value found by Thomson for the ratio e/m was about 1700 times that found for the same ratio for the hydrogen atom in electrolysis. A later value for the same ratio is 1.759×10^7 e.m.u., so that Thomson's value for the ratio was very good; on the other hand, his value for e, and consequently for m, was much too low, later values being $e = 4.803 \times 10^{-10}$ e.s.u. $= 1.601 \times 10^{-20}$ e.m.u and $m = 9.115 \times 10^{-28}$ grams.

Thomson's experimental determination of e/m was carried out in October 1897 and published in the *Philosophical Magazine* for that year. C. T. R. Wilson made his discovery the same year; it was used by Thomson for his separate determination of e during 1898.

In 1899 Thomson published his views on the nature of the atom. According to him, the atom contains a large number of negatively charged corpuscles—he later adopted the name *electron* [see p.

---

* $10^{-10} = \dfrac{1}{10^{10}} = \dfrac{1}{10,000,000,000}$.

12]—and, so that the normal atom may be electrically neutral, the space through which the corpuscles are spread in some way acts as if it had a positive charge. Electrification of a gas, e.g., by the action of X rays, he regarded as due to the splitting up of some of the atoms, corpuscles being detached and behaving as negative ions, while the remainder of each atom acts as a positive ion of much greater mass.

Early in 1904 Thomson published a theoretical investigation into the stability of systems of negatively charged corpuscles free to move about in a sphere of positive electrification. He showed, by a piece of brilliant mathematical reasoning, that when the corpuscles are constrained to move in one plane, they will arrange themselves in a series of concentric rings, the outer rings containing a large number of corpuscles, the innermost a small number; that if the corpuscles are not constrained to move in one plane, they will arrange themselves in a series of concentric shells. He then examined what properties would be conferred on an atom by this ring structure; he found that the properties of such an atom would be in many respects analogous to those possessed by the chemical elements, in particular that they would depend on the atomic weight in a manner similar to that expressed by the periodic law (see p. 414).

In 1886 Eugen Goldstein, of Berlin University, had discovered that if the cathode in a cathode-ray tube was so placed that it divided the tube into two approximately equal parts, and if the cathode was pierced with a number of holes, then, when the discharge was passed, bright-colored rays traveling in straight lines were seen to enter the space behind the cathode through the holes; the color of the rays varied according to the gas in the tube. To these rays he gave the name *Kanalstrahlen* (canal rays). W. Wien (*q.v.* 1911) measured the magnetic and electric deflections of the canal rays and found them to consist of positively charged particles with masses comparable with the masses of atoms or molecules.

These canal rays, or positive rays as they came to be called, formed the subject of Thomson's next great research, during the years 1906 to 1914. The investigation of these particles presented no little difficulty, chiefly owing to their relatively large mass and

to the fact that they have different velocities and are not all of the
same kind—they are actually atoms or molecules of the residual
gas in the discharge tube which carry one or more unit positive
charges due to the loss of an equal number of electrons. Thomson
overcame these difficulties by designing an ingenious form of discharge tube in which the cathode consisted of a metal rod bored
throughout its length with a hole 1/10 mm. or less in diameter;
some of the positive particles reaching the cathode passed through
it and entered a very high vacuum, where they were acted upon by
parallel magnetic and electrostatic fields; their path ended at a
photographic plate which, on being developed, showed a black
spot where each particle had struck it. These black spots were found
to form a series of parabolas, all having their vertices at the point
corresponding to zero deflection of the rays and all having the same
axes. Each parabola was due to particles having the same value for
the ratio of charge to mass, the different spots forming the parabola
being due to the different velocities with which the particles struck
the plate. From measurements on the photographic plate, combined
with a knowledge of the strengths of the magnetic and electrostatic
fields, it was possible to identify the various atoms and molecules
present. Other information was also obtained; thus, the mercury
atom was found to have from one to seven unit positive charges;
two parabolas were found for the gas neon, corresponding to atomic
weights of 20 and 22, the first experimental indication of the existence of *isotopes;* some molecules which are too unstable to be
found in nature or the laboratory were identified by this means,
thus with methane-gas molecules (CH_4) were also found molecules
corresponding to CH, CH_2, and CH_3.

CONSEQUENCES IN THEORY AND PRACTICE

J. J. Thomson announced his "discovery" of the corpuscle on
April 30, 1897, before the Royal Institution of Great Britain, a
date which may fittingly be taken as marking the dawn of modern
particle physics. Lorentz' electron theory of matter, though supported by Zeeman's discovery, still remained pure *theory;* Röntgen's
and Becquerel's discoveries, destined in course of time to con-

tribute so much to an unraveling of the subatomic mysteries of nature, were as yet unexploited; Lenard's explanation of the photoelectric effect as due to the emission of *quanten* of electricity was not published until 1899; it was Thomson's great achievement to establish, beyond all reasonable doubt, the existence of the electron. His method of investigating positive rays was developed by F. W. Aston, winner of the Nobel Prize in Chemistry in 1922, into the mass-spectrograph, which has played so large a part in the discovery of fresh isotopes, whose existence has served in turn to throw yet further light on the structure of the atom.

ALBERT ABRAHAM MICHELSON
(1852–1931)

*"For his optical precision instruments and for
the spectroscopic and metrological investigations
made with them."*

BIOGRAPHICAL SKETCH

ALBERT ABRAHAM MICHELSON WAS BORN ON DECEMBER 19,
1852, at Strelno, Posen (restored to Poland after the First World
War). His parents emigrated to the United States when he was two
years old, settling first in Nevada but moving fifteen years later to
San Francisco, where the boy attended high school. He obtained an
appointment at the Naval Academy at Annapolis, and in 1873 he
was graduated as Ensign, U. S. Navy. After a two-year cruise in the
West Indies he was an instructor in physics and chemistry at the
Naval Academy until 1879. During these five years he developed
a taste for physical problems, particularly the measurement of the
velocity of light, for which, in 1878, he obtained a remarkably good
value. As a result he was summoned in 1879 to the Nautical Almanac Office at Washington to assist Professor Simon Newcomb in
his experiments on the velocity of light. This investigation was
completed in 1880 and Michelson was granted leave of absence to
visit Europe; here, during 1880 and 1881, he studied under Helmholtz in Berlin, Quincke in Heidelberg, and Cornu and Lippmann
in Paris.

On his return to the United States he was appointed professor of physics at the Case School of Applied Science, Cleveland, Ohio; then, in 1890, professor of physics at Clark University, Worcester, Mass.; two years later he became professor of physics at the University of Chicago and head of the Ryerson Physics Laboratory there, appointments which he held until shortly before his death on May 9, 1931.

Michelson's high scientific achievements were recognized throughout the world by honorary degrees or membership in scientific societies. In 1887 he was vice-president of the American Association for the Advancement of Science and in 1900 president of the American Physical Society. The Royal Society of London awarded him the Rumford Medal in 1889, elected him a Foreign Member in 1902, and in 1907 conferred on him its highest award, the Copley Medal. In 1920 the Royal Society of Arts awarded him the Albert Medal.

DESCRIPTION OF THE PRIZE-WINNING WORK

From the beginning of his scientific career Michelson had one overriding interest: light, and particularly the velocity of light.

Olaf Römer in 1676 made the discovery, based on astronomical observations, that light travels with a finite velocity. This was confirmed by James Bradley half a century later, also as a result of astronomical observations. The first *terrestrial* determination of the velocity of light was made in 1849 by Hippolyte Fizeau, who used a rotating toothed-wheel method. By means of a suitable system of lenses, he arranged for a narrow beam of light to pass through one of the gaps in the wheel, be reflected at a mirror five miles away, and return to the eye of the observer, the path of the beam being parallel to the axis of the wheel. When the wheel was rotated slowly, a beam which had passed through out of the gaps would get back after reflection in time to pass through the *same* gap in the opposite direction. As the speed of rotation was increased, a point would be reached where the returning beam would be intercepted by a tooth of the wheel and so not reach the eye of the observer; the same thing would happen to the beam which passed through the next gap on the outward journey, and so on. To the observer the light would appear completely cut off. If the speed of rotation was doubled, all the returning beams passed through gaps and none of the light was cut off. From the speeds of rotation, the total distance traveled by the beam, and the number of teeth (720) in the wheel, the velocity of light could be calculated. Fizeau obtained the value 315,000 km. per sec. The same method, with modifications, was used by Marie Alfred Cornu, between the years 1872 and 1876; he obtained the value of 300,400 km. per sec.

In 1862 Jean Foucault determined the velocity by using a rotating-mirror method. In this case a beam of light falls on a plane mirror, is reflected into a concave mirror which in turn reflects it back to the plane mirror, and so along its original path back toward the source; here it is turned aside by a plane glass plate set at an angle of 45° to the path of the beam, and is viewed by the observer in a direction at right angles to the path. If the plane mirror has moved during the time taken by the beam to travel from it to the concave mirror and back, the final image seen by the observer will be displaced somewhat from its original position. The velocity of light can be calculated from the dimensions of the apparatus, the speed of rotation of the plane mirror, and the amount of the displacement of the image. In Foucault's experiment the distance between the two mirrors was 4 meters; the observed displacement was 0.7 mm.; the resulting value for the velocity of light was 298,600 km. per sec.

It was Foucault's method which Michelson adopted in principle, but modified in such a way that the distance between the two mirrors could be increased to 600 meters, with a resulting increase in the displacement of the image of 133 mm. In 1879 Michelson obtained the value 299,900 km. per sec. and in 1882 the value 299,850 km. per sec. Newcomb, of the Nautical Almanac Office, in the same year and using the same method, obtained the value 299,860 km. per sec. In 1926 Michelson, using a somewhat modified method, increased the distance between the two mirrors to 22 miles, one of the stations being at Mount Wilson, the other at Mount San Antonio in California; the result of this experiment was 299,796 km. per sec. *in vacuo.* Many determinations of this important quantity have been made since then, the generally accepted value being now 299,776 km. per sec. (= 186,281 miles per sec.) *in vacuo,* though a recent determination (autumn 1950) at the National Physical Laboratory, England, gives the somewhat higher value 299,792.5 km. per sec. (= 186,282 miles per sec.).

During the winter of 1880, while in Europe, Michelson devised a method which, it was hoped, would make it possible to measure the velocity of the earth through the ether. The idea was this: if the earth was moving through an ether at rest, then the time taken by a ray of light, a wave motion *in the ether,* to travel the distance between two objects fixed relative to the earth should be different, when the light is traveling in the direction of the earth's motion, from the time taken when it is traveling in a direction at right angles to that motion; from this difference, if it could be measured, the velocity of the earth relative to the ether could easily be calculated. The apparatus would have to be of extreme precision, but it was in the designing of such apparatus that Michelson excelled. The experiment was carried out first in the Physical Institute at Berlin and afterward in the Physical Observatory at Potsdam, but the result was entirely negative: no motion of the earth relative to the ether could be detected.

In 1887 the experiment was repeated with every possible refinement at the Case School of Applied Science; on this occasion Michelson was assisted by E. W. Morley, professor of chemistry at Western Reserve University. Figure 3 (page 62), which is a simplified version of the one given in Michelson's Nobel lecture, will help the reader to understand the method used in the now famous Michelson-Morley experiment. A beam of monochromatic light from a source *S* falls on a plate of glass *e* set at an angle of 45° to the path of the beam. This glass plate is lightly silvered at the back, so that part of the beam passes through to a mirror *g,* part is reflected to another mirror *f* at right angles to the first. A second glass plate *d,* identical with *e* except that it is unsilvered, is placed between plate *e* and the mirror *g* and parallel to *e;* its purpose is to make the paths of the two beams optically equal by compensating for the fact that the beam reflected at the back surface of *e* has to pass through an extra thickness of glass. The two beams are reflected back along their original paths by the two mirrors, and meet again at the silvered surface. Here they produce *interference fringes,* a series of dark and light bands caused by the wave trains alternately annulling and reinforcing each other. A slight movement of either mirror, by altering the relative lengths of the paths traversed, produces a displacement of the fringes. In the attempt to detect the earth's motion through the ether the whole apparatus was floated on mercury and slowly rotated so that the angles between the two beams and the direction of the earth's motion were constantly changing.

Now an earth moving through a stationary ether is indistinguishable from an ether flowing in the opposite direction past a stationary earth—that is, if the velocity of the earth in the first case and of the ether in the second are the same. A problem to be found in many textbooks of elementary mechanics requires the student to find the difference in time, if any, taken by a swimmer (1) to swim upstream at a steady speed relative to the water and back to the starting point, and (2) to swim the same distance across stream and back; the time in (1) is greater than in (2). The same thing applies to a train of light-waves in an ether flowing between two fixed points on a stationary earth when (*a*) the motion of the light-waves is first in the opposite direction to that of the ether, then, after reflection at a mirror, in the same direction, and (*b*) the motion of the light-waves is across the direction of motion of the ether. In (*a*) the effective optical path of the beam of light is increased more than in (*b*) and so, in the Michelson-Morley experiment, a displacement of the interference fringes was to be expected. No such displacement was observed. Other experiments, using entirely different methods, have been devised since then, but none has succeeded in detecting any motion of the earth relative to the ether—a fact which has in itself proved of the highest significance.

One important practical result came from these attempts on the part of Michelson: the application of the method used to the design of an interferometer of remarkable precision. We shall leave Michelson to speak of this part of his work himself, in the words of his Nobel lecture:

"The fame of Newton rests chiefly on his . . . laws of gravitational astronomy. . . .

"But in no less degree are we indebted to [him] . . . for that equally important brand of Astrophysics—in which the spectroscope plays so fundamental a role—by means of which we are enabled to discover the physical and chemical constitution of the heavenly bodies, as well as their positions and motions. As the number and the intricacy of the wonderful systems of stellar worlds which the telescope can reveal increase with its power, so also do the evidences of the innermost molecular structure of matter increase with the power of the spectroscope. If Newton's fundamental experiment of separating the colors of sunlight had been made under conditions . . . slightly different from those in his actual experiment . . . the science of spectroscopy would have been founded.

"So simple a matter as the narrowing of the aperture through which the sunlight streamed before it fell upon the prism which separates it into its constituent colors—would have sufficed to show that the spectrum was crossed by dark lines, named after their discoverer, the Fraunhofer lines of the Solar Spectrum. These may be readily enough observed, with no other appliances than a slit in a shutter which is observed through an ordinary prism of glass. Fraunhofer increased the power of the combination enormously by observing with a telescope—and this simple combination, omitting minor details, constitutes . . . the Spectroscope. As the power of a telescope is measured by the closeness of the double stars which it can 'resolve', so that of the Spectroscope may be estimated by the closeness of the spectral lines which it can separate. In order to form an idea of the advance in the power of spectroscopes let us for a moment consider the map of the Solar Spectrum.

"The portion which is visible to the unaided eye extends from the Fraunhofer line *A* to *H;* but by photography it may be traced far into the ultra-violet region and by bolometric measurements [see p. 101] it is found to extend enormously farther in the region beyond the red. In the yellow we observe a dark line marked *D,* which coincides in position with the bright light emitted by sodium —as when salt is placed in an alcohol flame. It may be readily shown by a prism of very moderate power that this line is double, and as the power of the instrument increases the distance apart or separation of this doublet furnishes a very convenient measure of its separating or resolving power. Of course this separation may be effected by simple magnification, but this would in itself be of no service, as the 'lines' themselves would be broadened by the magnification in the same proportion. It can be shown that the effective resolving power depends on the material of the prism which must be as highly dispersive as possible and on the size, or number, of the prisms employed—and by increasing these it has been found possible to 'resolve' double lines thirty or forty times as near together as are the sodium lines. It will be convenient to take the measure of the resolving power when just sufficient to separate the sodium lines as 1000. Then the limit of resolving power of prism spectroscopes may be said not much to exceed 40,000.

"This value of resolving power is found in practice to obtain under average conditions. Theoretically there is no limit save that imposed by the optical conditions to be fulfilled—and especially by the difficulty in obtaining large masses of the refracting material of sufficient homogeneity and high dispersive power. It is very likely that this limit has not yet been reached.

"Meanwhile another device for analysing light into its component parts had been found by Fraunhofer (1821), which at present has practically superseded the prism—namely, the diffraction grating. Fraunhofer's original grating consisted of a number of fine equidistant wires, but he afterwards made them by ruling fine lines on a glass plate covered with gold leaf and removing the alternate strips. They are now made by ruling upon a glass or a metal surface fine equidistant lines with a diamond point.

"The separation of light into its elements by a grating depends on its action on the constituent light-waves.

"Let Fig. 2 represent a highly magnified cross section of a diffraction grating with plane waves of light falling upon it normally,

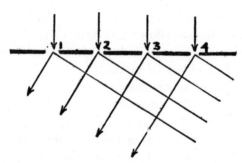

FIG. 2   *Michelson's Fig. 2*
[Diffraction grating.]

as indicated by the arrows. The wave motion will pass through the apertures, and will continue as a series of plane waves; and if brought to a focus by a telescope will produce an image of the slit source just as if no grating were present (save that it is fainter, as some of the light is cut off by the opaque portions). This image may be considered as produced by the concurrence of all the elementary waves from the separate apertures meeting in the same phase of vibration, thus re-inforcing each other. But this may also be true in an oblique direction, as shown in the figure, if the retardation of the successive waves is just one whole wave-length (or any whole number). . . . In this direction therefore there will also be an image of the slit source; and this direction is determined by the relation:

$$\sin \theta = \frac{m\,l}{s}$$

where l is the length of the light-wave of this particular color; s, the distance between the apertures (the grating space) and m the number of waves in the common retardation (1, 2, 3, etc.).

. . . . .

"A very great advance was made by Rutherford of New York, who (1868) ruled gratings two inches long on speculum metal and containing about 20,000 lines. These gratings exceeded in resolving power the best prism trains in use at the time. The next advance was made by Rowland of the Johns Hopkins University, who succeeded in ruling gratings six inches long (by two to three inches stroke) having about one hundred thousand lines, and capable (theoretically, at least) of resolving in the spectrum, double lines whose distance apart was only one-hundredth as great as that of the sodium lines. Practically this is about the limit of the power of the best Rowland grating which I have examined.

. . . . .

"The . . . importance of spectrum analysis, especially in determining the distribution of light in the so-called spectral lines under normal conditions, the resolution of complicated systems of lines, and in the investigation of the effects of temperature, of

pressure, and especially of a magnetic field—justified the under-
taking of much larger gratings than these. As an example of progress made in this direction, I have the honor of exhibiting a
grating having a ruled surface nine inches long by four and one half
inches stroke (220 $\times$ 110 mm). This has one hundred and ten
thousand lines and is nearly perfect in the second order; so that its
resolving power is theoretically 220,000 and this is very nearly realized in actual experiments.

"It will be observed that the effect produced at the focus of the
telescope depends upon the concurrence or opposition—in general
on the *interference* of the elementary trains of light-waves. We are
again indebted to the genius of Newton for the first observation
of such interference; and a comparatively slight modification of the
celebrated experiment of 'Newton's rings' leads to a third method
of spectrum analysis which, if more indirect and less convenient
than the methods just described, is far more powerful. If two plane
surfaces (say the inner surfaces of two glass plates) are adjusted
very accurately to parallelism, and sodium light fall on the combination at nearly normal incidence, the light reflected from the
two surfaces will interfere, showing a series of concentric rings
alternately bright and dark, according to the relative retardation of
the two reflected light beams.

"If this retardation change (by slowly increasing the distance
between the surfaces) the center of the ring system goes through
alternations of light and darkness, the number of these alternations
corresponding exactly to the number of light-waves in twice the increase in distance. Hence the measurement of the length of the
waves of any monochromatic light may be obtained by counting the
number of such alternations in a given distance. Such measurement
of wave-lengths constitutes one of the most important objects of
spectroscopic research.

"Another object accomplished by such measurement is the establishment of a natural standard of length in place of the arbitrary
standard at present in use—the meter.

.   .   .   .   .

"In the search for a radiation sufficiently homogeneous for the
purpose of a standard it became evident that the interference

method might be made to yield information concerning the distribution of light in an approximately homogeneous source when
such observations would be entirely beyond the power of the best
spectroscopes. To illustrate, suppose this source to be again the double radiation from sodium vapor. As the wave-lengths of these two
radiations differ by about one part in a thousand, then at a difference of path of five hundred waves (about 0.36 mm.) the bright
fringes of one wave train would cover the dark fringes of the
other, so that if the two radiations were of equal intensity, all
traces of interference would vanish. At twice this distance they
would reappear and so on indefinitely, if the separate radiations
were absolutely homogeneous. As this is not the case, however,
there would be a gradual falling off in the clearness or visibility of
the bands. Inversely, if such changes are observed in actual experiment, we infer that we are dealing with a double source.
Further, from the distance between the maxima of distinctness, we
may determine (and with extraordinary accuracy) the ratio of
wave-lengths of the components; from the ratio of maxima to
minima we may infer the ratio of their intensities; and finally the
gradual falling off when the distance becomes large gives accurate
information of the 'width' of the corresponding spectral lines.

"In this way it was found that the red line of hydrogen is a double with components about one fortieth of the distance apart of the
sodium lines. Thallium has a brilliant green radiation which is also
double, the distance being one sixtieth that of the sodium lines.
Mercury shows a brilliant green line, which is highly complex; but
whose chief component is a doublet, whose separation is only one
seven-hundredth of that of sodium. The interference fringes are
still visible when the difference of path is of the order of five hundred millimeters, corresponding to over a million light-waves; and
the corresponding width of spectral line would be less than a thousandth part of that which separates the sodium lines.

"The figure [3] illustrates the arrangement of the apparatus as
it is actually used. An ordinary prism spectroscope gives a preliminary analysis of the light from the source. This is necessary because
the spectra of most substances consist of numerous lines. For example, the spectrum of mercury contains two yellow lines, a very

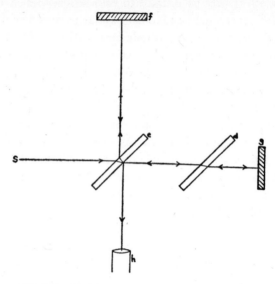

FIG. 3   *Michelson's Fig. 5*
[Principle of the Michelson interferometer.]

brilliant green line, and a less brilliant violet line, so that if we
pass all the light together into the interferometer, we have a combination of all four. It is usually better to separate the various radiations before they enter the interferometer. Accordingly, the light
from the vacuum tube passes through an ordinary spectroscope, and
the light from only one of the lines in the spectrum thus formed is
allowed to pass through the slit into the interferometer.

". . . the light divides at the plate *e*, part going to the mirror *f*,
which is movable, and part passing through, to the mirror *g*. The
first ray returns on the path *feh*. The second returns to *e*, is reflected,
and passes into the telescope *h*.

"The resolving power of the interferometer is measured by the
number of light-waves in the difference of path of the two interfering pencils, and as this is unlimited, the interferometer furnishes
the most powerful means for investigating the structure of spectral
lines or groups. Its use is, however, somewhat handicapped by the
fact that the examination of a single group of lines may require a
considerable number of observations which take some time and

during which it may be difficult to prevent changes in the light source. Nevertheless, it was found possible by its means to investigate the wonderful discovery of Zeeman—of the effect of a magnetic field on the character of the radiation from a source subjected to its influence; and the results thus obtained have been since confirmed by methods which have been subsequently devised."

During the two years as professor of physics at Clark University Michelson was busy studying the possible applications of his interferometer. In 1891 he succeeded by its aid in measuring the angular diameters of the satellites of Jupiter; this work was carried out at Lick Observatory. Another problem which occupied his attention at this time was the determination of the standard meter in terms of a suitable wave length—he refers to this in his Nobel lecture (p. 60). After a systematic study he found that the red light of cadmium vapor alone was sufficiently homogeneous to serve this purpose. He was later invited to carry out the determination of the meter in terms of the wave length of this light at the Bureau International des Poides et Mesures at Sèvres near Paris; the work was successfully concluded in 1893, the value found being 1,553,393 wave lengths to the standard meter; this result was afterward confirmed by others. Subsequent work was largely concerned with astronomical measurements, such as the estimation of the angular diameter of a star which he made at Mount Wilson Observatory in the early 1920's.

Michelson was greatly interested in Zeeman's discovery. His preliminary study of the phenomenon with his interferometer led to the design of an entirely new type of spectroscope—the echelon grating, consisting of a small number of thick glass plates arranged step-wise; this had a resolving power far greater than that of the largest diffraction grating then in existence (1907).

CONSEQUENCES IN THEORY AND PRACTICE

Michelson gave to optical science two of its most valuable aids: the interferometer and the echelon grating. Even more important, he set physical science as a whole one of its most profound prob-

lems: light and all electromagnetic waves seem to require a medium
through which they are propagated—the ether; why did the Michelson-Morley experiment fail to detect any motion of the earth
through this ether? The attempts to answer this question culminated
in Einstein's theory of relativity.

1 9 0 8

GABRIEL LIPPMANN
(1845–1921)

*"For his method of reproducing colors photo-
graphically, based on the phenomenon of interference."*

BIOGRAPHICAL SKETCH

GABRIEL LIPPMANN WAS BORN AT HOLLERICH, LUXEMBURG, ON
August 16, 1845. He received his early education at home; then,
when he was thirteen, his parents settled in Paris and he attended
the Lycée Napoléon; ten years later he entered the École Normale.
While he was still a student he collaborated in the publication of
the *Annales de Chemie et de Physique* by preparing abstracts of
German papers; in this way he became acquainted with contemporary research in electricity. In 1873 he was appointed to a scientific
mission and visited Germany, where he worked first at Heidelberg
under the physiologist Kühne and the physicist Kirchhoff, then at
Berlin under Helmholtz. In 1883 he was appointed professor of
mathematical physics in the Faculty of Science at Paris; three years
later professor of experimental physics and director of the Research
Laboratory, appointments which he held until his death. He died on
July 31, 1921, while returning from a visit to the United States and
Canada.

Lippmann was a member of the French Academy of Sciences
and of the Bureau des Longitudes. He was elected a Foreign Member of the Royal Society of London in 1908.

There is a pretty little experiment which can easily be carried out. A drop of mercury, covered with dilute sulphuric acid, is touched lightly with an iron nail near its upper edge; the mercury contracts, but recovers its original shape as soon as contact with the nail is broken. Lippmann was shown this experiment while he was at Heidelberg by Kühne and put it down to an increase in the surface tension of the mercury brought about by a change in the electrical conditions existing between the mercury and acid, the iron being in some way responsible. A systematic study of the phenomenon, which he made in Kirchhoff's laboratory at Heidelberg, led to the publication in 1873 of an account of his *capillary electrometer,* an instrument now in wide use for the measurement of very small differences in electromotive force.

Lippmann also studied the converse phenomenon, the change in the electromotive force between the mercury and the acid brought about by a mechanical deformation of the metallic surface. These electro-capillary phenomena are reversible, and Lippmann succeeded in devising a reversible electro-capillary engine which turned when a current was supplied to it but produced a current when it was turned mechanically. By applying to such an engine reasoning analogous to that used by Sadi Carnot (1824) in the case of a reversible heat engine, he arrived at a general theorem by which, given the direct phenomenon, it is possible to predict the existence of the converse phenomenon and to calculate its magnitude. For instance, from the existence of piezoelectricity (see page 4 above) he deduced that a crystal should lengthen in an electrostatic field, a result later confirmed experimentally by the Curie brothers. This theorem was published in 1881.

Faraday had suggested in 1838 that a moving charged body should produce the same effects as an electric current. In 1876 H. A. Rowland, of Johns Hopkins University, working in Helmholtz's laboratory at Berlin, showed experimentally that this is so: that a charged body in motion produces a magnetic field. The matter was investigated theoretically in 1881 by J. J. Thomson on the basis of Maxwell's theory. It is, of course, a fact of fundamental importance in modern electron theory. As early as 1879 Lippmann had pointed out to the French Academy of Sciences that there is an apparent increase in the mechanical inertia of a charged body, that is, that it requires a greater force to impart a given velocity to a body when it is charged than when it is uncharged—in other words, its effective mass is increased; he called this increase the "inertia of static electricity." W. Wien, physics laureate in 1911, suggested in 1900 that all mass might turn out to be electrical in origin (v. J. J. Thomson, 1906).

Lippmann rendered important service to astronomy by his invention of the *coelostat*, which gives a stationary image in a mirror of the portion of the sky under examination. Another instrument, the *uranograph*, provides a photographic chart of the sky with the meridians automatically impressed on it at equal intervals of time.

DESCRIPTION OF THE PRIZE-WINNING WORK

It was, however, Lippmann's method of color photography which gained him the Nobel Prize. The first to develop a photographic process giving reasonably permanent pictures were Nicéphore de Niepce and Louis Daguerre in the first half of the nineteenth century. About the same time attention was being paid to the possibility of reproducing colors photographically. That moist silver chloride reproduced the colors of the spectrum more or less faithfully was known at the beginning of the century and is mentioned in Goethe's *Farbenlehre* (1810). Edmond Becquerel (see above, p. 18) succeeded in 1848 in reproducing the colors not only of the spectrum but also of colored objects; he used a silver plate covered with a film of silver chloride. Becquerel, however, had no means of fixing the colors, which soon disappeared; nor could he offer any explanation of the effect. In 1868 Wilhelm Zenker explained the colors as due to the formation of stationary light-waves, i.e., waves formed by reflection in which the nodes, or points of zero displacement, are always at the same distance from the reflecting surface. This theory was further developed by Lord Rayleigh in 1887 and received experimental confirmation at the hands of Otto Wiener in 1890.

In Lippmann's method, published the following year, the sensitive film consisted of an emulsion of gelatine, silver nitrate, and potassium bromide; the plate was placed in the holder with the film *at the back* and in contact with a layer of mercury. On exposure, the light formed stationary waves in the substance of the film, the distance of the nodes from the mercury surface varying according to the color of the light. At the nodes there was no photographic action; at the loops there was a maximum. The result was that when the plate was developed strata of reduced silver were formed at a distance apart equal, for each color, to half the wave length of the incident light, the distance between the strata being different for different colors. When afterward the plate was viewed at right angles, each set of strata appeared in the color of the original incident light. Let us now see what Lippmann himself had to say on the subject in the very short Nobel lecture which he gave to the Royal Swedish Academy. Speaking in French, he said:

"The problem of reproducing colors by direct photography has engaged attention since the beginning of the last century. Edmond Becquerel . . . showed that the colors of the image in the camera are impressed on a layer of violet silver chloride. Zenker explained Becquerel's experiment as due to interference, but experiment can prove that this explanation is not correct and that Zenker's theory does not apply to silver chloride. Becquerel's photographs remained moreover as they were, unfixed, and disappeared in the light. Later, Otto Wiener fixed photographically a set of interference fringes in the neighborhood of a silver mirror, but this physicist had no thought of obtaining colors by an interference method. . . .

"[My] method is very simple. A plate covered with a sensitive layer, transparent and free from grains, is placed in a holder containing mercury. During the exposure the mercury is in contact with the sensitive layer, forming a mirror. After the exposure the plate is developed in the usual manner. When it is dry the colors appear, seen by reflection, and are permanent.

"This result is due to an interference phenomenon taking place inside the sensitive layer. During the exposure interference takes place between the incident rays and those reflected by the mirror, with the formation of interference fringes at a distance of half a wave length. It is these fringes that are impressed photographically within the thickness of the film and there form a sort of cast (*moulage*) of the luminous rays. When the photograph is afterward viewed by white light, the color is seen because there is selective reflection; the plate at each point sends back to the eye only that simple color which has been impressed on it, the other colors being destroyed by interference. Thus the eye sees at each point the color present in the image; but it is only a phenomenon of selective reflection, as in the case of the soap bubble or mother of pearl, the photograph itself being formed of colorless material. . . .

"This explanation can be verified by an experiment. . . . Here is a photograph of the spectrum, which I will project on the screen: you see the colors are brilliant. We now moisten the photograph and project it again on the screen: now there is no color; this is because the gelatine has swollen and the intervals between the images of the interference fringes (Zenker's laminae) have become two or three times too great. Wait a minute while the water evaporates: we see the colors reappear as the drying proceeds; and they reappear in an order we might have foreseen: the red, corresponding to the longest wave length, reappears first, then the orange, the green, the blue, and the violet."

CONSEQUENCES IN THEORY AND PRACTICE

Lippmann's most valuable contribution to science lay in his electro-capillary work. Though he received the Nobel Prize for his method of color photography, this method was not developed to any great extent, mainly because the time of exposure was too great —as much as 15 min. in his earlier experiments, reduced later to 1 min. The successful development of modern color photography took place along quite different lines, namely, the three-color process first suggested by Clerk Maxwell nearly a hundred years ago.

1 9 0 9

GUGLIELMO MARCONI
(1874–1937)

CARL FERDINAND BRAUN
(1850–1918)

"For their development of wireless telegraphy."

BIOGRAPHICAL SKETCH

MARCONI

GUGLIELMO MARCONI WAS BORN AT BOLOGNA, ITALY, ON APRIL 25, 1874, and was educated privately. While still a student he became convinced that Hertz's electric waves could be used for signaling. Marconi's first experiments were made in 1895; in spite of his crude apparatus he succeeded in sending signals over distances of more than a mile. In 1896 Marconi went to England, and in that year he took out the first patent ever granted for radiotelegraphy. He carried out demonstrations for the Post Office, ranges up to nine miles being obtained. In June 1897 he went to Spezia at the invitation of the Italian Government; here a land station was erected and wireless communication established with Italian warships at a distance of twelve miles; shortly after, successful demonstrations were shown in Rome to the King and Queen of Italy. A few weeks later a company was formed in London to acquire Marconi's patents; its activities were at first mainly concerned with the development of Marconi's pioneer work: tests and demonstrations were undertaken in Britain and abroad, and permanent stations were erected. In March 1899 Marconi established wireless communication between Chelmsford in England and Wimeureux in France, a distance of 85 miles.

Marconi's experiments had convinced him that the curvature of the earth was no obstacle to long-distance wireless telegraphy and he now decided to attempt to transmit messages across the Atlantic. Stations were erected at Poldhu in Cornwall and Cape Cod in Massachusetts. The masts and aerials at both stations were wrecked by storms; those at Poldhu were repaired, but to save time a temporary station was set up, on the American side, at St. John's, Newfoundland, the aerial being attached to a kite kept at a height of 400 feet. On December 12, 1901, the first signal—the Morse letter S—was received at St. John's from Poldhu, a distance of 1800 miles. In February 1902 Marconi, on board the *Philadelphia* of the American Line, received clear and distinct signals from Poldhu at a distance of 1550 miles and test letters at a distance of 2100 miles. During 1902 he also carried out experiments between the station at Poldhu and a receiving installation erected on the Italian cruiser *Carlo Alberto,* placed at his disposal by the King of Italy. With the encouragement and financial assistance of the Canadian Government a station was erected at Glace Bay in Nova Scotia, and on December 16, 1902, the first official messages were exchanged between this station and Poldhu. Shortly after, the Cape Cod station was in operation and during the latter part of March and early part of April 1903 the London *Times* published messages sent by its New York correspondent.

As a result of the data and experience gained from these and from tests made for the British Government between England and Gibraltar, Marconi was able to erect a new station at Clifden, Ireland, where several improvements were introduced, and to enlarge the one at Glace Bay; in October 1907 commercial communication was established between these stations. In 1910 Marconi, in Buenos Aires, received messages sent from Clifden, 6000 miles away; in September 1918 the first wireless messages were transmitted from England to Australia.

For some time before the erection of the Clifden station Marconi had been experimenting with various types of multiple aerial. The system finally adopted, and used for the long-distance stations between England and Canada, consisted of a number of horizontal parallel aerials; with this arrangement he found it possible to confine the emitted radiations mainly to the direction of their vertical plane and pointing away from the earthed end.

Prior to 1916 it was generally considered that long waves, e.g., 12,000 feet, were essential for long-distance transmission, but in that year Marconi began experimenting in Italy with short waves with the object of devising a directive or beam system for war purposes. Later, successful results were obtained with 15-meter waves between London and Birmingham. In 1923 excellent reception was obtained up to 1200 miles with 92-meter waves, and in October Marconi discovered that short waves of about 30 meters could be transmitted and received over the greatest distances during daylight. As a result the short-wave beam system was adopted for long-distance wireless communication in the British Empire. In 1931 Marconi turned his attention to the systematic study of waves of about one meter in length; successful experiments were carried out in Italy, where the system was installed between Vatican City and the Papal Palace at Castel Gandolfo.

During the First World War Marconi served in both the Italian army and navy. He was a member of the Italian war mission to the United States. In 1919 the King of Italy appointed him plenipotentiary delegate to the Peace Conference in Paris and it was he who signed on behalf of Italy the Peace Treaties with Austria and Bulgaria. He died on July 20, 1937.

Marconi's work brought him the highest honors from governments, universities, and learned societies throughout the world. In Italy he was created a marquis and a member of the Senate; the Tsar of Russia conferred on him the Order of St. Anne, the King of England the Grand Cross of the Victorian Order. Among the many scientific awards conferred on him for the invention of wireless telegraphy were the Franklin Medal and the John Fritz Medal in the United States and the Albert Medal of the Royal Society of Arts in England.

DESCRIPTION OF THE PRIZE-WINNING WORK

MARCONI

When Marconi began his experiments in 1895 two pieces of apparatus were available: the Hertzian *oscillator* and the Branly *coherer,* the first to produce the electromagnetic waves, the second to detect them. In the Hertzian oscillator two square metal plates (40 by 40 cm.) were placed edge to edge about 60 cm. apart and joined by light metal rods to two metal balls forming a spark gap; the plates were connected to the terminals of the secondary winding of an induction coil; on operating the coil, sparks passed across the gap and an oscillatory discharge occurred between the plates, with the emission of electromagnetic waves. The Branly coherer, invented by Professor Branly of Paris, was based on a discovery made by Sir Oliver Lodge in the late 1880's; it consisted of metal filings in a tube connected in series with an electric battery; normally the loosely packed filings possessed such high electrical resistance that practically no current passed, but if electric oscillations fell on them they *cohered* and their resistance fell to a small fraction of its previous value, so that a current now passed; this current could be used to operate an ordinary telegraph sounder or a Morse printer. How Marconi improved on these pieces of apparatus may be told in the words of his Nobel lecture, delivered in English.

"My first tests were carried out with an ordinary Hertz oscillator and a Branly coherer as detector, but I soon found out that the Branly coherer was far too erratic and unreliable for practical work.

"After some experiments I found that a coherer consisting of nickel and silver filings placed in a small gap between two silver plugs in a tube, was remarkably sensitive and reliable. This improvement together with the inclusion of the coherer in a circuit tuned to the wave-length of the transmitted radiation, allowed me to gradually extend up to about a mile the distance at which I could affect the receiver.

"Another, now well-known, arrangement which I adopted was to place the coherer in a circuit containing a voltaic cell and a sensitive telegraph relay actuating another circuit, which worked a tapper or trembler and a recording instrument. By means of a Morse telegraph key placed in one of the circuits of the oscillator or transmitter it was possible to emit long or short successions of electric waves, which would affect the receiver at a distance and accurately reproduce the telegraphic signs transmitted through space by the oscillator.

"With such apparatus I was able to telegraph up to a distance of about half a mile.

"Some further improvements were obtained by using reflectors with both transmitters and receivers, the transmitter being in this case a Righi oscillator.

"This arrangement made it possible to send signals in one defi-

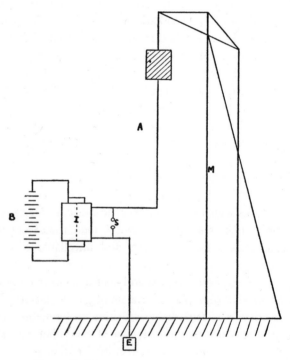

FIG. 4   *Marconi's Fig. 2*

[Transmitting system. S—Hertzian oscillator.]

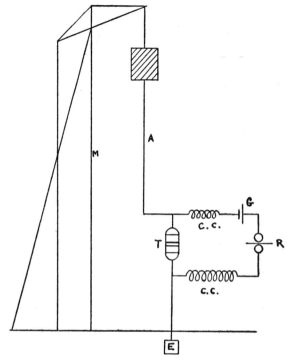

FIG. 5　　　*Marconi's Fig. 3*
[Receiving system.]

nite direction, but was inoperative if hills or any large obstacle happened to intervene between the transmitter and receiver.

"In August 1895 I discovered a new arrangement which not only greatly increased the distance over which I could communicate, but also seemed to make the transmission independent from the effects of intervening obstacles.

"This arrangement consisted in connecting one terminal of the Hertzian oscillator, or spark producer, to earth and the other terminal to a wire or capacity area placed at a height above the ground, and in also connecting at the receiving end one terminal of the coherer to earth and the other to an elevated conductor (Figs. 2 and 3) [Figs. 4 and 5].

"I then began to examine the relation between the distance at which the transmitter could affect the receiver and the elevation of the capacity areas above the earth, and I very soon definitely ascertained that the higher the wires or capacity areas, the greater the distance over which it was possible to telegraph.

"Thus I found that when using cubes of tin of about 30 cms. side as elevated conductors or capacities, placed at the top of poles 2 meters high, I could receive signals at 30 meters distance, and when placed on poles 4 meters high, at 100 meters, and at 8 meters high at 400 meters. With larger cubes 100 cms. side, fixed at a height of 8 meters, signals could be transmitted 2,400 meters all round.

"These experiments were continued in England, where in September 1896 a distance of 1¾ miles was obtained in tests carried out for the British Government at Salisbury. The distance of communication was extended to 4 miles in March 1897, and in May of the same year to 9 miles. . . .

"In all these experiments a very small amount of electrical power was used, the high tension current being produced by an ordinary Ruhmkorff coil.

. . . . .

"From the beginning of 1898, instead of joining the coherer or detector directly to the aerial and earth, I connected it between the ends of a secondary of a suitable oscillation transformer containing a condenser and tuned to the period of the electrical waves received. The primary of this oscillation transformer was connected to the elevated wire and to earth (Fig. 6).

"This arrangement allowed of a certain degree of syntony, as by varying the period of oscillation of the transmitting antennae, it was possible to send messages to a tuned receiver without interfering with others differently syntonized.

. . . . .

"In 1900 I constructed and patented a complete system of transmitters and receivers which consisted of the usual kind of elevated capacity area and earth connection, but these were inductively coupled to an oscillation circuit containing a condenser, an inductance, and a spark gap or detector, the conditions which I found essential for efficiency being that the periods of electrical oscillation of the

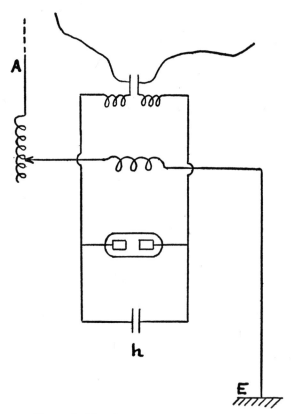

FIG. 6 *Marconi's Fig. 6*
[Syntonized receiving system.]

elevated wire or conductor should be in tune or resonance with that
of the condenser circuit, and that the two circuits of the receiver
should be in electrical resonance with those of the transmitter
(Fig. 8) [Fig. 7].

"The circuits consisting of the oscillating circuit and the radiating circuit were more or less loosely 'coupled' by varying the distance between them. By the adjustment of the inductance inserted
in the elevated conductor and by the variation of capacity of the
condenser circuit, the two circuits were brought into resonance, a
condition . . . essential in order to obtain efficient radiation.

"Part of my work regarding the utilisation of condenser circuits

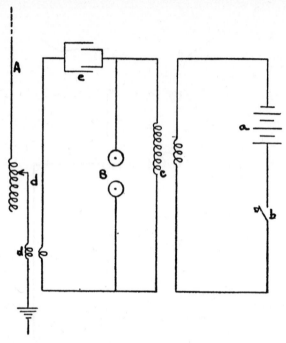

FIG. 7   *Marconi's Fig. 8*
[Inductively coupled system.]

in association with the radiating antennae was carried out simultaneously to that of Professor Braun, without, however, either of us knowing at the time anything of the contemporary work of the other.

. . . . .

"The belief that the curvature of the earth would not stop the propagation of the waves, and the success obtained by syntonic methods in preventing mutual interference, led me in 1900 to decide to attempt the experiment . . . to detect electric waves over a distance of 4000 kilometers, which, if successful, would immediately prove the possibility of telegraphing without wires between Europe and America.

". . . I was convinced that . . . the exact knowledge of the real conditions under which telegraphy over such distances could be carried out, would do much to improve our understanding of the phenomena connected with wireless transmission.

"The transmitter erected at Poldhu, on the coast of Cornwall, was similar in principle to the one I have already referred to, but on a very much larger scale than anything previously attempted.

"The power of the generating plant was about 25 kilowatts.

. . . . .

"My previous tests had convinced me that when endeavouring to extend the distance of communication, it was not merely sufficient to augment the power of the electrical energy of the sender, but that it was also necessary to increase the area or height of the transmitting and receiving elevated conductors.

"As it would have been too expensive to employ vertical wires of great height, I decided to increase their number and capacity, which seemed likely to make possible the efficient utilization of large amounts of energy.

"The arrangement of transmitting antennae which was used at Poldhu consisted of a fan-like arrangement of wires supported by an insulated stay between masts only 48 meters high and 60 meters apart. These wires converged together at the lower end and were connected to the transmitting apparatus contained in a building.

. . . . .

"The tests were commenced early in December 1901 and on the 12th of that month the signals transmitted from England were clearly and distinctly received at the temporary station at St. John's in Newfoundland.

. . . . .

"A result of scientific interest which I first noticed during the tests on S.S. *Philadelphia* and which is a most important factor in long distance Radiotelegraphy, was the very marked and detrimental effect of daylight on the propagation of electric waves at great distances, the range by night being usually more than double that attainable during daytime.

"I do not think that this effect has yet been satisfactorily investigated or explained. . . .

"I am now inclined to believe that the absorption of electric waves during the daytime is due to the electrons propagated into space by the sun, and that if these are continually falling like a shower upon the earth, in accordance with the hypothesis of Professor Arrhenius, then that portion of the earth's atmosphere which is facing the sun will have in it more electrons than the part which is not facing the sun, and therefore it may be less transparent to electric waves.

"Sir J. J. Thomson has shown . . . that if electrons are distributed in a space traversed by electric waves, these will tend to move the electrons in the direction of the wave, and will therefore absorb some of the energy of the wave. Hence, as Professor [J. A.] Fleming has pointed out, . . . a medium through which electrons or ions are distributed acts as a slightly turbid medium to long electric waves.

"Apparently the length of wave and amplitude of the electrical oscillations have much to do with this interesting phenomenon, long waves and small amplitudes being subject to the effect of daylight to a much lesser degree than short waves and large amplitudes.

"According to Professor Fleming the daylight effect should be more marked on long waves, but this has not been my experience. Indeed, in some very recent experiments in which waves of about 8000 meters long were used, the energy received by day was usually greater than at night.

"The fact remains, however, that for comparatively short waves, such as are used for ship communication, clear sunlight and blue skies, though transparent to light, act as a kind of fog to these waves. . . ."

Whereas Marconi was the brilliant amateur not altogether indifferent to the commercial value of his spectacular achievements, Braun, who shared the Nobel Prize with him, was the highly trained physicist applying his scientific knowledge, both theoretical and practical, to this new branch of electrical science, with little thought beyond the solution of the problem immediately before him. Marconi protected his inventions by patents, Braun gave his discoveries freely to the scientific world; Marconi's name is a household word, Braun's almost unknown. Yet in many ways it was

Braun's work, carried out in the laboratory or at the modest experimental station at Strasbourg, that pointed the way to modern radio development.

BIOGRAPHICAL SKETCH

BRAUN

CARL FERDINAND BRAUN was born on June 6, 1850, at Fulda, in the Prussian province of Hesse-Nassau. He was educated first at the *Gymnasium* in his home town, then at the universities of Marburg and Berlin, obtaining his doctor's degree at Berlin in 1872. For the next two years he was Quincke's assistant at Würzburg; then for two years lecturer at the St. Thomas *Gymnasium* at Leipzig. In 1876 he returned to Marburg as professor extraordinary of theoretical physics; from 1880 to 1883 he filled a similar post at the University of Strasbourg. In 1883 he was appointed professor of physics at the Technical High School at Karlsruhe, but two years later went to Tübingen, where he was largely concerned with the establishment of the new Physical Institute. In 1895 he returned to Strasbourg as professor of physics and director of the Physical Institute; here he remained, in spite of a tempting offer of the chair of physics at Leipzig made vacant by the death of Gustav Wiedemann in 1899.

He died on April 20, 1918, in New York, where he had been detained for several years on account of the war.

DESCRIPTION OF THE PRIZE-WINNING WORK

BRAUN

Braun's doctoral thesis dealt with the vibrations of elastic rods and strings, an investigation which he resumed later at Marburg. Apart from this and a theoretical investigation, based on thermodynamical reasoning, into the effect of pressure on the solubility of solids (1887), most of his work dealt with electricity. In 1897 he published an account of a modified cathode-ray tube which enabled him to make a study of electric oscillations with frequencies of over 100,000 per second; a narrow beam of the cathode rays was passed between the plates of a condenser or across a coil at right angles to its axis; the beam was then allowed to fall on a fluorescent screen, where the motion of the luminous spot followed the oscillations of the periodic electric or magnetic field through which the beam had passed; precise information could be obtained by studying the image of the moving spot in a rapidly rotating mirror. This oscillograph was of great assistance to Braun in his later investigations in connection with wireless telegraphy.

In the course of his electrical studies he came across a phenomenon which was later to make possible the "crystal set" so familiar in the mid-1920's, namely, that a large number of substances, mostly crystals of binary compounds, possessed the peculiar property of offering more resistance to a current passing in one direction than to one passing in the other; such a crystal, when placed in an alternating-current circuit, partially suppressed the current in one direction but allowed that in the other to pass through, thus acting as a valve or "rectifier." As early as 1901, when audible reception first came in, Braun urged that the possible use of these substances should be given a thorough technical examination.

Marconi's original system had its weak points. One was the comparative weakness of the oscillations emitted, due to rapid damping; another that the waves from different transmitters jammed one another at the receiving station. When, in the spring of 1898, Braun turned his attention to wireless telegraphy, these were the first problems that engaged his attention. It was already known that a mere increase in the length of the spark gap would not necessarily help and might even have an adverse effect on the strength of the signals, the spark itself using up too large a proportion of the energy. Braun's idea was to have the spark in a separate circuit "coupled" with the aerial directly or inductively or by a mixture of both methods. Experiments were carried out at Cuxhaven in the second half of 1899 and the beginning of 1900, with satisfactory results. An essential feature of Braun's system was the inclusion of a condenser in the circuit containing the spark gap. At the receiver he used direct coupling between the condenser circuit and the aerial; the oscillations from the transmitting station produced, through resonance, the maximum effect at the receiving station, with the added advantage that the waves effective at the receiving station were of the same period as those emitted by the transmitter.

In the summer of 1902 two research stations were erected at Strasbourg, and Braun set himself the problem of investigating the most favorable conditions in the transmitter and in the receiver; he was surprised to find that when the coils forming the coupling were moved further apart, not only was the resonance sharper but the intensity was increased—at least up to a certain limit, after which it began to fall off again. By using known capacities combined with calculated self-inductances, the oscillations resulting from the coupling could be determined for a large number of wave lengths. One result of the introduction of these metrical methods into wireless telegraphy was the designing of a wave meter by Braun's assistant Dönitz.

Another series of experiments, carried out at Strasbourg between 1901 and 1905, dealt with directional transmission and reception. For directional transmission Braun used three vertical antennae arranged to form an equilateral triangle, the currents in two of the antennae being in phase, that in the third having a phase retardation of a quarter-period; when this was the case, waves having a wave length equal to twice the height of the triangle were more or less confined to a direction between the first two antennae and away from the third. For directional reception he found that an aerial inclined at 10° to the horizontal gave the best results.

The following extract, translated from the German of Braun's Nobel lecture, gives an account of the considerations which led him to introduce his "coupled" system.

". . . The year 1897 saw, among others, his [Marconi's] experiments in Spezia Harbor, in which he reached a distance of about 15 km.; in the autumn of the same year Slaby, using essentially the same arrangement, reached a distance overland of 21 km., but only by using wires 300 meters long supported by air balloons. The question then arose: Why was so much difficulty experienced in increasing the range? If the arrangement worked over a distance of 15 km., why was it not possible to reach a distance two or more times as great by increasing the output energy, for which the means were at hand? It appeared, however, that a constant increase in the length of the antenna was necessary. . . . I set myself the problem of obtaining more powerful transmission.

". . . What facts were available and what conclusions could be drawn from them? It was known how sensitive Hertzian oscillations were to changes in the length of the spark gap; further, that a lengthening of the spark could actually prove detrimental, since the spark became 'inactive.' Hertz, in his first work, had already referred to the strong damping of the oscillators and had compared their electrical vibrations to the badly defined acoustical vibrations of wooden rods. Bjerknes in 1891 had measured the damping and found the logarithmic decrement (the measure, of course, of the damping) to be 0.26 for a linear oscillator with only a small spark gap. But if the spark gap was increased to 5 mm. the decrement rose to 0.40. This and a number of other facts suggested that considerable damping occurred with sparks. Everything became understandable if we assumed that with small capacities the spark used up a large fraction of the energy—the more, the longer the spark. On the other hand, it had been known for a long time that the discharge of large capacities in the usual closed circuits was always oscillatory; obviously they were (in radiation-free paths, of course) much more weakly damped; even as long ago as 1862 Feddersen had directly photographed up to 20 half-periods.

"It was to these oscillations that I turned my attention. With the larger quantities of energy which could be conveniently collected in condensers there was hope, too, that the radiation of energy would continue for some time. All things considered, I came to the conclusion that if it were possible to excite fluctuations of potential in a *sparkless* antenna by means of a closed condenser circuit of large capacity, whose mean value was equal to the initial charge in the Marconi sender, then we should have a more efficient transmitter. The only question was: Could it be done? Moreover, experiment over a distance would have to decide whether any disturbing factor had been left out of consideration. The desired result was achieved by the use of exciting circuits of suitable dimensions, and comparative experiments carried out over a distance decided in favor of the new system.

"This at once gave rise to three possible arrangements, which I called inductive excitation of the sender, direct excitation, and a

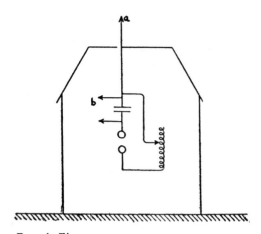

FIG. 8   *Braun's Fig. 1*
[Transmitting system with direct coupling.]

combination of the two. Fig. 1 [Fig. 8] shows the direct system, Fig. 2 [Fig. 9] the inductive system.

"My system brought the so-called coupled circuits into general use in wireless telegraphy, and this is the place to say something of their properties. For purposes of illustration I prefer to use the pendulum model we owe to Oberbeck, although it does not altogether correspond with the electrical case. Two pendulums (Fig. 4) [Fig. 10] of the same period are 'coupled' by means of a loaded thread. If I displace the first pendulum from its position of rest

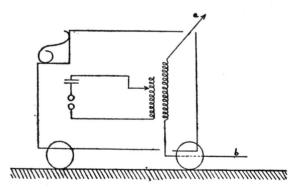

FIG. 9   *Braun's Fig. 2*
[Transmitting system with inductive coupling.]

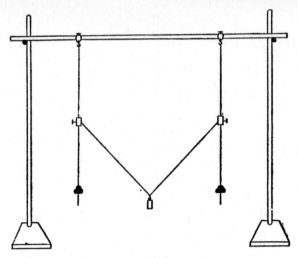

FIG. 10   *Braun's Fig. 4, modified.*
[Mechanical illustration of a "coupled" system.]

and then let it go, its motion is transferred to the second pendulum, the energy of the latter increasing at the expense of the energy of the exciting pendulum, until after a time all the energy is in the second; the process is then repeated in the opposite direction. If I make the first pendulum heavy and the second light, I can make the amplitude of the second greater than that of the first. The first pendulum represents the condenser circuit, the second the sender, to which, in this case, the whole energy of the condenser circuit is transferred. By altering the ratio of the capacities the electric tension can be increased or, if it is desired, made smaller."

CONSEQUENCES IN THEORY AND PRACTICE

Alfred Nobel's will stipulated that the prizes should go to those who had "conferred the greatest benefit on mankind." The part played by "wireless" in modern life, not only as a means of communication, instruction, and entertainment, but also in its many technical applications such as radar, leaves little doubt that few awards could have been more in conformity with Nobel's wishes than the physics award for the year 1909.

1 9 1 0

JOHANNES DIDERIK
VAN DER WAALS
(1837–1923)

"For his work concerning the equation of state of gases and liquids."

BIOGRAPHICAL SKETCH

JOHANNES DIDERIK VAN DER WAALS WAS BORN AT LEIDEN, Holland, on November 23, 1837. He studied at Leiden University from 1862 to 1865. For the next few years he taught physics in schools at Deventer and The Hague. In 1873 he obtained his doctor's degree for a dissertation which at once attracted attention and was subsequently translated into German (1881), English (1888), and French (1894). In 1877 he was appointed professor of physics in the University of Amsterdam, a post which he held until his retirement in 1907. He died in Amsterdam on March 9, 1923.

DESCRIPTION OF THE PRIZE-WINNING WORK

The title of van der Waals's doctoral dissertation was "On the continuity of the gaseous and liquid states"; this theme, namely, that a substance passes from the gaseous to the liquid state without any *essential* change, though its *physical* properties differ in the two states, dominated the whole of van der Waals's work. As he

said in his Nobel lecture, his idea came to him through reading a
paper by Rudolph Clausius, who played an important part in the
development of the kinetic theory of gases. According to this theory
the molecules of a gas are in violent motion; the pressure of the
gas is due to the impacts of the molecules on the walls of the containing vessel, and the temperature of the gas depends on the mean
velocity of the molecules.

From the kinetic theory of gases can be deduced two important
laws: (1) For a given mass of gas at constant *temperature* the
product

$$\text{pressure} \times \text{volume}$$

is constant (Boyle's law, 1662); (2) For a given mass of gas at
constant *pressure,* the quotient

$$\frac{\text{volume}}{\text{absolute temperature}}$$

is constant, the absolute temperature being the temperature measured from the absolute zero, $-273°$ C. These two laws combined
are expressed by the equation

$$\frac{pv}{T} = R \qquad \text{or} \qquad pv = RT$$

where p is the pressure, v the volume, T the absolute temperature,
and R a constant depending only on the mass of the gas. Such an
equation is called an *equation of state,* because it shows the connection between the three factors which determine the state or condition of the gas; this particular one is known as the *perfect gas
equation.* Why *perfect* gas? A gas which really obeyed this law
would behave perfectly regularly throughout the whole range of
possible values of pressure, temperature, and volume: the graph
showing pressure plotted against absolute temperature, the volume
being kept constant, would be a straight line which, when produced, would meet the temperature axis at the point marked
$-273°$ C; the graph showing pressure plotted against volume, the
temperature being kept constant, would be a rectangular hyperbola.
No *real* gas exists which behaves in this perfectly regular manner:
there are always discrepancies, sometimes large, sometimes small,
and particularly marked when the pressure is high; for many pur-

poses, however, it is convenient to imagine that there is such a *perfect* or *ideal* gas. It was the discrepancies which interested van der Waals: they called for explanation; further, when the cause of the discrepancies was once known it should be possible to construct an equation which would correctly represent the state of the gas for all possible values of the three factors involved.

Van der Waals approached the problem from the point of view of the kinetic theory. In deducing the perfect gas equation from this theory it had been assumed that the molecules of the gas were mere points, having mass but no volume; also no account had been taken of collisions between the molecules or of intermolecular forces. How van der Waals, by taking these factors into account, arrived at an improved equation of state, is told in the following extract, translated from the German of his Nobel lecture:

"The first impulse toward my life's work came, after I had left the University, through my becoming acquainted with a work by Clausius, published in 1857, on the kind of motion we call heat. In this work . . . Clausius showed how easily Boyle's law could be deduced if we assumed that a gas consists of material points moving with great velocity; he showed, too, that this velocity is of the order of magnitude of the velocity of sound and is proportional to the square root of the absolute temperature. It was later realized that this is only the mean value of the square of the velocity and that, as Maxwell said, it gives a law for the distribution of velocities, now known as Maxwell's law. . . .

"Clausius' work was a revelation to me, but at the same time it occurred to me that if an extremely rarefied gas, one whose volume is so large that the molecules may be regarded as points, consists of small bodies in motion, then it is surely obvious that it must still do so when the volume is diminished; that, in fact, this must still be the case when the gas reaches its highest density, and even for the so-called liquids, which, indeed, are to be regarded simply as gases condensed at low temperatures. This gave me the idea that there is no essential difference between the gaseous and liquid states of matter—that although those factors which, in addition to the motion of the molecules, go to determine the pressure must be

assumed to change quantitatively with changes in density and perhaps also with changes in temperature, yet they must be the same
factors that operate over the whole range. This brought me to the
idea of continuity. . . .

"The two factors I suggested as responsible for the fact that in
a nonrarefied state an aggregate of particles in motion does not obey
Boyle's law were, . . . (1) the attraction between the particles,
(2) their own proper volume. . . . I had originally expected that
the total volume must simply be diminished by the collective volume
of the molecules in order to find what volume was left over for the
motion. A closer investigation, however, soon showed . . . that
the quantity by which the volume must be diminished is variable:
that in extremely rarefied states this quantity, which I denoted by b,
is four times the molecular volume, but that with reduction of the
external volume it becomes less and falls by degrees to about half.
The law governing this falling-off has, however, not yet been
found. It has turned out that it is just this point that presents the
greatest difficulty in the study of the equation of state. . . . I thought
at first that it was merely necessary to examine the reduction in the
mean free path between the molecular collisions which results from
the fact that the molecules can no longer be considered as material points but, like all bodies known to us, must be considered as
possessing a real volume. . . . Boltzmann has shown that this is
not sufficient.

·　·　·　·　·

"As for . . . the mutual attractions of the molecules, . . .
here too the last word has not yet been spoken. Following the
method used by Laplace in his theory of capillarity, I, in my theory
of continuity, reduced this attraction, which acts throughout the
volume, to a surface force acting inward and thus, combined with
the external pressure, holding the moving molecules together.
Laplace considered his liquid purely as a continuum, as yet knowing nothing about molecules; in fact, if we were dealing with
molecules devoid of motion the reduction of the attractive forces
within the liquid to a surface force alone would not be permissible.
Since, however, the molecules are in motion, each point in the

liquid will not, at each moment, be filled with matter. We can, however, consider the space as continually filled with matter of average density. . . . As a result of the considerations I have mentioned I arrived at the equation

$$p = \frac{RT}{v - b} - \frac{a}{v^2} . \text{''}$$

This equation is usually written:

$$\left(p + \frac{a}{v^2}\right)(v - b) = RT$$

which may be compared with the perfect gas equation $pv = RT$. In van der Waals's equation a expresses the mutual attractions of the molecules, b their volume. Both a and b have different values for different gases.

The attractions between the molecules cause the pressure on the walls of the vessel due to their impacts to be less than would be the case if these attractions did not exist, so that the pressure *inside* the gas is greater by this amount than the observed pressure p. It is this *internal pressure,* as van der Waals called it, that is measured by a/v^2. As the volume v decreases due to an increase in the external pressure, a/v^2 increases, but more rapidly, and may ultimately equal or exceed the external pressure, in which case no external pressure is needed to keep the gas within the vessel, that is, it has now become a liquid. It was one of the essential features of van der Waals's theory that the equation applied equally well to the gaseous and liquid states of a substance, the transition from the gaseous to the liquid state being marked by a very big decrease in the value of v and consequently by a very big increase in the value of the internal pressure a/v^2. Van der Waals calculated the pressure inside a drop of water and found it to be about 10,000 atmospheres, ten times the pressure at the bottom of the ocean.

A gas cannot, however, be liquefied by mere increase of pressure unless its temperature is below a certain *critical temperature;* thus carbon dioxide, critical temperature 31° C, can be liquefied by pressure alone at ordinary temperatures, but the so-called *permanent* gases—oxygen (crit. temp. —118° C), nitrogen (crit. temp. —146° C), hydrogen (crit. temp. —234° C)—must first be cooled below these temperatures before they can be liquefied by pressure. Associated with the critical temperature of a gas are also the critical pressure and the critical volume, these three quantities occurring at what is called the *critical point*. At this critical point a gas or liquid possesses interesting properties; for instance in the case of carbon dioxide it is almost impossible to distinguish between the liquid substance and its vapor, the liquid and vapor states being apparently continuous, without any visible surface of separation between the two.

Van der Waals succeeded in expressing these critical constants of a substance in terms of the a and b occurring in his equation of state, finding that the critical volume $v_c = 3b$, the critical pressure $p_c = a/(27b^2)$, and the critical temperature $T_c = 8a/(27bR)$. Now the known temperature, pressure, and volume of a gas can always be expressed as multiples of its critical temperature, pressure, and volume, i.e., by putting $T = kT_c$, $p = lp_c$, $v = mv_c$, where k, l, m are ordinary numbers; thus for carbon dioxide ($T_c = 31°$ C) $46\frac{1}{2}°$ C can be expressed as $1\frac{1}{2}T_c$. If T_c, p_c, and v_c are now replaced by their values in terms of a and b and the results are substituted for T, p, and v in van der Waals's equation, a little straightforward algebraic manipulation results in the equation

$$\left(l + \frac{3}{m^2}\right)\left(m - \frac{1}{3}\right) = \frac{8}{3}k$$

This does not contain a or b, which are characteristic of the particular gas or liquid, but only the numbers k, l, m, which depend on the temperature, pressure, and volume, respectively. Hence this equation is independent of the *nature* of the gas or liquid. It means that if l and m are the same for any two gases, then k must also be the same, as otherwise the equation would not be satisfied; hence if the temperature of one of the gases is known, that of the other is also known, provided the critical temperatures of both gases are known. Thus as soon as the behavior of a single gas and the corresponding liquid is known at all temperatures and pressures, the state of any gas or liquid at any temperature and pressure can be calculated, if the state at the critical temperature is known. This is van der Waals's *law of corresponding states* and is the most important result of his work.

CONSEQUENCES IN THEORY AND PRACTICE

Van der Waals's equation of state is by no means perfect; he and others, including Clausius (died 1888), continued to work on the subject, Clausius finding that a was not a constant for a given substance but varied with temperature, a fact already suspected by van der Waals, who was fully aware that b varied with temperature.

In spite of its imperfections this equation, and the theory underlying it, marked a most promising attack on a very difficult problem. For practical purposes, when combined with the law of corresponding states, it is of great value, and most tables of physical constants list, in addition to the critical data, the values of a and b for various gases and liquids. One of the most important practical applications lies in the fact that the theory makes it possible to predict the conditions necessary for the liquefaction of a gas: thus it was of great assistance to Dewar in the liquefaction of hydrogen and to Kamerlingh Onnes (*q.v.* 1913) in the liquefaction of helium. It also plays an important part in the theory of modern freezing technique.

1911

WILHELM WIEN
(1864–1928)

"For his discoveries concerning the laws of heat radiation."

BIOGRAPHICAL SKETCH

WILHELM WIEN WAS BORN ON JANUARY 13, 1864, AT GAFFKEN, East Prussia, where his father was a landowner. In 1866 his parents settled in Drachenstein, near Rastenburg, East Prussia. Wien received his schooling first at the *Gymnasium* at Rastenburg, then at the Alstadt *Gymnasium* at Königsberg, capital of East Prussia. In the spring of 1882 he entered the University of Göttingen to study mathematics and science, but in the following autumn went to Berlin University, where from 1883 to 1885 he worked in Helmholtz' laboratory, obtaining his doctor's degree in 1886.

His further studies were interrupted through his having to return home to assist his sick father in the administration of the estate, and between the years 1886 and 1890 he was able to spend only one semester in Helmholtz' laboratory. In 1890, however, the estate was sold and Wien returned to Berlin. Helmholtz was now director of the Physikalisch-Technische Reichsanstalt, or State Physicotechnical Institute, the German equivalent of the National Bureau of Standards (Washington), and here Wien went as his assistant, remaining until 1892, when he was appointed lecturer at Berlin University. In 1896 he went to Aachen as lecturer in physics at the

Technical High School. In 1899 he was appointed professor of physics at the University of Giessen, but the following year went to Würzburg as Röntgen's successor. Here he remained until 1920, when he accepted the chair of physics at Munich, again succeeding Röntgen. He was still at Munich at the time of his death on August 30, 1928.

Wien's doctoral dissertation dealt with the diffraction of light at sharp metallic edges and with the influence of the material on the color of the diffracted light. His subsequent work falls roughly into two periods. While he was at Berlin, that is, from 1890 to 1896, he was engaged chiefly on problems connected with radiation: in a theoretical study he extended the concept of temperature to radiation existing in empty space; he investigated experimentally the thermoelectric method of measuring high temperatures; in 1893 he published his displacement law and in 1896 his distribution law, the work for which he received the Nobel Prize.

At the same time, probably as a result of his association with Helmholtz, he investigated a number of problems in hydrodynamics. From the time he went to Aachen almost to the time of his death his work dealt mainly with the discharge of electricity through rarefied gases. His investigations in this field were hardly less important than those on radiation. While at Aachen he began a series of pioneer researches on the canal rays discovered by Goldstein (p. 49) and in 1896 read a paper to the German Physical Society on the magnetic and electrostatic deflections of these rays. He showed that, although the value of the ratio of the charge to the mass for the carriers of *negative* electricity (cathode rays) was about 2000 times that of the hydrogen ion in electrolysis, the value of this ratio for the carriers of *positive* electricity (canal rays) was very much smaller, being of the right order of magnitude for these carriers to be positively charged atoms. In later researches, made at Würzburg in 1902, he showed that the canal rays did in fact consist of atoms of the residual gases in the discharge tube. Wien was also the first to arrive at an estimate for the wave length of X rays; he did this in 1905 from a determination of the ratio of the energy of the X rays to that of the cathode rays by which they were excited.

DESCRIPTION OF THE PRIZE-WINNING
WORK

Wien's work on radiation dealt with two closely connected problems: the distribution of heat energy in the spectrum and the effect of a change of temperature on this distribution. Of these two problems it was the second which first engaged his attention. His treatment was a theoretical one in which he applied thermodynamical reasoning to the radiation existing in a constant-temperature enclosure.

When radiation, whether associated with the phenomenon of light or not, falls on a surface, part is reflected, part absorbed, part may be transmitted; if the surface is rough the reflected radiation will be *scattered,* that is, reflected in all directions. The proportions absorbed and reflected depend on the nature of the surface: thus a highly polished metallic surface reflects a large proportion of the incident radiation and absorbs very little, whereas lampblack reflects very little and absorbs most. Again, surfaces differ in their absorbing powers for different wave lengths, a red object appearing red because it absorbs blue rays more readily than red, which are for the most part reflected; the same thing applies, of course, to radiation which does not excite the sensation of light, that is, to *dark radiation.* A surface in a steady state as regards temperature must be giving out, or emitting, as much radiation as it receives, so that high absorbing power is always accompanied by high emitting power. Since the absorbing power is not the same for all wave lengths, a surface is a good emitter only of those wave lengths which it absorbs; lampblack, which absorbs radiation of nearly all wave lengths, is in turn an emitter of nearly all wave lengths. But no substance, not even lampblack, is a perfect absorber of all wave lengths—some are always reflected.

Gustav Kirchhoff, who, about 1860, made a theoretical study of the connection between absorbing and emitting powers, introduced the idea of a *perfectly black body,* defining it as a body which absorbs *all* the radiation falling on it, reflecting none. Such a body, if one really existed, would also emit radiation of *all* wave lengths. Kirchhoff then showed on theoretical grounds that a completely enclosed cavity having its walls at a uniform temperature possessed the properties of such a black body, and deduced that the distribution of wave lengths in the radiation contained in the cavity depended only on the temperature and not at all on the nature of the material forming the walls of the cavity.

We may get some idea of what this means if we carry out what Wien calls in his Nobel lecture a mental experiment: we imagine that it is possible for us to enter such an enclosure, without of course disturbing the radiation there, and that the temperature is such that the wave lengths corresponding to the red end of the spectrum predominate; then the walls of the enclosure will appear a uniform red; if they are made of different substances, say partly of lampblack, partly of polished silver, it will be quite impossible to distinguish the boundaries between the two substances, since the silver will be reflecting predominantly red radiation, while the lampblack will be absorbing, and therefore also emitting, predominantly red radiation. Of course, all other wave lengths will also be present in various proportions, but the red will predominate.

Obviously the name *black-body radiation* is not a happy one when applied to the particular distribution of wave lengths we have chosen, and the term *full radiation* is sometimes preferred. A close approximation to a constant-temperature enclosure may be seen in a cavity in a very hot coal fire, where small pieces of various substances such as metal, china, and glass become indistinguishable as soon as they have reached the temperature of their surroundings.

By a somewhat similar mental experiment Kirchhoff established the important law that bears his name: that the ratio of the emitting power to the absorbing power is the same for all bodies at the same temperature and is equal to the emitting power of a black body at that temperature. This applies to the totality of wave lengths emitted and absorbed, but he also showed that the same thing holds for any small range of wave lengths.

In the following extracts, translated from the German of his Nobel lecture, Wien outlines the argument by which he arrived at his displacement law.

". . . In the application of thermodynamics to the theory of radiation use is made of those ideal processes which have proved so fruitful in other respects. They are mental experiments which frequently cannot be carried out in practice but yet lead to reliable results. . . . Kirchhoff used them in the proof of his famous law. . . .

. . . . .

"Boltzmann also made use of ideal processes when, assuming the pressure of radiation, at that time only inferred from the electro-magnetic theory of light, he deduced from thermodynamics the law already arrived at empirically by Stefan, that the radiation of a black body is proportional to the fourth power of the absolute temperature.

"In this case, however, the deductions to be obtained from ther-modynamics were not exhausted: the change which the individual colors in the radiation underwent as a result of the change of tem-perature still remained to be determined. The calculation of this change again rests on an ideal process. For this we must assume the possibility of *perfectly reflecting* bodies, but such that all the radia-tion falling on them is scattered in the process of reflection; such bodies we can therefore describe as perfectly white. If we allow the radiation from a black body to enter an enclosure whose walls are formed of perfectly white bodies, the radiation will ultimately spread out just as if the walls of the enclosure were themselves radiating and were at the same temperature as the black body. If we now shut off the black body from our white space, we obtain something never realizable in practice, namely, radiation passing backward and forward continually between reflecting walls.

"But we carry the mental experiment further: we imagine the volume of our space to become smaller through a contraction of the walls, so that all the radiation is now confined in a smaller space. Since the radiation exerts a definite pressure, the pressure of light, on the walls on which it falls, we must do a certain amount of work in making the space smaller, just as if we had compressed a gas. Since the pressure of light is very small, this work is very small, but it can be calculated exactly, and that is the only thing that matters here. This work, according to the principle of the conserva-tion of energy, cannot be lost; it is converted into radiation, so that the density of the radiation is still further increased.

"This change in density produced by the movement of the white walls is not the only change the radiation has undergone. When a ray of light is reflected by a moving mirror it suffers a change in color due to the change in frequency determining the color. This change, obeying the so-called Doppler principle, plays a great part in astrophysics. The spectral lines which an approaching heavenly body sends to us appear to be displaced toward the shorter wave lengths in the ratio of the velocity of the body to the velocity of light. The same thing happens when a ray of light is reflected from a moving mirror, only here the change is twice as great. We are therefore in a position to calculate fully the change the radiation has undergone through the movement of the walls. The pressure of light, essential for these considerations, was first demonstrated by Lebedew much later; Arrhenius used it to explain the existence of comets' tails. Previously it had only been a deduction from Maxwell's electromagnetic theory.

"We now calculate on the one hand the change in the density of the radiation, on the other the change in the individual wave lengths. From these mental experiments we can draw an important conclusion: we can deduce from the second law of thermodynamics that the spectral composition of the radiation, which we have changed as a result of the compression of the space with reflecting walls, is precisely the same as if we had produced the increased density by raising the temperature, since otherwise we could, by means of a color filter, produce unequal density of the radiation in the two spaces and so obtain work from heat without compensation. Also, since we can calculate the change in the individual wave lengths caused by the compression, we can deduce how the spectral composition of the radiation from a black body changes with temperature. I shall not go further into this calculation, but merely give the result, namely, that the radiation energy of a given wave length so changes with temperature that the product of the temperature and the wave length remains constant."

Wien's displacement law is expressed by the relation:

$$\lambda T = \text{constant}$$

where λ is the wave length and T the absolute temperature. The value of the constant is about 0.288 when λ is measured in centimeters. Of course, if the distribution of wave lengths in black-body radiation were uniform, a general shortening of all wave lengths would result in a state indistinguishable from that which existed before the shortening took place, at least as far as the wave lengths are concerned, for, by the definition of black-body radiation, all wave lengths were already present in the radiation. The distribution is, however, far from uniform, the intensity of the radiation rising to a maximum in the neighborhood of some particular wave length and then falling off again. Wien's law tells us that this maximum shifts toward the region of shorter wave lengths as the temperature rises, a fact often indicated by stating his law as:

$$\lambda_{max}T = \text{constant}$$

where λ_{max} is the wave length for which the intensity of the radiation is a maximum.

That something of this sort happens may be seen from the successive appearances of a platinum wire when it is gradually heated electrically. At first the radiation is "dark," corresponding to wave lengths beyond the red end of the visible spectrum. As the temperature rises the wire becomes in turn dull red, red, bright red, orange, yellow, and finally white, corresponding to a gradual shift of λ_{max} toward the blue end of the spectrum, the region of shorter wave lengths; when λ_{max} lies in the blue, all the wave lengths constituting white light are being copiously emitted and the wire is *white hot.*

It was this problem of the distribution of energy among the wave lengths constituting black-body radiation that Wien investigated next. Unfortunately thermodynamical reasoning alone was not sufficient and Wien had to make certain arbitrary assumptions regarding the part played by the molecules in the emission of the radiation, assumptions which were by no means obviously true. The formula at which he arrived was

$$E_\lambda = \frac{c_1}{\lambda^5 e^{c_2/\lambda T}}$$

where E_λ is the energy corresponding to unit range of wave length at wave length λ; c_1 and c_2 are constants; and e is, of course, the base of the natural system of logarithms.

CONSEQUENCES IN THEORY AND PRACTICE

To what extent are Wien's two laws, the displacement law and the distribution law, supported by experiment? To provide an answer to this question a very sensitive instrument was required for detecting and measuring the small differences in the heating effect of the various parts of the spectrum. Fortunately such an instrument was available. In 1881 S. P. Langley, working at the Allegheny Observatory, Pennsylvania, had devised what he called a *bolometer,* in which radiant heat, falling on a thin strip of metal, caused a change in the electrical resistance of the metal, the resistance increasing with rise of temperature; from this increase in resistance the amount of heat received could be calculated. Langley himself used this bolometer to make the first thorough investigation into the distribution of energy in the solar spectrum; he found that at the base of the atmosphere it was a maximum in the yellow. In 1899 Lummer, who had worked with Wien at the Reichsanstalt, and Pringsheim, using a modified form of Langley's bolometer, examined the black-body radiation emerging from a small hole in a constant-temperature enclosure. Their results fully confirmed Wien's displacement law. The distribution law, however, did not fare so well, since it was found to agree with observation only when the product λT was small; but for small values of λT the agreement was excellent.

It was the failure of Wien's formula to represent correctly the distribution of energy throughout the spectrum which was directly responsible for one of the greatest discoveries in the history of physics: Max Planck (*q.v.* 1918) took up the problem and solved it by making a slight change in the form of Wien's expression, a change which nevertheless was of the greatest significance and led Planck to the formulation of his quantum theory of radiation.

1 9 1 2

NILS GUSTAF DALÉN
(1869–1937)

*"For his invention of automatic regulators to be
used in conjunction with gas accumulators for
lighting beacons and light buoys."*

BIOGRAPHICAL SKETCH

NILS GUSTAF DALÉN WAS BORN ON NOVEMBER 30, 1869, AT
Stenstorp, in southern Sweden. His education was directed mainly
to fitting him to follow his father's occupation: agriculture, horti-
culture, and dairy-farming. Even as a child, however, Dalén showed
a marked mechanical turn of mind, and as he grew older his lean-
ing toward an engineering career increased. In 1892, as a result of
private study combined with some private lessons, he was able to
enter the Chalmer technical school at Göteborg, from which he
was graduated in 1896 as a mechanical engineer. He completed his
studies by spending a year at the Federal Polytechnic at Zurich. On
his return to Sweden in 1897 Dalén busied himself with experimental work on hot-air turbines, compressors, and air-pumps, some
of his experiments being carried out in the workshops of the de
Laval steam turbine company at Stockholm; several improvements
in detail were the outcome of his work.

From 1900 to 1905 Dalén was a member of the engineering
firm of Dalén and Celsing, founded for the purpose of exploiting
inventions. It was through his connection with this firm that he
came into contact with the Swedish Carbide and Acetylene Com-

pany, which had in 1901 acquired the patent rights in Scandinavia of a French invention called "Acetylène Dissous," acetylene dissolved in acetone contained in a porous filling to form an acetylene gas accumulator. It was as works chief of this company from 1901 to 1903 and as chief engineer from 1906 of the Gas Accumulator Company, which in that year took over the Swedish Carbide and Acetylene Company, that Dalén did his most important work, laying the technical foundations of the world-wide industry which arose out of his inventions. When, in 1909, the Gas Accumulator Company was re-formed as the Swedish Gas Accumulator Company, he was appointed managing director.

On September 12, 1912, Dalén was injured in a serious explosion while carrying out tests. For some time his life was in danger, but he recovered to continue his work, though he lost the sight of both eyes. This occurred a few weeks before he was awarded the Nobel Prize; his brother, Professor Albin Dalén of the Caroline Medico-Chirurgical Institute in Stockholm, attended the Nobel ceremony in his place. Dalén died on December 10, 1937.

DESCRIPTION OF THE PRIZE-WINNING WORK

Dalén's interest in gas accumulators arose out of his connection with the Swedish Carbide and Acetylene Company. The original accumulators suffered from the serious defect that they were liable to explode if roughly handled. Dalén took the matter up, and it was one of his greatest achievements that he ultimately succeeded in discovering a filling, the famous *agamassan,* or *aga*-mass, which freed the accumulators from this danger. The most obvious explanation of the name AGA is that it was formed from the initial letters of the component words of *acetylengasackumulator,* acetylene gas accumulator, though it may have been suggested by the initials of the Swedish name of the Gas Accumulator Company, *Aktiebolaget Gasackumulator,* of which Dalén was chief engineer at the time of the discovery.

Dalén's interest in gas accumulators naturally directed his attention to problems connected with their use. He invented a regulator for controlling the pressure of the gas and, in 1905, an apparatus for use in beacon lighting which increased enormously the number of flashes obtainable from a given quantity of acetylene. His cleverest and most important invention, made in 1907, was, however, the sun-valve, *solventil,* for use, in conjunction with acetylene gas accumulators, for the automatic lighting up of beacons when dusk fell. It was based on the fact that a blackened metal rod is a greater absorber of radiant heat than a polished rod of the same metal and therefore expands more when exposed, for example, to the heat of the sun. As a result of a number of preliminary experiments, mostly carried out on a window-sill of his house, Dalén found that the difference in the expansion of a blackened and a polished rod, though very small, was yet sufficient for his purpose. The sun-valve which he finally evolved consisted of a glass cylinder containing three vertical polished metal rods arranged in a circle round a vertical blackened metal rod, all four being fixed at their upper ends. When, through absorption of heat, the blackened rod expanded, it depressed a lever and so closed the gas vent; when cooling caused the rod to contract, a spring set in one of the polished rods raised the lever from the vent and allowed the free passage of the gas, which was ignited by a by-pass jet. The apparatus could be adjusted to light up at any desired degree of darkness; this was done by raising or lowering the four rods by means of a differential screw.

Owing to his accident Dalén did not give the customary Nobel lecture; nor does he appear to have published any account of his work. The following is a translation of part of the address, given in Swedish, by Professor H. G. Söderbaum, President of the Swedish Royal Academy of Science at the time of the presentation:

"Ever-increasing sea routes demand more and more devices for the safety of navigation; among these safeguards, lighthouses and luminous buoys play no small part and their number has increased enormously during recent years. At the same time ways have been sought for increasing the strength of the light and for making the individual lights more easily distinguishable. Also efforts have been made to render the lights as far as possible self-regulating, a matter of considerable importance, since no country can afford to pay for constant supervision of all the beacons it needs. . . .

"In the mid-1890's the preparation from calcium carbide of the gaseous hydrocarbon acetylene first became possible on an industrial scale. This gas burns brilliantly with a particularly strong white light, but the first attempts to use it for the lighting of beacons were not very satisfactory. The oil gas previously employed could be compressed into large metal containers, but to treat acetylene in the same way was found to be dangerous, since it explodes at the least shock if it is under a pressure of two or more atmospheres. For luminous buoys the method was tried of putting the calcium carbide inside the buoy and letting the acetylene escape gradually through the automatic admission of water, but unfortunately this method proved inconvenient, unreliable, and impracticable in the cold.

"In 1896 the two French chemists Claude and Hess discovered the property possessed by acetone of dissolving large quantities of acetylene. This solution is not explosive, but it cannot be used for the storage of acetylene since, even if the container is filled originally with a saturated solution under high pressure, the volume of the liquid soon diminishes through use or cooling, with the result that a vacuum forms above the surface of the liquid and becomes filled with explosive acetylene gas.

"It was then found that the explosiveness disappeared if the acetylene solution was forced into a porous mass. Many unsuccessful attempts were now made to prepare a porous mass sufficiently durable and elastic to withstand jolting and shaking, for instance during transport, without cracking and crumbling and the consequent formation of cavities which, becoming full of acetylene, could cause an explosion.

"The honor of having finally found the formula for such a porous mass, the so-called *aga,* belongs to the engineer [Nils] Gustaf Dalén. By a complicated and carefully studied process this mass is introduced into steel containers, which thus become in effect acetylene gas accumulators. The pores of the mass are half filled with acetone, and the acetylene is then forced in under a pressure of ten atmospheres. Under this pressure and at a temperature of 15° C the container holds a hundred times its own volume of acetylene. Such a container can be used to supply the gas required for a lighthouse or luminous buoy.

"The advantage of this method would not, however, be great if the acetylene light had to burn uninterruptedly: on the one hand it would prove quite costly, on the other it would be impossible to distinguish the lights of different lighthouses from one another or from other lights. Several methods had indeed already been devised for rendering beacon lights intermittent, for instance by the use of moving screens or by causing the lantern itself to revolve. But these methods require constant supervision and consequently entail great expense. In the use of compressed oil gas as illuminant it had been found possible to arrange for the escaping gas to actuate the mechanism for producing the flashes. The duration of the flash was about 5 to 7 sec., which in view of the feeble illumination from oil gas was perhaps an advantage. But with the strong light given by acetylene such long flashes are unnecessary; moreover, they do not allow of enough variation in the signals. In the large lighthouses they have therefore for the most part already been replaced by flashes of only $1/10$ to $1/30$ sec. duration.

"It was about the year 1904 that Dalén took up the study of this problem. In the apparatus employing oil gas not more than 50 flashes could be obtained from one liter of gas. Using an absolutely new principle, Dalén constructed an apparatus for producing flashes by the instantaneous opening and closing of the gas vent, with the result that one liter of gas produced several thousand extremely short but very distinct flashes. This ingenious invention was subjected to lengthy trials from which it emerged victorious, proving to be very reliable. Later methods for the application of the so-called *aga* light in lighthouses were very completely worked out by Dalén. . . . The burner is fitted with a small by-pass jet which, in the most usual arrangement, produces a flash of $3/10$ sec. duration every three seconds.

"In 1907 Dalén achieved his crowning success by constructing a so-called sun-valve; this extinguishes the light at sunrise and relights it at nightfall. It consists of four metal bars enclosed in a glass tube, the inner bar being blackened, the others gilded and bright. Daylight is absorbed by the blackened bar, which expands as a result of the heating and so closes the gas valve; as the light fails, the black bar comes to the same temperature as the other three and the resulting contraction allows the valve to re-open. The apparatus can be adjusted to the degree of sensitivity desired; for greater security it is preferable to arrange for it to light up as soon as fog or cloud obscures the sun.

"Thanks to the sun-valve combined with intermittent light, a saving in gas of 93 percent is secured; a greater saving is possible if the duration of the eclipses is lengthened.

"Aga-lighting makes it possible for lighthouses and buoys to be established in the most inaccessible spots among islands and in seas where there are dangerous reefs. With a very small number of easily transportable gas accumulators these lights can, without supervision, unerringly send out their regular warning and guiding signals for a whole year or more. This has resulted in a previously unattainable degree of safety for navigation and at the same time in an enormous saving in cost. . . .

"Most maritime nations have begun to instal Dalén's apparatus. . . .

"The *aga* light has proved to be extremely useful in other respects, for instance for the lighting of railway carriages, for railway track signals, for the headlights of cars, for welding, for smelting and cutting metals."

CONSEQUENCES IN THEORY AND PRACTICE

The passage of time has not lessened the importance of Dalén's work. It is true that where electricity is available this has largely displaced acetylene as a source of illumination; but the vast majority of beacons are far removed from sources of electrical power and still rely largely on Dalén's aga-lighting and on Dalén's sun-valve.

1 9 1 3

HEIKE KAMERLINGH ONNES
(1853–1926)

"For his investigations into the properties of bodies at low temperatures, which led, among other things, to the preparation of liquid helium."

BIOGRAPHICAL SKETCH

HEIKE KAMERLINGH ONNES WAS BORN AT GRONINGEN, HOLland, on September 21, 1853. He received his early schooling at the Groningen High School under J. M. van Bemmelen, who later became professor of chemistry at Leiden University and did important work on colloids. In 1870 Kamerlingh Onnes entered the University of Groningen, but in October of the following year went to Heidelberg, where he studied under Kirchhoff and Bunsen. He returned to Groningen University in April 1873 and remained there until 1878, when he was appointed assistant to the professor of physics at the Delft Polytechnic. In 1879 he obtained his doctor's degree at Groningen University for a dissertation on the rotation of the earth. In 1882, when only twenty-nine years of age, he was appointed professor of experimental physics at Leiden University. He held this chair until 1923, when he resigned on reaching the retirement age of seventy. He died at Leiden on February 21, 1926.

In 1904 Kamerlingh Onnes was created Chevalier of the Order of the Netherlands Lion, and in 1923, Commander. The Royal Society of London awarded him the Rumford Medal in 1912 and elected him a Foreign Member in 1916. Honorary degrees were conferred on him by the universities of Delft and Berlin. The Prussian Academy of Sciences in Berlin elected him a Corresponding Member in 1923.

In 1904, the silver jubilee of his doctorate, his students and collaborators issued a *Gedenkboek,* which surveyed the work done in his laboratory at Leiden during the period 1882 to 1904. In 1922 a second *Gedenkboek,* covering the period 1904 to 1922, was issued in commemoration of his forty years as professor of experimental physics at Leiden.

DESCRIPTION OF THE PRIZE-WINNING WORK

In his inaugural lecture at Leiden Kamerlingh Onnes said that every physics laboratory should bear the motto: "Through measurement to knowledge"; certainly no better label could be found for the work done during the next forty-one years in the laboratory which he was to organize at Leiden—a laboratory destined to become world-famous as the Leiden cryogenic laboratory. In selecting low-temperature work as the main field of research in the laboratory Kamerlingh Onnes was largely influenced by the work of his friend van der Waals (*q.v.* 1910), professor of physics at Amsterdam. He was particularly interested in the law of corresponding states and had in 1881, while at Delft, published an important paper on the general theory of fluids, treating the subject from the point of view of the kinetic theory. He realized, however, that the great need was for accurate measurements of volume, pressure, and temperature over as wide a range of values as possible, and to that end turned his attention to the problem of attaining very low temperatures and holding them constant.

The problem of producing low temperatures is bound up with that of the liquefaction of gases. A supply of liquid oxygen, for example, makes available for experimental work a temperature of −183° C, since that is the temperature at which liquid oxygen boils at normal atmospheric pressure; liquid nitrogen boils at −195.7° C, liquid hydrogen at −252.7° C, liquid helium at −269° C, four degrees above the absolute zero. Originally, of course, the liquefac-

tion of gases was an end in itself; it was only in the cryogenic laboratory at Leiden that it became a means to an end: the investigation
of the physical properties of bodies at very low temperatures.

Three methods of cooling a gas below the temperature of its
surroundings were known and each had been made the basis of a
method of liquefaction. L. P. Cailletet in France used the cooling
effect due to the sudden expansion of a gas at high pressure (see
above, p. 46); oxygen under a pressure of several hundred atmospheres was cooled by liquid sulphur dioxide to −29° C and then
allowed to expand suddenly: a mist formed, which Cailletet took
to be droplets of liquid oxygen.

In the same year (1877) R. P. Pictet of Geneva used the cooling
effect due to the rapid evaporation of a liquid; he devised a *cascade*
method in which the cooling took place by stages: oxygen was surrounded by liquid carbon dioxide, the temperature of which had
been previously reduced to about −70° C by passing it through a
tube surrounded by liquid sulphur dioxide boiling under reduced
pressure; rapid evaporation of the carbon dioxide lowered the temperature of the oxygen to about −140° C; this being below its critical temperature (see above, p. 91), the oxygen could now be
liquefied by pressure alone (about 500 atmospheres). Z. F. Wroblewski and K. S. Olszewski, both of Cracow, in 1883 modified
Pictet's method by using liquid ethylene at −100° C and cooling it
to −136° C by rapid evaporation into a vacuum; at this temperature oxygen was liquefied by a pressure of about 20 atmospheres.
In the same year they succeeded in liquefying nitrogen. In 1884
Wroblewski, using Cailletet's method, with liquid oxygen as the
cooling agent, obtained a mist of liquid hydrogen, but it was not
until 1895 that liquid hydrogen was obtained in any quantity; in
that year Olszewski obtained enough to be able to estimate its boiling point. Neither Cailletet's nor Pictet's method yielded more than
small quantities of the liquefied gases, though James Dewar in
England, using a modified form of Pictet's cascade method, succeeded in 1892 in obtaining about a pint of liquid oxygen. However, valuable information and experience were gathered during
the course of these early experiments.

The third method made use of a fact discovered about 1850 by
J. P. Joule and W. Thomson (later Lord Kelvin), namely, that

when a gas under pressure escapes through a small orifice its temperature is lowered—it is due to this *Joule-Thomson effect* that the stream of air issuing from a small puncture in an inflated tire feels cold. The amount by which the temperature is lowered depends on the nature of the gas; it increases with the pressure difference on the two sides of the orifice and is greater the lower the initial temperature: thus for air at ordinary temperatures it is about $\frac{1}{4}°$ C per atmosphere difference of pressure. For hydrogen and helium there is a slight *rise* of temperature unless the gas is initially at a sufficiently low temperature, about −80° C for hydrogen.

In 1895 Professor Carl Linde of Munich constructed a liquid air plant in which this cooling effect was combined with a process known as the *regenerative* process: air from an air compressor passed through the inner of two concentric tubes coiled into a spiral —the *regenerator* or *heat-interchanger;* it was then cooled by expansion through a fine nozzle and flowed back through the outer of the concentric tubes, thus cooling the incoming air in the inner tube before that air reached the nozzle; the cooled air then reentered the compressor and was forced round the circuit a second time, being further cooled. The process was continued until the air liquefied, when it could be drawn off into one of the vacuum flasks invented by Dewar in 1892. Almost simultaneously W. Hampson in England invented a similar process. In the case of hydrogen or helium the gas must first be sufficiently cooled before the regenerative process can be used to liquefy it. Dewar, working in the laboratories of the Royal Institution of Great Britain, London, where he was Fullerian Professor of Chemistry, succeeded in 1896 in applying the process to the liquefaction of hydrogen, first cooling the gas by means of boiling liquid air to −190° C and then expanding it in a regenerative coil from a pressure of 200 atmospheres; however, he was unable to collect the liquid in an open vessel owing to its low specific gravity (0.07); this difficulty was overcome in 1898 by enclosing the regenerative coil in a vacuum vessel so designed that the liquid could be drawn off, and on May 10 of that year a small quantity of liquid hydrogen was for the first time collected in an open vessel.

The method used by Kamerlingh Onnes was a combination of Pictet's cascade method and Linde's regenerative process. It is described in the following extracts translated from the German of his Nobel lecture.

"The work done at Leiden owed its distinctive character from the beginning to the fact that I was guided by the theory put forward by van der Waals shortly before, in particular by the law of corresponding states. This law had an additional attraction for me in that I thought to find a basis for it in the mechanical similarity of substances; from this point of view the study of the deviations shown by substances of simple chemical structure and low critical temperatures seemed to me especially important. . . . For this purpose larger constant-temperature measuring apparatus had to be obtained and suitable constant-temperature baths constructed for the whole range of low temperatures. . . .

"Just as I was considering how to put these ideas into effect, the fundamental classical work of Wroblewski and Olszewski on the static liquefaction of oxygen was published. It now became a matter of high value to use a bath of liquid oxygen for the determination of the isothermals of hydrogen—particularly with a view to the liquefaction of hydrogen. These determinations could not be carried out until more than ten years after the foundation of the cryogenic laboratory, nor the results published until many years after Dewar had already succeeded in liquefying hydrogen. Also it was ten years before the first great step forward in the development of the cryogenic laboratory, the rendering possible of the carrying out of measurements in a liquid oxygen bath, was attained. By that time Olszewski and Dewar had already solved the problem of pouring the oxygen into open vessels.

"The Leiden procedure differed from the others in this respect: in order to have a permanent bath at our disposal, the vaporized oxygen was again liquefied and led round in a closed circuit. With the further development of the resources of the Leiden laboratory we again turned our attention to circuits of this kind, only now the researches to be made were transferred to still lower temperatures. Earlier experience could thus be applied in the attack on a later problem. For the liquefaction of helium this was even decisive. Thus the whole cryogenic laboratory still bears the impress of its first investigation.

. . . . .

"I now ask you to follow me into the Leiden laboratory.

"As I have already briefly indicated, the measurements are carried out in baths of liquid gases, preserved as long as one wishes in cryostats (apparatus for the maintenance of constant low temperatures), the vaporized gas making a circuit in the course of which it is again liquefied.

"As in Pictet's famous experiment, the cycles for the different gases are arranged in cascade, so that the low-temperature bath from an immediately preceding cycle also serves to liquefy at a lower temperature the gas circulating in the cycle immediately following.

"The first cycle contains methyl chloride. The liquid methyl chloride passes from a water-cooled condenser into a refrigerator, where it evaporates under the pressure corresponding to the desired temperature, namely, that for the liquefaction of ethylene. The vapor is drawn by means of a large vacuum pump through a regenerator, in which it flows in the opposite direction past the ethylene to be cooled; it is returned by a conjugate compressor to the condenser, where it is liquefied. The second cycle contains ethylene, the circulation taking place in the same way as in the first. In the third cycle oxygen circulates; the liquefied oxygen can serve to produce liquid air in the oxygen refrigerator.

"The cryostat with the liquid-oxygen bath which I have just mentioned was arranged without the use of vacuum flasks; it was connected to the liquefaction apparatus, so that at that time the measurements could be made only in the immediate neighborhood of the latter. Dewar, by his introduction of silvered vacuum flasks, revolutionized work at low temperatures; the liquid oxygen could be kept in these flasks and carried from the liquefaction apparatus to the spot where it was to be used. In the working of the cycles as well as in my subsequent work I later derived the greatest assistance from this ingenious idea of Dewar's.

"The fourth cycle serves for the preparation of liquid air. While the other cycles are closed, this one can be interrupted. Atmospheric air is drawn in and a supply of liquid air can be kept in open vacuum flasks.

"Shortly after our success in providing a permanent bath of liquid oxygen, . . . Linde discovered the process by which he created the liquid air industry. This ingenious discovery permits air initially at normal temperature to be liquefied without the use of intermediate steps. You will see that the production of liquid hydrogen and liquid helium in the following cycles, which requires each time a similar great reduction in temperature without intermediate steps, rests on the principle of Linde's process. For the production of liquid air, however, we continued to use the cycles arranged in cascade that I have described; this arrangement works economically and yields about 14 liters an hour.

· · · · ·

"Let us now pass on to the hydrogen cycle. . . . I started from the principle of mechanical similarity. . . . From this and the critical data determined . . . by Olszewski it could be inferred that, if one succeeded in constructing as model a suitable apparatus which, starting from *normal* temperature, liquefied *oxygen,* then with apparatus constructed on this model it would be possible, starting from the temperature of *liquid oxygen,* to liquefy *hydrogen.* Long before I had an opportunity of applying this principle, hydrogen had already been liquefied by Dewar. . . . In liquid hydrogen a source of cold was placed at our disposal which took us five times nearer the absolute zero than did liquid air. In Leiden a continuously working cycle was arranged in which hydrogen was used. . . . The compressed hydrogen leaves the refrigerator, in which liquid air evaporates under reduced pressure, and enters a regenerator coil fitted with a throttle valve which, following Dewar's example, we placed in a silvered vacuum flask. The coil itself was constructed on the model of Hampson's extremely practical apparatus for the liquefaction of air. The liquid hydrogen collects in a Dewar's flask and is siphoned over into portable silvered vacuum flasks.

· · · · ·

"The determination of the isothermals of helium was of the greatest importance for the liquefaction of this gas. They could show whether the gas, like other substances, obeyed the law of corresponding states, and, if this was the case, what were the critical data of helium. From this it would be possible to judge whether, starting from the freezing point of hydrogen, the lowest tempera-

ture to which it was possible to cool it, the helium could be liquefied with the help of Linde's process. If that was so, the principle
of similarity could again be applied to arrange the helium cycle,
just as the liquefaction of hydrogen was built on the model of
Hampson's liquefaction of air. It was now a question of determining whether the Boyle temperature, that is, the temperature at
which the compression of the helium begins to obey Boyle's law,
lay above the melting point of hydrogen. If this were the case, a
static liquefaction might be hoped for if a closed helium cycle were
arranged in a suitable manner on the model of the hydrogen cycle.
The question was answered in the affirmative by the determination
of the isothermals. . . .

· · · · ·

"After suitable previous cooling, the compressed helium enters
the refrigerator, where hydrogen evaporates under reduced pressure; then flows through the regenerator coil and expands through
the throttle valve. As in the Linde process, the liquid collects in the
bottom of the vacuum flask. So that it may be possible to observe
the liquid helium, the bottom of the flask is kept transparent and is
surrounded by a vacuum flask kept full of liquid hydrogen, which
in its turn is protected by a transparent vacuum flask containing
liquid air, and this again by a flask in which warmed alcohol
circulates.

· · · · ·

"The refrigerator is supplied with liquid hydrogen from a transparent auxiliary reservoir into which the liquid hydrogen is siphoned from the supply flasks. Before it is cooled in the refrigerator
the helium flows through a tube cooled with liquid air and containing charcoal to free it from traces of air with which it may have
become contaminated during the circulation. For the use of this
property of charcoal we are indebted to Dewar. . . .

· · · · ·

". . . the experiment began at half past five in the morning and
was concluded at half past nine in the evening, the first liquid

helium having been observed at half past six in the evening. . . .
It was a wonderful sight when the almost ethereal-looking liquid
first appeared; it was not noticed as it flowed in, its presence only
being detected when the vessel was already full—then its surface
stood out sharp as a knife edge against the glass.

"It gave me the greatest pleasure to be able to show the liquid
helium to my revered friend van der Waals, whose theory had
remained to the end my guide in the liquefaction of gases."

CONSEQUENCES IN THEORY AND PRACTICE

From the point of view of the work of the cryogenic laboratory
the importance of the successful outcome of the experiment lay in
the fact that it made available a temperature only a little more than
four degrees above the absolute zero, the boiling point of liquid
helium being found to be −268.8° C. In order to get still lower
temperatures Kamerlingh Onnes next attempted to obtain solid
helium; in this, however, he was not successful, though in 1910,
by boiling liquid helium under reduced pressure, he reached a temperature only slightly more than one degree above absolute zero,
and in 1921 came within one degree. It was not until 1926, after
the death of Kamerlingh Onnes, that his successor at Leiden, Professor W. H. Keesom, succeeded in obtaining solid helium by
cooling the liquid to about −272° C under pressure.

Concurrently with these attempts to get nearer and nearer to the
absolute zero, Kamerlingh Onnes and his collaborators were making use of the lower temperatures as they became available to
extend the range of their investigations into the physical properties
of substances at low temperatures. The results of their work were
published regularly in English as "Communications from the Physical Laboratory at Leyden" and distributed to scientists throughout
the world. These *Communications,* together with the two *Gedenk-
boeken* already mentioned, form a most valuable record of researches of outstanding accuracy carried out over a wide range of
physical problems.

One of the problems investigated was the effect of very low temperatures on electrical resistance. It had been known since the early

years of the nineteenth century that the resistance of metals decreased when they were cooled, so that a considerable falling off at very low temperatures was expected; Kamerlingh Onnes, in 1911, made the completely unexpected discovery that near the absolute zero the resistance of certain metals practically disappears, so that a current once started in a coil of one of these metals may continue to flow for hours or even days. The temperature at which this occurs is quite definite for a given metal, but varies from one metal to another. The phenomenon, which is known as superconductivity, has not yet been satisfactorily explained, though much work has since been done on it by, among others, Kamerlingh Onnes himself (who discovered that the effect can be annulled without change of temperature by a suitably applied magnetic field), by Gabriel Lippmann, and by Max von Laue.

Although Kamerlingh Onnes's greatest single achievement was the liquefaction of helium, his contributions to physics must be measured by the mass of precise data on low temperature phenomena gathered at the Leiden cryogenic laboratory—a laboratory which, with its unrivaled equipment for low-temperature research, is in itself a monument to his genius.

1 9 1 4

MAX THEODOR FELIX VON LAUE
(1879–)

"For his discovery of the diffraction of Röntgen rays in crystals."

BIOGRAPHICAL SKETCH

MAX THEODOR FELIX VON LAUE WAS BORN ON OCTOBER 9, 1879, at Pfaffendorf, near Coblenz, Prussia. His father, a military official, was frequently moved from place to place, so that von Laue lived in turn in Brandenburg, Altona, Posen, Berlin, and Strasbourg. In each of the last three places he attended the *Gymnasium* for the study of the humanities. His interest in the exact sciences was first aroused through the excellent teaching of Professor Goering at the Protestant *Gymnasium* in Strasbourg. He obtained his leaving certificate in 1898 and, after serving his year in the army, entered the University of Strasbourg in 1899, but soon transferred to Göttingen, where W. Voigt's lectures on theoretical physics so influenced him that he decided to devote himself to that subject. After a semester at the University of Munich he spent three semesters at Berlin studying under Max Planck (*q.v.* 1918), whose lectures on optics and thermodynamics determined von Laue's special line of research. In experimental optics he was especially indebted to two short lectures, one on interference spectroscopy, the other on heat radiation, given by O. Lummer (see above, p. 101), who at that time was still at Berlin.

After obtaining his doctor's degree at Berlin in 1903 he went back to Göttingen, but returned to Berlin in 1905 as Planck's assistant, being appointed a lecturer the following year. In 1909 he went as *privatdozent* to Munich, and it was while there that he did the work on the interference of X rays for which he received the Nobel Prize. In 1912 he was appointed assistant professor at Zurich, and in 1914 professor at Frankfort on the Main. From 1916 until the end of the First World War he was engaged on technical war work at Würzburg, doing research on the high vacuum tubes used in telephony and wireless telegraphy. In 1919 he was appointed professor of theoretical physics at Berlin, where he remained until he resigned the appointment in 1943. Since 1946 he has been honorary professor at Göttingen University.

Von Laue was awarded the Max Planck Medal by the German Physical Society in 1932. He received an honorary D.Sc. from Manchester University in 1936 and from the University of Chicago in 1948. In 1949 he visited London to be admitted as a Foreign Member of the Royal Society. He is a member of the Berlin Academy of Sciences and of many other scientific bodies.

DESCRIPTION OF THE PRIZE-WINNING WORK

In the extract from his Nobel lecture which we give below von Laue tells how he came to be particularly interested in the phenomena of interference (see p. 55); his doctoral dissertation dealt with this subject, as did the paper which qualified him for his lectureship at Berlin; this latter, like several other papers published during the next few years, dealt with the thermodynamics of interference phenomena. When, in 1909, he went to Munich, he found himself at the same university as Röntgen, with the natural result that to his interest in interference he added an interest in X rays. At Munich, too, was Arnold Sommerfeld, actively engaged in the study of X rays and γ rays, and later to play an important part in the development of the theory of atomic structure. It was through Sommerfeld that von Laue undertook a mathematical investigation of the theory of *cross-gratings*—diffraction gratings having two sets of lines, one at right angles to the other—and thus prepared the way for dealing later with the problem of *space-gratings*.

Munich was also the home of the Bavarian national museum, which housed one of the finest scientific collections in existence. Here Paul von Groth, professor of mineralogy, was curator of the minerals section. Von Groth upheld the theory, put forward by Auguste Bravais in 1848 and developed by L. Sohncke in 1879, and by J. S. von Federow and A. Schoenflies in 1891, that in a crystal the atoms are not closely packed but are arranged in an open lattice according to a definite three-dimensional pattern—von Federow and Schoenflies, by independent methods, arrived at 230 possible types of lattice. This theory had attracted little attention on the part of physicists, but von Laue heard of it from von Groth and was greatly impressed by it; soon it was to play a fundamental part in his own work.

At this time (1912) there was still considerable uncertainty as to the nature of X rays—whether they were particles or ether waves or, as some thought, pulses in the ether. If they were ether waves —and by 1912 what little evidence there was tended to support this view—they should, like light, show interference effects. Röntgen, very soon after making his discovery, had looked for such effects but without success; nor had he been able to detect any signs of reflection, refraction, or polarization. He thought it possible that, whereas ordinary light consisted of transverse vibrations in the ether, X rays might consist of longitudinal vibrations.

At the beginning of the century H. Haga and C. H. Wind, of the University of Groningen in Holland, passed a narrow pencil of X rays through a very fine triangular slit 4 cm. long and only 25-thousandths of a millimeter wide at the base; a photographic plate showed a broadening of the image of the slit at the vertex, possibly due to diffraction. In 1909 B. Walter and R. Pohl at Hamburg, using Haga and Wind's method, found from measurements on the photographic plate the value 1.2×10^{-9} cm. for the hypothetical wave length of X rays, which agreed reasonably well with values already obtained by Wien (*q.v.* 1911) and by Stark (*q.v.* 1919) independently by applying Planck's theory of radiation to the transfer of energy between very slow cathode rays and the X rays produced by them. In 1912 Sommerfeld, using a microphotometric method of measurement for which he was indebted to his colleague at Munich, P. P. Koch, obtained the value 4×10^{-9} cm. In the meantime C. G. Barkla (q.v. 1917) in England had found evidence of at least partial polarization with X rays. It therefore seemed probable that X rays were electromagnetic waves, but of very much shorter wave length than visible light—about ten thousand times shorter than the wave length of sodium light. Since the distance between the lines of a diffraction grating must be of the same order of magnitude as the wave length of the incident light, it was clearly impossible to construct an artificial grating for producing interference effects with X rays.

How von Laue was led to his brilliant idea that a crystal, with its ordered arrangement of atoms, might provide a suitable natural diffraction grating, is told in the extract from his Nobel lecture, though his own part in the subsequent development receives but summary treatment at his hands. Friedrich and Knipping carried out the crucial experiment, but von Laue, treating the array of atoms in a crystal as a space-grating, had already determined theoretically what would happen if very short electromagnetic waves were passed through such a grating. The problem was a difficult one, but by extending his earlier work on cross-gratings, he was able to show mathematically that a pencil of X rays should, after passing through a crystal, produce a dark spot where the primary pencil struck a photographic plate, with other spots, due to the diffracted pencils, arranged in a regular pattern round the central spot. This prediction was fully confirmed by the Friedrich and Knipping experiment.

We now give * a translation from the German of that part of the Nobel lecture which dealt particularly with von Laue's own work. He himself always uses the name "Röntgen rays," but we have preferred to use the more familiar "X rays."

"As far back as I can remember . . . optics, and particularly the wave theory of light, has held an attraction for me. . . . As I finally acquired almost a sure instinct for wave processes, it naturally came about that my first independent work, which was on the

---

* By kind permission of Professor von Laue.

propagation of ordinary radiation in dispersive bodies and on the thermodynamics of interference phenomena, also lay in this field. It was a piece of great good fortune that Sommerfeld entrusted me with the task of writing the article on wave optics for the *Encyklopädie der mathematischen Wissenschaften,* for I had to find a mathematical treatment of the theory of gratings which—without being entirely new—could be applied as simply as possible to crossgratings. Even at that time I thought of the wider application to space-gratings, but did not follow the matter up. . . .

"Then, when in 1909 I came to Munich, my thoughts turned repeatedly to the nature of X rays, partly as a result of Röntgen's work at this university, partly through Sommerfeld's lively interest in X rays and in γ rays, matters on which he had also published several works. There was yet another important circumstance. Mineralogists since Haüy and Bravais had explained the fundamental crystallographic law of rational indices simply and clearly as due to the arrangement of the atoms in a space-lattice. Sohncke, as well as Federow and Schoenflies, had brought the mathematical theory of the possible space-lattices to the highest degree of perfection. But these ideas led to no further physical deduction and so continued to exist as a doubtful hypothesis comparatively unknown to physicists. In Munich, however, where models of the Sohncke space-lattices were to be seen in more than one Institute of the University, P. [von] Groth in particular advocated the theory orally and in writing, so that I too became acquainted with it. It gripped me all the more strongly as, in spite of all doubts as to the reality of atoms . . . , I had early become convinced that, while sound theoretical grounds were not to be found, yet experience constantly afforded new confirmation of this reality.

"That is how matters stood when in February 1912 P. P. Ewald came to me one evening. At Sommerfeld's request he was working on a mathematical investigation into the behavior of long electromagnetic waves in a space-grating, . . . and asked my advice. Now I must admit that I was unable to help him, but during the conversation the thought occurred to me to examine at some time or other the behavior of waves which are short in comparison with the grating constant of the space-lattice. And here my instinct for optics told me at once that a diffraction spectrum would be produced.

That the lattice constant in crystals is of the order of magnitude of 10^{-8} cm. was sufficiently well known by analogy with other atomic distances in solid and liquid bodies, and besides was easily confirmed from the density, the molecular weight, and the mass of the hydrogen atom, for which an especially good value had at that time just been found. The order of magnitude of the wave length of X rays estimated by Wien and Sommerfeld was 10^{-9} cm. Hence, if X rays were passed through a crystal, the ratio of the wave length and the lattice constant was extraordinarily favorable. I told Ewald at once that I expected interference effects with X rays.

"W. Friedrich also soon heard of this. Although he at once declared himself ready to carry out a suitable experiment, the idea was at first received with some scepticism by those acknowledged masters of our science to whom I had opportunity of mentioning it. A little diplomacy was necessary in order that Friedrich and Knipping should be allowed to make the experiment according to my plan, using at first quite simple means. Copper sulphate was used as the crystal, since large and regular pieces of it were easily obtainable. We left the direction in which the radiation passed through the crystal to chance. At the very first attempt there appeared on the photographic plate behind the crystal, near the track of the primary rays coming straight from the cathode, a large number of deflected rays, the expected diffraction spectrum.

"Friedrich and Knipping continued the work, ... Instead of the triclinic copper sulphate, with the radiation passing through in any direction, they used crystals of the highest possible symmetry, and therefore regular, and irradiated them in the direction of the crystallographic axes. The theoretical work had already been done, taken over from ordinary gratings and cross-gratings, so that on June 8, 1912, Sommerfeld was able to give the Munich Academy an account of the joint work of Friedrich, Knipping, and myself on X-ray interference, an account which contained, besides the theory, a series of very characteristic photographs."

CONSEQUENCES IN THEORY AND PRACTICE

The success of the experiment provided strong evidence in favor not only of the wave nature of X rays but also of the lattice theory of crystal structure. The diffraction of X rays by crystals, once established, made possible a precise determination of the wave length of X rays, and in the hands of the Braggs (*q.v.* 1915) was developed into a powerful method for exploring the arrangement of atoms in crystals. X-ray spectra have played a fundamental part in the investigation of the structure of the atom; they enter into the work of several of the later Nobel laureates.

1 9 1 5

WILLIAM HENRY BRAGG
(1862–1942)

WILLIAM LAWRENCE BRAGG
(1890–   )

"For their contributions to the study of crystal structure by means of X rays."

BIOGRAPHICAL SKETCH

WILLIAM HENRY BRAGG

WILLIAM HENRY BRAGG WAS BORN AT WESTWARD IN CUMBER-land, England, on July 2, 1862. On the death of his mother when he was barely seven years old, Bragg was sent to the old grammar school at Market Harborough in Leicestershire. After six years here, he went to King William's College in the Isle of Man, where he developed a marked liking for mathematics. In 1881 he entered Trinity College, Cambridge, and studied mathematics under Dr. E. J. Routh. After passing the Mathematical Tripos, Part I, in 1884, as Third Wrangler, he remained on at Cambridge, attending lectures in physics given by J. J. Thomson, who had been appointed Cavendish Professor at the end of 1884.

Toward the end of 1885 the professorship of mathematics and physics at Adelaide University, Australia, fell vacant. Bragg, al-though only twenty-three years of age, obtained the post, and the next twenty-three years of his life were spent in Australia. In 1908 he was offered the Cavendish Professorship of Physics at the University of Leeds; he accepted the offer and returned to England the following year. He remained at Leeds until 1915, when he was appointed Quain Professor of Physics at University College, London.

During the First World War, however, he was engaged on research work for the Admiralty, being a member of the Board of Inventions and Research; when the submarine menace became acute, he and his team of workers invented and developed the hydrophone for the detection of underwater craft. It was not until 1919 that he was free to take up his appointment at University College, London. In 1923, on the death of Sir James Dewar, Bragg was appointed director of the Royal Institution of Great Britain, London; under him the Davy-Faraday Laboratory became a world-famous center of research, particularly into problems of crystal structure. He died on March 10, 1942, after a very short illness.

Bragg was elected a Fellow of the Royal Society of London in 1907, was awarded its Rumford Medal in 1916 and the Copley Medal in 1930, and was elected president in 1935. Some sixteen British and foreign universities conferred honorary doctorates on him. He was knighted in 1920.

Sir William Bragg's Christmas lectures at the Royal Institution—lectures traditionally intended for a "Juvenile Auditory"—were famous. They included "The World of Sound," "Concerning the Nature of Things," "Old Trades and New Knowledge," "The Universe of Light"; all have been published and are masterpieces of clear exposition.

For several years after taking up his post at Adelaide, Bragg was occupied almost entirely with teaching and administrative work. Then, in 1903, he was called upon to give the presidential address to the mathematical and physical section of the Australasian Association for the Advancement of Science, the following January. He decided to review the recent developments in physics, particularly the researches of Lenard on the passage of cathode rays through matter, the work of J. J. Thomson on the electron, and the work of Becquerel, the Curies, and Rutherford on radioactivity. The preparation of his address aroused in him so great an interest in radioactivity that as soon as possible he obtained some radium salt and embarked on a series of experiments which, carried out between the years 1904 and 1908, made his name world famous.

These researches dealt mainly with the passage through matter of the α, β, and γ rays emitted by radioactive substances (see p. 26). Of special importance were those dealing with α rays. Lenard had shown (p. 38) that cathode rays were able to pass through thin layers of metal and also through several centimeters of air at normal pressure, though in the latter case a fluorescent screen or photographic plate placed in various positions in the stream showed a considerable amount of scattering, the boundaries of the stream becoming ill-defined because of the deflection of individual electrons from the main stream. On J. J. Thomson's theory of the structure of the atom (p. 48) this scattering could be put down to collisions between electrons of the cathode stream and constituent electrons of the atoms of the air through which the stream passed. It seemed to Bragg that an α particle, with a mass some seven thousand times as great as that of an electron, would not be deflected from its path by such an encounter, but would pursue a perfectly rectilinear course, so that a beam of α particles should show no appreciable scattering; also that, whereas the absorption of β rays—fast electrons with initial velocities approaching that of light—was mainly due to scattering, that of an α particle was due to loss of energy in producing ions along its track by removing electrons from the atoms through which it passed. These considerations led Bragg to the conclusion that an α particle should have a definite *range*— that the ionizing effect should end suddenly at a definite distance from the point of origin, a distance which would depend on the initial velocity of the particle and on the nature of the material traversed. These ideas were put forward in the presidential address of 1904.

When, a few months later, some radium bromide was placed at his disposal, Bragg proceeded to put his ideas to the test of experiment, using a modified form of the ionization chamber method introduced by Mme. Curie. The α rays from a thin film of radium bromide at R (Fig. 11) were restricted to a narrow pencil by lead stops C, C. The rays entered a shallow ionization chamber AB, A being a metal plate connected to an electroscope or electrometer, B

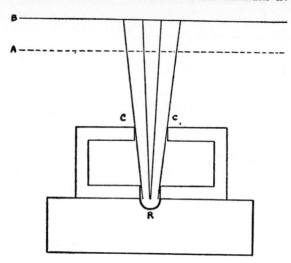

FIG. 11

W. H. Bragg's determination of the range of α particles.

a piece of metal gauze. If the plate A and the electroscope were given a positive charge, then, when the pencil of α rays entered the chamber, the negative ions formed moved to the plate, neutralized some of the charge, and so caused the leaves of the electroscope to collapse. The rate of collapse of the leaves was a measure of the strength of the ionization current. Bragg found that the first α particles entered the ionization chamber at a distance of 7 cm., and that the current increased uniformly with lessening distance, but at 3.5 cm. it suddenly began to increase more rapidly. This suggested that α particles of more than one range were being emitted and lent support to Rutherford's theory of radioactive change, according to which several distinct radium derivatives existed in a radium compound, namely, radium itself, radium emanation (a gas), radium C, and radium A, all of which emitted α particles—radium B emitted β particles only. Later experiments, carried out with far more elaborate and precise apparatus, gave ranges of 7 cm., 4.8 cm., 4.2 cm., and 3.5 cm., these being assigned to α particles from radium C, radium A, radium emanation, and radium itself, respectively. By interposing metallic screens in the path of the rays Bragg determined the stopping powers of the metals, finding them to depend on the atomic weight alone for screens of the same thickness. These investigations, as well as fundamental researches on the β rays and γ rays, were published in English scientific periodicals at the time, and later (1912) in book form under the title *Studies in Radioactivity.*

It was while Bragg was Cavendish Professor at Leeds that von Laue announced his discovery of the diffraction of X rays by crystals. Bragg immediately became interested, but it was his son William Lawrence, then still a student at Cambridge, who took the first step in their epoch-making investigations.

BIOGRAPHICAL SKETCH

WILLIAM LAWRENCE BRAGG

WILLIAM LAWRENCE BRAGG was born at Adelaide on March 31, 1890. He was educated at St. Peter's College, Adelaide, and afterward at the University of Adelaide, where he took First Class Honours in Mathematics in 1908. In 1909, when he went with his parents to England, he entered Trinity College, Cambridge. Here he studied physics and took First Class Honours in the Natural Science Tripos in 1912.

In the autumn of that year he began his investigation of the von Laue phenomenon and published his first paper on the subject in the *Proceedings* of the Cambridge Philosophical Society in November. During the next two years he at Cambridge and his father at Leeds continued their study of crystal structure by means of X rays, their results being collected in *X-Rays and Crystal Structure,* published in their joint names in 1915. In 1914 Lawrence Bragg was elected Fellow and lecturer at Trinity College, Cambridge, and in 1919 was appointed Langworthy Professor of Physics at Manchester University, where he remained until 1937. From 1937 to 1938 he was director of the National Physical Laboratory. Since 1938 he has been Cavendish Professor of Physics at Cambridge.

During the First World War he was technical adviser on sound ranging at General Headquarters, France. He was awarded the Military Cross and made an Officer of the British Empire in 1918.

Sir Lawrence Bragg—he was knighted in 1941—is a member of

many British and foreign learned societies and has been awarded honorary doctorates by seven universities. He was elected a Fellow of the Royal Society of London in 1921, and received the Hughes Medal in 1931, the Royal Medal in 1946.

DESCRIPTION OF THE PRIZE-WINNING WORK

Von Laue had passed the X rays *through* the crystal and obtained a diffraction pattern on a photographic plate placed behind it; his mathematical treatment of the problem as one of diffraction through a space-grating was somewhat complicated. W. L. Bragg was able to simplify the problem by treating it as a case of reflection, the reflecting surfaces being in effect the various planes in which atoms arranged in a regular space-lattice must lie. That there are many such planes may be seen by considering the simple cubic lattice shown in Fig. 15 (p. 136); this lattice is built up of cubes having an atom at each corner. In addition to the planes through each of the six faces such as *CGFB*, there are such planes as *CHEB*, *eaclh*, *CAPM*, as well as such planes as *cbl*, where *l* is a corner of an adjoining cube. Any one of these planes passes through an enormous number of atoms similarly situated at the corners of other cubes. Again, each plane is repeated over and over again in parallel positions throughout the lattice, at distances readily calculated once the length of the side of the unit cube is known. Reflection of the X rays at one of these planes does not, of course, take place at *all* points in the plane, in the way that a beam of light is reflected at a mirror: there is nothing in the planes to intercept the rays except at those points where atoms lie.

But W. L. Bragg showed that, under certain conditions, the total effect of any one system of parallel planes is to produce a reflected beam of X rays, just as if the reflection had taken place at a single reflecting surface; and that the reflected beam, like a beam of light reflected at a mirror, makes an angle with the reflecting surface which is equal to the glancing angle*. Figure 12, which is taken from *X-Rays and Crystal Structure,* shows how the incident wave front *PP* is affected by its passage over the atoms represented by

---

* The angle made by the incident beam with the reflecting surface.

the dots. The portion of the wave front which meets an atom is scattered, forming a number of diffracted wavelets which combine in a certain direction to form a reflected wave front $P'P'$, this direction being such that the angle of reflection equals the angle of incidence. Parts of the incident wave front which pass between the atoms of the first plane will be scattered by atoms in the next plane; parts which pass between the atoms of this plane will similarly

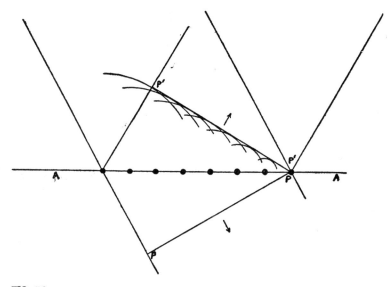

FIG. 12

Scattering of X rays by the atoms of a crystal.

be scattered at the next, and so on. Although the reflected wave fronts will all be in the same direction, the reflected wave trains will be in phase and so will reinforce one another only if the glancing angle θ has one of the values given by

$$n\lambda = 2d \cdot \sin \theta$$

where λ is the wave length, d the distance between the planes, and n has one of the values 1, 2, 3. . . . If this condition, which is known as the "Bragg condition," is not satisfied, the wave trains reflected at the different planes will be out of phase with one another and so will more or less cancel one another out, producing at best a very weak reflected beam. Strong reflection takes place, therefore, only for certain quite definite values of the glancing angle. Thus in a certain experiment strong reflection was found at angles of 5.9°, 11.85°, and 18.15°; the sines of these angles are in the ratio 1:2:3 very nearly, corresponding to $n = 1, 2, 3$ in the above relation.

The position and strength of the reflected beams was found by using an ionization chamber connected to an electroscope. By plotting ionization current against glancing angle, curves were obtained which showed peaks at those angles at which strong reflection occurred. Figure 13 illustrates the type of X-ray spectrum obtained in this way; the three sets of peaks are the first-, second-, and third-

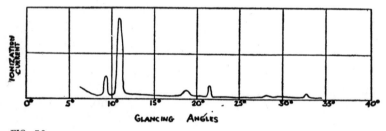

FIG. 13

X-ray spectrum (sylvine; [100]* plane).

order spectra, corresponding to $n = 1, 2, 3$ respectively. Generally there are two or more predominating wave lengths, with a number of others not strong enough to give rise to peaks.

In order to measure the angles and intensities precisely, the Braggs designed the X-ray spectrometer, shown diagrammatically in Fig. 14, which is also taken from *X-Rays and Crystal Structure*. The cathode is indicated by *P; Q* is the *anticathode* where the X rays originate through the interception of the cathode stream; *A* and *B* are slits to limit the rays to a fine pencil; *C* is the crystal mounted on a revolving table with a pointer moving over a graduated circle; *D* is an adjustable slit through which the reflected beam passes into the ionization chamber *E*, which can be rotated about the same vertical axis as the table carrying the crystal. The strength of the ionization current produced is measured by the deflection of the leaves of the electroscope.

---

* See p. 355.

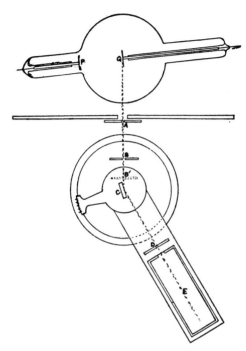

FIG. 14
Bragg X-ray spectrometer.

Owing to the First World War the customary Nobel lecture had to be postponed; it was finally given in September 1922 at Stockholm by Professor W. L. Bragg. It is from this lecture that the following extracts are taken.*

"You have already honoured with the Nobel Prize Professor Laue, to whom we owe the great discovery which has made possible all progress in a new realm of science, the study of the structure of matter by the diffraction of X-rays. . . . In trying to think of some way in which diffraction effects with X-rays might be found, and the question of their true nature answered, he came to the realization that Nature had provided, in a crystal, a diffraction grating exactly suited for the purpose. It had already been surmised that the X-rays, if they were in truth electromagnetic waves, would

---

* By kind permission of Sir Lawrence Bragg.

be found to have a very short wave length, of the order of 10^{-9} centimetre. The work of Sohncke, Federow and others on the geometry of crystal structure had shown that the atoms or molecules in a crystal must be arranged in a geometrical pattern with perfect regularity, and it was possible to calculate that the spacing of the pattern must be of the order of 10^{-8} centimetre. The relation between this spacing and the conjectured wave length of the X-rays was precisely that required to give diffraction effects. Laue, in collaboration with Friedrich and Knipping, tried the experiment of passing a narrow beam of X-rays through a crystal, and they were immediately successful in obtaining undoubted evidence of regular diffraction. . . .

"Professor Laue had made some of his earliest experiments with a crystal of zinc sulphide, and had obtained results which proved that the diffracted pencils showed the symmetry of the underlying crystal structure, which in this case was cubic. He developed a mathematical theory of diffraction by a space lattice, and proved that these diffracted pencils were in directions which were to be expected for a series of diffracting points arranged on a cubic space lattice. In pursuing the analysis still further, he tried to account for the fact that, whereas there were a large number of directions in which one would expect to find a diffracted beam, only a certain number of these appeared on the photographic plate used to record the effect. He suggested that this might be accounted for by the existence, in the X-ray beam, of certain wave lengths alone; and that a diffracted beam only appeared when conditions were right for diffracting these wave lengths.

"In studying his work, it occurred to me that perhaps we ought to look for the origin of this selection of certain directions of diffraction in the peculiarities of the crystal structure, and not in the constitution of the X-ray beam; this might be of the nature of white light and be composed of a continuous range of wave lengths. I tried to attack the problem from a slightly different point of view, and to see what would happen if a series of irregular pulses fell on diffracting points arranged on a regular space lattice. This led naturally to the consideration of the diffraction effects as a reflexion of the pulses by the planes of the crystal structure. The points of a space lattice may be arranged in series of planes, parallel and equidistant from each other. As a pulse passes over each diffracting point, it scatters a wave, and if a number of points are arranged on a plane the diffracted wavelets will combine together to form a reflected wave front, according to the well-known Huygens' construction.

"The pulses reflected by successive planes build up a wave train, which analysis shows to be composed of the wave lengths given by the formula

$$n\lambda = 2d \cdot \sin \theta$$

. . . . .

"To regard the diffraction as a reflexion of the X-rays involved no new principle that was not already contained in Laue's mathematical treatment. It still left open the question why certain planes in the zincblende structure appeared to reflect strongly, while others which were apparently equally well adapted to do so were not represented by diffracted pencils. In analysing Laue's result, however, I found that the selection of the effective planes could be accounted for by assuming that the diffracting centres were arranged in a face-centred cubic lattice, and not in a simple cubic lattice. The structural unit of the face-centred cubic lattice is a cube with a point at each corner and at the centre of each face. When the planes of such a lattice are arranged in the order of those most densely packed with atoms, and so most effective for reflexion, this order is rather different to that for a simple cubic lattice. By assigning a face-centred cubic lattice structure to zincblende, it seemed possible to explain satisfactorily the Laue photograph as due to the diffraction of white radiation with a maximum intensity in a certain part of the spectrum. I made a further test of two simple cubic crystals, sodium chloride and potassium chloride. While the Laue photographs obtained with sodium chloride indicated a face-centred lattice, those obtained with potassium chloride were of a simpler nature, and were such as one would expect from an arrangement of points at the corners of cubes. Since it seemed probable that these two crystals had a similar structure, I was led to conjecture that the atoms were arranged as shown in Figure 1 [Fig. 15], where every corner of the cube is occupied by an atom, whereas the atoms of one kind considered alone are arranged on a face-centred lattice.

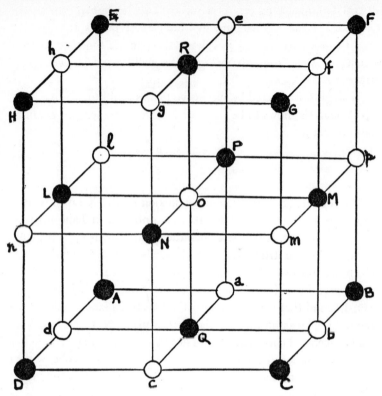

FIG. 15   *Bragg's Fig. 1*

[Arrangement of atoms in a crystal of sodium chloride or potassium chloride.]

In potassium chloride the atoms are so nearly equal in their weight that they act as equivalent diffracting centres and the structure may be regarded as a simple cubic one.

"Although it seemed certain that the Laue effect was due to the diffraction of very short waves, there remained the possibility that they might not be X-rays. My father, in order to test this, examined whether the beam reflected by a crystal ionized a gas; this he found to be the case. He examined the strength of the reflexion at various angles, and the instrument which was first used for the purpose was developed later into the X-ray spectrometer with which we have done the greater part of our work. . . .

"In examining the effect for varying angles of incidence my father discovered that a very strong reflexion appeared when a given crystal face was set at certain definite angles. Since the relationship which has been mentioned above must hold between glancing angle and wave length, this constituted the first evidence of the existence of characteristic 'lines' in the radiation given off by the anticathode. These same lines could be recognised in the reflexions from other faces, and the measurement of the angles at which they appeared proved a most powerful method of finding the arrangement of the atoms in the crystal. The structures of sodium chloride and potassium chloride, which had been suggested by the Laue photographs, were established on a firm basis by means of the spectrometer, and more complex structures such as calcite, zincblende, fluor-spar, and iron pyrites, were analyzed.

"On the other hand, since the arrangement of atoms in these crystals was known, it was possible to calculate the spacings of the reflecting planes and so to assign a definite wave length to the characteristic lines in the spectrum. By using tubes with anticathodes of platinum, osmium, tungsten, nickel, and other metals, it became clear that each gave off a radiation containing characteristic lines which agreed in their properties with the K or L radiations first discovered by Barkla. Further, Whiddington had measured the energy of the cathode rays required to excite Barkla's K and L radiations. The results obtained with the spectrometer gave the frequency of these radiations, and my father was able to show that the product of the frequency and Planck's constant h was equal to the cathode ray energy required to excite the rays; this was a first proof of the quantum law as applied to X-rays.

"These two lines of investigation, into X-ray spectra and into crystal structure, are the two great branches of research to which Laue's discovery led. Moseley was the first to make a survey of X-ray spectra. His famous researches established the law which governs the number and order of the elements. He found that, in passing from one element to the next in the periodic table, there was a regular progression of the frequency in the K and L radiations given out by the elements, and that its regularity was so great that it was possible to assign with absolute certainty each element to its proper place in the list, and to find the gaps where an element was not known. . . . Since then the technique of X-ray spectrometry has been very highly developed. No one has done more in this line than Professor Siegbahn . . . who has attained such a marvellous accuracy and delicacy in his measurement of X-ray spectra.

• • • • •

"A single crystal is employed in the X-ray spectrometer. We used large crystals in our first experiments, reflecting from natural or artificially prepared faces. It is not essential to do this, however, for the ionization chamber is so sensitive a detector of X-radiation that small crystals a millimetre or two in breadth can be examined. In this case the rays are reflected throughout the whole volume of the crystal, which is not sufficiently thick to absorb them too much. A small crystal can be set at the centre of the instrument, adjusted so that a zone is parallel to the axis, and then turned round so that the reflexion of various faces is observed in turn. The X-ray spectrometer may be thus used in a manner very similar to that employed by a crystallographer when he measures a crystal with a goniometer. It is a more searching method, however. The goniometer can only measure the angles between faces which have been developed on the crystal, whereas the X-ray spectrometer measures the angles between planes of the crystal structure, and the spacings of the planes, although the crystal may have no regular external form."

CONSEQUENCES IN THEORY AND PRACTICE

By the time Professor W. L. Bragg delivered his lecture, ten years after von Laue's discovery and the commencement of his own and his father's researches, experience had amply shown that a most powerful means of investigating the structure of matter had been placed at the disposal of science. The study of crystallography in particular was revolutionized, since it was now possible to determine with the greatest accuracy the arrangement of atoms in a crystal, and during these ten years and those that followed the Braggs and their co-workers determined the crystal structure of a large variety of substances. Their results have proved of the greatest significance in chemistry, where a knowledge of the space-lattices has thrown light on many problems.

One surprising fact became apparent almost at the outset, namely, that it is the *atoms* that count, the *molecules* appearing to have no separate existence as such in a crystal. Thus in sodium chloride (Fig. 15) the atoms of sodium and chlorine are separated from each other and are not in any way associated as chemical molecules. In the physics of the atom the Bragg method has produced the profoundest results. Here the X-ray spectrometer, by extending the powerful method of spectroscopic analysis to X rays, has proved a most effective tool not only in confirming results obtained by other methods, but also in providing fresh data which have to be taken into account in building up a picture of the structure of the atom itself.

Pioneer work in this direction was done by H. G. J. Moseley in the year or so immediately preceding the outbreak of the First World War. But for his untimely death at the age of twenty-eight —he was killed in the Dardanelles in 1915—Moseley's name would almost certainly have been numbered among those of the Nobel laureates in physics. We shall deal with his work in some detail, since it plays a fundamental part in later developments, but shall be in a better position to do so when we have considered Bohr's theory of the atom.*

---

* Moseley's work is described on pp. 221-223.

1 9 1 6

No award

CHARLES GLOVER BARKLA

(1877–1944)

*"For his discovery of the characteristic X radia-
tion of the elements."*

BIOGRAPHICAL SKETCH

CHARLES GLOVER BARKLA WAS BORN ON JUNE 7, 1877, AT
Widnes, Lancashire, twelve miles from Liverpool, England. After
receiving his early education at the Liverpool Institute, he entered
University College, Liverpool, in 1894, where he was graduated
with honors in mathematics. He then specialized in physics, studying under Professor (later Sir) Oliver Lodge; while still a student
he used to give the professor's lectures when Lodge was ill. After
obtaining First Class Honours in Physics, he went in 1899 as an
1851 Exhibition Scholar to Trinity College, Cambridge, to work
as a research student under J. J. Thomson in the Cavendish Laboratory. Barkla left Trinity College after eighteen months to enter
King's College so as to join the celebrated King's College Chapel
Choir. In 1902 he returned to Liverpool University as Oliver Lodge
Fellow, obtaining his D.Sc. in 1904.

For several years he devoted most of his time to original investigation and during this period he did the work which won him
the Nobel Prize. In 1907 a lectureship in advanced electricity was
created for him at Liverpool University, a post which he held until
1909, when he was appointed Wheatstone Professor of Physics at
King's College, University of London. In 1913 he became pro-

fessor of natural philosophy at the University of Edinburgh, where he remained for the rest of his life.

The loss of his youngest son, a surgeon of great promise who was killed in a flying accident in North Africa in 1943, was largely responsible for Barkla's failure in health, followed by his sudden death on October 23, 1944.

Barkla was elected a Fellow of the Royal Society of London in 1912, and was awarded the Hughes Medal in 1917. In 1931 Liverpool University conferred on him an honorary LL.D. In 1913 he gave the annual lecture to the German Scientific and Medical Congress, choosing as his subject his researches in X radiation.

DESCRIPTION OF THE PRIZE-WINNING WORK

Röntgen in 1898 noticed that a photographic plate was affected when X rays passed through air, though the plate was screened from the direct action of the rays. He put the effect down to secondary radiation produced in the air by the passage of the X rays. Secondary radiation from metals was studied shortly afterward by G. Sagnac of France, who, with P. Curie, in 1902 made the discovery that the radiation consisted in part of negatively charged corpuscles (electrons).

It was Barkla, however, who first examined the phenomenon in detail. While a research student at the Cavendish Laboratory he began an investigation of the secondary radiation produced by the passage of X rays through gases; this work was continued during his first year at Liverpool and the results were published in 1903. In these experiments the X-ray tube was enclosed in a wooden box completely covered with thick sheet lead, with the exception of a small window in the side of the box through which the rays escaped in a definite beam. An electroscope placed out of the path of the beam showed by the gradual collapse of its leaves that the air in the electroscope had become ionized. Barkla satisfied himself that this ionization was due to secondary radiation produced in the air through which the X rays were passing.

His next step was to compare this secondary radiation with the primary radiation producing it. To do this he assumed the amount of ionization in the electroscope to be proportional to the intensity of the radiation passing through it. He then tested both the primary and the secondary radiation by interposing a thin aluminum plate in the path of the rays and noting the effect on the ionization as indicated by the rate of collapse of the leaves. He found that the absorption in the aluminum plate was of the same order of magnitude in both cases.

The investigations were next extended to gases other than air: hydrogen, carbon dioxide, sulphur dioxide, and hydrogen sulphide. The gas under test was enclosed in a metal box with two parchment windows, one at the end to admit the primary X-ray beam, the other at the side to allow the secondary radiation to escape. An electroscope placed opposite the side window always indicated the presence of secondary radiation. The intensity of the radiation, as measured by the ionization produced, increased with the density of the gas, being proportional to the density. On the other hand, the absorbability test with the aluminum plate showed that the secondary radiation was of the same character as the primary, the intensity being reduced by the same percentage in each case. Barkla therefore concluded that the secondary radiation was simply *scattered* primary radiation. He concluded further that, as the scattering was proportional to the mass of the atom, the number of scattering particles in the atom (i.e., electrons) was proportional to the atomic weight. Hence: *"This gives further support to the theory that the atoms of different substances are different systems of similar corpuscles, the number of which in the atom is proportional to its atomic weight."* This is the first suggestion of a connection between the number of electrons in the atom of an element and the position of the element in the periodic table.

Barkla's next series of researches, begun in 1904, went far toward establishing the true nature of X rays. When a beam of ordinary light is scattered by minute particles, the light which is scattered in a direction at right angles to the beam is found to be polarized, the transverse vibrations constituting the light being confined to a plane at right angles to the original beam. It can be shown that this applies to any electromagnetic waves passing through a medium containing particles small enough to produce scattering. If, therefore, X rays consist of electromagnetic waves, they too when scattered should give rise to a polarized beam in a direction at right angles to the original beam. The difficulty lay in detecting this polarization, if it existed, the simple method used with ordinary light being of no use in the case of X rays.

However, Barkla succeeded in devising a method. He allowed the primary X-ray beam to fall on a block of carbon, and the radiation scattered at right angles to the primary beam to fall on a second carbon block. On examining with an electroscope the intensity in different directions of this twice-scattered beam, Barkla found moderately strong radiation in a direction parallel with the primary beam, but no radiation, or at most very weak radiation, in a direction perpendicular to the plane containing the primary beam and the first scattered beam. This result showed that the first scattered beam was highly polarized and therefore that X rays consisted of transverse waves like ordinary light.

The next phase of Barkla's work was the most important. In investigating the intensity in different directions of the scattered radiation from various substances, he found that the light elements carbon (at. wt. 12), aluminum (at. wt. 27), and sulphur (at. wt. 32) showed the most marked variation in intensity with direction; calcium (at. wt. 40) showed much less; with iron (at. wt. 56) and heavier elements there was practically no difference in intensity in different directions. This led him to investigate more closely the relation between atomic weight and absorbability. He did this by interposing thin plates of aluminum in the path of the X-ray beam before the latter entered the ionization chamber, the resulting loss in intensity being measured by means of the electroscope. At this time (1906) Barkla used the term *percentage absorption,* meaning the percentage reduction in ionization due to the passage of the beam through the plate. He took equal percentage absorption in a given plate as an indication of similarity in the radiation—it must be borne in mind that at this time, six years before von Laue's discovery, there were no means of measuring the wave lengths of X rays. In this way Barkla found that for light elements the scattered radiation closely resembled the primary radiation producing it, but that for elements of higher atomic weight than calcium the secondary radiation was quite different from the primary.

Following this up, he proceeded to examine the secondary radiation more closely. In this phase of his work Barkla made the assumption that if interposing a second plate identical with the first produced a further percentage reduction in intensity equal to that produced by the first, then the secondary radiation was homogeneous, or at least very nearly so, the wave lengths present in the beam being approximately equal. His investigations showed that the secondary radiation from metals contained not only scattered radiation of the same character as the primary, but also homogeneous radiation which was characteristic of the element irradiated. The emission of this homogeneous radiation occurred only when the incident X-ray beam was more penetrating, or *harder,* than the characteristic radiation, just as fluorescent substances fluoresce only when exposed to light of shorter wave length than that of the fluorescent light emitted by the substance (Stokes's law), a fact which led Barkla to give the name "fluorescent Röntgen radiation" to this type of secondary radiation, the term "characteristic radiation" coming into general use later.

From his absorption measurements Barkla identified two series of homogeneous characteristic radiation, a penetrating radiation which he called K radiation and a less penetrating, or *soft,* radiation which he called L radiation. In both series the radiation became more penetrating as the atomic weight of the element increased. The elements from calcium (at. wt. 40) to rhodium (at. wt. 103) emitted K radiation only; those from silver (at. wt. 108) to cerium (at. wt. 140) emitted both K and L radiation; and elements from tungsten (at. wt. 184) to bismuth (at. wt. 208) emitted L radiation only. These results suggested that the emission of characteristic radiation was an atomic property.

For many years Barkla held the view that evidence pointed to the existence of a more penetrating radiation than the K series, namely, a J series. Subsequent research has not, however, supported this view. A *less* penetrating series, the M series, was identified by Siegbahn (*q.v.* 1924) in the characteristic radiation of heavy elements, and a still softer N radiation, and even an O radiation, has since been found in the characteristic radiation of the heaviest elements.

Soon after Barkla's discovery of characteristic secondary radiation it was found by others that these characteristic X rays were also emitted, under the action of cathode rays, when the element in question was used as the anticathode in an X-ray tube—they were the cause of the peaks in the Bragg curves (see Fig 13, p. 132), systematically studied by Moseley (see p. 221).

Barkla's Nobel lecture was delivered in 1920, fourteen years after the discovery for which the award was made. By then his work was well known in scientific circles. Barkla therefore restricted himself in his address to two points of more recent interest —the results of his own experiments which had a bearing on the quantum theory of radiation, and the evidence for the existence of a J series. The extract given below is taken from the first of these.

"Phenomena of Scattering. . . . When X-rays traverse matter of any kind, this matter becomes a source of a radiation similar in character to that of the primary radiation falling upon it. A variation in the intensity of this scattered radiation with direction around the primary beam shows slight polarization of the primary radiation proceeding direct from an X-ray tube.

"The scattered radiation proceeding in a direction at right angles to that of propagation of the primary radiation is highly polarized in the manner of light scattered from the sky.

．　．　．　．　．

"[I] early concluded that neither atoms, molecules nor gaseous ions were the scattering units, but that these were the constituent electrons in matter, and that in general the number of electrons per atom, for light atoms at any rate, was proportional to the atomic weight. . . . It at first appeared that the number of electrons per atom was several times the atomic weight. As the data available for the values of N, e/m and e * were more accurately determined, the calculated value for the number of electrons per atom became smaller, until with the most recent values the number indicated is one electron per atom of hydrogen, 6 per atom of carbon, 7 per atom of nitrogen, 8 for oxygen, 15 or 16 for sulphur and so on.

"As these conclusions regarding the number of electrons (outer electrons) within the atom have been confirmed by the researches

---

* N is the number per cubic centimeter of particles of charge e and mass m.

of Rutherford, Bohr and Moseley, it is perfectly legitimate to use the agreement as evidence in support of the theory of radiation upon which it was based. . . . [This theory] is the spreading wave theory. It assumes that the scattered radiation is the radiation resulting from the disturbance in electrons while under the influence of the electrostatic field in the primary radiation.

"The theory assumes that radiation can take place from these electrons in any quantity whatever, and is not confined to units or quanta; that the radiation is a continuous process not depending on any limiting or critical condition.

"Again, I have found that the intensity of the radiation scattered from light elements over considerable ranges varies little with the wave-length of the primary radiation. This is in perfect agreement with the theory based on the assumption of independent action of the electrons. Further experiments have shown that the intensity of scattered radiation from the heavy atoms in which the constituent electrons are more closely packed, increases rapidly and apparently continuously with the wave-length of the radiation, unless this is fairly small. Also, in general, the rate of increase of intensity with wave-length is greater, the heavier the atom from which the scattered radiation proceeds. Such results are, again, to be expected on the wave-theory when the wave-length becomes comparable with the size of the atom, for there is very close agreement in phase of the radiations set up by neighbouring electrons; ultimately a group of electrons and not an individual electron moves as a whole and becomes the scattering unit. . . .

• • • • •

"There is thus in the phenomena of scattering, not only no suggestion of a quantum or entity of radiation, or of any discontinuity in the process of radiation involved, but there is some of the strongest positive evidence against any such theory. The results appear conclusive, for the tests which have been applied are the most searching and sensitive. The phenomena observed become meaningless on any quantum or entity theory. This conclusion is true also of absorption, for in the transmission of X-rays, particularly of short wave-length through matter consisting of light elements only, the energy absorbed is practically all re-emitted as scattered radiation. The quantities radiated by each electron are approximately identical with those absorbed. It follows that *this* process of absorption is also a process which takes place in any quantity whatever, and is unlimited by any critical condition.

"Characteristic Radiation. Each element when traversed by X-rays emits X-radiations characteristic of the element; each characteristic radiation is unaffected by changes in the physical condition or state of chemical combination of the radiating element, and its quality is independent of that of the exciting primary radiation. But only primary radiations of shorter wave-length are able to excite the characteristic X-radiations—an extension of Stokes's fluorescence law.

"All the radiations hitherto definitely observed have fallen into three series, the *K: L:* and *M* series; . . . . The absorption method of analyzing a radiation showed the radiation of the *K* series from a particular element to be so homogeneous, that it was regarded as giving a spectral line, the *K* line; but the possibility of the *L* radiation consisting of more than one line was suggested by an obvious heterogeneity in the *L* radiation.

"The interference experiments of Bragg, Moseley and others have shown, however, that both the *K* and *L* radiations give spectra consisting of a number of neighbouring lines.

"The uniformity in the distribution of the characteristic radiation around the radiating substance, even when the primary beam is polarized, shows that, in contrast with the process of emission of scattered radiation, the emission of a characteristic radiation is absolutely uncontrolled by the primary radiation exciting it. The phenomenon of emission is not an immediate consequence of the passage of the primary beam, but arises only indirectly from it; the process is dependent on some critical condition, as evidenced by Stokes's law. Here we see the possibility of the applicability of some kind of quantum theory. The most significant evidence as to the origin of the characteristic radiation comes from the study of the accompanying phenomena of the absorption of the exciting primary radiation and the emission of electrons by the radiating substance in the form of a corpuscular radiation. I have shown that the total absorption of a primary radiation in the substance traversed can be analyzed into what are apparently independent absorptions, each—

with the exception of that due to the process of scattering—definitely associated with the emission of a characteristic X-radiation. Thus there are the *J,K,L,M* absorptions. Similarly, a corpuscular radiation may be analyzed into *J,K,L,M* corpuscular radiations, each associated with the emission of the corresponding characteristic X-radiations.

"The results obtained from a study of the energy of the primary beam absorbed, of the energy of the characteristic radiation emitted, and of the corpuscular radiation emitted, are very significant. In certain substances—bromine and probably substances of high atomic weight—nearly all the energy of the primary beam absorbed in association with the emission of *K* characteristic radiation is re-emitted partly as characteristic X-radiation of the *K* series, and partly as corpuscular radiation of the *K* series. Not only this, but there is a definite relation between the intensity of the *K* radiation and the number of electrons emitted in the associated corpuscular radiation. For various wave-lengths of the primary radiation it appears that the number of quanta of *K* fluorescent radiation per *K* electron emitted is approximately 1. . . .

.   .   .   .   .

"Whatever the process of radiation may be, there can be little doubt that characteristic radiation is emitted in quanta by those atoms merely from which an electron has been ejected. . . . All the evidence suggests that the characteristic radiation is emitted immediately after the ejection of the electron from the atom."

Barkla's remarks on the absence of quantum effects in the scattering of X rays will be better understood when the work of some of the later Laureates has been read. It must be said at once, however, that his views on this point were not supported by subsequent researches, in particular those of A. H. Compton (*q.v.* 1927).

The corpuscular (electronic) secondary radiation to which Barkla refers has already been mentioned (p. 142) as having been discovered in 1902 by Sagnac and P. Curie in the secondary radiation. W. H. Bragg in 1907 put forward the view that the part played by X rays in the ionization of gases was mainly an indirect one—that β particles (high-speed electrons) ejected by the action of the rays from the atoms of the gas were the chief cause. This view was later confirmed by Wilson's cloud track experiments (see C. T. R. Wilson, 1927). Barkla's experiments on the subject, begun in 1913 and continued over a number of years, applied the ionization method to the measurement of the energy of the corpuscular radiation; they led to the important result that the ejection of each electron was accompanied by the emission of one quantum (frequency $\times$ Planck's constant h; see below, p. 165) of energy in the form of secondary radiation.

CONSEQUENCES IN THEORY AND PRACTICE

Barkla's discovery of the characteristic X radiation of the elements has proved of the greatest importance in the investigation of the structure of the atom and of the events occurring within the atom—investigations in which Barkla himself played no small part. The next step forward, however, is to be found in the work of Moseley and Siegbahn, who developed the powerful method of X-ray spectroscopic analysis and applied it to the more precise determination of relations foreshadowed by Barkla's work.

1 9 1 8

MAX KARL ERNST LUDWIG PLANCK

(1858–1947)

"For his contribution to the development of physics by his discovery of the element of action."

BIOGRAPHICAL SKETCH

MAX PLANCK WAS BORN AT KIEL, PRUSSIA, ON APRIL 23, 1858. In 1867 the family moved to Munich, where Planck received his early education. In 1874 he finished at the *Gymnasium* and devoted himself to the study of mathematics and physics, first for three years at Munich under Professor von Jolly, then for a year under Helmholtz and Kirchhoff at Berlin. It was at Berlin that Planck made first-hand acquaintance with the works of Rudolf Clausius and through them turned his attention to the study of thermodynamics, his doctor's thesis of 1879 dealing with this subject.

In 1880 he became *privatdozent* at Munich University. In 1885 he received an appointment which gave him great happiness—that of professor extraordinary of theoretical physics at Kiel. In 1889, on the death of Kirchhoff, Planck accepted an invitation to go to Berlin as professor extraordinary of theoretical physics; he became ordinary professor in 1892. He retired in 1928 on reaching the age of seventy, but continued his scientific activities for many years. He died on October 4, 1947.

Planck bore with fortitude the many misfortunes which befell him in his later years. His elder son was killed in action before Verdun in 1916. Of his twin daughters, one died in childbirth in 1917; the other married the widower and herself died in childbirth a year later. His younger son was accused of complicity in the anti-Hitler plot of July 1944 and was executed by the Nazis. Planck's home was destroyed in an air raid on Berlin and he lost all his possessions, including his fine library. He and his wife took refuge near Magdeburg, but found themselves between the retreating Germans and the advancing Allies. The Americans heard of their plight and sent a military car to bring them to Göttingen, where Planck spent the remaining years of his life.

One of the greatest theoretical physicists of all time, whose work has changed the whole aspect of physics, Planck received most of the honors the learned world has to offer. He was elected a member of the Prussian Academy of Sciences in 1894; in 1912 he was appointed permanent secretary of the Academy. He was elected a Foreign Member of the Royal Society of London in 1926 and was awarded the Copley Medal in 1929. In 1930 he became president of the Kaiser Wilhelm Society of Berlin, since renamed the Max Planck Society. In 1946 he was a guest at the Royal Society's Newton Celebrations, this occasion being the last of several visits to Britain. Planck was a member of many scientific societies in Europe and America, and held honorary doctorates in a number of universities, including London and Edinburgh. One of the minor planets was "given" to him for his eightieth birthday and named "Planckiana."

DESCRIPTION OF THE PRIZE-WINNING WORK

Throughout his long and active scientific career Planck's main interest lay in thermodynamics. His doctoral thesis dealt with this subject; so did the paper of 1880 through which he qualified for the position of *privatdozent* at Munich. During the next twelve years or so he published a number of papers on thermodynamics which were later embodied in his famous *Vorlesungen über Ther-*

modynamik, published in 1897. . . . Four important papers dealt with the principle of the increase of entropy.

Since the concept of entropy played an important role in Planck's treatment of the problem of radiation and will be met again in Einstein's work on the photoelectric effect, we must say something about it here.

Clausius, who, in the early 1850's, was largely responsible for giving to thermodynamics its present form, derived the second law of thermodynamics—"heat cannot of itself pass from a colder to a hotter body"—by considering a reversible cyclic process—*cyclic,* because the body, after passing through a series of changes, returns to its original state; *reversible,* because the whole cyclic process can be carried out in the reverse order, the body reaching exactly the same final state.

For the process to be reversible, all heat exchanges, such as that between the source of heat and the body, must take place at a constant temperature; for, as Clausius pointed out, it is only then that the direction of the exchange can be reversed. Since, however, a transfer of heat cannot take place without at least a slight difference in temperature between the bodies, a perfectly reversible process is an *ideal* one, never actually realizable in practice. All heat transfers must therefore be supposed to be made in such ideally infinitesimally small amounts that the temperature remains unchanged, that is, in amounts dQ, where dQ does not mean "d multiplied by Q," but an infinitesimal amount of Q. Clausius then showed that in a reversible cyclic process the sum of all the dQ's divided by the temperature at which the transfers take place is equal to zero, or, in the notation of the calculus, for the complete cycle,

$$\int \frac{dQ}{T} = 0$$

where T is the temperature. Denoting dQ/T by dS, he then showed that S is a quantity which depends only on the condition of the body at the moment, being fully determined as soon as that condition is known. To this quantity S Clausius gave the name *entropy.* He showed further that in any *irreversible* change the entropy can only increase, never decrease.

Whereas Clausius began with the reversible process, Planck

began with the irreversible process, which he defined as a process which cannot be exactly retraced by any means whatever, all other processes being defined as reversible. Planck preferred to regard irreversible processes as *natural* processes: in any ordinary process in nature bodies are brought from an initial state A to a final state B; if a complete return to state A cannot be brought about in any way, the process is irreversible. He once described this by saying that in an irreversible process Nature has a greater predilection for state B than for state A, whereas in a reversible process she has as much liking for the initial state as for the final state, and a transition between them can be made in either direction. The physical quantity which serves as a measure of Nature's predilection for any state is the entropy associated with that state. Ludwig Boltzmann in 1877 had shown that the entropy S of a given state and the probability W that the molecules of the system will have the arrangement corresponding to that state are connected by the relation

$$S = k \cdot \log W$$

where k is a constant (*Boltzmann's constant*). This enabled Planck to interpret his "predilection of Nature for a certain state" as meaning simply that Nature prefers more probable states to less probable ones. He pointed out that Boltzmann's relation gave a means of calculating the entropy of a system without the necessity of introducing a reversible process, as Clausius had had to do.

Planck's familiarity with thermodynamics stood him in good stead when he turned his attention to the problem of the distribution of energy in the spectrum of black-body radiation. His interest in this was aroused about 1896 by the investigations by Lummer and Pringsheim and by Rubens and Kurlbaum in the Berlin Reichsanstalt. Wien had just published his distribution law (see p. 100), which was confirmed for low temperatures and short wave lengths, but which Lummer and Pringsheim found did not fit their observations for high temperatures and long wave lengths; and researches by Rubens and Kurlbaum in the infrared region showed that here the energy was simply proportional to the absolute temperature, a result at which Lord Rayleigh arrived on theoretical grounds about the same time.

In his first attack on the problem Planck based his hopes on classical electrodynamics. At this time he was not convinced of the correctness of Lorentz' electron theory; the laws of the emission of electromagnetic radiation by a linear oscillator had, however, been established by Hertz on the basis of classical electromagnetic theory —one of these *Hertzian oscillators* is illustrated in Fig. 4 (p. 74). Planck therefore imagined the walls of the constant-temperature enclosure (see p. 97) to be composed of tiny elementary Hertzian oscillators, which by their oscillations caused the emission of electromagnetic waves and to which the laws of the Hertzian oscillator could be applied—he suggested that these elementary oscillators might be thought of as in some way connected with the atoms of the substance composing the walls of the enclosure. The oscillators would not only emit radiation, but would also, through resonance, selectively absorb the radiation falling on them, until finally a steady state would be reached. Planck therefore frequently referred to them as *resonators*. The attempt to solve the problem of the distribution of energy in the spectrum of black-body radiation on these lines did not succeed, but it did lead to the result that the energy of the radiation could be replaced by the energy of the oscillator—a result which gave Planck great satisfaction, since it enabled him to deal with the oscillator responsible for the radiation instead of with the radiation itself.

Planck now decided to see what could be achieved by the application of thermodynamics. His procedure and the basic mathematics involved are presented in the following paragraphs.

He fell back on Wien's formula (see p. 100), which he wrote in the form

$$U = a \cdot e^{-b/T} \quad \ldots \ldots \ldots \ldots \ldots \quad (1)$$

where U is the mean energy of the oscillator at the temperature T, and a and b are constants for the oscillator (both involve the wave length λ of the emitted radiation, since a is Wien's C_1/λ^5 and b is Wien's C_2/λ). He then proposed to combine this formula with the one which fitted the results obtained by Rubens and Kurlbaum for the infrared spectrum, namely,

$$U = cT \quad \ldots \ldots \ldots \ldots \ldots \ldots \quad (2)$$

where c is a constant for the oscillator. In this way Planck hoped to derive a formula which approximated to Wien's for short wave lengths and to that of Rubens and Kurlbaum for long wave lengths. To effect the combination it was natural for him, in view of the importance he attached to entropy, to study the relation between the entropy S of the oscillator and its energy U. By a slight extension of the meaning of entropy, the entropy S of the oscillator is given by

$$dS = \frac{dU}{T}$$

where T is the temperature, dS and dU being, of course, infinitesimally small elements of S and U. Then

$$\frac{dS}{dU} = \frac{1}{T}$$

dS/dU being the differential coefficient of S with respect to U. By differentiating a second time we obtain

$$\frac{d^2S}{dU^2} = \frac{-\dfrac{1}{T^2}}{\dfrac{dU}{dT}} \quad \cdots \cdots \cdots \cdots \quad (3)$$

Now when

$$U = ae^{-b/T}, \qquad \frac{dU}{dT} = \frac{bU}{T^2}$$

and when

$$U = cT, \qquad \frac{dU}{dT} = c$$

When these expressions for dU/dT are substituted in turn in Equation (3) we find, in the first case,

$$\frac{1}{\dfrac{d^2S}{dU^2}} = -bU$$

and in the second case,

$$\frac{1}{\dfrac{d^2S}{dU^2}} = -\frac{U^2}{c}$$

The quantity $\dfrac{1}{\dfrac{d^2S}{dU^2}}$ is the one Planck refers to as R in his Nobel lecture.

Planck now assumes that

$$\frac{1}{\dfrac{d^2S}{dU^2}} = -bU - \frac{U^2}{c}$$

and then solves this differential equation, obtaining

$$\frac{dS}{dU} = \frac{1}{b} \log \left(1 + \frac{bc}{U} \right)$$

But from the definition of entropy

$$\frac{dS}{dU} = \frac{1}{T}$$

Therefore

$$\frac{1}{T} = \frac{1}{b} \log \left(1 + \frac{bc}{U} \right)$$

which, with a little manipulation, gives

$$U = \frac{bc}{e^{b/T} - 1}$$

This is the original form of Planck's famous radiation formula, first published in October 1900 in the "Proceedings" of the German Physical Society.

So far Planck has been dealing with the energy U of the *oscillator*. To change over to the energy E_λ of the *emitted radiation*, b and c must be expressed in terms of the wave length of the radiation (a, it will be noticed, does not occur in the final result). Now b is proportional to $1/\lambda$ (Wien) and c is proportional to $1/\lambda^4$ (Rubens and Kurlbaum); therefore

$$E_\lambda = \frac{A}{\lambda^5} \cdot \frac{1}{e^{B/(\lambda T)} - 1}$$

where A and B are constants, B being Wien's c_2. For small values of λT, for which Wien's formula holds, $e^{B/(\lambda T)}$ is large compared with 1, so that

$$E_\lambda = \frac{A}{\lambda^5} \cdot \frac{1}{e^{B/(\lambda T)}}$$

very closely. This is Wien's formula (p. 100), with A in place of c_1 and B in place of c_2. But if λT is large, $B/(\lambda T)$ is small and $e^{B/(\lambda T)}$ approximates * to

$$1 + \frac{B}{\lambda T}$$

---

* Note that

$$e^x = 1 + x + \frac{x^2}{1 \cdot 2} + \frac{x^3}{1 \cdot 2 \cdot 3} + \cdots$$
$$= 1 + x \quad \text{(very nearly)}$$

when x is small.

Planck's formula then becomes

$$E_\lambda = \frac{A}{\lambda^5} \cdot \frac{1}{\dfrac{B}{\lambda T}}$$

$$= \frac{A}{B} \cdot \frac{T}{\lambda^4}$$

which fits the Rubens and Kurlbaum results and is in effect the formula obtained about the same time by Lord Rayleigh, who deduced it from the laws of classical dynamics.

By a stroke of genius Planck had succeeded in so combining the formula known to hold for small values of λT with that holding for large values that he obtained one which held for both—but the fact remains that he *did* start from the two known formulas and did obtain his final result by mathematical "juggling" based on the concept of entropy. To a man of Planck's caliber it would be more satisfactory if the correct radiation law could be deduced directly from the physical principles involved in the process of radiation. Here too Planck's efforts were crowned with success—but with a success which depended on the introduction of a principle at variance with one of the most fundamental ideas regarding energy. This second stage of Planck's work on the radiation law was published in the "Proceedings" of the German Physical Society in December 1900, and also, in a slightly modified form, in the *Annalen der Physik* for March 1901; it is this latter account that we follow in our treatment. The mathematics is essential for an understanding of Planck's work.

Planck began by calculating the entropy of a resonator as a function of its energy. The entropy S_N of a system of N resonators is connected with the probability W of the state of the system by Boltzmann's relation

$$S_N = k \log W$$

Let the combined energy of the N resonators be U_N. Planck now wishes to obtain an expression for the probability W of any particular distribution of this total energy among the resonators. To do this he must find the number of ways in which the total energy can be distributed among the resonators.

Now there is no great difficulty in calculating the number of ways in which, say, 10 cups of water can be distributed among 4 vessels, *pro-*

vided all the water in each cup is emptied into the same vessel, so that, for example, the first vessel contains 3 cupfuls, the second 2, the third 1, and the fourth 4; the number is 286. But if it is permissible to divide the contents of each cup among the vessels, the problem becomes insoluble, or rather, the number of ways in which the distribution can be made is infinite. According to the generally accepted ideas of energy, the problem of distributing the total energy U_N among the N resonators is that of dividing the water, in *any* quantities, among the vessels; Planck, however, reduced it to the soluble problem of distributing *cupfuls* among the vessels by making the bold assumption that the total energy U_N is made up of an integral number P of elements of energy each equal to ε, so that $U_N = P\varepsilon$; these P elements of energy are distributed among the N resonators in integral multiples of ε. As an illustration Planck takes the case of 100 elements of energy distributed among 10 resonators; then one possible distribution would be 7ε, 38ε, 11ε, O, 9ε, 2ε, 20ε, 4ε, 4ε, 5ε. Obviously, even with only 10 resonators and 100ε, the number of possible distributions is very large.

It must be pointed out that at this stage Planck does not particularly emphasize his assumption: it is simply a device to enable him to replace an insoluble problem by a soluble one; ε, though small, is finite and so can be treated as a discrete quantity—it is as if, in our cups-of-water analogy, the water were distributed among the vessels, not in *any* quantities, but in *drops of a definite size;* the number of possible distributions could then be calculated. In either case, the number of possible distributions is given, to a reasonable degree of accuracy, by

$$\frac{(N + P)^{N+P}}{N^N \times P^P}$$

where N and P have the meanings given them by Planck. For this formula to hold even approximately either N or P or both must be very large*; but this is so in the case Planck is considering, since N, the number of resonators, is determined in some way by the number of atoms in the radiating substance, and P is large because ε is very small. Planck next takes the number of possible distributions as a measure of the probability of the system and puts, for the entropy S_N,

$$S_N = k \log W = k \log \frac{(N + P)^{N+P}}{N^N \times P^P}$$

and therefore

$$S_N = k[(N + P) \log (N + P) - N \log N - P \log P]$$

---

* In the example given above, for instance, where P and N are both small (10 and 4 respectively), the formula gives 4340 (approx.) instead of 286!

The next step is to get rid of P. If U is the mean energy of a single resonator, then

$$U_N = UN$$

and

$$P\epsilon = U_N = UN$$

so that

$$P = \frac{UN}{\epsilon}$$

Therefore

$$S_N = k\left[\left(N + \frac{UN}{\epsilon}\right)\log\left(N + \frac{UN}{\epsilon}\right) - N\log N - \frac{UN}{\epsilon}\log\frac{UN}{\epsilon}\right]$$

$$= kN\left[\left(1 + \frac{U}{\epsilon}\right)\log N\left(1 + \frac{U}{\epsilon}\right) - \log N - \frac{U}{\epsilon}\log N\frac{U}{\epsilon}\right]$$

$$= kN\left[\left(1 + \frac{U}{\epsilon}\right)\left\{\log\left(1 + \frac{U}{\epsilon}\right) + \log N\right\}\right.$$

$$\left. - \log N - \frac{U}{\epsilon}\left\{\log\frac{U}{\epsilon} + \log N\right\}\right]$$

$$= kN\left[\left(1 + \frac{U}{\epsilon}\right)\log\left(1 + \frac{U}{\epsilon}\right) - \frac{U}{\epsilon}\log\frac{U}{\epsilon}\right]$$

since all the terms involving $\log N$ cancel out.

The entropy S of a *single* resonator is therefore given by

$$S = k\left[\left(1 + \frac{U}{\epsilon}\right)\log\left(1 + \frac{U}{\epsilon}\right) - \frac{U}{\epsilon}\log\frac{U}{\epsilon}\right]$$

Planck now brings in Wien's displacement law (p. 99), namely,

$$\lambda T = \text{constant}$$

From this law it follows, from the definition of entropy, that

$$\frac{dS}{dU} = \frac{1}{T} = \frac{\lambda}{\text{constant}}$$

or, in terms of the frequency ν of the resonator,

$$\frac{dS}{dU} = \frac{c}{\nu \times \text{constant}}$$

since $\lambda\nu = c$, the velocity of light. Therefore

$$dS = \frac{c \cdot dU}{\nu \times \text{constant}}$$

The entropy S is therefore a function of U/ν alone; in other words, the expression obtained above for S must contain only U/ν and constants. To comply with this, Planck puts

$$\epsilon = h \cdot \nu$$

where h is a constant, so that

$$S = k\left[\left(1 + \frac{U}{h\nu}\right)\log\left(1 + \frac{U}{h\nu}\right) - \frac{U}{h\nu}\log\frac{U}{h\nu}\right]$$

Differentiation with respect to U gives

$$\frac{1}{T} = \frac{dS}{dU} = \frac{k}{h\nu}\log\left(1 + \frac{h\nu}{U}\right)$$

so that

$$\frac{h\nu}{kT} = \log\left(1 + \frac{h\nu}{U}\right)$$

or

$$1 + \frac{h\nu}{U} = e^{h\nu/(kT)}$$

whence

$$U = \frac{h\nu}{e^{h\nu/(kT)} - 1}$$

To pass over from the energy U of the resonator to the energy u of the emitted radiation Planck makes use of a relation which he had already established, namely,

$$u\,d\nu = \frac{8\pi}{c} \cdot \frac{\nu^2}{c^2} \cdot U\,d\nu$$

where c is the velocity of light; u is defined as the space density of energy of radiation in the range of frequency ν to $\nu + d\nu$. Substituting in this relation the value found for U gives

$$u\,d\nu = \frac{8\pi\nu^3 h}{c^3} \cdot \frac{1}{e^{h\nu/(kT)} - 1}\,d\nu$$

To express this relation in terms of the wave length λ, we have

$$\nu = \frac{c}{\lambda}$$

and therefore, differentiating,

$$d\nu = -\frac{c}{\lambda^2}d\lambda$$

Hence for the energy of the radiation in the range of wave length λ to $\lambda + d\lambda$ we have numerically:

$$E_\lambda\,d\lambda = \frac{8\pi ch}{\lambda^5} \cdot \frac{1}{e^{ch/(k\lambda T)} - 1}d\lambda$$

or, as Planck gives it in his paper,

$$E = \frac{8\pi ch}{\lambda^5} \cdot \frac{1}{e^{ch/(k\lambda T)} - 1}$$

This is the formula already obtained (p. 157), with $A = 8\pi ch$, and $B = ch/k$.

By making use of the experimental results of Kurlbaum on the one hand, and of Lummer and Pringsheim on the other, Planck calculated the values of both h and k, obtaining

$$h = 6.55 \times 10^{-27} \text{ erg sec.}$$
$$k = 1.346 \times 10^{-16} \text{ erg per deg. C}$$

Later values are 6.622×10^{-27} and 1.381×10^{-16}, respectively.

We now give some extracts translated from the German of Planck's Nobel lecture.

"An indispensable hypothesis, even if it is far from guaranteeing a result, is often the outcome of the pursuit of a definite object, the importance of which is not lessened by initial failure.

"For me, such an object has long been the solution of the problem of the distribution of energy in the normal spectrum of radiant heat. Gustav Kirchhoff showed that the character of the heat radiation produced in a space bounded by emitting and absorbing bodies at the same temperature is independent of the nature of the bodies. Since then it has been proved that there exists a universal function which depends only on the temperature and the wave lengths, a function independent of any special properties of any one substance. The discovery of this remarkable function promised a deeper insight into the connection between temperature and energy, which forms the chief problem of thermodynamics and so of the whole of molecular physics. The only way to obtain this function is to select from among all the various bodies occurring in nature any one of known powers of emission and absorption, and to calculate the character of the heat radiation when the exchange of energy is stationary. This must then, according to Kirchhoff's law, be independent of the nature of the body.

"It seemed to me that a body specially suited for this purpose was Heinrich Hertz's linear oscillator, for which the laws of emission for a given frequency had shortly before been fully developed by Hertz.

. . . . .

"The result of this long series of investigations . . . was the establishment of a general relation between the energy of the resonator and the radiant energy of the corresponding region of the spectrum in the surrounding space when the energy exchange was stationary. The remarkable result was obtained that the relation does not depend at all on the nature of the resonator, in particular not on its damping coefficient— . . . the whole problem could [therefore] be simplified by replacing the energy of the radiation by the energy of the resonator. . . . This result was nothing but a preliminary step to starting on the real problem. . . .

. . . . .

"The only course now open to me was to attack the problem from the opposite direction, that is, through thermodynamics, with which I felt more familiar. In this my previous investigations into the second law of thermodynamics helped me. It at once occurred to me to connect the entropy, not the temperature, of the resonator with the energy, or rather, not the entropy itself but its second differential coefficient with respect to energy, since this has a direct physical meaning for the irreversibility of the exchange of energy between the resonator and the radiation. . . . In 1899 . . . the law of the distribution of energy had been discovered by W. Wien, the experimental proof being provided by F. Paschen at the *Hochschule*, Hanover, and by O. Lummer and E. Pringsheim at the *Reichsanstalt*, Charlottenburg. This law expresses the intensity of the radiation as an exponential function of the temperature. When it is used to determine the relation between the entropy and the energy of the resonator, the remarkable result is obtained that R, the reciprocal of the differential coefficient mentioned above, is proportional to the energy. This exceedingly simple relation is a full and complete expression of Wien's law for the distribution of energy. . . .

"The whole problem deals with one of the universal laws of nature, and I believed then, as I do now, that the more general a law of nature is, the simpler will be its form. . . . I therefore thought for a long time that the above relation, namely, that R is proportional to the energy, should be considered the foundation of the law of distribution of energy. Later results soon showed, however, that this idea was untenable. Although Wien's law was confirmed for small values of the energy, i.e., for small wave lengths, Lummer and Pringsheim found large deviations in the case of long wave lengths. Finally, observations by H. Rubens and F. Kurlbaum on infrared rays after their passage through fluorspar or rock salt showed an entirely different relation, but one which, under certain conditions, was still very simple. In this case R is proportional, not to the energy, but to the square of the energy, a relation which becomes more accurate as the energies and wave lengths increase.

"Thus direct experiments fixed two simple limits for the function R: for small values of the energy it is proportional to the energy, for large values to the square of the energy. The next step was obviously to express R as the sum of two terms, one involving the first power of the energy, the other the second power, so that the first term predominated for small values of the energy, the second for large values. This gave a new formula for the distribution of the radiation, which so far has stood the test of experiment fairly satisfactorily. . . .

· · · · ·

"According to Boltzmann, entropy is a measure of physical probability. . . . A comparatively simple combinatory method was derived for calculating the physical probability of a certain distribution of energy in a system of resonators. This method led to the same expression for the entropy as that obtained from the radiation theory.

"For numerical applications of this method of probability two universal constants are required, each having an independent physical meaning. . . . The first constant is of a more or less formal nature and depends on the definition of temperature.

· · · · ·

"The interpretation of the second universal constant in the radiation formula was much more troublesome. As it represented the product of energy by time, I called it the elementary quantum of action; according to my first calculation it has the value 6.55×10^{-27} erg per sec. Although it was absolutely indispensable for obtaining the correct expression for the entropy . . . it proved itself cumbersome and unmanageable in all attempts to make it fit in any suitable form into the framework of the classical theory. As long as this constant could be considered infinitesimally small, as when large energies or long periods were involved, everything was in beautiful order; in the general case, however, a gap appeared which became more marked as the oscillations became weaker and more rapid. The failure of all attempts to bridge this gap left no doubt that either the quantum of action was merely a fictitious quantity—in which case the entire deduction of the radiation formula was illusory in principle and represented nothing more than empty juggling with symbols—or else the deduction of the radiation formula rested on an actual physical fact, in which case the quantum of action must play a fundamental part in physics and appears as something quite new and hitherto unheard-of, compelling us to recast our ideas from the very bottom—ideas which since the invention of the infinitesimal calculus by Leibniz and Newton rested on the assumption of continuity in all causal relations.

"Experience has decided in favor of the second alternative. That the decision could come so soon and with so little doubt is due, not to the verification of the law of energy distribution in heat radiation, still less to my special deduction of that law, but to the tireless, ever-advancing labors of those workers who have made use of the quantum of action in their investigations."

CONSEQUENCES IN THEORY AND PRACTICE

Planck's derivation of the correct radiation formula—it has since been confirmed for a wide range of wave lengths and temperatures —was in itself an important achievement, but of far greater importance was the assumption on which this derivation rested, namely, that the energy emitted or absorbed by the resonator must be treated as made up of discrete units of energy, each equal to the frequency of the vibration multiplied by the same constant h. This was to give to energy something of an atomic nature, each of the infinite number of possible frequencies v having associated with it a definite "atom" of energy hv, so that any transfer of energy at the frequency v took place only in integral multiples of hv.

The idea was too revolutionary to receive immediate acceptance. The first to see its possibilities was Einstein (*q.v.* 1921), who, in 1905, showed that other radiation phenomena besides that of heat, in particular the photoelectric effect, could be explained on the assumption of quanta of energy and later showed that Planck's radiation formula could be derived very simply and directly from Bohr's conception of transitions of atoms from one stationary state to another. Then in 1913 Bohr (*q.v.* 1922) embodied Planck's quantum hypothesis in his electron theory of the atom and so was able to explain quantitatively the emission of spectral lines by atoms. Since that time Planck's "quantum of action" h, now recognized as perhaps the most fundamental of the universal constants, has played a major part in the development of theoretical physical science. It will figure frequently in our accounts of the work of later laureates.

1 9 1 9

JOHANNES STARK
(1874–   )

"For his discovery of the Doppler effect in canal rays and of the splitting of spectral lines in an electric field."

BIOGRAPHICAL SKETCH

JOHANNES STARK WAS BORN ON APRIL 15, 1874, IN SCHICKEN-hof, Bavaria. He attended the *Gymnasiums* in Bayreuth and Regensburg, and from 1894 to 1898 studied physics, chemistry, mathematics, and crystallography at the University of Munich, becoming assistant in the Physical Institute there in 1898. In 1900 he was appointed *privatdozent* in physics at the University of Göttingen; in 1906 professor extraordinary at the Technical High School in Hanover; and in 1909 ordinary professor at the Technical High School in Aachen. In 1917 he went as professor to the University of Greifswald, and in 1920 to Würzburg. In 1933 he became president of the Physikalisch-Technische Reichsanstalt at Charlottenburg.

DESCRIPTION OF THE PRIZE-WINNING WORK

In 1842 Johann Christian Doppler predicted that the color of a luminous body moving toward a stationary observer should appear different from its color when it is moving away from the observer, the apparent frequency of the light emitted by the body being greater in the former case, less in the latter, than when the source is at rest. Doppler thought it probable that all stars emitted white light, the colored appearance of some of them being due to their motion of approach or recession. C. H. D. Buys-Ballot, however, pointed out in 1845 that no change in the color of a source emitting white light would occur, since the whole visible spectrum would still be emitted in spite of the motion, radiation from the infrared or ultraviolet entering to make up for any color lost by the displacement. In 1848 Fizeau predicted that the spectral *lines,* for instance those of hydrogen, would be shifted slightly toward the violet end of the spectrum when the source of light is approaching, and toward the red end when the source is receding, but it was not until about 1870 that spectroscopy was sufficiently developed for the predicted shift to be detected. Since then, this so-called *Doppler effect* has enabled the velocity of approach or recession of stars and other heavenly bodies to be calculated from the observed shifts of known spectral lines.

Up to the end of the nineteenth century the Doppler effect had not been observed with terrestrial sources of light because it was not possible to impart a sufficently high velocity to any source of light.*
In 1902, however, Stark predicted that the high-velocity luminous atoms which constituted the canal rays (see p. 49) should show the effect when the spectrum emitted by them was viewed in the direction of motion of the particles, and pointed out that since the amount of the shift is proportional to the velocity of the particles, it must be possible in this way to determine that velocity. He first detected the effect in 1905, when, using canal rays consisting of hydrogen atoms, he found that each of the known hydrogen lines was shifted toward the violet end of the spectrum when the particles were approaching the observer, and in the opposite direction when they were receding from him. The effect was observed in all other chemical elements examined. This was additional proof that the canal rays do consist of luminous atoms.

The splitting of the spectral lines in a magnetic field had been discovered by Zeeman (see p. 13), but all attempts to detect a

---

* Professor Herbert Dingle has drawn my attention to a successful laboratory demonstration of the effect made in 1900 by Belopolsky, who used two systems of mirrors revolving at very high speed in opposite directions.

similar effect in an electric field had failed. In 1913 Stark, by placing a third electrode behind the perforated cathode and at a distance
of only a few millimeters from it, with an electric field of 20,000
volts per cm. or more between the two, observed the effect when
the canal rays emerging from the perforations were examined with
a spectrometer at right angles to the rays.

Stark's own account of his discovery of the Doppler effect with
canal rays and of the splitting of the spectral lines in an electric
field is given in the following extracts, translated from the German
of his Nobel lecture.*

"For the last twenty years or so I have been preoccupied in investigating experimentally the connection between changes in the
structure of chemical atoms and changes in their spectra. The first
[question] concerns the phenomenon of the change in the structure
of the surface of the atom. We will start with a single atom whose
parts are all in equilibrium with one another. Experience shows that
through the impact of electrical radiation one electron (under certain circumstances a second or a third) can be removed from the
surface of an atom. The question of the structure of the neutral
atom is now replaced by that of the structure of the remaining
one-, two-, or three-valued ion. . . . What are the two spectra
belonging to the two atomic structures, the neutral atom and the
positive ion? . . . Is a special spectrum emitted when the positive
ion again becomes a neutral atom?

. . . . .

"It is possible to impart a velocity to the positive ions by allowing them to fall through an electric field and in this way we can
distinguish them from the neutral atoms at rest. If we can correlate
this velocity with the spectral lines emitted by the atoms, we shall
thereby show that the moving ions are the carriers of the displaced
spectral lines. The proof of the motion of the carriers of spectral
lines rests on the Doppler principle.

"Thus, we can arrange the beam of positive ions first at right
angles to the axis along which we view the spectral lines emitted

---

* By kind permission of Professor Stark.

by them. The lines then appear in their normal positions in the spectrum, where they lie when their carriers are at rest. Secondly, we can let the beam of positive ions approach us along the line of vision; then the spectral lines emitted by them appear to us to be displaced from their normal positions toward the side of the shorter wave lengths by an amount which is proportional to the velocity of the carriers of the lines. If, in the third place, the ions are moving away from us along the line of vision, their spectral lines appear displaced from their normal positions in the opposite direction.

"In 1905 I set to work to put this idea to the test of experiment. According to the state of research at that time, the canal rays, which stream toward the cathode of the discharge tube and pass to the back of it through 'canals,' were to be pictured as positive ions. I therefore first directed the collimator of my spectrometer in a direction at right angles to the axis of a beam of hydrogen canal rays; secondly, I let the rays enter the collimator along its axis. On a comparison of the two spectra thus obtained there appeared the looked-for Doppler effect in the series spectra of hydrogen; the same result was later obtained in the series spectra of numerous other chemical elements.

"Thus at the beginning of 1906 it appeared established that the carriers of the series spectra of the chemical elements were their positive ions. This interpretation of my observations was, it is true, soon called into question. For, as W. Wien and J. J. Thomson in particular showed, the canal rays generally contain neutral rays in addition to the positive ions, so that the question whether the series spectra of the former or of the latter were to be associated with the Doppler effect had to be regarded as unsettled. However, cases later became known in which canal rays containing only positive ions showed the Doppler effect in the spectral lines emitted by them.

·   ·   ·   ·   ·

"The removal of an electron from the surface of an atom, and therefore the ionization of the atom, means in any case a profound change in the structure of its surface. That it is accompanied by just as profound a change in the spectrum was to be expected from the first. Matters are otherwise with the second type of structural change which I made the subject of experimental investigation.

"Bear in mind that the atom is a closed structure consisting of positive and negative electrical entities. If we let an external electric field act on and through it, this will act on both the positive and negative entities of the atom, displacing the one to one side, the other to the other. It is true the displacement soon reaches a limit as a result of the opposing forces produced between the oppositely displaced entities, but the displacement remains, and it means a deformation, a change in the atomic structure. . . . Does this kind of change . . . manifest itself in a change in the spectrum of the atom? In other words, Has the electric field any effect on the spectral lines?

". . . Voigt had already developed a mathematical theory of the electrical counterpart of the Zeeman effect. The result of this theory was not encouraging, since it led to the conclusion that the change in the frequency, or wave length, of the spectral lines due to an electric field was immeasurably small. This result seemed to be confirmed by the lack of success met by several years' search for the effect in question.

"I could not, however, admit the assumption on which the theory was built, namely, that the emission of a spectral line on the part of an atom was merely a matter of a single electron moving by itself in the atom. I visualized the atom as a single complex structure, and the emission of a spectral line appeared to me to be the result of the interconnection and interaction of several electrical entities. So I expected a change in the atomic structure due to an external electric field to be accompanied by a corresponding change in the spectrum. I therefore gave my full attention to the problem of producing a strong electric field in a luminous gas. This I achieved by letting the canal rays, after they had passed through the channels in the cathode, enter a strong electric field between the cathode and an electrode placed opposite it.

"My very first photographs with the canal rays from hydrogen and helium showed the effect of the electric field on a series of spectral lines, and foreshadowed the wealth of phenomena this fresh field of research was to produce. . . . Theory had predicted that in the case where the luminous electric field is viewed at right angles, each spectral line would be split up by the field into two components, both appearing displaced from the normal line toward the longer wave lengths, one of the vibrations being parallel, the other perpendicular, to the field. How different the reality! For example, the red hydrogen line was split symmetrically with respect to the normal line into nine components, six of them vibrating parallel, three of them perpendicular, to the field."

CONSEQUENCES IN THEORY AND PRACTICE

In 1916 P. Epstein gave a quantum theory explanation of the Stark effect, based on an extended form of Bohr's theory of the atom. In 1926 Schrödinger (*q.v.* 1933) explained the effect by means of wave mechanics. In both cases the complete qualitative and quantitative agreement with observation provided strong evidence in support of the theories.

1 9 2 0

CHARLES-ÉDOUARD GUILLAUME

(1861–1938)

"For the services he rendered to precision physics by his discovery of the anomalies in nickel-steel alloys."

BIOGRAPHICAL SKETCH

CHARLES-ÉDOUARD GUILLAUME WAS BORN ON FEBRUARY 15, 1861, at Fleurier in the Swiss Jura. He was educated first at the *Gymnasium,* then at the Academy, at Neuchâtel, becoming assistant to the professor of physics at the latter institution. From 1878 to 1882 he attended the Federal Polytechnic School at Zurich, where he studied the mathematical sciences, particularly physics. He obtained his doctor's degree in 1883 for a dissertation on electrolytic condensers. On October 1, 1883, he entered the Bureau International des Poids et Mesures at Sèvres, near Paris, where he worked under the direction of J.-René Benoît, later in collaboration with him. He became director of the Bureau in 1915, a position which he held until his retirement in 1936. He died on June 13, 1938.

Guillaume's outstanding contributions to the science of metrology were recognized by honors and decorations from all parts of the world. France made him a Grand Officer of the Legion of Honor.

In 1790 the French National Assembly appointed a committee

to consider replacing the somewhat chaotic units of weights and measures in use by a system based on some constant unit of length. The result was the metric system, in which the unit of length, the meter, was defined as the ten-millionth part of the earth's quadrant through Paris; the unit of volume, the liter, as the volume of a cube of one decimeter ($1/10$ meter) side; and the unit of mass, the kilogram, as the mass of one liter of pure water at $4°$ C, the temperature of the maximum density of water. A committee appointed to determine the length of the meter reported its results in 1799, and in the same year a platinum standard meter (the *mètre des archives*) and a platinum standard kilogram (the *kilogramme des archives*) were prepared.

Later, more accurate, determinations of the earth's quadrant showed that the original meter was not, in fact, the ten-millionth part of the quadrant, so the original *mètre des archives* was itself adopted as the standard. Similarly, the original platinum kilogram was found to differ slightly from the mass of a cubic decimeter of pure water at $4°$ C; the original *kilogramme des archives* therefore became the standard unit of mass, with the liter, the standard unit of volume, as the volume occupied by one kilogram of pure water at $4°$ C. The liter is therefore not precisely equal to a cubic decimeter or 1000 cu. cm.

In 1875 the International Bureau of Weights and Measures was established to ensure that the meter and kilogram were standardized throughout the world. To this end the old platinum standards were replaced, about 1889, by platinum-iridium standards conforming as closely as possible to the originals; they are called the International Prototype Metre and International Prototype Kilogramme and are kept at the Bureau. At the same time *national* prototype meters and kilograms were prepared for distribution to the various governments concerned.

When Guillaume joined the Bureau one of his first tasks was a careful investigation into the sources of error in the mercury-in-glass thermometer, and the corrections to be applied. Obviously the precise and accurate measurement of temperature is a matter of first importance in dealing with metal standards, even though the coefficient of expansion of the platinum-iridium alloy used is exceptionally low. The results of Guillaume's researches on precision thermometry were published in a treatise on the subject in 1889.

Another task was the re-determination of the mass of a cubic decimeter of pure water in terms of the standard kilogram. In 1904 he determined the volume of a kilogram of pure water at 4° C and 760-mm. pressure as being 1000.029 cu. cm.; in 1927 he obtained the value 1000.028 cu. cm. Since the liter is by definition the volume occupied by a kilogram of pure water at 4° C, Guillaume's result, which is still accepted, means that 1 liter measures 1000.028 cu. cm., not the 1000 cu. cm. originally intended.

DESCRIPTION OF THE PRIZE-WINNING WORK

Guillaume's most important work arose out of the desirability of finding a cheaper material for the national prototype standards than the very expensive platinum-iridium alloy. Alloys of iron and nickel showed some promising features, one alloy having a co-efficient of expansion above that of iron or nickel alone, another below. Guillaume undertook a systematic and exhaustive series of investigations, extending over many years, in which he determined the coefficients of expansion of alloys of nickel and iron having different percentage compositions. He found that an alloy containing 35.6 percent nickel had a coefficient of expansion far lower than that of any pure metal or previously known alloy, less than 1/10 that of either nickel or iron alone and nearly 1/10 that of the platinum-iridium alloy. To this alloy he gave the name "invar," a contraction of *invariable*. Figure 16 (p. 178) shows how the co-efficient of expansion changes with increasing nickel content. At A (all iron, no nickel), the coefficient of expansion is about 11.9×10^{-6}; with 20 percent nickel, it has risen to about 19×10^{-6}; with 36 percent nickel it has dropped to about 1×10^{-6}; with further increase of nickel content the coefficient increases at first sharply, then gently until at B it is that of pure nickel (11×10^{-6}).

Another steel alloy discovered by Guillaume was "elinvar," in which the elasticity remained constant over a wide range of temperature.

The following extracts are taken from Guillaume's Nobel lecture, delivered in French, and describe the steps by which he was led to the discovery of invar.

"These prototypes [i.e., those adopted in 1889] were indeed admirable. They were made of an alloy of platinum and iridium, first prepared by Henri Sainte-Claire Deville, which combines all the properties of hardness, permanence, and resistance to chemical agents, thus being well fitted for the construction of standards intended to last throughout the centuries. But their high price put them out of reach for ordinary scientific purposes. . . .

"The search for a less expensive solution became pressing, for between these precious prototypes and standards of doubtful reliability there existed a gap which nothing could fill.

"It was to this problem that, in 1891, I devoted my first research. The really excellent qualities of pure nickel steel soon became evident. . . . However, a difficulty stopped me from extending its use. It concerned essentially the construction of a geodesic standard four meters long, and no factory was willing to undertake to supply the bar, perfectly sound and free from fissures, capable of filling the need.

"The continuation of the researches was guided by certain fortunate chances. In 1895 J. R. Benoît had undertaken . . . the investigation of a standard made of an alloy of 22 percent nickel and 3 percent chrome, and had found it to have an expansion near that of brass. This alloy was nonmagnetic, so that it showed a double anomaly.

"The curious phenomena discovered by John Hopkinson had been known for several years. They may be described briefly as follows. Certain alloys of iron and nickel, in the neighborhood of 25 percent of the latter, are, when they first come from the forge, nonmagnetic and lacking in hardness; but when they have been chilled, for example in solid carbon dioxide, they become strongly magnetic and hard; moreover, in this transformation their volume increases by about 2 percent.

"The phenomena discovered by Hopkinson and Benoît were evidently related. But, . . . alloys which undergo a change or which increase in expansibility are of no use for the construction of standards of length.

". . . in 1896, I was put on the track of a new and unexpected fact, closely related to those I have just mentioned. A bar of steel containing 30 percent nickel had reached the Bureau International, and I found that its expansibility was about one-third less than that of platinum. . . .

"For metrology the question of expansion is fundamental; indeed, an error made in the measurement of temperature is passed on to the measurement of length in proportion to the expansibility of the standard, and the continually renewed efforts made by metrologists to protect their measuring instruments against the disturbing effects of temperature show clearly the importance they attach to errors due to expansion. . . .

"Before the discovery of the anomaly I have just mentioned, every physicist would have affirmed that there was no hope of solving the problem by means of metals or alloys having an expansibility much lower than the values known, for the law of mixtures had always been considered to hold in practice.

"My first care was to verify the direction in which the expansion changed as a function of the composition of the alloys. This precaution was not a waste of time, for between the nonmagnetic 22 percent alloy and the magnetic 30 percent alloy there might have been a break in continuity. Experiments made on two alloys straddling the second . . . established the continuity.

. . . . .

"A first examination consisted in determining the curve of the anomaly as a function of the nickel content, without worrying about the additions of manganese, carbon, and silicon present in the alloys in varying quantities, which left the curve a little uncertain. Next I investigated series of alloys containing proportions of manganese and carbon up to the workable limit. Having thus determined the coefficients relative to these additions for all the values of the nickel content, I was able to reduce the results to the constant proportions of additions of 0.1 percent manganese and 0.4 percent carbon; those which contained these proportions I called *typical alloys*.

. . . . .

"For normal nickel-steel alloys the coefficients of expansion (a) at 20° C are shown in the curve in Fig. 2 [Fig. 16].

"The anomaly varies between wide limits, the expansibility varying in the ratio 1 to 15 and reaching a value which is only a quarter of the lowest expansibility found in a pure metal. Moreover, . . . these low expansibilities are obtained here by the use of inexpensive metals and form an altogether continuous scale. . . .

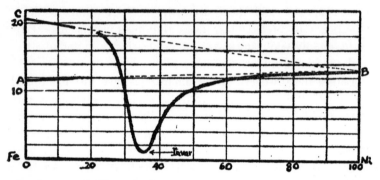

FIG. 16   *Guillaume's Fig. 2*

The expansion of nickel-steel alloys as a function of the composition. (The scale at the bottom gives the percentage nickel in the alloy.)

"The name 'invar' . . . has been given to the alloys whose coefficients of expansion differ little from the minimum. The coordinates for the minimum are: nickel, 35.6 percent; coefficient of expansion (a), 1.2×10^{-6}.

·   ·   ·   ·   ·

"As soon as he learned of the existence of invar, M. Jäderin, who was busy with preparations for measuring the bases in the Russo-Swedish expedition to Spitzberg, asked me to place the necessary wire at his disposal. I had already given my mind to the question and had had wires answering the requirements of base measurements made at the Imphy steelworks; these had been used in some preliminary experiments. The effect of drawing on the expansibility was already partly known, and it was possible to provide the Mission with wires practically free from expansibility.

"The success of the measurements at Spitzberg, carried out in

1899, was altogether outstanding. A letter from M. Jäderin, dated Treurenberg Bay, September 13, 1899, ran as follows: '. . . We measured, coming and going, a base 10,024 meters long. So far, we have made only a provisional calculation, and it shows a variation of only 19 millimeters. We made no allowance for the expansion of the wires. . . .'

"This message . . . was, for me, supremely encouraging. Benoît and I pushed on with our own experiments and when, a year later, the Geodesic Association met in Paris, we were able . . . to state that a very high degree of precision was likely to be attained by a still further development of the method. . . .

"A mural base-line, constructed immediately, has served since 1901 for studies pursued uninterruptedly.

"The observations . . . number hundreds of thousands. But our labor has . . . enabled us to determine the conditions under which the invar wires, first specially treated, then tested at the Bureau or in any standardization laboratory, can be transported, rolled up, to the site of the base-line, unrolled and used, all without any modification to their equation."

CONSEQUENCES IN THEORY AND PRACTICE

Guillaume's discovery, the outcome of a search for an alloy to serve one particular purpose, is of the utmost importance wherever change in length with temperature is to be avoided. The accuracy which geodetic measurements attained through the use of invar wires is shown by the example given in Guillaume's lecture. Apart from precision scientific instruments, the widest use of invar is in the clock- and watch-making industry; well over one hundred million watches with invar balance wheels are in existence, and millions are manufactured annually; high-grade watches and chronometers are fitted with elinvar hair springs.

1 9 2 1

ALBERT EINSTEIN
(1879–   )

"For his contributions to mathematical physics, and especially for his discovery of the law of the photoelectric effect."

BIOGRAPHICAL SKETCH

ALBERT EINSTEIN WAS BORN OF JEWISH PARENTS ON MARCH 14, 1879, at Ulm, in Württemberg, Germany. His father had a small electrochemical factory which he operated with the help of his brother, a trained engineer; his mother was of an artistic temperament and fond of music, qualities which Einstein inherited. When he was six years old, the family moved to Munich, where he received his primary education at the Catholic school.

At the age of ten he entered the Luitpold *Gymnasium* in Munich. Here Latin and Greek grammar were little to his liking, but he began to develop an interest in mathematics, not through the teaching at school, but through his uncle, who gave him his first insight into algebra; he found geometry an especially absorbing study. His interest in science was aroused mainly by popular works on the subject. Normally he would have remained at the *Gymnasium* until he was eighteen and had taken the diploma which would entitle him to become a university student. When he was fifteen, however, his father closed his factory in Munich and went to Milan, where he opened a similar one. Einstein was left in Munich to complete his schooling, but after six months followed his parents to Italy.

The electrochemical factory not proving very successful, it became necessary for Einstein to think of supporting himself. It seemed best that he should train for a practical profession. He therefore tried to gain admission to the Swiss Federal Polytechnic School, but failed in the entrance examination, in spite of his exceptionally high standing in mathematics. However, after attending a school in Aarau for a year he obtained the necessary diploma and was admitted to the Polytechnic without further examination.

On the conclusion of his studies at the Polytechnic Einstein tried without success to obtain a post there. After a period as private tutor he secured a position as a junior official in the Patent Office at Berne. Here it was his duty to make a preliminary report on inventions submitted; this served to keep alive his interest in scientific apparatus and to develop his rapid grasp of essential details. He also had ample time to pursue his studies and in 1902 his first paper, one dealing with thermodynamics, was published in the *Annalen der Physik*. In 1905 three other papers by him were published in the same journal: the paper on photoelectricity from which our extract is taken, one on the Brownian motion, and his first paper on relativity. In the same year he received his doctor's degree from the University of Berne.

His published work was of such outstanding merit that Einstein was advised to apply for a post as *privatdozent* at Berne University, such an appointment being a necessary prelude to a professorship. Einstein, able to retain his post at the Patent Office, since he would not be obliged to give more lectures than he wished, followed the advice, and became *privatdozent* at Berne in 1909. Shortly afterward, however, he was offered an appointment as professor extraordinary at the University of Zurich; Einstein accepted and now gave up his post at the Patent Office.

In 1910 the chair of theoretical physics at the German university, a part of the University of Prague, was offered to Einstein. He accepted, but shortly after his arrival at Prague in 1911 he was offered the chair of theoretical physics at the Polytechnic School in Zurich. Einstein accepted the offer, chiefly because his wife (a former fellow-student there whom he had married while working in Berne) preferred Zurich to Prague, and at the end of 1912 took up his new duties.

In 1913, Einstein was invited to Berlin to become first director of the newly founded Kaiser Wilhelm Physical Institute, with the status of professor at Berlin University, and to become a member of the Prussian Academy of Sciences, a much coveted honor. Einstein accepted and left Zurich at the end of 1913. For the next twenty years Berlin was his home.

Shortly after his arrival in Berlin Einstein separated from his wife, who returned to Switzerland with their two sons; later in the First World War, Einstein married his cousin Elsa.

A few months after the war ended Einstein's general theory of relativity received its dramatic confirmation and Einstein became a world celebrity.

In 1921 he accepted an invitation to accompany the Zionist leader Chaim Weizmann on a visit to the United States to encourage wealthy American Jews to support the plan for the establishment of a Jewish national home in Palestine and for the foundation of a Hebrew university there. After spending some time in the States, he returned to Berlin in June 1921, visiting England on his way home. In March 1922 he visited Paris at the invitation of the Collège de France. In the autumn of 1922 he traveled to the Far East, returning home via Palestine and Spain in the spring of 1923. In 1925 he visited South America. During the winters of 1930-1931 and 1932-1933 he was visiting professor at the California Institute of Technology.

On his return to Europe in 1933 conditions inside Germany made it inadvisable for him to enter the country, and he and his wife took up their residence near Ostend. In the following autumn they returned to the United States, and in the winter of 1933 he went to Princeton University as professor at the recently founded Institute for Advanced Study there. He resigned his professorship in 1945, but still continues to work at the Institute. He became a United States citizen in 1940.

Einstein's outstanding position as the greatest theoretical physicist of our time has been recognized by learned bodies throughout the world. He was elected a Foreign Member of the Royal Society of London in 1921 and received the Copley Medal in 1925. He was awarded the Gold Medal of the Royal Astronomical Society in 1926, and the Franklin Medal of the Franklin Institute in 1935.

Some fourteen universities, including Harvard, Princeton, Oxford, Cambridge, London, and Paris, have conferred honorary doctorates on him.

DESCRIPTION OF THE PRIZE-WINNING WORK

We have already mentioned that in 1905 Einstein published three papers in the *Annalen der Physik*. He was then a young man still in his twenties, holding no academic appointment, but those three papers have served to render that particular volume of the *Annalen* famous in scientific literature. The first, dated March 1905, made use of Planck's quanta of energy (see p. 165) to explain radiation phenomena other than heat radiation, in particular the photoelectric effect (see p. 38). The second paper, dated May 1905, developed a mathematical theory of the Brownian motion (see p. 251) and showed that the suspended particles should obey the gas laws—a theory which was later confirmed experimentally by Perrin (*q.v.* 1926). The third paper, dated June 1905, marked the first step in the development of the theory with which Einstein's name has become synonymous—the theory of relativity.

Though by the time of the Nobel award Einstein's fame as a physicist rested on his theory of relativity, there was some doubt as to whether a *theory*, however important, could be regarded as sufficient qualification for the award, since Nobel's will stipulated that the prizes were to be for *discoveries* conferring great benefit on mankind. Einstein therefore received the prize, not for the theory of relativity, but for "the discovery of the law of the photoelectric effect." Partly for this reason, but mainly because it is Einstein's quantum theory of light rather than his theory of relativity that enters into the work of several of the later laureates, we have taken our extracts from his first paper of 1905 and not from his Nobel lecture, which dealt with the theory of relativity.

In his later work on the photoelectric effect (see p. 39) Lenard made the important discovery that the velocity of the ejected electrons was quite independent of the intensity of the incident ultraviolet light: weakening the light by placing the source further away or by interposing screens merely reduced the number of electrons emitted, but did not reduce their velocity. Not all the electrons were ejected with the same velocity, but none had a velocity greater than a certain definite maximum as measured by the retarding potential (see p. 39) which had to be applied to prevent the emission of the electrons. Lenard found this retarding potential to be rather less than 5 volts, but it varied slightly with the substance. That velocities less than the maximum occurred was accounted for by E. Ladenburg in 1903, the year after Lenard published his discovery; Ladenburg showed that the photoelectrons were ejected from a layer of a definite thickness for each substance irradiated, the fastest electrons being those ejected from the surface, the slower ones those which had come from deeper in the layer and so had had their velocities reduced by collisions with atoms. There was, however, no satisfactory explanation of the existence of the maximum velocity of ejection independent of the intensity of the light; Lenard himself suggested a sort of trigger action: the incident light, however weak, released explosive forces within the atom which caused the ejection of the electron; stronger light could do no more than release the same forces.

Lenard's idea made the energy imparted to the electron come from the atom; Einstein's theory made it come from the light. According to Einstein, light consists of streams of minute bundles of energy, light quanta—or *photons,* as they are now called; the amount of energy in each quantum is $h\nu$, where h is Planck's constant and ν is the frequency of the light. When a light quantum falls on an electron, the latter cannot receive more energy than the light quantum has to give it, namely $h\nu$. Thus the maximum velocity of ejection is explained. At this time it was not known that this velocity varied with the frequency of the light; Einstein's theory required that it should, and later (1912) Richardson (*q.v.* 1928) and K. Compton found that the retarding potential required to prevent emission of electrons increased with the frequency of the incident light.

In the following passages, translated from the paper of 1905*, Einstein develops his quantum theory of light and uses it to explain the photoelectric effect.

---

* By kind permission of Professor Einstein.

THE EXCITATION AND TRANSFORMATION
OF LIGHT

"Between the theoretical ideas which physicists have formed regarding gases and other ponderable bodies and Maxwell's theory of electromagnetic processes in so-called empty space there lies a profound formal difference. For although we regard the state of a body as fully determined by the positions and velocities of a very large yet finite number of atoms and electrons, we employ continuous space functions for the determination of the electromagnetic state of a region of space, so that a finite number of magnitudes is not therefore to be regarded as sufficient for the complete determination of this state. According to Maxwell's theory, in all purely electromagnetic phenomena, and therefore also in light, the energy is to be conceived as a continuous function of space; whereas the energy of a ponderable body is, according to the current ideas of physicists, to be represented as a total distributed among the atoms and electrons. The energy of a ponderable body cannot be divided into as many parts as we please, each part as small as we please; whereas the energy of a ray of light emitted by a point source of light is, according to Maxwell's theory of light (or, more generally, according to any undulatory theory) distributed continuously throughout an ever-increasing volume.

"The undulatory theory of light employing continuous space functions has proved excellent for the representation of purely optical phenomena. . . . But . . . optical observations apply to time averages and not to instantaneous values; in spite of the complete experimental confirmation of the theories of diffraction, reflection, refraction, dispersion, and so on, it is quite conceivable that the theory of light employing continuous space functions may lead to contradictions with experience when it is applied to the phenomena of the excitation and transformation of light.

"It seems to me, in fact, that the observations on 'black-body radiation,' photoluminescence, the production of cathode rays by ultraviolet light, and other groups of phenomena involving the excitation and transformation of light, appear more understandable on the assumption that the energy of light is spread discontinuously in space. According to the assumptions to be put forward here, the energy of a ray of light proceeding from a point is not distributed continuously throughout an ever-increasing volume, but consists of a finite number of quanta of energy localized at points in space, quanta which move as wholes and which can be absorbed or emitted only as wholes.

"In what follows I shall give the train of ideas and cite the facts which have led me along this path. . . .

· · · · ·

"We turn for a moment from the radiation emitted and absorbed by resonators, and enquire into the condition for dynamical equilibrium in the interaction (collisions) between molecules and electrons. The kinetic theory of gases supplies this condition: it is that the mean total energy of an electron, considered as a resonator, must be equal to the mean kinetic energy of linear motion of the gas molecule. If we resolve the motion of the electron into three vibratory motions at right angles to one another, we find that the mean value $\bar{E}$ of the energy of such a linear vibration is given by

$$\bar{E} = \frac{R}{N} T$$

where R is the absolute gas constant*, N the number of 'effective molecules' in a gram equivalent, and T the absolute temperature.

· · · · ·

"We now apply similar considerations to the interaction between the resonators and the radiation present in the enclosure. Planck has deduced the condition for dynamical equilibrium in this case. He found that

$$\bar{E}_\nu = \frac{L^3}{8\pi\nu^2} \rho_\nu$$

where $\bar{E}_\nu$ is the mean energy of a resonator of natural frequency ν (per component of the vibration), L † the velocity of light, ν the

---

* $R = 8.315 \times 10^7$ ergs per deg. C.
† Velocity of light (now always denoted by c) = 2.998×10^{10} cm. per sec.

frequency, and $\rho_\nu \, d\nu$ the energy per unit volume of that part of the radiation whose frequency lies between ν and $\nu + d\nu$.

"If the radiation energy of frequency ν is to be on the whole neither continually decreased nor increased, we must have

$$\frac{R}{N} T = \bar{E} = \bar{E}_\nu = \frac{L^3}{8\pi\nu^2} \rho_\nu$$

and therefore

$$\rho_\nu = \frac{R}{N} \cdot \frac{8\pi\nu^2}{L^3} \cdot T$$

This relation, which we have found for the dynamical equilibrium, not only does not agree with experience, but also implies that in our representation there can be no question of a definite distribution of energy between ether and matter; for the larger the frequency of the resonator is made, the greater is the radiation energy in the enclosure, and in the limit it becomes infinite.

$$\cdot \quad \cdot \quad \cdot \quad \cdot \quad \cdot$$

"Planck's formula for the energy density ρ_ν, which so far experience has shown to be satisfactory, is

$$\rho_\nu = \frac{\alpha\nu^3}{e^{\beta\nu/T} - 1}$$

where $\alpha = 6.10 \times 10^{-56}$; $\beta = 4.866 + 10^{-11}$. For large values of T/ν, that is, for large wave lengths and radiation density, this formula becomes, in the limit,*

$$\rho_\nu = \frac{\alpha}{\beta} \nu^2 T$$

We know that this agrees with the one deduced from Maxwell's theory and the electron theory. By comparing coefficients in the two formulas we obtain

$$\frac{R}{N} \cdot \frac{8\pi}{L^3} = \frac{\alpha}{\beta}$$

---

* Since

$$e^{\beta\nu/T} = 1 + \frac{\beta\nu}{T} + \left(\frac{\beta\nu}{T}\right)^2 + \left(\frac{\beta\nu}{T}\right)^3 + \cdots$$

$$= 1 + \frac{\beta\nu}{T}$$

if $\frac{\nu}{T}$ is very small.

or

$$N = \frac{\beta}{\alpha} \cdot \frac{8\pi R}{L^3} = 6.17 \times 10^{23}$$

Therefore the mass of an atom of hydrogen $= 1/N$ gram* $= 1.62 \times 10^{-24}$ gram. This is exactly the value found by Planck, and agrees satisfactorily with values found by other means.

. . . . .

"It is true that the results of observations made so far on 'black-body radiation' show that the radiation law put forward by Wien, namely,

$$\rho = \alpha \nu^3 e^{-\beta\nu/T}$$

does not hold precisely. It does, however, agree very well with experiment for large values of ν/T. We make this formula the basis of our calculations, but bear in mind that our results are valid only within certain limits.

"First, from Wien's formula we obtain

$$\frac{1}{T} = -\frac{1}{\beta\nu} \log \frac{\rho}{\alpha\nu^3}$$

"Let radiation of energy E and frequency between ν and $\nu + d\nu$ occupy a volume v. . . . When the radiation occupies a volume v_0 let the entropy be S_0. Then, for the change of entropy as a function of the volume occupied, we have †

$$S - S_0 = \frac{E}{\beta\nu} \log \left(\frac{v}{v_0} \right)$$

"The equation shows that the entropy of monochromatic radiation of sufficiently small density varies with volume according to the same law as the entropy of an ideal gas or a dilute solution. The equation just found is to be interpreted in what follows on the basis of the principle introduced into physics by Boltzmann, according to which the entropy of a system is a function of the probability of its state.

---

* Since N is the number of molecules in 2 grams of hydrogen (diatomic) or the number of *atoms* in 1 gram.

† Einstein's derivation of this result is too long to give here. It involves the definition of entropy (p. 153), the expression for $1/T$ derived from Wien's formula, and $\rho_0/\rho = v/v_0$.

"If S_0 denotes the entropy for a certain initial state of the system under consideration, and W the relative probability of a state for which the entropy is S, we obtain the following general relation:

$$S - S_0 = \frac{R}{N} \log W$$

"We deal first with the following special case. In a volume v_0 let there be a number n of moving points (e.g., molecules), on which we fix our attention. Besides these there may be present in the space any number of other moving points of any kind. Let no assumption be made about the laws governing the motion of the points under consideration in the space except that, so far as this motion is concerned, no portion of the space and no direction is distinguished from any other. Further, let the number of moving points under consideration be so small that the action of the points on one another can be disregarded.

"A certain entropy S_0 is associated with the system under consideration, which may be, for example, an ideal gas or a dilute solution. We imagine a portion of magnitude v of the volume v_0, and suppose that all n moving points are transferred to this volume v without otherwise changing the system in any way. Clearly another value S of the entropy will be associated with this system. We shall now determine the change in entropy with the help of Boltzmann's principle.

"We ask: What is the probability of the latter state relative to the original state? Or, what is the probability that at any arbitrarily chosen moment of time all n points, moving independently of one another, in a given volume v_0, will happen to be in the volume v ?

"The value of this probability, which is a 'statistical probability,' is obviously

$$W = \left(\frac{v}{v_0}\right)^n$$

From this, applying Boltzmann's principle, we obtain *

$$S - S_0 = R\left(\frac{n}{N}\right)\log\left(\frac{v}{v_0}\right)$$

---

* $S - S_0 = \frac{R}{N} \log W = \frac{R}{N} \log \left(\frac{v}{v_0}\right)^n = \frac{R}{N} n \log \left(\frac{v}{v_0}\right)$

"We have found (above, p. 188) that the entropy of monochromatic radiation is given as a function of the volume by the equation

$$S - S_0 = \frac{E}{\beta \nu} \log \left(\frac{v}{v_0} \right)$$

If we write this as

$$S - S_0 = \frac{R}{N} \log \left[\left(\frac{v}{v_0} \right)^{(N/R)\,(E/\beta\nu)} \right] \; *$$

and compare it with the general formula expressing Boltzmann's principle, namely,

$$S - S_0 = \frac{R}{N} \log W$$

we arrive at the following conclusion:

"If monochromatic radiation of frequency ν and energy E is enclosed (by means of reflecting walls) in a volume v_0, the probability that at any arbitrarily chosen moment of time all the energy of the radiation will be in the partial volume v of the total volume v_0 is given by

$$W = \left(\frac{v}{v_0} \right)^{(N/R)\,[E/(\beta\nu)]}$$

From this we conclude further that monochromatic radiation of small density (within the limits of validity of Wien's radiation law) behaves, from the point of view of the theory of heat, as if it consisted of independent quanta of energy (*Energiequanten*) of magnitude $R\beta\nu/N$.

· · · · ·

"Now if monochromatic radiation (of sufficiently small density) behaves, as regards the dependence of its entropy on the volume, as a discontinuous medium consisting of quanta of energy of magnitude $R\beta\nu/N$, then the obvious thing to do is to investigate whether the laws of the excitation and transformation of light are such that light might consist of these energy quanta. We shall deal with these questions in what follows.

---

* $\frac{E}{\beta \nu} \log \left(\frac{v}{v_0} \right) = \log \left(\frac{v}{v_0} \right)^{E/\beta\nu} = \frac{R}{N} \log \left(\frac{v}{v_0} \right)^{(N/R)\,(E/\beta\nu)}$

"*The production of Cathode Rays by Illumination of Solid Bodies.* The customary view that the energy of light is distributed continuously throughout the space traversed by the radiation meets with especially serious difficulties in the attempt to explain photo-electric phenomena. These were pointed out by Lenard in his pioneer work.

"On the view that the exciting light consists of quanta of energy $(R/n)\beta\nu$, the production of cathode rays by light may be explained as follows. Quanta of energy penetrate the surface layer of the body and their energy is converted, at least in part, into kinetic energy of the electrons. The simplest view to take is that a light-quantum gives up its entire energy to a single electron, and we shall assume that this is the case. That electrons only partially take up the energy of light-quanta is not, however, to be excluded. An electron inside the body, endowed with kinetic energy, will, when it has reached the surface, have lost a part of its energy. Furthermore, it must be assumed that each electron must do an amount of work P (characteristic of the body) in leaving the body. Electrons excited right on the surface and normal to it will leave the body with the greatest normal velocity. The kinetic energy of such electrons is

$$\frac{R}{N}\beta\nu - P$$

"If the body is charged to a positive potential Π and is surrounded by conductors at zero potential, and if Π is just able to prevent loss of electricity by the body, then we must have

$$\Pi e = \frac{R}{N}\beta\nu - P$$

where e is the charge on the electron, or

$$\Pi E = R\beta\nu - P'$$

where E is the charge on a gram equivalent of a monovalent ion and P' the potential of this quantity of negative electricity with respect to the body.

"If we put $E = 9.6 \times 10^3$ [e.m.u.], then $\Pi \times 10^{-8}$ is the potential in volts which the body acquires through irradiation in a vacuum.

"To see, first of all, whether the relation we have deduced agrees with experiment, we put $P' = 0$, $v = 1.03 \times 10^{15}$ (corresponding to the limit of the solar spectrum at the ultraviolet end), and $\beta = 4.866 \times 10^{-11}$ [see above, p. 187]. We then obtain $\mathrm{II} = 4.3$ volts, which agrees in order of magnitude with Lenard's results.

"If the formula we have found is correct, then the values of II, when plotted as a function of the frequency of the exciting light, must lie on a straight line whose gradient is independent of the nature of the substance under test.

"Our view is not in conflict, as far as I can see, with the phenomena of the photoelectric effect observed by Lenard. If each quantum of energy of the exciting light gives up its energy to electrons independently of all the rest, then the velocity-distribution of the electrons, that is, the quality of the cathode rays produced, will be independent of the intensity of the exciting light; on the other hand, the number of electrons leaving the body will be proportional to the intensity of the exciting light, other conditions being the same."

Einstein's equation is now usually given in one or the other of the forms

$$\tfrac{1}{2}mv^2 = h\nu - p$$
$$Ve = h\nu - p$$

In the first equation m is the mass of the electron, v the velocity with which it leaves the surface, $\tfrac{1}{2}mv^2$ being the kinetic energy. In the second, V is the retarding potential required to prevent the emission of electrons and e the electronic charge. In both, $h\nu$ is the energy of the incident light-quantum and therefore the energy which is imparted to the electron; p is the part of this energy which is required to get the electron up to and away from the surface. If $h\nu$ is less than p, the electron cannot escape from the surface.

Einstein's equation was confirmed experimentally over a wide range of frequencies by Millikan (*q.v.* 1923) and his collaborators at the Ryerson Laboratory, Chicago, the results being published in 1916 (see p. 215).

Turning now to the theory of relativity, all we can do is to indicate how it arose and the general lines along which it developed; the subject is too big and too mathematical for discussion in any detail here.

Relativity is no new thing, as anyone who has studied elementary mechanics will appreciate when he recalls the problems he had to solve dealing with the motion of one body relative to another. But in all these problems one body, usually the earth, could be regarded as at rest. In fact, in one sense, relativity is as old as science itself. In ancient times the motions of the planets were described relative to the earth—generally held to be *really* motionless. Copernicus described the motions of the planets, including that of the earth, relative to the sun, treated as motionless. Newton, reaching out beyond the solar system, could find no motionless body to which to refer the motions of the heavenly bodies; he therefore gave reality to empty space and took this as his "frame of reference." With the advent of the wave theory of light, some medium was needed in which there could be waves, so Newton's empty space was filled with an all-pervading ether, which also served as the medium in which the electromagnetic waves predicted by Maxwell and demonstrated experimentally by Hertz could be transmitted. Given a fixed ether and light traveling through it with a definite velocity, it should be possible to find the velocity of the earth relative to the ether. Many attempts to measure this velocity were made, the most famous being that of Michelson and Morley (see p. 56); but all failed to detect any motion of the earth relative to the ether. Various explanations of this negative result were suggested, for example that the ether in the immediate neighborhood of the earth was dragged along with the earth, but all involved serious difficulties.

Another matter giving trouble when motion was involved concerned Maxwell's equations—six famous equations connecting the electric and magnetic quantities associated with any given point in an electric field; when the coordinates of the point are changed to new coordinates referred to axes moving with respect to the first set of axes, the equations assume a different form—that is, if the change in coordinates is made according to the transformation rules used in Newtonian mechanics. Yet obviously the electric and magnetic states at a point cannot be affected by a change in the system of coordinates used to describe the position of the point. For example, when a magnet is moved in the neighborhood of a coil of wire, electric and magnetic effects are produced in the coil and in the surroundings; but when the Newtonian transformations are applied to change the axes of reference from the coil (fixed system) to the magnet (moving system), Maxwell's equations assume a form which indicates a different electric and magnetic state in the coil and surroundings. Yet common experience shows that it is immaterial whether the magnet is moved toward the coil or the coil toward the magnet: it is only the *relative* motion that matters.

The first to make a successful attack on the problem was H. A. Lorentz (*q.v.* 1902), who in 1904 published a paper on electromagnetic phenomena in a moving system. In his treatment Lorentz made use of a hypothesis which he and G. F. Fitzgerald of Dublin had put forward independently in 1892 to account for the negative result of the Michelson-Morley experiment, namely, that a body, such as a measuring rod, suffered, as a result of its motion through the ether, a contraction in the direction of motion which was just sufficient to mask the velocity of the earth relative to the ether. The transformations at which Lorentz arrived were completely satisfactory when applied to Maxwell's equations and constitute one of his greatest achievements, the "Lorentz transformation" replacing the Newtonian in electrodynamics when moving bodies are involved.

Einstein, who at the time did not know of Lorentz' paper, attacked the same problem in his paper of 1905, which bore the title: "Zür Elektrodynamik bewegter Körper" (On the Electrodynamics of Moving Bodies). Einstein's approach was entirely different from Lorentz'. Where Lorentz gave the chief role to the ether, Einstein dispensed with it altogether, or at least ignored it. Instead, he laid down two postulates as fundamental. The first asserted the general validity of Maxwell's equations: "the same laws of electrodynamics and optics will be valid for all frames of reference for which the equations of mechanics hold good*." To this postulate Einstein gave the name "the principle of relativity." The second postulate stated that "light is always propagated in empty space with a definite velocity c which is independent of the state of motion of the emitting body" *—this postulate, self-evident on the ether theory, had to be introduced if no appeal was to be made to the properties of the ether.

---

* Quoted from *The Principle of Relativity,* by Einstein and others, (London: Methuen & Co., Ltd., 1923), pp. 37, 38.

In the subsequent treatment Einstein first showed that the constancy of the velocity of light was consistent with the "principle of relativity" and that this velocity is unaltered by being compounded with another velocity (e.g., that of the earth) less than that of light —thus accounting for the negative result of the Michelson-Morley experiment. That the velocity of light is the same for all observers, whether in motion or not, became one of the cornerstones of the theory of relativity. Turning to Maxwell's equations, Einstein deduced a transformation which was, in fact, equivalent to the Lorentz transformation. When applied to mechanics, however, this required that at very high velocities bodies should behave so strangely that at first very few were prepared to accept such a solution of the problem.

The next step in the development of the theory of relativity was taken by Hermann Minkowski. In a Newtonian transformation from stationary to moving axes *time* remains the same, but Lorentz had found that time, like each of the three space coordinates, must assume a different value when the change to moving axes is made; he used the term "local time" to distinguish time for the moving system from time for the stationary system. Einstein, early in his paper of 1905, discusses the relation between time for a stationary and time for a moving system, and draws the conclusion that no absolute meaning can be attached to simultaneity—that two events which are simultaneous when viewed from a stationary system of coordinates no longer appear as simultaneous events when viewed from another system moving relatively to the first. Einstein specified an event by four "coordinates" (x,y,z,t), where x,y,z are the space coordinates of the point, referred to stationary axes, where the event occurs, and t is the time of the occurrence; if the coordinates of the point where the event occurs are x',y',z' referred to *moving* axes, then the time of the event must also be changed to a definitely specified value t', the coordinates of the event now becoming $(x',\ y',\ z',\ t')$. Einstein at this stage still keeps space and time distinct. Minkowski, however, linked the two inseparably together by considering the four variables as the coordinates of a *world-point* in a four-dimensional space-time continuum; he was then able to study the metrical properties of this continuum in the same way as is done for space in ordinary analytical geometry of three dimensions.

In 1916 Einstein published his second great paper on relativity—that which introduced the *general* theory, so called because the theory was now extended to include accelerated frames of reference, whereas the original one (the special theory of relativity) was restricted to frames of reference in uniform rectilinear motion. In this paper Einstein lays down as his fundamental postulate: *the laws of physics must be of such a nature that they apply to systems of reference in any kind of motion.* Making full use of Minkowski's four-dimensional space-time continuum and of the tensor analysis developed by the two Italian mathematicians Ricci and Levi-Civita, Einstein then proceeded to develop the consequences of this hypothesis, and thus arrived at a law of gravitation more general than that of Newton, the latter, however, approximating very closely to it in ordinary circumstances. The new law gave an immediate explanation of the already known but unexplained motion of the perihelion of the planet Mercury, and required also a displacement of spectral lines produced in a strong gravitational field and a bending of a ray of light which passed through such a field. The latter requirement was confirmed during the total eclipse of the sun on May 29, 1919.

CONSEQUENCES IN THEORY AND PRACTICE

Of all the far-reaching results arising out of the theory of relativity one of the most important was a deduction which Einstein drew shortly after putting forward the special theory. This was, that if a body gives off energy in the form of radiation, its mass is diminished by an amount equal to the energy given off divided by the square of the velocity of light, and an increase in the energy of a body is accompanied by an increase in its mass; the mass of a body is a measure of its energy-content, the two being connected by the relation

$$\text{mass (in grams)} = \frac{\text{energy (in ergs)}}{c^2},$$

where $c = 3 \times 10^{10}$ cm per sec., the velocity of light. This is of special importance in the physics of fast-moving particles, since the high velocity of these particles, often approaching that of light itself, makes it necessary to take into account the increase in the mass of the particle caused by the particle's speed—one of the remarkable requirements of the postulates of the special theory which has received some experimental confirmation. It also provides an explanation of a discovery made by Anderson (*q.v.* 1936) in 1933 that a gamma-ray photon on striking a nucleus gave rise to a positive and a negative electron, the interpretation being that the greater part of the energy of the gamma ray (radiation) had been converted into the rest-mass of the material particles, the balance appearing in their kinetic energy.

Einstein has recently formulated a "unified field theory" combining the general theory of relativity and electromagnetic field theory, but so far has not found a practicable way to confront the results of the theory with experimental evidence.

1 9 2 2

NIELS HENRIK DAVID BOHR
(1885–   )

*"For his studies on the structure of atoms and the
radiation emanating from them."*

BIOGRAPHICAL SKETCH

NIELS BOHR WAS BORN ON OCTOBER 7, 1885, AT COPENHAGEN,
where his father was professor of physiology at the university. He
attended the Gammelholm Grammar School, and, largely owing to
his father's influence, became interested in physics. In 1903 he
entered the University of Copenhagen, where he studied physics
under Professor C. Christiansen, obtaining his master's degree in
1909 and his doctor's degree in 1911, the latter with a dissertation
in which he applied the electron theory to the explanation of the
properties of metals. In the autumn of 1911 he went to Cambridge,
England, to work in the Cavendish Laboratory under J. J. Thomson, and in the spring of 1912 to Victoria University, Manchester,
to work in Rutherford's laboratory. From 1913 to 1914 he held a
lectureship in physics at the University of Copenhagen; from 1914
to 1916 he was reader in mathematical physics at Manchester. In
1916 he was appointed professor of theoretical physics at Copenhagen and since 1920 has been head of the newly established Institute for Theoretical Physics there.

Bohr is a Member or Honorary Member of very many European
and American scientific societies. He was elected a Foreign Member of the Royal Society of London in 1926. Universities in all
parts of the world have conferred honorary doctorates on him.

DESCRIPTION OF THE PRIZE-WINNING WORK

The modern theory of the atom as a complex structure arose out of J. J. Thomson's discovery of the electron in 1897. From Lenard's experiments on the passage of cathode rays through matter it appeared that an atom must consist largely of empty space; J. J. Thomson suggested in 1904 that it might consist of a sphere of positive electricity in which electrons revolved (p. 48). Then in 1911 Rutherford put forward his *nuclear* theory of the atom. This theory arose out of some Wilson cloud-track photographs (see below, p. 271) taken in Rutherford's laboratory; these showed that occasionally an alpha particle emitted by a radioactive substance suffered a sharp deflection from its straight-line path. To account for this, Rutherford suggested that the atom consisted of a minute but relatively heavy positively charged nucleus around which a sufficient number of electrons revolved to render the atom as a whole electrically neutral, the sharp deflection being due to the passage of the a particle through the intense electric field surrounding the central charge. In 1913 Bohr, at that time working in Rutherford's laboratory, put forward his modification of Rutherford's theory.

According to the classical electromagnetic theory, an electron describing an orbit about a nucleus should radiate continuously, losing energy as it does so, with the result that the orbit should become smaller and smaller until the electron ultimately falls into the nucleus. An incandescent gas therefore, if it could exist long enough, should emit light of all wave lengths, forming a continuous spectrum. But the spectrum of every gas—even that of hydrogen, the gas with, it may be assumed, the simplest of all atoms—consists of a number of separate *lines*. It is evident, therefore, that any particular atom is capable of emitting light of certain frequencies only. This Bohr met by postulating that emission of light occurred, not as a result of the periodic motion of the electron in its orbit, but as the result of a "jump" on the part of the electron from one of a limited number of possible orbits to another in which the electron possessed less energy, the difference in energy between the two orbits being equal to the frequency of the emitted light multiplied by Planck's constant h. As long as the electron revolves in the *same* orbit, no radiation takes place. Bohr's "stationary orbits" mark a definite departure from classical electromagnetic theory, according to which the frequency of the emitted light is identical with the frequency of the periodic orbital motion of the electron. Otherwise, apart from this introduction of nonradiating orbits and the emission of energy in quantum jumps, Bohr's theory adhered to classical electrodynamics and mechanics.

At the time Bohr was working on his theory, two important generalizations in connection with spectral lines were at his command. The first of these was a discovery made in 1885 by J. J. Balmer that the wave lengths of the lines in the visible region of the hydrogen spectrum can be expressed by the formula

$$\lambda = \text{constant} \times \frac{m^2}{m^2 - 4}$$

where m is any whole number greater than 2. Later (1890) J. R. Rydberg expressed the relation in the form

$$n = R\left(\frac{1}{2^2} - \frac{1}{m^2}\right)$$

m still being a whole number greater than 2. Here R is a constant having the value 109,678 if n is, not the frequency itself, but the reciprocal of the wave length, or, as it is called, the *wave number,* that is, the number of wave lengths in one centimeter. The frequency is equal to the wave number multiplied by the velocity of light (3×10^{10} cm. per sec.). Many other spectra also were found to contain series of lines represented by a similar formula, with the same value of R (the *Rydberg constant*) but with nonintegral values of m.

The second generalization was the *combination principle* put forward by W. Ritz in 1908. This principle, which has been fully confirmed by later observations, applies to all spectra, but we shall restrict ourselves to that of hydrogen. The principle states that the wave number of every line of the spectrum can be expressed as the difference of two "terms," the same "terms" taking part in a large number of combinations; the hydrogen terms are of the form R/m^2. To give an example:

$$n_1 = R\left(\frac{1}{2^2} - \frac{1}{3^2}\right) \quad \text{and} \quad n_2 = R\left(\frac{1}{2^2} - \frac{1}{4^2}\right)$$

are both lines of the hydrogen spectrum; the combination principle suggests that $R\left(\frac{1}{3^2} - \frac{1}{4^2}\right)$ might also be a line—it is, in fact, the first line of a series later discovered by F. Paschen in the infrared spectrum of hydrogen.

Bohr's theory accounted most satisfactorily for the Ritz combination principle as applied to the hydrogen spectrum and for the existence of such series of spectral lines as the Balmer series; it was one of the earliest triumphs of the theory that Bohr was able to deduce from it almost the exact value of the Rydberg constant in terms of known physical constants.

We now give * translations of some extracts from Bohr's Nobel lecture, which he delivered in Danish.

"Rutherford's discovery of the nucleus of the atom in 1911 made it clear that the classical conceptions did not offer any basis for an understanding of the most essential properties of the atom. One was therefore led to seek a formulation of the principles of the quantum theory which should meet at once the demands of the stability of the structure of the atom and the character of the radiation emitted by the atoms. . . . I proposed such a formulation in 1913 by laying down two postulates, which can be expressed as follows:

I. Among the conceivable states of motion in an atomic system there are a number of *stationary states*. In spite of the fact that the motion of the particles in these states is assumed largely to obey the laws of classical mechanics, these states are distinguished by a strange, mechanically inexplicable, stability which causes every change occurring in the motion of the system to consist in a complete transition from one stationary state to another.

II. Although, contrary to classical electromagnetic theory, no radiation takes place in the stationary states themselves, a transition between two stationary states can be accomplished by an emission of electromagnetic radiation, which will have the same character as that which, according to the classical theory, would be emitted by an electrical particle exciting an

---

* By kind permission of Professor Bohr.

harmonic vibration with constant frequency. This frequency ν has, how-ever, no simple relation to the motion of the particles in the atom, but is given by the condition

$$h\nu = E' - E''$$

where h is Planck's constant, and E', E'' are the values of the energy of the atom in the two states forming the initial and final states of the radiation process. Conversely, an irradiation of the atom with electro-magnetic waves of this frequency can give rise to a process of absorption by which the atom is brought back from the last-named state to the first state.

"Whereas the first postulate is directed at the general stability behavior of the atoms, which, for instance, manifests itself in the chemical and physical properties of substances, the second postulate is directed, first of all, at the existence of spectra consisting of sharp lines. Also the fact that the quantum-theory condition enters into the second postulate offers a starting point for the interpretation of the empirical laws for the spectra of substances. The most general of these laws, the *combination principle* put forward by Ritz, states that the frequency ν of each of the lines in the spectrum of a sub-stance can be expressed by the formula

$$\nu = T'' - T'$$

where T'', T' are two so-called 'spectral terms' belonging to a num-ber of such terms characteristic of the substance in question.

"According to our postulates this law is immediately explained by assuming that the spectrum is emitted in transitions between a number of stationary states in each of which the numerical value of the energy of the atom is equal to the value of the spectral term multiplied by Planck's constant. This interpretation of the combina-tion principle differs from our customary electrodynamic concep-tions in two respects. Not only do we assume that there is no simple relation between the motion of the atom and the radiation emitted, but—and this perhaps shows most clearly to what extent we have departed from the basis on which our customary description of nature rests—our interpretation of the production of the spectral lines corresponding to combinations of a given spectral term with various others means that the character of the radiation emitted by the atom is dependent not only on the state of the atom at the beginning of the process of radiation, but also on the state to which the atom is brought as a result of that process. At first glance it might perhaps be expected that this formal interpretation of the combination principle could hardly be reconciled with our knowledge of the component parts of the atom. . . . A closer examination, however, shows that, on the basis of the postulates, it is possible to arrive at a connection of an intimate kind between the spectra of the different substances and the structure of their atoms.

"Of all the spectra we know, that of hydrogen shows the simplest behavior. The frequencies of its spectral lines can, as is well known, be represented with great exactness by Balmer's formula

$$\nu = K\left[\frac{1}{(n'')^2} - \frac{1}{(n')^2}\right]$$

where K is a constant and n', n'' are two whole numbers. We have therefore in the spectrum a single series of spectral terms of the form K/n^2, which decrease regularly with increasing term number n. In accordance with the postulates we consider therefore that each of the spectral lines of hydrogen is emitted in the transition between two among a number of stationary states of the hydrogen atom, in each of which states the energy of the atom is equal to hK/n^2. According to our picture of the structure of the atom, the hydrogen atom consists of a positive nucleus and one electron which, if the customary mechanical conceptions can be applied with a high degree of approximation, will describe a periodic elliptical path with the nucleus at one focus. As a simple calculation shows, the major axis of the path is inversely proportional to the work that must be done to remove the electron completely from the atom, and in this connection we shall now assume that this work in the stationary states just equals hK/n^2. We thus arrive at a multiplicity of stationary states for which the major axis of the electron's path assumes a series of discrete values proportional to the squares of the whole numbers.

"The accompanying figure [Fig. 17] illustrates this behavior schematically. For the sake of simplicity, the paths of the electrons in the stationary states are shown as circles, although the theory does not in fact impose any restrictions on the eccentricity of the path, but only determines the length of the major axis. The arrows indi-

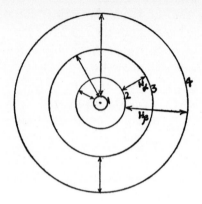

FIG. 17

[Bohr's model of the hydrogen atom: electron orbits and transitions. (*See also Fig. 26, p. 241.*)]

cate the transitions corresponding to the red and green hydrogen lines, the frequencies of which are given by Balmer's formula when we put 2 for n'' and 3 and 4 in turn for n'. The figure also shows the transitions corresponding to the first three lines in the ultra-violet series discovered by Lyman in 1914, the frequencies of which are given by the formula when n'' is put equal to 1; also the first line in the infrared series, which was discovered some years ago by Paschen and which is given by the formula when n'' is put equal to 3.

"This explanation of the production of the hydrogen spectrum leads naturally to something else: that this spectrum may be looked on as evidence of a process by which electrons are 'bound' to the nucleus. The largest spectral term, with term number 1, corresponds to the final stage of the binding process, and the small-valued spectral terms, which correspond to large values of the term number, belong to stationary states marking the initial stages of the binding process, where the path of the electron still has large dimensions and where the work that has to be done to pull the electron completely free from the nucleus is still small. The final stage of the binding process we can describe as the 'normal state' of the atom; it is distinguished from the other stationary states by the property that, according to the postulates, the state of the atom can be changed only through a supply of energy whereby the electron is transferred to a path of larger dimensions corresponding to an earlier stage of the binding process.

"The size of the electron path in the normal state, calculated on the basis of the explanation we have given, agrees approximately with the values for the size of the atoms of the elements calculated from the properties of the gases by means of the kinetic theory of gases."

CONSEQUENCES IN THEORY AND PRACTICE

Even in its original form, in which the orbits of the electron were restricted to circles, Bohr's theory proved remarkably successful in interpreting the complex structure of spectra. When, in 1915, Arnold Sommerfeld of Munich extended the theory to include elliptical orbits, it was applied with equal success to the explanation of the *fine structure* shown by certain spectral lines when examined with instruments of sufficiently high resolving power. By ascribing spin to the electron and to the nucleus it was possible to account for yet more of the data provided by spectroscopic examination.

On the whole it seemed that the Bohr-Sommerfeld theory of the atom had come to stay—that only comparatively minor adjustments were necessary to bring all the results of spectroscopic analysis within its scope; certainly from 1913 until the mid-1920's Bohr's theory held undisputed sway and was at the root of the great advances made in atomic physics. Yet in spite of its many brilliant successes in explaining experimental facts, theoretical physicists were not too happy about the fundamental assumptions of the theory. These had been, so to say, imposed on Nature from without; it would be more satisfying if they could be arrived at by deduction from some simpler, more fundamental, theory. Such a theory was later found in the *wave mechanics* constructed on de Broglie's conception of matter waves (see below, pp. 289, 295, 315 *ff*).

1 9 2 3

ROBERT ANDREWS MILLIKAN
(1868–   )

*"For his work on the elementary electric charge
and on the photoelectric effect."*

BIOGRAPHICAL SKETCH

ROBERT ANDREWS MILLIKAN WAS BORN ON MARCH 22, 1868, at Morrison, Illinois. He attended the Maquoketa (Iowa) High School, and, from 1886, Oberlin College, Ohio. Though he took physics for one semester, his great interest in the subject did not develop until after his graduation in 1891. From 1891 to 1893 he taught physics at Oberlin College. After obtaining his A.M. degree in 1893 he was appointed Fellow in physics at Columbia University, where he took his doctor's degree in 1895. The next two years were spent in Europe, where he studied physics at Göttingen and Berlin. On his return in 1896 he was appointed assistant in physics at the University of Chicago, where he remained for the next twenty-five years, being appointed professor of physics in 1910. In 1921 he went to the California Institute of Technology at Pasadena as director of the Norman Bridge Laboratory of Physics, an appointment which he held until his retirement in 1945.

In 1917 Millikan became chairman of the National Research Council and chief of the Science and Research Division of the Signal Corps, U. S. A., with the rank of lieutenant-colonel.

Millikan has been awarded the Hughes Medal of the Royal Society of London, the Comstock Prize of the National Academy of Sciences, and the Edison Medal of the American Institute of Electrical Engineers. Many American universities and colleges have conferred honorary doctorates on him, as has also the University of Dublin. He is a member of numerous scientific societies and academies.

DESCRIPTION OF THE PRIZE-WINNING WORK

The work for which Millikan is most famous is his precise determination of the electronic charge e, work which, begun in 1906, extended over more than ten years. In 1897 C. T. R. Wilson (*q.v.* 1927) invented his cloud chamber (p. 271) and in the following year Sir J. J. Thomson in the Cavendish Laboratory, Cambridge, England, used the apparatus to measure e. His procedure, which he described in his Nobel lecture (see extract, p. 47), involved the estimation of the number of drops in the cloud. To obtain this number he first calculated from the degree of supersaturation the total amount of water in the cloud and then determined the volume of each droplet. To find the volume of a droplet—he had, of course, to assume that all the droplets were of the same size—he made use of Stokes's law of fall. This law expresses the limiting velocity attained by a small body falling through a viscous fluid in terms of the radius and density of the body and the density and viscosity of the fluid. Since the other quantities were known, the radius of a drop could be calculated from the observed velocity with which the cloud fell under gravity, and from this the mass. The total mass of the cloud having been found and the mass of a single drop, the number of drops in the cloud could at once be calculated. The total charge on the cloud was measured by means of an electrometer. The charge on each ion was then found by dividing the total charge by the number of drops, the assumptions being made that each ion carried only unit charge e and that each drop formed on a single ion, so that the number of ions equaled the number of drops. The value obtained by Thomson for e was 3.1×10^{-10} e.s.u.—the value accepted today is about 50 percent higher than this. In 1903 H. A. Wilson, also in the Cavendish Laboratory, modified Thomson's method so as to remove some at least of the experimental uncertainties involved. In the expansion chamber he fitted two horizontal plates about a centimeter apart and connected them to the terminals of a 2000-volt battery. The rate of fall of the *top* of the cloud was observed (*a*) when gravity alone acted, and (*b*) when the electric field was applied. The value of *e* was then calculated from the two observed rates of fall and the strength of the field, the only other quantities involved being the density of the drops, the coefficient of viscosity of the gas, and the acceleration of gravity. By observing only the top of the cloud, Wilson avoided the assumption that each drop formed on a single ion; since the more heavily charged drops were more strongly attracted to the oppositely charged lower plate, the top layer contained only those drops which carried the least charge. But he had to introduce the serious assumption that the size of the drops was the same in two successive expansions. The values which Wilson obtained for *e* varied between 2×10^{-10} and 4.4×10^{-10}, their mean being close to the value obtained by Thomson. Though Wilson's method was a decided improvement on Thomson's, it, like Thomson's, depended to a very large extent on the validity of Stokes's law, which had never been tested for bodies of such minute size as the droplets forming the clouds. Moreover, in both methods it had to be assumed that no decrease in the size of the droplets occurred during the time of observation, yet such a decrease was bound to occur as a result of evaporation due to the rise of temperature following the cooling caused by the expansion.

When, in 1906, Millikan took up the problem, he began by repeating Wilson's experiments in the hope of obtaining greater consistency in the results. In this he did not succeed at first, but in 1908, by shortening the time of observation so as to reduce the error due to evaporation, he obtained values lying between 3.66 and 4.37, the mean value for *e* being 4.06×10^{-10} e.s.u. Millikan, however, was not satisfied, since evaporation, though greatly reduced, was still present and remained an unknown quantity. So instead of changing the rate of fall by means of the electric field, he adjusted the strength of the field until the top of the cloud remained *stationary,* hoping to be able to observe the rate of evaporation and make allowances for it. The method did not come up to his expectations, but he made the important discovery that it was possible to hold individual droplets stationary for nearly a minute.

This gave him the means he required for studying the effect of evaporation; for, by changing the strength of the field, he could allow the drop to fall and could time its passage between the first and second and then between the second and third of three equally spaced parallel cross hairs, observing the motion of the drop through a telescope. If the two times were equal, no appreciable evaporation had taken place during the process. The subsequent calculation of e was made in the same way as in Wilson's work, the value obtained being 4.70×10^{-10} e.s.u.

In these experiments Millikan found that in practically every case the droplets carried multiple charges. He also noticed that sometimes, when he had failed to screen off the rays from the radium used to produce the ionization, a "balanced drop" suddenly began to move up or down in the electric field, having evidently "captured" a positive or a negative ion. This suggested that measurements of the speed of the drop before and after it had captured an ion would enable him to calculate the charge on the captured ion. So far he had used the Wilson expansion chamber in his investigations, but now, in the autumn of 1909, he discarded this altogether in favor of the apparatus shown schematically in Fig. 18 and in

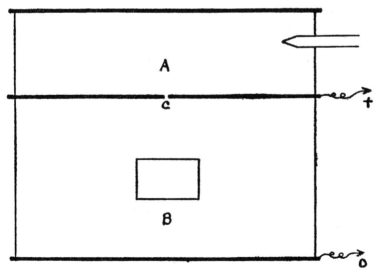

FIG. 18
Millikan's oil-drop apparatus. Simplified diagram.

greater detail in Fig. 19 (p. 212). Minute droplets of oil, about one-thousandth of a millimeter in diameter, were sprayed into the space A (Fig. 18), where they fell slowly under gravity; occasionally a droplet would find its way through the pinhole C and enter the space B, where it was illuminated by a powerful beam of light and showed up as a bright star against the ebonite walls of the chamber when viewed through a telescope. Friction due to the spraying had caused the droplets to become electrified, so that when an electric field was applied the drop rose or fell according to the direction of the field, falling under gravity when the field was turned off.

Millikan found that in the absence of the field the time taken to fall the distance between two cross hairs was always the same, but that when the field was on, the times of successive transits differed from one another, but always had one or another of a few recurring values. Thus in one set of experiments the time of fall under gravity was always 13.6 sec. (very nearly); when the field was applied, the time of transit was 12.5 sec., the drop, positively charged, falling faster because of the attraction of the negatively charged lower plate. The drop was then raised by reversing the direction of the field. The next downward transit took the same time, but the next took 21.8 sec., showing that a negative ion had been captured. The following transits took 34.8 and 85.5 sec., but the next only 34.6 sec., indicating the capture of one or more *positive* ions. When the velocity of the droplet changed between two timings, the increase or decrease was, in the set of experiments from which the above data are taken, always very nearly 0.0088 cm. per sec., or an integral multiple of this value.

In these experiments Millikan used an ordinary stop-watch, but later (1910) he carried out far more precise experiments using a chronometer reading to one-thousandth of a second. Part of his researches included an examination of the validity of Stokes's law when applied to the minute droplets used in the experiments: he found that a small correcting term had to be inserted. The calculation of e was made in the same way as before except that the amended law of fall under gravity was used, the value obtained in 1913 being $e = 4.807 \times 10^{-10}$ e.s.u. In 1917, as a result of still more refined oil-drop experiments, Millikan confirmed this value, with a possible error of 5 in the last decimal place.

We have chosen for our extracts those portions of Millikan's Nobel lecture which deal with the determination of the charge on the electrons.*

"The conception of electrical particles or atoms goes back . . . to Benjamin Franklin who wrote, about 1750: 'The electrical matter consists of particles extremely subtle, since it can permeate common matter, even the densest, with such freedom and ease as not to receive any appreciable resistance.'

". . . the experimentalist's answer . . . to the . . . query: 'What is electricity?' . . . is naive, but simple and definite. He admits at once that as to the *ultimate* nature of electricity he knows nothing.

. . . . .

"He begins rather with a few simple and familiar experiments and then sets up some definitions which are only descriptions of the experiments and therefore involve no hypothetical elements at all.

"He first notes the fact that a pith ball, after contact with a glass rod that has been rubbed with silk, is found to be endowed with the new and striking property that it tends to move away from the rod with a surprisingly strong and easily measurable force. He describes that fact, . . . by inventing a new word and saying that the pith ball has been put into a *positively electrified state,* or simply has received *a charge of positive electricity.* He then measures the amount of its charge by the strength of the observed force.

"Similarly he finds that the pith ball, after contact with an ebonite rod that has been rubbed with cat's fur, is attracted, and he . . . [says] that it has now received a *charge of negative electricity.* Whenever the pith ball is found to have been put . . . into a condition to behave in either of the foregoing ways, it has, *by definition,* received a charge of either positive or negative electricity. The whole of our thinking about electrical matters starts with these two simple experiments and these two definitions.

". . . to get the most crucial possible test of . . . Franklin's conception of a particle, or an atom, of electricity it was clearly nec-

* The following extracts are quoted by kind permission of Professor Millikan.

essary to reduce the charge on the pith ball to the smallest possible amount, to change that charge by the most minute possible steps, and then to see whether the forces acting upon it at a given distance from the glass rod (i.e. in a constant field) had any tendency to increase or decrease by *unitary* steps.

"The success of the experiments, first performed in 1909, was wholly due to the design of the apparatus, i.e. to the relation of the parts.

"The pith ball . . . had of course to be the smallest spherical body . . . which would remain of constant mass; for a continuously changing gravitational force would be indistinguishable in its effect upon the motion of the charged body from a continuously changing electrical charge.

"A non-homogeneous or non-spherical body also could not be tolerated; for the force acting on the pith ball had to be measured by the speed of motion imparted to it by the field, and this force could not be computed from the speed unless the shape was spherical and the density absolutely constant. This is why the body chosen to replace the pith ball was an individual oil-droplet about a thousandth of a millimeter in diameter blown out of an ordinary atomizer and kept in an atmosphere from which convection currents had been completely removed by suitable thermostatic arrangements. The glass rod, the purpose of which was to produce a constant electrical field, was of course replaced by the two metal plates C and D (Fig. 1) [Fig. 19] of an air condenser, one of the plates (D) being attached to the positive, the other (C) to the negative termi-

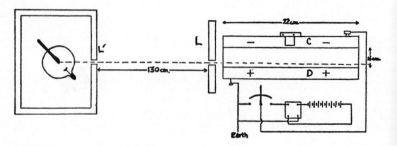

FIG. 19   *Millikan's Fig. 1*

[Millikan's oil-drop apparatus for determining the charge on an ion.]

nal of a battery, and a switch being added . . . to make it possible to throw the field on or off at will.

"In order to be able to measure very accurately the force acting upon the charged oil-droplet it was necessary to give it about a centimeter of path in which the speed could be measured. This is one of the most important elements in the design. . . . The centimeter of path and the constancy of field then fixed the approximate size of the plates, the diameter of which was actually 22 cm. They were placed 16 millimeters apart.

"The field strength, too, about 6,000 volts per cm., was vital. . . . It was the element which turned possible failure into success. Indeed, nature . . . left only a narrow range of field-strengths within which such experiments as these are at all possible. They demand that the droplets be large enough so that the Brownian movements are nearly negligible, that they be round and homogeneous, light and non-evaporable, that the distance be long enough to make timing accurate, and that the field be strong enough to more than balance gravity by its pull on a drop carrying but one or two electrons. Scarcely any other combinations of dimensions, field strengths, and materials could have yielded the results obtained. Had the electronic charge been one-tenth its actual size, or the sparking potential in air a tenth of what it is, no such experimental facts as are here presented would ever have been seen.

"The observations which gave an unambiguous answer to the questions as to the atomic nature of electricity consisted in putting a charge upon the drop, in general by the frictional process involved in blowing the spray, letting the charged drop drift through a pin-hole in the center of the plate C into the space between C and D, and then in changing its charge in a considerable number of different ways: for example, by ionizing the air just beneath it by alpha, beta, or gamma rays from radium and letting the field throw these ions into the drop; by illuminating the surface of the drop itself with ultra-violet light; by shooting X-rays both directly at it and beneath it, etc. The results of those changes in charge in a constant field, as is now well known, were

(1) that it was found possible to discharge the droplet completely so that within the limits of observational error—a small fraction of one per cent—*it fell its centimeter under gravity, when the 6,000 volt electrical*

field was on, in precisely the same time required to fall the same distance when there was no field;

(2) that it could become endowed with a particular speed in the electrical field, which *could be reproduced as often as desired, but which was the smallest speed that the given field ever communicated to it,*— nor was this change in speed due to the capture of an electron a small one, difficult to observe and measure. It was often larger than the speed due to gravity itself;

(3) that *speeds exactly two times, three times, four times, five times, etc.* (always within the limits of observational error—still less than one percent) *could be communicated to the droplet, but never any fraction of these speeds.*

"He who has seen that experiment . . . has literally *seen* the electron. For he has measured (in terms of a speed) the smallest of the electrical forces which a given electrical field ever exerts upon the pith ball with which he is working and with the aid of whose movements he defines electricity itself. Further, he has found that something which he has chosen to call electricity may be placed upon or removed from his pith ball only in quantities which cause the force acting upon it either to drop to zero, or else to go up by definite integral multiples of the smallest observed force.

. . . . .

"The measurement of the electron . . . in absolute electrostatic units involved observations of the foregoing sort upon thousands of drops of various sizes, made from a number of different substances, surrounded by a large number of different gases at widely differing pressures, varying from atmospheric down to a millimeter and a half of mercury.

"It involved also years of work in finding accurate values of gaseous viscosities, and in determining just how 'Stokes's Law' must be modified to yield the complete law of fall of a particle through a gas at any density whatever."

Hardly less important than Millikan's work on the electronic charge was his work on the photoelectric effect. Einstein in 1905 had succeeded in explaining this effect by extending to light the concept of quanta of energy introduced by Planck in his work on black-body radiation, and had arrived at the equation given on p. 191, namely,

$$\Pi e = \frac{R}{N} \beta \nu - P$$

where e is the charge on the electron, Π the potential required to prevent the emission of photoelectrons, R the gas constant (8.315×10^7 ergs per deg. C), N Avogadro's number (6.0×10^{23} molecules per gram-molecule), β a constant having the value 4.866×10^{-11}, ν the frequency of the incident light, and P the work in ergs required to get the electron out of the metal. The expression $\frac{R}{N} \beta \nu$ is the quantum of energy of the exciting light, that is, $h\nu$, where h is Planck's constant (6.6×10^{-27} erg sec.). Einstein's equation is now usually written as:

$$V e = h\nu - P$$

where V is the equivalent of Einstein's Π.

The task which Millikan set himself and his collaborators in the Ryerson Laboratory at Chicago was the thorough testing of the validity of this equation. The work extended over many years and entailed the devising and construction of elaborate and ingenious apparatus. Einstein's equation predicted that the kinetic energy with which the photoelectrons leave the metal should be directly proportional to the frequency of the incident light after allowing for P; to test this it was obviously desirable to use as wide a range of frequencies as possible. Unfortunately ordinary metals do not show any marked photoelectric effect for wave lengths longer than the ultraviolet, so that it was necessary to use the alkali metals sodium, potassium, and lithium, which respond to all wave lengths in the visible spectrum below the red. These metals, however, oxidize very rapidly, so that the experiments had to be carried out in a very high vacuum. Specimens of the three metals, in the form of small cylinders, were mounted on a wheel which could be rotated by means of an electromagnet outside the vacuum tube; any one of the three cylinders could thus be brought into line with the incident light. To ensure that a perfectly clean surface was presented to the light, a knife, also controlled by an electromagnet, sliced thin shavings off the cylinder to be used—the alkali metals are soft and easily cut with a knife. The photoelectrons emitted by the metal entered a gauze cylinder which formed part of the vacuum tube and was connected to a sensitive electrometer. For each frequency of the incident light the positive potential was found which had to be applied to the surface of the metal cylinder in order to prevent the emission of electrons. The results of the researches, which were published in the *Physical Review* in 1916, fully confirmed Einstein's equation and led to the value 6.56×10^{-27} erg sec. for h.

The discovery made in 1912 by Hess (*q.v.* 1936) of a very penetrating radiation entering the earth's atmosphere from space aroused wide interest, but, largely owing to the First World War, little progress was made in the study of the phenomenon during the next ten years. Then, in 1922, Millikan took the subject up and sent self-registering electroscopes, barometers, and thermometers in balloons to a height of 50,000 feet. The results could not be interpreted satisfactorily, the difficulty being that no direct measurement of the penetrating power of the rays had so far been made. During the next three years Millikan and his collaborators at the Norman Bridge Laboratory therefore made a series of investigations into this particular problem. They sank self-registering electroscopes in turn in each of two lakes in California, one of which was 11,800 feet above sea-level, the other 5,100 feet. In the lower lake the reading of each electroscope at any given depth below the surface was always identical with the reading at a depth six feet greater in the higher lake, the six feet of water having the same absorbing power for the rays as the amount of atmosphere between the surface levels (6,700 feet) of the lakes. This seemed to Millikan conclusive evidence that the rays did not originate in the earth's atmosphere, and in an article written in 1925 he named them "cosmic rays."

Since that time Millikan has continued to play a leading part in cosmic-ray research, not only in the investigations which he has carried out himself, but also in the suggestions and guidance which he has given to others working in his laboratory and elsewhere; it was he, for instance, who entrusted Anderson (*q.v.* 1936) with the organization of the large-scale researches at Pasadena which led to Anderson's identification of the positron in cosmic radiation.

CONSEQUENCES IN THEORY AND
PRACTICE

Millikan's great contribution to science lies in his having established beyond all reasonable doubt theories which were for the most part already generally accepted. Probably no one doubted that the electron was the ultimate unit of electricity: Millikan, by a series of experiments which have already become classic, established that it was so; the accuracy with which he determined the electronic charge is relatively unimportant compared with the fact that he showed that electricity *always* consists of exact multiples of this unit. Few doubted the correctness of Einstein's equation, but Millikan submitted it to the severest possible tests and established its validity.

1 9 2 4

KARL MANNE GEORG SIEGBAHN

(1886–   )

"For his discoveries and investigations in X ray spectroscopy."

BIOGRAPHICAL SKETCH

KARL MANNE GEORG SIEGBAHN WAS BORN ON DECEMBER 3, 1886, at Orebro in southern Sweden. After receiving a high-school education he entered the University of Lund (Sweden) in January 1906, where he obtained his doctor's degree in 1911. From 1907 to 1915 he served as assistant to Professor J. R. Rydberg in the Physics Institute of the university, being appointed deputy professor of physics in 1915 and, on the death of Rydberg, professor in 1920. During the summer terms of 1908 and 1909 he studied at the universities of Göttingen and Munich, and he visited a number of universities in several countries in later years. In 1923 he became professor of physics at the University of Uppsala and in 1937 professor of physics at Stockholm. He is now director of the Institute of Experimental Physics of the Swedish Royal Academy of Sciences, Stockholm.

DESCRIPTION OF THE PRIZE-WINNING WORK

Up to 1914 Siegbahn's researches were mainly concerned with problems in electricity and magnetism, but since then he has devoted himself to the study of X rays, in particular to X-ray spectroscopy.

Barkla (*q.v.* 1917), using the only property of X rays then open to measurement, their penetrating power, had discovered that when X rays fall on a substance they give rise to X radiation which differs in penetrating power from the primary rays and is characteristic of the particular substance; he identified two types of this radiation, K radiation and L radiation, the former being the more penetrating, or harder. He found, too, that in both types the radiation increased in hardness with the atomic weight of the element used as target. Barkla achieved remarkable results with his limited resources, but the means for true X-ray spectroscopy were not yet available.

In 1912, the Braggs, following up von Laue's discovery of the diffraction of X rays by a crystal, invented their X-ray spectrometer and so gave to science a means of measuring precisely the wave lengths of X rays. Interest at first centered rather on the use of the spectrometer to investigate the structure of crystals than on its use in the investigation of X-ray wave lengths, but, even so, the Braggs soon found evidence of the effect of the material of the anticathode on the X radiation originating there. X rays are produced when high-speed electrons, such as those forming the cathode stream, are brought to a sudden stop by striking some obstacle—in Röntgen's apparatus the stoppage was caused by the walls of the discharge tube, in the later X-ray tubes by the anticathode, a block of metal of high melting point placed in the path of the cathode stream and in electrical communication with the anode. Barkla had used X rays to excite the characteristic radiation of an element; in 1908 G. W. C. Kaye showed that it is also excited by the direct bombardment of the element by cathode rays.

The Braggs found that, with a given anticathode, the same set of peaks, of the same relative magnitude, always occurred in the ionization curve, though the angles at which they occurred varied with the crystal plane used to produce the reflection. Figure 20, which is taken from their *X-Rays and Crystal Structure,* shows the curves obtained by plotting ionization current against glancing angle when X rays from a tube with a platinum anticathode were reflected from each of two different planes of a crystal of rock salt. In both cases the same three peaks, *A, B, C,* occur, *C* being rather weak, *B* strong,

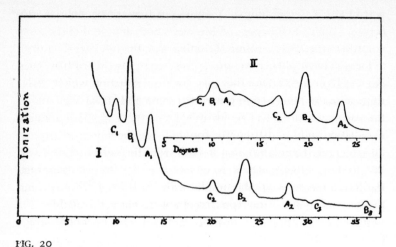

FIG. 20

Characteristic X-ray spectrum of platinum.

A moderate. Both curves show the first- and second-order spectra, the lower showing in addition traces of the third order. When crystals of other substances were used, the same three peaks still occurred. In all cases the wave length λ of, for instance, the middle peak came out the same value when calculated from the Bragg formula

$$n\lambda = 2\,d \cdot \sin\theta$$

in which n equals 1, 2, or 3 according to the order of the spectrum, d is the appropriate crystal spacing, and θ is the glancing angle. When, however, the anticathode was composed of nickel, tungsten, or rhodium, the peaks occurred in positions corresponding to quite different wave lengths. The Braggs therefore concluded that these peaks were the X-ray spectrum of the element composing the anticathode and were as characteristic of that element as the yellow lines in sodium, for example, are characteristic of that metal. The next step was taken by H. G. J. Moseley.

As we have already remarked (p. 139), had it not been for his untimely death, Moseley would undoubtedly have won a Nobel Prize in physics. We must give more than passing attention to his work, for not only did it play an important part in the development of X-ray spectroscopy, but it also provided strong evidence in support of the theory of atomic structure put forward by Bohr shortly before—Bohr's first paper and Moseley's both appeared in the same number of the *Philosophical Magazine,* that for July 1913.

Henry Gwyn-Jeffreys Moseley (1887-1915), who had been educated at Eton and Oxford, was a lecturer and research worker under Rutherford at Manchester, where for some time Bohr was among his contemporaries. His first researches with the Bragg spectrometer were carried out, in collaboration with C. G. Darwin, soon after its introduction, the results being published in the paper of July 1913. While these experiments were in progress, the Braggs discovered the X-ray spectrum of platinum already mentioned; Moseley and Darwin, using much finer slits, were able to show that each of the peaks *B* and *C* (Fig. 20) really consisted of close doublets which the wider slits used by the Braggs had been unable to separate.

On the completion of this first investigation Moseley embarked on researches in which he examined systematically the X-ray spectra of all the known elements, the results being published in December 1913 and April 1914 in the *Philosophical Magazine*. Kaye had used a magnetic device to bring each of the elements under examination in turn into the cathode stream, the elements being mounted on a small truck inside the vacuum tube. Moseley adopted a similar arrangement. Instead of the ionization chamber used in his earlier experiments, he used special X-ray plates to record the characteristic X radiation, each radiation of definite wave length producing a fine line on the photographic plate when the slit was sufficiently narrow. Moseley found that the K radiation of each element consisted of two lines, a stronger, which he called the α line, and a weaker β line. When the wave lengths corresponding to these lines had been determined and the elements had been arranged in order of decreasing wave length (i.e., increasing frequency), the elements, with one or two outstanding exceptions, were found to be in the same order as when arranged according to increasing atomic weight, the exceptions being cases where the arrangement according to increasing atomic weight disagrees with that according to chemical properties. Earlier in 1913 Van den Broek had drawn attention to the advantage of denoting the elements by numbers indicating their position in the periodic table and had pointed out that these *atomic numbers* are very nearly halves of the corresponding atomic weights. Moseley found that, in all but a few cases, the square root Q of the frequency of, for example, the α line of the K radiation increased by a constant amount in passing from one element to the element of next higher atomic weight; the same thing applied to the β line and to the L lines. The significance of this discovery is best given in Moseley's own words, taken from his paper of December 1913:

". . . It is at once evident that Q increases by a constant amount as we pass from one element to the next, using the chemical order of the elements in the periodic system. Except in the case of nickel and cobalt, this is also the order of the atomic weights. While, however, Q increases uniformly the atomic weights vary in an apparently arbitrary manner, so that an exception in their order does not come as a surprise. We have here a proof that there is in the atom a fundamental quantity, which increases by regular steps as we pass from one element to the next. This quantity can only be the charge on the central positive nucleus, of the existence of which we already have definite proof. Rutherford has shown, from the magnitude of the scattering of α particles by matter, that this nucleus carries a $+$ charge approximately equal to that of $A/2$ electrons, where A is the atomic weight. Barkla, from the scattering of X rays by matter, has shown that the number of electrons in an atom is roughly $A/2$, which for an electrically neutral atom comes to the same thing. Now atomic weights increase on the average by about 2 units at a time, and this strongly suggests the view that N * increases from atom to atom always by a single electronic unit. We are therefore led by experiment to the view that N is the same as the number of the place occupied by the element in the periodic system. This atomic number is then for H 1 for He 2 for Li 3 . . . for Ca 20 . . . for Zn 30, etc. This theory was originated by Broek and since used by Bohr. We can confidently predict that in the few cases in which the order of the atomic weights A clashes with the chemical order of the periodic system, the chemical properties are governed

---

* Moseley does not define N, but it is evidently the number of extra-nuclear electrons in the neutral atom, the charge on the nucleus being $+Ne$. Bohr uses N with this meaning in a paper published in the *Philosophical Magazine* in September 1913.

by N, while A is itself probably a complicated function of N. The very close similarity between the X-ray spectra of the different elements shows that these radiations originate inside the atom, and have no direct connexion with the complicated light-spectra and chemical properties which are governed by the structure of its surface."

The keynote of Siegbahn's work is supplied by the last sentence of the passage quoted: X-ray spectra originate in the innermost parts of the atom. Siegbahn clearly recognized that the only way to lay bare the inner secrets of the atom was to develop X-ray spectroscopy to such perfection that the spectral line produced by every electron transition should be accurately recorded on the photographic plate. Through years of patient and unremitting work Siegbahn and his co-workers at Lund went far toward attaining this objective. The vacuum spectrograph was devised, in which the whole spectrometer, the photographic plate, and the X rays themselves in their passage from the anticathode were enclosed in a high vacuum. Improvements in the X-ray tube made it possible to use much shorter exposures than the five minutes required in Moseley's experiments, and improvements in the spectrometer were carried so far that each of the two K lines discovered by Moseley was clearly shown on the photographic plate to consist of a doublet; in the L series, where Moseley found four or five lines, Siegbahn found in some cases as many as twenty-eight. In a systematic and exhaustive study of the X-ray spectra of the elements, the various lines of the K and L series were investigated and the corresponding wave lengths were measured with an accuracy of 1 part in 100,000; a new M series was discovered with elements of moderately high atomic weight, and an N series with the heaviest elements of all, thorium and uranium; an O series has since been discovered with these two elements. No less important than the accumulation of all these experimental data was the interpretation of the material in the light of Bohr's theory of the atom. For this we turn to Siegbahn's Nobel lecture, the following extracts being translated * from the Swedish of his address.

---

* By kind permission of Professor Siegbahn.

"But the study of X rays is justified not merely by the possibilities of their use in the various sciences, to which I have just referred; they give us, besides, an insight into the world of phenomena lying within the outer boundaries of the atom. All the messages they bring us from this domain of physical reality are expressed, so to say, in the X-ray language, and if we wish to understand these messages we must learn that language.

"The X-ray language is a language of electromagnetic waves. What we see, record, and interpret are first and foremost *wave lengths* and *intensity* of electromagnetic radiation. If we fix our attention on a particular atom, experience shows that from this atom there is emitted a system of waves of quite definite composition in relation to the incident wave lengths. The emitted wave lengths are also, as a matter of fact, quite independent of external circumstances such as the chemical or physical forces acting on the atom in question; the wave system is determined entirely by the field of force of the atom itself.

"The first problem we have to solve . . . is therefore that of measuring up and analyzing the wave systems emitted by the atoms of the 92 elements.

". . . certain spectra in ordinary optics consist of several thousand different wave lengths which still defy all attempts at even a preliminary systematization. Nature has, however, been kinder in the case of the X rays emitted by the atom. Not only is the wave system belonging to each kind of atom reasonably free from complications, but also the wave systems belonging to different atoms show great conformity among themselves, a conformity which is not, as in ordinary spectroscopy, confined to the vertical columns in Mendeléeff's periodic table, but extends to all the elements. It is therefore remarkable that the general type of X-ray spectra bears a particularly close resemblance to just that type in the ordinary optical spectra which is to be found in the first vertical column of Mendeléeff's scheme, that is, in the spectra of the alkali metals.

"To be able to demonstrate this, I must first say a few words on the derivation of an energy diagram from the observed wave system.

"Assume that at a certain instant the atom is in such a state that its total energy has the value E_1, and that at this instant there occurs

a change of such a nature that the total energy of the atom is reduced to E_0. During this change a quantity of energy $E_1 - E_0$ is
therefore set free.

"This quantity of energy we assume, with Bohr, to be emitted
in the form of a wave belonging to the wave system characteristic
of the atom in question. Its wave length may be denoted by λ and
the corresponding frequency by ν, the frequency being defined as
the reciprocal of the wave length*, so that $\nu = 1/\lambda$.

"According to the Einstein-Bohr formula, the relation between
the frequency ν_1 of the wave and the energy set free from the atom
is then

$$\nu_1 = \frac{E_1 - E_0}{h}$$

where h is a universal constant (Planck's constant).

"We next suppose that in another such transition the energy of
the atom changes from E_2 to E_0, a wave of frequency ν_2 being
emitted. Then

$$\nu_2 = \frac{E_2 - E_0}{h}.$$

The series can be extended further:

$$\nu_3 = \frac{E_3 - E_0}{h}$$

and so on. By measuring the wave lengths the series of ν values ν_1,
ν_2, ν_3, . . . can be determined experimentally.

"A separate and not always simple analysis of the wave-length
material is required in order to pick out and combine the frequency
values belonging to one and the same series. It was the Swede J. R.
Rydberg who first succeeded, in the field of ordinary spectroscopy,
in solving this difficult but, for subsequent investigation, fundamental problem.

"Rydberg found a general formula for the relation between the
ν values belonging to one and the same series. He then made use
of this formula to group together in various series the available

---

* The reciprocal of the wave length is the *wave number,* the number of wave
lengths per centimeter. Strictly, *frequency* $= c/\lambda$, where c is the velocity of light,
but is sometimes, as here, used for the wave number $(1/\lambda)$ (see also p. 242 and
Figs. 25 and 27).

wave-length material for the spectrum of each individual substance. In particular, he found for the alkali spectra three different types of series, which he named the *principal series,* the *sharp secondary series,* and the *diffuse secondary series.* Later, as a result of fresh measurements, another series, generally called the *Bergmann series,* was added to these.

"By applying the Einstein-Bohr formula we can now calculate, from the known ν values, four series of energy values. These are usually represented in the manner shown in the figure [Fig. 21].

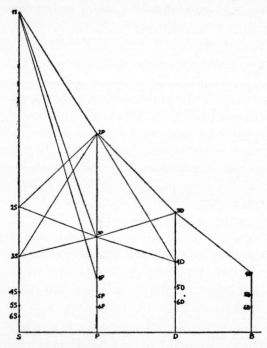

FIG. 21

[Energy levels for an alkali atom, with some of the transitions producing spectral lines. Simplified. (*See also Fig. 27, p.243.*)]

For each point the height above the horizontal base line is a measure of the quantity of energy corresponding to the state of the atom. The four series, each of which is represented by a vertical line, are usually labeled the *s, p, d,* and *b* series.*

---

* The Bergmann is now usually called the *fundamental* series and denoted by *f*.

"From the energy series we come back via the formula

$$\nu_1 = \frac{E_1 - E_0}{h}$$

to the frequency series. These are represented in the figure by the oblique lines.

.   .   .   .   .

"If we now turn from the optical spectra to X-ray spectra, we find, on examining the collective results of measurement, that the X-ray spectra for all the elements can be represented by an energy diagram of exactly the same character as that already found for the alkali spectra. Besides the energy-levels corresponding to the *s*, *p*, *d*, and *b* series (the vertical lines) there are also the observed transitions—spectral lines—indicated by lines joining the two energy-levels which correspond to the initial and final states of the atom when the spectral line in question is emitted. It is clear from this that the *K* series in X-ray spectra corresponds to the principal series in ordinary optics. The *L* series, on the other hand, is made up of both the secondary series in optics together with some other lines of principal series type.

"The most important reason for giving the X-ray energy diagram this form lay in this, that in this way the combination rules become identical with those valid for the alkali spectra. In both cases, for instance, transitions occur only between points on two *adjacent* vertical lines; further, transitions do not occur between points on the *same* vertical line."

Siegbahn's spectroscopic work was continued at Uppsala, where he extended his researches to include the region of the spectrum lying between X rays and the ultraviolet. In 1924 he at last succeeded in demonstrating an effect which had been looked for since Röntgen's time—the refraction of X rays by a prism; by letting a narrow pencil of the rays fall on a wide-angled prism near the edge and at almost grazing incidence he obtained photographs which showed the four K lines clearly separated.

CONSEQUENCES IN THEORY AND PRACTICE

The importance of Siegbahn's work needs no stressing. His book, *Spektroscopie der Röntgenstrahlen,* which has been translated into English, is the standard work on X-ray spectroscopy. Whenever exact figures for X-ray wave lengths are given, the authority quoted is almost invariably Siegbahn.

1 9 2 5

JAMES FRANCK
(1882–   )

GUSTAV HERTZ
(1887–   )

"For their discovery of the laws governing the impact between an electron and an atom."

BIOGRAPHICAL SKETCHES

FRANCK

JAMES FRANCK WAS BORN ON AUGUST 26, 1882, IN HAMBURG, Germany. On completing his studies at the Wilhelm *Gymnasium* in Hamburg he spent two semesters at the University of Heidelberg, where chemistry was his chief study. He then went to the University of Berlin, where he studied physics under Warburg and Drude, taking his doctor's degree in 1906. After a short period as assistant at Frankfort on the Main, he returned to Berlin as assistant to Professor Rubens, becoming a lecturer in 1911.

On the conclusion of the First World War he became a member and head of one of the departments of the Kaiser Wilhelm Institute of Physical Chemistry at Berlin-Dahlem, which was then under the direction of Fritz Haber (winner of the 1918 Nobel Prize in *Chemistry*). In 1920 he was appointed professor of experimental physics at the University of Göttingen and director of the Physical

Institute. In 1935 Franck came to the United States to serve as professor at the Johns Hopkins University, and in 1938 he became professor of physical chemistry at the University of Chicago. He is now a United States citizen.

HERTZ

GUSTAV HERTZ was born on July 22, 1887, in Hamburg. After attending the *Realgymnasium* in Hamburg, Hertz, between the years 1906 and 1911, studied at the universities of Göttingen, Munich, and Berlin, obtaining his doctor's degree at Berlin for a dissertation dealing with the infrared absorption spectrum of carbonic acid.

In 1913 he became an assistant in the Physical Institute of the University of Berlin. He was severely wounded early in the First World War and resumed his academic life in 1917, when he became *privatdozent* at Berlin. From 1920 to 1925 he worked in the physical laboratory of the Philips incandescent lamp factory at Eindhoven, Holland. In October 1925 he was appointed professor of physics and director of the Physical Institute at the University of Halle, but returned to Berlin in 1928 as professor of physics at the *Technische Hochschule,* or Technical University, Berlin-Charlottenburg. He resigned his professorship in 1934 for political reasons and shortly afterward became director of Research Laboratory II (*Forschungslaboratorium* II) of the Siemens industrial concern, a position which he held until the end of the Second World War*. He is known to have been in Berlin when the Russians entered the city in 1945, but what befell him then and how he has fared since are matters of complete uncertainty; according to a press report he is believed to be engaged on nuclear research somewhere in the Caucasus area.

DESCRIPTION OF THE PRIZE-WINNING WORK

In our account of Lenard's work on the photoelectric effect we described (p. 39) how he prevented the electrons ejected from

---

* I am indebted to Professor Hertz's son, Mr. Hellmuth Hertz, of the University of Lund, Sweden, for details of his father's career between 1928 and 1945.

the metal by the ultraviolet light from reaching a disk placed in
their path, by giving the disk a negative charge. This was the basis
of a method by which he showed, in some pioneer work on the
ionization of gases by electrons, that an electron must possess a
certain minimum velocity before it is capable of causing ionization.
The apparatus he used is shown diagrammatically in Fig. 22. Slow
electrons, emitted by an electrically heated metal filament Z, were

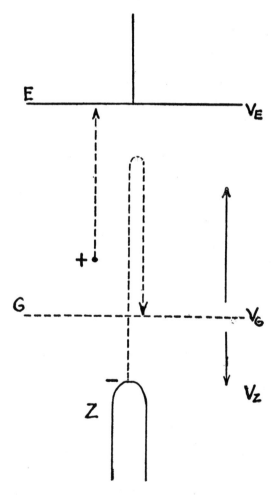

FIG. 22

Diagram showing Lenard's method of measuring critical potentials.

accelerated toward a positively charged metal gauze G. The distance
between Z and G was small enough to ensure that practically all
the electrons emitted by the filament reached the gauze without
having made collisions with the molecules of the gas and therefore
with the full velocity imparted to them by the potential difference
$V_G - V_Z$ between the filament and the gauze, that is, with a kinetic
energy equal to $(V_G - V_Z)e$, where e is the charge on an electron.
Those electrons which pass through the gauze enter a much larger
space GE, where collisions with molecules of the gas cause positively charged ions to be produced—one is indicated in the figure
by a dot marked $+$. These positive ions are attracted to a plate E,
which is negatively charged. To prevent any electrons from reaching E and so counterbalancing the positive ions, the potential difference between G and E is made greater than that between G and Z,
so that even electrons that have made no collisions are sufficiently
retarded by the field GE to be stopped before they reach E and to
be returned to the gauze. By gradually increasing the potential of
the gauze Lenard found what minimum potential difference $V_G -
V_Z$ was necessary to give the electrons just enough energy ($\frac{1}{2}mv^2$,
where m is the mass of the electron and v its velocity on reaching
G) to be able to produce ions and so cause an electrometer connected to E to register a positive charge. Lenard found this minimum potential difference, or *ionization potential,* to be about 11
volts for the gases hydrogen, nitrogen, and oxygen.

It was a modification of Lenard's method that Franck and Hertz
used in their researches on electron impact, the purpose of which
was to investigate the changes of energy within the atom by direct
measurement of the quantity of energy transferred to the atom in
an electron collision. Both Franck and Hertz delivered Nobel addresses. Between them they covered the ground so thoroughly that
we may leave the rest to them. Franck, speaking in German, introduced the subject and then described the method of the experiments.*

"A slow electron with a given kinetic energy should, on striking
an atom at rest, be deflected by the atom practically without loss of

* The following extracts are given here by kind permission of Professor Franck.

energy, rather like a rubber ball striking a hard wall. It is now possible to study this elastic impact quantitatively in various ways.

"I shall pass over the proof of the case where a single deflection occurs and go rather fully into the case where a succession of impacts allows the loss of energy, immeasurably small in a single impact, to be determined by means of a simple experimental arrangement.

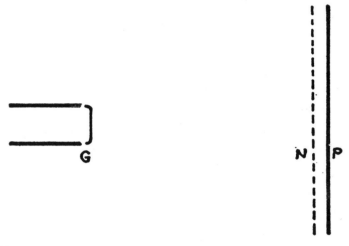

FIG. 23

[Diagram illustrating the method used by Franck and Hertz for investigating the energy distribution of electrons.]

"[In Fig. 23] *G* denotes a source of electrons. It consists of a thin tungsten wire brought to a bright red heat by an electric current. That such hot wires are strong sources of slow electrons I may assume known in these days of wireless. At a distance of several centimeters from the hot wire is a wire-gauze electrode *N*. If, by means of an accumulator, we charge the gauze positively with respect to the hot wire, the electrons emitted by the wire will be accelerated to the gauze. We can easily find an expression for the kinetic energy which the electrons must attain as a result of the accelerating potential if there is no gas between *G* and *N*, that is, if the electrons fall freely through the field of force without collisions. The relation is

$$\tfrac{1}{2}mv^2 = eV$$

where $\frac{1}{2}mv^2$ is the kinetic energy of each electron, e its electric charge, and V the applied potential difference. If, for example, we measure the last in volts, then the kinetic energy of an electron due to a potential difference of 10 volts is approximately 10^{-11} erg.

"It has become customary to speak of 'x-volt electrons' and to use the accelerating potential, x-volts, as a measure of the energy of the electron. In our arrangement, therefore, the electrons strike the gauze with an energy of x-volts, where x is the potential difference between G and N in volts. Some of the electrons are caught by the gauze, the rest pass through the meshes. These latter, if there is no field between N and P to drive them back, all reach the electrode P and constitute a negative current, which flows to earth through a galvanometer. By applying an electric field between N and P we can determine the energy distribution of the electrons passing through the gauze. If, for example, we have a 4-volt beam passing at right angles through the gauze, the electron current, measured by the galvanometer as a function of the potential difference applied between N and P to retard the electrons, remains constant until P is 4 volts negative with respect to N. At this point the current must fall suddenly to zero, since now all the electrons will be repelled from P and will return to N. If we now admit an inert gas such as helium or a metal vapor between the electrodes and adjust the pressure so that the electrons make many collisions with atoms between G and N, but traverse the distance NP unhindered, we can, by constructing the energy distribution curve for the electrons reaching P, determine whether these electrons have lost energy as a result of their collisions with atoms.

. . . . .

"From an examination of the curves obtained, it was found that, for not too high pressures and with monatomic gases of high atomic weight, the kinetic energy of slow electrons was equal to that acquired in a vacuum with the same accelerating potential.

. . . . .

". . . It is only at high pressures, that is, where many thousands of collisions occur, that the loss of energy due to elastic collision can be detected. A calculation of the number of collisions was later

made by Hertz. From his result and the curves obtained at higher
pressures, we find, for example, that for the helium atom a quantity
of energy is transferred equal to a value between 1.2×10^{-4} and
3.0×10^{-4} times the energy of the electron before the collision;
for purely mechanical impact the value calculated from the ratio
of the masses is 2.9×10^{-4}, so that we are justified in describing
these impacts as 'elastic.'

. . . . .

"Now can the conformity to the law of elastic impact, found to
hold for *slow* electrons in their impacts with atoms, also hold for
electrons of higher velocity? Clearly not, since the fundamental experiment of the discharge through gases shows that *fast* electrons,
namely, the cathode rays, when they strike atoms excite the latter
to luminescence, in other words, the atoms are ionized. In this case
the energy of the colliding electron must be converted into energy
within the atom; the impacts are now *inelastic,* and the electrons
lose a larger quantity of energy. A determination of the least value
of the kinetic energy which an electron must possess in order to
ionize an atom was therefore of interest. Measured in volts, this
energy is called the *ionization potential.*

. . . . .

"We therefore repeated Lenard's experiment, taking full advantage of the improvements in vacuum-pump technique made in
the meantime; we found, for the different gases, characteristic and
markedly different values. In Lenard's experiment electrons,—
again, for instance, those emitted by a hot wire—were accelerated
through a suitable electric field and then passed through a gauze
into a space where they made collisions with atoms. By means of a
strong opposing field these electrons are prevented from reaching
an electrode connected to a measuring instrument. If, however,
atoms are ionized as a result of the collisions, the newly formed
positive ions are accelerated to the negatively charged electrode by
that same electric field which drives back the electrons. There is
therefore a positive current as soon as the energy of the electrons is
sufficient to produce ionization.

. . . . .

"In any case, as I have already explained, it was to be expected that the collisions between electrons and atoms would, at these characteristic critical potentials—characteristic, that is, for each kind of atom—be inelastic. That this really was the case turned out to be easily demonstrable with the same apparatus as had served previously in the case of elastic collisions. Measurement of the energy distribution of the electrons, as the accelerating potential was increased beyond the critical value, yielded the result that electrons endowed with the critical energy of translation could lose their entire kinetic energy on collision, and that electrons whose energy exceeded the critical value gave up, in an inelastic collision, only this same quantity of energy, the excess being retained as energy of motion. . . . The measurement consisted in determining, as a function of the accelerating potential, the number of electrons possessing, after many collisions, an energy appreciably greater than zero.

"The diagram [Fig. 24] shows the result of the measurement of such an electron current in mercury vapor. In this case all electrons with energy greater than $\frac{1}{2}$ volt came under measurement. We see that in mercury vapor these partial electron currents increase with increase of accelerating potential until the critical energy is reached, when the current drops suddenly almost to zero. Since the electrons give up neither more nor less than the critical amount of energy, the process begins afresh with further increase of potential; the number of electrons with energy greater than $\frac{1}{2}$ volt again rises to the critical value, when the current again drops. The process repeats periodically, whenever the accelerating potential passes a multiple of the critical potential. The distance between the maxima gives the exact value of the critical potential. For mercury vapor it is 4.9 volts.

· · · · ·

"Some six months before the completion of these researches Niels Bohr's first work on his theory of the atom appeared. Let us compare briefly the fundamental hypothesis of this theory with our results.

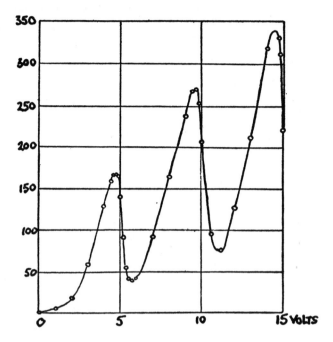

FIG. 24

[Results of the electron collision experiments. The electron current is plotted as a function of the accelerating potential.]

"According to Bohr an atom can take up only discrete quantities of energy as internal energy, namely, those that transform the atom from one stationary state to another stationary state. If, through a supply of energy, a transition to a stationary state of higher energy, an excited state, has resulted, the energy taken up will be given out again in quanta as radiation, in accordance with the $h\nu$ relation. The frequency of the longest wave-length absorption line, the resonance line, multiplied by Planck's element of action, gives the energy used to attain the first excited state. These fundamental ideas agree in all respects with our results. The elastic collisions with slow electrons show that in these no energy is taken up by the atom as internal energy, and the first critical energy-level gives just that quantity required for the excitation of the longest wave-length absorption line of mercury."

Hertz, who also spoke in German, then went on to discuss the significance of the experiments in the light of Bohr's theory of the atom.*

"The main significance of the results of the researches carried out on the electron collision method lies in their having provided direct experimental proof of the fundamental assumptions of Bohr's theory of the atom. In what follows I shall review the most important of these results and shall show that they are in fact in agreement in all the observational details so far available with what is to be expected on Bohr's theory.

"The fact that atoms are able to take part in an exchange of energy with electromagnetic radiation led, in classical physics, to the conclusion that moving electrical charges must be present in the atoms; that it was the oscillations of these charges which caused the emission of light, whereas the absorption of light was attributed to their forced oscillations under the influence of the electric field due to the incident light-waves. On the basis of the Lorentz theory of the normal Zeeman effect—the magnetic splitting of the spectral lines—it was concluded that the moving charges in question must be electrons, already known to us in the cathode rays. If each kind of atom had emitted only one or a few spectral lines, it might have been assumed that for each spectral line there was present in the atom one electron of the corresponding proper frequency. In reality, however, each atom emits an infinite number of spectral lines. These are not distributed irregularly: certain regularities are to be found among their frequencies, but these regularities are of such a kind that it is not possible to explain them, on the basis of classical physics, in terms of the proper oscillations of a system of electrons.

"It is here that Bohr came in with his theory of the atom, in which he applied Planck's quantum theory to the problems of atomic structure and the emission of light, at the same time considerably extending the theory. . . . Planck was led in his deduction of the law of heat radiation . . . to the conclusion that the processes of emission and absorption of light did not take place

---

* I am indebted to Professor Hertz's son, Mr. Hellmuth Hertz, for permission to include the following extracts from his father's Nobel lecture.

according to the laws of classical mechanics and electrodynamics. Although in Planck's quantum theory the assumption is retained that the emission and absorption of monochromatic radiation can occur only through an electric oscillator of the same frequency, it is assumed that the energy in such processes is emitted or absorbed only in discrete quantities—*quanta.* The magnitude of such a quantum is, according to Planck, proportional to the frequency of the radiation in question, the constant of proportionality being Planck's constant h (6.55×10^{-27} erg sec.), which plays a fundamental part in the whole subsequent development of the theory. Bohr realized that to explain the laws of line spectra it was necessary to give up the simple picture of emission and absorption as due to an oscillating electron, and with it the connection between the frequency of the light-wave and that of the electron. From Planck's theory, however, he adopted the fundamental connection between the magnitude of the emitted or absorbed quantum of energy and the frequency of the radiation, and arrived at the following fundamental assumptions of his theory of the atom:

(1) For each atom there exists an infinite series of discrete stationary states which are characterized by definite values of the internal energy of the atom and in which the atom can exist without emitting radiation.

(2) Emission or absorption of radiation is always associated with the transition of the atom from one of the stationary states to another— emission with a transition from a state of higher energy to one of lower, absorption with a transition in the opposite direction.

(3) The frequency of the radiation emitted or absorbed in such a transition is given by the equation

$$h\nu = E_2 - E_1$$

where h is Planck's constant, and E_1, E_2 the energy of the atom in the two stationary states.

"To these fundamental assumptions were added other special assumptions dealing with the mode of motion of the electron in the atom, Bohr following Rutherford in conceiving the atom as consisting of a positive nucleus and a number of electrons of equal charge. By means of equations of condition, which also contain Planck's constant, from among all the possible states of motion those are distinguished which are permissible as stationary states.

"Although these laws for the motion of the electrons in the atom constitute an essential part of Bohr's theory, and in particular have made possible the quantitative determination of Rydberg's constant from thermal and electrical data, as well as the explanation of the periodic system of the elements, we need not go into details here. For the electron collision experiments only one fact is of significance, namely this, that the series of stationary states of an atom belonging to a series spectrum must correspond to an ever-lessening bond between the electron and its atom, and that the consecutive stationary states differ from each other by ever-lessening quantities of energy as the bond between the electron and the atom becomes less, and converge to the state of complete loosening of the electron from the atom.

"As typical of all series spectra we consider first the simplest case, the spectrum of hydrogen. The frequencies of all the lines of this spectrum are given with a high degree of accuracy by the formula

$$v = R\left(\frac{1}{m^2} - \frac{1}{n^2}\right)$$

if any chosen whole numbers are put for m and n. All the lines belonging to a definite value of m, while n takes all integral values from $m + 1$ to infinity, together form a series. Thus if, for example, $m = 2$, the well-known Balmer series is obtained. This series is shown schematically in Fig. 1 [Fig. 25]. The characteristic

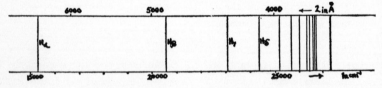

FIG. 25   *Hertz's Fig. 1*

[The Balmer series in the hydrogen spectrum. The lower scale gives the frequency (v) in wave numbers (see p. 225, note), or *reciprocal centimeters*. The upper scale gives the corresponding wave lengths (λ) in angstroms (10^{-8} cm).]*

---

* For example, v for the first line (H_α) is obtained by putting R (Rydberg's Constant) $= 109678$ cm^{-1}, $m = 2$, $n = 3$ in the above formula, the value obtained being $15,233$ cm^{-1}. Then $\lambda = 1/v$ cm $= 10^8/v$ angstroms $= 6563$ angstroms.

ILLUSTRATIONS

HENDRIK ANTOON LORENTZ

WILHELM KONRAD RÖNTGEN

PIETER ZEEMAN

ANTOINE HENRI BECQUEREL

PIERRE CURIE

MARIE SKLODOWSKA CURIE

PHILIPP LENARD

JOHN WILLIAM STRUTT

JOSEPH JOHN THOMSON

ALBERT ABRAHAM MICHELSON

GABRIEL LIPPMANN

JOHANNES DIDERIK VAN DER WAALS

CARL FERDINAND BRAUN

GUGLIELMO MARCONI

WILHELM WIEN

NILS GUSTAF DALÉN

HEIKE KAMERLINGH ONNES

MAX THEODOR FELIX VON LAUE

WILLIAM HENRY BRAGG

WILLIAM LAWRENCE BRAGG

CHARLES GLOVER BARKLA

JOHANNES STARK

MAX KARL ERNST LUDWIG
PLANCK

CHARLES-ÉDOUARD GUILLAUME

NIELS HENRIK DAVID BOHR

ALBERT EINSTEIN

ROBERT ANDREWS MILLIKAN

KARL MANNE GEORG SIEGBAHN

JAMES FRANCK

GUSTAV HERTZ

JEAN PERRIN

ARTHUR HOLLY COMPTON

CHARLES THOMSON REES WILSON

OWEN WILLANS RICHARDSON

LOUIS-VICTOR DE BROGLIE

CHANDRASEKHARA VENKATA
RAMAN

WERNER KARL HEISENBERG

ERWIN SCHRÖDINGER

PAUL ADRIEN MAURICE DIRAC

JAMES CHADWICK

CARL DAVID ANDERSON

VICTOR FRANCIS HESS

GEORGE PAGET THOMSON

CLINTON JOSEPH DAVISSON

ENRICO FERMI

ERNEST ORLANDO LAWRENCE

ISIDOR ISAAC RABI

OTTO STERN

PERCY WILLIAMS BRIDGMAN

WOLFGANG PAULI

EDWARD VICTOR APPLETON

PATRICK MAYNARD STUART
BLACKETT

CECIL FRANK POWELL   HIDEKI YUKAWA

crowding together of the lines as a definite limiting frequency, the series limit, is approached, is found in all series spectra.

"In the above formula the frequency of a spectral line is put equal to the difference between two quantities each of which can assume an infinite number of discrete values. The meaning of these quantities in terms of Bohr's theory is obtained immediately from the fundamental assumptions of the theory: they are, except for a numerical factor, equal to the energy of the atom in its various stationary states; a closer study shows that the energy is to be taken with negative sign, so that the smaller energy goes with smaller values of m and n. The lines of a series therefore correspond to transitions from a series of stationary states of higher energy to one and the same final state. In Fig. 2 [Fig. 26] the production of the series belonging to the first six stationary states of the hydrogen atom is shown schematically.

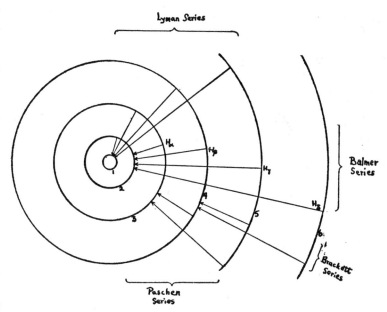

FIG. 26   *Hertz's Fig. 2*

[The Bohr orbits of hydrogen, showing the transitions producing the Lyman series ($m=1$), the Balmer series ($m=2$), the Paschen series ($m=3$), and the Brackett series ($m=4$). The first lies in the ultra-violet, the last in the infra-red.]

"The relations for the other elements are to a greater or lesser degree more complicated than for hydrogen. One feature, however, all series spectra possess in common with that of hydrogen, namely that expressed by the Ritz combination principle, according to which the frequencies of the individual spectral lines can always be expressed as the differences of discrete numerical values. These numerical values, the so-called *terms,* take the place of the quantities R/n^2 with hydrogen; they differ from these quantities in that their values, as dependent on the term number, are represented by a complicated formula; but they agree with them in so far that the differences between consecutive terms become smaller and smaller, and that the term *values* themselves converge to zero as the term *number* increases. As an example, the spectrum of sodium * is shown graphically in Fig. 4 [Fig. 27]. The individual term values are represented by short horizontal lines, with the term number written alongside, their magnitudes being arranged from above downward in such a way that the value of a term is given by its distance from the top boundary of the figure. . . .

. . . . .

"The essential thing is that the frequency of each spectral line is equal to the difference between two term values. To each line, therefore, there belongs a definite combination of two terms. In the figure some of the lines of the sodium spectrum are shown, represented by the straight lines joining the two terms of the spectral line in question. . . . The scale marked on the figure, by the way, gives the term values, not in frequencies, but, as is customary in spectroscopy, in wave numbers, i.e., reciprocals of wave lengths.

"The explanation of this term scheme on the Bohr theory, to which we now turn, is precisely similar to that already given for hydrogen. From the relation between the frequency of a spectral line and the two terms belonging to it, viz.

$$\nu = T_1 - T_2$$

---

* Hertz chose mercury as his example. We have taken sodium throughout as being simpler.

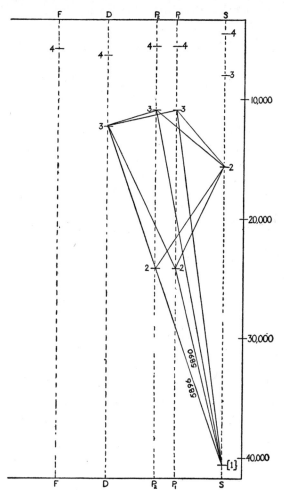

FIG. 27   *Hertz's Fig. 4*

[Part of the term scheme for sodium. The wave number of any chosen spectral line, for example that represented by the line joining $1S$ to $2P_2$, is the *difference* between the corresponding values given in the scale of wave numbers on the right. For the line $1S—2P_2$ this difference is very nearly 17,000 (see Table I)—*the diagram is only approximately to scale.* The two wave lengths marked on the figure are those of the D_1 and D_2 sodium lines, two lines close together in the yellow region of the visible spectrum.]

on the one hand, and the Bohr frequency condition

$$h\nu = E_2 - E_1$$

on the other, we obtain the relation

$$T_n = -\frac{E_n}{h}.$$

The spectral terms thus denote, according to Bohr, the values of
the energy of the atom in the different stationary states divided by
Planck's constant and with the negative sign prefixed. That the
energy value is here negative is due merely to the omission of an
arbitrary constant which always has to be added to the energy;
since it is always only energy *differences* that come into question
here, this constant in any case always cancels out. Since the term
values in Fig. 4 [Fig. 27] are arranged according to their magnitude from above downward, the corresponding energy values increase from below upward; the term scheme therefore enables us
to see at a glance the energy-levels in which the atom can exist in
its stationary states.

. . . . .

"The connection between the terms of the series spectrum and
the energy of the atom in its various stationary states is fundamental
for Bohr's theory. The possibility of using the electron collision
method to test this connection experimentally rests on this, that the
quantities of energy transferred in the collisions between electrons
and atoms can be directly measured and, further, that the phenomena which occur when quite definite quantities of energy are
imparted to the atom can be observed. What, on Bohr's theory, is
to be expected when electrons of definite velocity collide with
atoms? If in such a collision energy is transferred to the atom, the
result can only be that the atom is transformed from its normal
state to a stationary state of higher energy. Therefore only quite
definite quantities of energy can be transferred to the atom; moreover, each of the possible quantities of energy is equal to the excitation work corresponding to a definite excited state of the atom. It

must therefore, according to the above considerations, be calculable from the relevant series term.

"Among the excited states of an atom there is always one for which the excitation work is smallest. The excitation work corresponding to this state represents therefore the smallest quantity of energy which can be transferred to the atom in an electron collision. As long as the energy of the colliding electron is less than this smallest excitation work, no energy at all can be transferred to the atom in the collision and the collision occurs as a perfectly elastic impact, the electron losing only the extremely small quantity of energy which appears as kinetic energy of the atom, in accordance with the law of impact. As soon, however, as the energy of the electron exceeds the smallest excitation work, energy can be transferred on collision to the atom, which is thereby brought to the first excited state. If the energy of the electron is further increased, so that by degrees it reaches and exceeds the excitation work corresponding to excited states of higher energy, then in a collision the atom can also be transformed to these higher states, the quantity of energy transferred always being equal to the excitation work corresponding to the excited state. Finally, if the energy of the electron is equal to the ionization work, then in a collision the electron can break away entirely from the atom, which is thus left as a positive ion.

"In the experimental investigation of these processes a definite energy is usually imparted to the electrons by accelerating them through a definite potential difference, and on the other hand the energy of the electrons after collision is investigated by determining what potential difference they are just able to overcome. In this way, instead of the excitation work for a definite state, we introduce the potential difference through which an electron with initial velocity zero must fall freely so that its energy is equal to the excitation work. This excitation potential is thus equal to the excitation work divided by the charge on the electron. In the same way, the ionization potential corresponds to the ionization work. The aim of the electron collision experiments was, then, in the first place to measure the excitation and ionization potentials. The methods used for this may be divided, in their essentials, into three groups. Those of the first group are based on Lenard's method, the one used by us in our first experiments. . . .

. . . . .

"By comparing the values found experimentally for the excitation and ionization potentials with those calculated from the series terms, we shall now show that in all the cases so far investigated there is in fact excellent agreement. The alkali metals show the simplest relationships. The series scheme for sodium is represented graphically in Fig. 4 [Fig. 27] (p. 243); the spectra of the other metals of this group are of similar structure. The ground term is the term denoted by $1S$; going from this to the terms corresponding to higher energy, we come first to two terms differing only slightly in their energy; these are denoted by $2P_1$ and $2P_2$.

"The transitions of the atom from the stationary states corresponding to these terms into the normal state are accompanied by the emission of the so-called resonance lines; in the case of sodium these are the two components of the well-known yellow sodium line. These lines are called resonance lines because an atom which has been excited by the absorption of radiation of the frequency of these lines must, when it returns to the normal state, again emit all the energy taken up in the absorption as radiation of the same frequency, so that as regards radiation of this frequency the atom behaves as an electric oscillator of this proper frequency.

"The first excitation potential V_a of the alkali metals is obtained not only, as in every other case, from the difference between the ground term and the next smallest term, but also in an especially simple manner, by making use of the Bohr frequency condition, from the frequency ν_r of the resonance line. It is

$$V_a \cdot e = h\nu_r$$

where e is the charge on the electron. As the term scheme at once shows, in electron collisions above this first excitation, potential emission of the resonance line must occur, so that the name *resonance potential* has been introduced for this excitation potential. It must be mentioned, however, that it is only in the case of the alkali metals that the resonance potential is identical with the first excitation potential.

"The Table [1] shows the spectroscopic data (frequency and wave length) for the alkali metals*, the ionization and resonance potentials calculated from these data on Bohr's theory, and the observed values given by the electron collision experiments. The agreement between the calculated and observed values shows that the deductions from Bohr's theory are in fact fully confirmed by the electron collision experiments."

TABLE I. Sodium (Na); Atomic Number 11

| | Frequency (ν) | Wave Length (λ) $\times 10^8$ cm. | Volts | |
			Calculated	Observed
$1S$	41,448.59		5.116**	5.13 5.18
$1S$–$2P_2$	16,955.88	5,895.9	2.093†	2.12
$1S$–$2P_1$	16,973.52	5,889.9		2.13

** 5.116 is the value of the energy, in electron volts, required to remove the electron from the ground state ($1S$) completely from the atom.
† 2.093 is the value of the energy required to raise the atom from the ground state ($1S$) to the first excited state ($2P_1$ or $2P_2$).

Later, Franck did valuable work on the dissociation of molecules, determining from the molecular spectra (band spectra) the energy-levels at which dissociation takes place; the values obtained by his method were more accurate than those previously found by the thermal methods used in physical chemistry. Hertz, while professor of physics at the Berlin Technical University, developed a gas-diffusion method for separating the isotopes of neon; his method was later applied with success in the separation of the heavy isotope of hydrogen, the samples of heavy hydrogen obtained being particularly free from impurities.

* Only that part of the table which refers to sodium is given here. The table includes similar data for lithium, potassium, rubidium, and cesium.

CONSEQUENCES IN THEORY AND PRACTICE

The great importance of the work of Franck and Hertz on electron impact lies in the experimental support it gave to Bohr's theory of discrete energy states in the atom. It also provided as direct a method as could be desired for determining the value of Planck's quantum of action h.

1 9 2 6

JEAN PERRIN
(1870–1942)

"For his work on the discontinuous structure of matter, and especially for his discovery of the equilibrium of sedimentation."

BIOGRAPHICAL SKETCH

JEAN PERRIN WAS BORN ON SEPTEMBER 30, 1870, AT LILLE, France. After receiving his early education there, he attended the École Normale Supérieure, or training college for teachers, Paris, where he was himself a teacher of physics from 1894 to 1897. In 1897 he obtained the degree of D-ès-Sc and also became a lecturer in physical chemistry at the University of Paris. He was appointed professor of physical chemistry there in 1910 and held this post for the next thirty years, except for the years 1914 to 1918, when he served as an officer in the Engineers. He died in New York on April 17, 1942.

Many honors were conferred on Perrin. The Royal Society of London awarded him the Joule Prize in 1896 and elected him a Foreign Member in 1918. He was elected a member of the French Academy of Sciences in 1923 and its president in 1938. In 1938 he was also elected president of the French Government Department of Scientific Research. In 1926 he was made a Commander of the Legion of Honor. Many foreign universities conferred honorary doctorates on him: Berlin (1910), New York (1913), Manchester (1918), Oxford (1920).

In the extract which we have quoted from Sir J. J. Thomson's Nobel lecture there is a reference (see above, p. 45) to the important part played by Perrin in the early investigation of the cathode rays. Crookes had shown (see p. 36) that the cathode rays are deflected by a magnetic field in a manner consistent with their being streams of negatively charged particles, but for many years opinion was divided as to the nature of the rays, English physicists favoring the idea that they consisted of negatively charged particles, German physicists that they were some form of ether waves.

In 1895 Perrin devised an experiment which should settle the matter. The arrangement of his apparatus is shown in Fig. 28. Rays

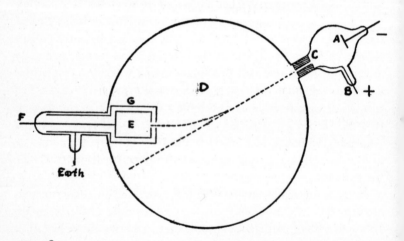

FIG. 28

Perrin's apparatus (as modified by J. J. Thomson) by which he showed that the cathode rays consist of negatively charged particles.

from the cathode A pass through a narrow opening C opposite the cathode and enter a larger vessel D, where they produce fluorescence on the opposite wall. An insulated metal cylinder E is placed out of the direct path of the rays and is shielded from electrical disturbances by an outer cylinder G, which is earthed. When the discharge was passed, an electrometer connected to E registered a small negative charge, but if the rays were deflected by a magnetic field so as to fall on the opening in the double vessel, the electrometer recorded a very much larger negative charge. This afforded conclusive proof that the cathode rays carried negative charges.

DESCRIPTION OF THE PRIZE-WINNING WORK

Perrin's best known work, however, is that which he did on the motions and distribution of microscopic particles suspended in a liquid, in particular his study of what is known as *Brownian motion*. In 1827 Robert Brown, a botanist, observed under his microscope that pollen grains suspended in water were in violent and irregular motion. At first this was put down to temperature irregularities, but Christian Wiener suggested (1863) that the motion might be due to bombardment of the grains by the molecules of the liquid, a view which was also put forward by Sir William Ramsay in 1879. By the end of the century it had become generally accepted that this so-called Brownian motion was due to molecular bombardment. We have already mentioned (p. 183) Einstein's theoretical investigation of the subject in 1905; Einstein showed that the suspended particles should obey the gas laws, and that Avogadro's number (see below) could be expressed in terms of known or measurable quantities and the average displacement of the particles.

Perrin's researches, begun in 1908, provided the experimental confirmation of Einstein's theoretical work. First of all he established that small particles in suspension in a liquid did in fact obey the gas laws, and could therefore be regarded as enormous molecules. Then, having obtained molecules of appreciably uniform size, he studied the variation with height in the concentration of the particles when the equilibrium state had been reached. In this way he found the change in height necessary to halve the number of particles per cubic centimeter. Knowing the change in height (5 km.) required to halve the concentration of oxygen molecules in the atmosphere, he could then calculate by simple proportion the mass of a particle in terms of that of the oxygen molecule, and so find the "molecular weight" of the particle on the scale in which the oxygen atom has mass 16.

Now according to *Avogadro's hypothesis* equal volumes of all gases at the same temperature and pressure contain equal numbers of molecules. Since the total mass of a volume of gas is equal to the mass of the individual molecule multiplied by the number of molecules in the volume, it follows that the "gram-molecule" (M grams, where M is the molecular weight) of all gases at the same temperature and pressure contains the same number of molecules. At normal temperature and pressure (0° C and 76 cm. of mercury) this number—*Avogadro's number*—is 6.1×10^{23}. Perrin had found the "molecular weight" of the particles from their equilibrium distribution, and therefore knew how many grams went to the "gram-molecule." His next step was to determine the mass of the individual particles. This presented great difficulties, but Perrin overcame them. When he divided the "gram-molecule" by the mass in grams of a single particle, he obtained the number 6.8×10^{23}, which is remarkably close to Avogadro's number. The significance of this agreement need hardly be stressed: clearly, uniform particles in suspension behave like gas molecules even to the extent that they lead to the same value of Avogadro's number.

The following extracts, translated from the French of Perrin's Nobel lecture, amplify our brief account of this part of Perrin's work.

"When we know the ratio of the weights of the molecules of two compounds, we can say that masses proportional to these weights (and which must therefore contain the same number of molecules) occupy, in the gaseous state, equal volumes under the same conditions of temperature and pressure. That is to say, for these bodies equal numbers of molecules, heavy or light, exert equal pressures at the same temperature when the volumes are equal. Since it is the mass of the molecule and not its nature which must influence the effect of the impact of the molecule on the wall of the containing vessel, I see in this a justification . . . for the following proposition, stated as a postulate or hypothesis by Avogadro: *Gaseous masses which, at the same temperature and pressure occupy equal volumes, all contain the same number of molecules.*

"These *equimolecular* masses are fixed for the different chemical substances as soon as any particular one of them has been chosen as standard. They are called *gram-molecules* when they are the masses

which, in the gaseous state, occupy at the same temperature and
pressure the same volume as 32 grams of oxygen. The number N
of the molecules in a gram-molecule is *Avogadro's number.*

. . . . .

"In brief, if molecules and atoms do exist, their relative weights
are known to us, and their absolute weights would be known as
soon as Avogadro's number is known.

. . . . .

". . . Every microscopic particle placed in water (or in any
liquid), instead of falling uniformly, is seen [with the miscoscope]
to be in a state of continuous and quite irregular agitation. It comes
and goes, at the same time twisting and turning, rises, falls, rises
again, without any tendency at all to come to rest, and maintaining
indefinitely the same average state of agitation. This phenomenon,
foreshadowed by Lucretius, foreseen by Buffon, definitely established by Brown, constitutes the *Brownian motion.*

"The nature of the particles is immaterial, but the smaller the
particle, the more violent its agitation. There is, moreover, complete independence between the movements of two particles even
when very close to each other, which excludes the hypothesis of
general convections due to disturbance or to differences of temperature.

. . . . .

"Briefly, the Brownian motion (an experimental fact) brings
us back to the molecular hypothesis: we imagine that each particle
situated in a liquid is ceaselessly bombarded by the neighboring
molecules, receiving impacts from them which in their totality
have less chance of being in equilibrium the smaller is the particle,
so that the particle must needs be tossed about irregularly.

"This applies to any particles whatever. If a large number of
particles, all of the same nature, are brought into suspension in a
liquid, the result is called an *emulsion.* The emulsion is stable if
the particles in suspension do not coalesce when they happen to be
brought into contact by the Brownian motion and if they return
into the liquid after striking the walls of the containing vessel or

the surface of the liquid. Such a *stable emulsion* is, from this two-fold point of view, comparable to a *solution*. It was just in following up this analogy that I was able to achieve a simple determination of molecular magnitudes. . . .

. . . . .

"It will be sufficient for us to establish for emulsions a property, open to experiment, which is logically equivalent to the gas laws.

"I found such a property (in 1908) by extending to emulsions this fact, well known to you in a qualitative way, that in a vertical column of a gas in equilibrium the density decreases as the height increases. We all know that the air is more rare on a mountaintop than at sea-level. Broadly speaking, the pressure of the air must become less as we go higher, since the weight of the atmosphere, which this pressure has to sustain, becomes less.

"We follow Laplace in rendering this somewhat vague reasoning more precise. . . .

. . . . .

"Two important facts are expressed by this very simple equation

$$dp = n_\pi \, dh$$

where dp is the change in pressure (p) for the small difference in height dh, π the weight of a single molecule, n the number of molecules in unit volume, i.e., the concentration. First, as the molecular concentration n is, for each given temperature, proportional to the pressure p, we see that for a column of a given gas (π given), of uniform temperature, the relative drop in pressure, dp/p, or equally well, the relative drop in concentration dn/n, which can be said to measure the rarefaction, always assumes the same value for equal differences dh in level, at whatever level we are. For example, in air, every time you go up a step of a staircase, the pressure (or molecular concentration) drops by one forty-thousandth of its value. Adding these effects step by step, we see that, at whatever height we were at first, every time we rise through an equal height, in air at a uniform temperature, the pressure (or the density) will be divided by the same number; for example, in oxygen at 0° the rarefaction will double for each increase of height of 5 km.

"The other fact which at once emerges from our equation concerns the weight π of the molecule. For the same value dh of the difference between the levels, the relative rarefaction dp/p (or relative concentration dn/n) varies as the weight of the molecule. Here again, adding the effects step by step, we see that in two different gases at the same temperature, the increases in height which are accompanied by the same rarefaction are inversely as the molecular weights. For example, since we know that the molecule of oxygen (if it exists, and behaves according to the laws summarized above) should weigh 16 times as much as the molecule of hydrogen, the height must be increased 16 times as much in hydrogen as in oxygen, that is, to 80 km., for the rarefaction to be doubled.

. . . . .

"Now let us assume that Avogadro's law is valid for emulsions as for gases. We then assume that a stable emulsion consisting of particles of equal size has been prepared and left to itself at a constant temperature and under the sole influence of gravity. We now repeat the preceding argument without any change other than that which results from the fact that the space between the particles, instead of being empty, is filled with a liquid which exercises on each particle, in accordance with the principle of Archimedes, a thrust in the opposite direction to the weight. As a result, the effective weight of the particle in question is its real weight diminished by this thrust.

"Now if our generalization is justified, the emulsion, once equilibrium is established, will present a *miniature atmosphere consisting of visible molecules,* in which equal increases in height are accompanied by equal rarefactions. But if, for example, to double the rarefaction the height must be increased by an amount a billion times less in the emulsion than in oxygen, then the effective weight of the particle must be a billion times greater than that of the molecule of oxygen. It is sufficient, then, to determine the effective weight of the visible particle, which forms a link between magnitudes on our scale and molecular magnitudes, in order to obtain by

simple proportion the weight of any molecule whatever and consequently Avogadro's number. . . .

"I first of all prepared some stable emulsions consisting of spherical droplets of various resins in suspension in a liquid, generally
water. This is done by dissolving the resin in alcohol and adding
to this clear solution a large quantity of water. The resin, quite
insoluble in water, is then precipitated in microscopic droplets of
all sizes. Prolonged centrifuging, similar to that by which the red
corpuscles of blood serum are separated, allows the particles to be
collected in the form of a sediment; when this sediment is shaken
up in pure water, after the alcohol on top has been poured off, it
breaks up again into a stable emulsion consisting of separate
particles.

"It was then necessary, starting with an emulsion in which the
particles were of very different sizes, to separate the particles according to their diameters, so as to produce *uniform* emulsions
(particles of equal size). The method I used can be compared to
fractional distillation: just as, during a distillation, the fractions
which pass over first are richest in the more volatile constituents,
so, in centrifuging a *pure* emulsion (particles of the same substance), the first deposits are richer in large particles, and thus we
have a means of separating the particles according to their size,
following certain rules which it would be of no interest to give here.
For the rest, one has to be patient: in my most careful fractionization I treated one kilogram of gamboge daily for several months
to obtain a fraction containing a few decigrams of particles with
diameters sensibly equal to that I wished to obtain (about three-
fourths of a thousandth of a millimeter).

. . . . .

"To study the equilibrium distribution of the emulsion under the
action of gravity, a drop of emulsion is enclosed in a covered trough
(evaporation must be made impossible) arranged for microscopic
examination. The distribution of the particles is at first uniform,
but . . . they progressively accumulate in the lower layers until a
limiting distribution is established, the particles sinking or rising
reversibly according as the temperature is lowered or raised. There

are two methods of observation. In the one (microscope horizontal) we see at one glance the rarefaction of the emulsion with height, and the likeness to an atmosphere in miniature is most striking; instantaneous photographs allow of precise measurements. But it is difficult to give the emulsion a height of less than (say) one millimeter, and the time necessary for the establishment of permanent conditions becomes considerable (several days), with consequent complications and difficulties.

"In the other method of observation, the microscope is vertical and the emulsion, enclosed between the stage of the microscope and the cover-glass, is of the order of 1/10 mm. in thickness. An object glass of high magnification and short focal length is used, so that a very thin layer of the emulsion (of the order of 2 microns *) is clearly seen; an instantaneous photograph is taken. This gives us the concentration at a definite level, just as an airman could take the density of the air at each level. The concentrations at different levels can be compared at leisure.

[At this point a motion picture was shown of the equilibrium distribution of an emulsion consisting of particles agitated by the Brownian motion.]

"This film sums up for you the qualitative and quantitative results which prove that the perfect gas laws apply to dilute emulsions. This generalization was foreseen as a consequence of the molecular hypothesis through reasoning so simple that its verification assuredly constitutes a very strong argument in favor of the existence of molecules. . . . The different emulsions studied lead, within the limits of possible error, to the same value for Avogadro's number. I have, in fact, varied the mass of the particles (from 1 to 50), their nature (gamboge, mastic), their density (1.20 to 1.06), the nature of the surrounding liquid (water; a strong solution of sugar and water; glycerin, in which the particles of mastic, being lighter, accumulated in the upper layers), and finally the temperature (from $-9°$ to $+60°$). My most careful measurements, made with an emulsion for which each elevation of 6 microns doubled the rarefaction, give a value for N of 68×10^{22}."

---

* 1 *micron* $(\mu) = \dfrac{1}{1000}$ mm.

CONSEQUENCES IN THEORY AND PRACTICE

By these researches and a great variety of others carried out over a long period of time, Perrin established that the laws which, according to the kinetic theory of gases, govern the behavior of the invisible molecules of a gas apply equally well to the behavior of the visible particles in a suspension. In this way he may be said to have provided one of the most striking pieces of experimental evidence in support of the existence of the molecule.

1 9 2 7

ARTHUR HOLLY COMPTON
(1892–   )

"For his discovery of the effect named after him."
(The award for 1927 was shared with Charles
Thomson Rees Wilson; see below, pp. 269-277.)

BIOGRAPHICAL SKETCH

ARTHUR HOLLY COMPTON WAS BORN ON SEPTEMBER 10, 1892, at Wooster, Ohio. After receiving his B.S. degree at the College of Wooster in 1913, he studied for three years at Princeton University, where he obtained his M.A. in 1914 and his Ph.D. in 1916. The next year he spent at the University of Minnesota as an instructor in physics; then two years (1917-1919) as a research engineer with the Westinghouse Lamp Company at Pittsburgh, for part of this time being attached to the U. S. Signal Corps for work on the development of airplane instruments. In 1919 he went as a National Research Fellow to the Cavendish Laboratory, Cambridge, England. On his return in 1920 he was appointed professor of physics and head of the Physics Department at Washington University in St. Louis. From 1923 till 1929 he was professor of physics at the University of Chicago, and from 1929 to 1945 was Charles H. Smith Distinguished Service Professor. Since 1945 he has been Chancellor of Washington University.

From 1926 to 1945 Compton was consulting physicist to the General Electric Company. During the Second World War he was director of the Metallurgical Atomic Project (1942-1945). In

1946 he was a member of the Technical Advisory Committee to the United Nations Atomic Energy Commission.

In addition to the Sc.D. which he received in 1927 from the College of Wooster, Compton holds honorary doctorates of most of the leading American universities and of many foreign ones. He was awarded the Rumford Medal of the American Academy of Arts and Sciences in 1927, the Matteucci Medal of the Italian Academy of Sciences in 1930, the Hughes Medal of the Royal Society of London in 1940, the Franklin Medal of the Franklin Institute in 1940, and the Franklin Medal of the American Philosophical Society in 1945. In 1947 he was made an Officer of the Legion of Honor. He is a member of many leading American and foreign scientific societies.

DESCRIPTION OF THE PRIZE-WINNING WORK

Barkla's researches (see p. 145) had shown that when X rays fall on matter the secondary radiation produced consists in part of purely scattered radiation of the same character as the primary, in part of X radiation which differs from the primary and is characteristic of the scattering substance; he was led to this discovery through having observed a considerable difference between the absorbability of the primary rays and that of the secondary rays due to scattering by elements of higher atomic weight than calcium, whereas in the case of light elements the difference was slight.

It was this secondary radiation from substances of low atomic weight that Compton made the subject of investigation on his return to the United States in 1920. Barkla's absorbability measurements were only capable of detecting the quite considerable change in the character of the radiation caused by the presence in the secondary radiation of the characteristic radiation due to the scattering substance. Compton, however, had at his command far more refined methods of measurement and was able to detect with a Bragg X-ray spectrometer a slight change in the character of the scattered radiation itself. He found that X rays scattered by graphite, an allotropic form of the light element carbon, contained, in addition to radiation of the same wave length as the primary rays, other radiation

of slightly longer wave length. At first it seemed that this might be
a new type of characteristic (or fluorescent) radiation, but the
change in wave length proved to be independent of the scattering
substance and to depend only on the angle between the incident
and scattered rays. Compton therefore concluded that the primary
X rays had, in the process of scattering, undergone a slight increase
in wave length—an effect which is now known as the *Compton
effect;* the analogous effect for visible light was discovered by
Raman (*q.v.* 1930) a few years later.

Figure 29 (p. 263) shows the results of one set of Compton's
observations. As primary radiation he used the K radiation (see
p. 145) from a molybdenum target. When this radiation fell directly on the crystal (calcite) of the X-ray spectrometer and the
resulting ionization current was plotted against the glancing angle,
the upper curve was obtained. When the K radiation was allowed
to fall on carbon and the *scattered* radiation was examined with the
spectrometer, the lower curve was obtained; here the smaller of the
two peaks occurred at exactly the same wave length as the peak for
the primary radiation, but the higher peak occurred at a slightly
longer wave length, the wave length λ being found from the glancing angle θ by means of the Bragg relation

$$n\lambda = 2d \cdot \sin \theta$$

where d is the crystal spacing and $n = 1$ (first-order spectrum).

The increase in wave length occurring as a result of the scattering could not be explained by the classical theory of scattering
(according to which the primary and the scattered rays should have
precisely the same wave length), since the incident radiation produces forced vibrations of its own frequency in the atoms over
which it passes, these vibrations in their turn producing electromagnetic waves (X rays) of still the same frequency.

Now, as we have already explained (p. 184), Einstein in 1905
had succeeded in accounting for the photoelectric effect by assuming that light consists of light quanta, small bundles of energy $h\nu$,
where h is Planck's constant and ν is the frequency of the incident
light. This, in effect, was to assign to light something of a corpuscular nature. Compton was able to explain the effect he had discovered by applying to it Einstein's theory of light quanta, or *photons*

as they are now called. He assumed that when a light quantum falls on a *free* electron, or on an electron which is so loosely bound to its atom that it may be regarded as free, the same thing happens as when one billiard ball strikes another: both move off in directions depending on their state of motion at the moment of impact; also that both the total energy and the momentum are the same after the impact as before, i.e., they are conserved. The energy of the scattered photon is therefore less than that of the incident photon by an amount equal to the kinetic energy acquired by the electron responsible for the scattering; the frequency of the scattered photon must therefore be less than that of the incident photon, that is, its wave length must be greater. The process is illustrated diagrammatically in Fig. 29 (p. 263), where the incident photon on striking an electron is scattered in a direction making an angle ϕ with the original direction, and the electron recoils at an angle θ.

When Compton put forward this theory in 1923 there was no experimental evidence in support of the existence of these recoil electrons, but shortly afterward C. T. R. Wilson, using the cloud chamber described below (p. 271) observed tracks which could be readily explained on Compton's theory. This is illustrated in Fig. 31 (p. 266). An incident X-ray photon strikes an electron at O; the recoiling electron starts off at an angle θ with the direction of the incident photon, but the collisions which produce the ions and so render the track visible also cause the electron to follow an irregular path until at B its velocity is so reduced that it is no longer able to produce ions and the track disappears. In the upper part of the figure another irregular track begins abruptly at A and ends at C; this is interpreted as due to the scattered photon which, starting at O, produced no effect until it reached A, where it ejected an electron from an atom, the irregular track being due to the ionizing collisions subsequently made by the electron. The angle ϕ which the line OA makes with the direction of the incident photon agrees closely with that calculated by Compton for the scattered photon, as does the angle θ for the calculated direction of the recoil electron.

We now give some extracts from Compton's Nobel lecture.*

---

* By kind permission of Professor Compton.

"The Scattering of X-rays and Light. A series of experiments performed during the last few years has shown that secondary X-rays are of greater wave length than the primary rays which produce them. . . . On the other hand, careful experiments to find a similar increase in wave length in light diffusely scattered by a turbid medium have failed to show any effect. An examination of the spectrum of the secondary X-rays shows that the primary beam has been split into two parts, as shown in Fig. 8 [Fig. 29], one of the same wave length and the other of increased wave length. When different primary wave lengths are used, we find always the same difference in wave length between these two components; but the relative intensity of the two components changes. For the longer wave lengths the unmodified ray has the greater energy, while for

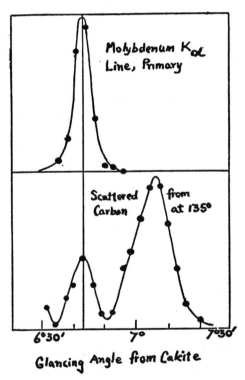

FIG. 29   *Compton's Fig. 8*

A typical spectrum of scattered X rays, showing the splitting of the primary ray into a modified and an unmodified ray.

the shorter wave lengths the modified ray is predominant. In fact when hard γ-rays are employed, it is not possible to find any radiation of the original wave length.

"Thus in the wave length of secondary radiation we have a gradually increasing departure from the classical electron theory of scattering as we go from the optical region to the region of X-rays and γ-rays.

"The question arises, are these secondary X-rays of increased wave length to be classed as scattered X-rays or as fluorescent? An important fact bearing on this point is the intensity of the secondary rays. From the theories of Thomson, Debye, and others it is possible to calculate the absolute intensity of the scattered rays. It is found that this calculated intensity agrees very nearly with the total intensity of the modified and unmodified rays, but that in many cases the observed intensity of the unmodified ray taken alone is very small compared with the calculated intensity. If the electron theory of the intensity of scattering is even approximately correct, we must thus include the modified with the unmodified rays as scattered rays.

"Information regarding the origin of these secondary rays is also given by their state of polarization. We have called attention to the fact that the electron theory demands that the X-rays scattered at 90 degrees should be completely plane polarized. If the rays of increased wave length are fluorescent, however, we should not expect them to be strongly polarized. . . . [In] the experiments performed by Barkla . . . he observed strong polarization in X-rays scattered at right angles, . . . which gave us our first strong evidence of the similar character of X-rays and light. But . . . the intensity of the secondary rays at 90 degrees dropped only to one third its maximum value, whereas for complete polarization it should have fallen to zero.

"The fact that no such unpolarized rays exist was established by repeating Barkla's experiment with scattering blocks of different sizes. When very small blocks were used, we found that the polarization was nearly complete. The lack of complete polarization in Barkla's experiments was due chiefly to the multiple scattering of the X-rays in the large blocks that he used to scatter the X-rays. It would seem that the only explanation of the complete polarization of the secondary rays is that they consist wholly of scattered rays.

"According to the classical theory, an electromagnetic wave is scattered when it sets the electrons which it traverses into forced oscillations, and these oscillating electrons re-radiate the energy which they receive. In order to account for the change in wave length of the scattered rays, however, we have had to adopt a wholly different picture of the scattering process, as shown in Fig. 9 [Fig. 30]. Here we do not think of the X-rays as waves but as

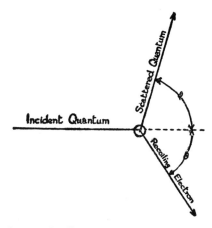

FIG. 30   *Compton's Fig. 9*

An X-ray photon is deflected through an angle φ by an electron, which in turn recoils at an angle θ, taking a part of the energy of the photon.

light corpuscles, quanta, or . . . photons. Moreover, there is nothing here of the forced oscillation pictured on the classical view, but a sort of elastic collision, in which the energy and momentum are conserved.

"This new picture of the scattering process leads at once to three consequences that can be tested by experiment. There is a change of wave length

$$\delta\lambda = \frac{h}{mc} (1 - \cos \varphi)*$$

---

* In this equation m is mass of electron; c, velocity of light; h, Planck's constant; θ and ϕ the angles shown in Fig. 9 [30]; ν, the frequency of the incident quantum.

which accounts for the modified line in the spectra of scattered X-rays. Experiment has shown that this formula is correct within the precision of our knowledge of h, m, and c. The electron which recoils from the scattered X-rays should have the kinetic energy

$$h\nu \cdot \frac{h\nu}{mc^2} \cos^2 \theta$$

approximately. When this theory was first proposed, no electrons of this type were known; but they were discovered by C. T. R. Wilson and W. Bothe within a few months after their prediction. Now we know that the number, energy, and spatial distribution of these recoil electrons are in accord with the predictions of the photon theory. Finally, whenever a photon is deflected at an angle ϕ, the electron should recoil at an angle θ given by the relation

$$\cot \tfrac{1}{2}\varphi = \tan \theta$$

approximately.

"This relation we have tested using the apparatus shown diagrammatically in Fig. 10 [Fig. 31]. A narrow beam of X-rays

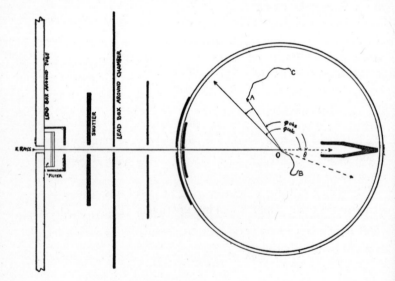

FIG. 31   *Compton's Fig. 10*

An electron recoiling at an angle θ should be associated with a photon deflected through an angle ϕ.

enters a Wilson expansion chamber. Here it produces a recoil electron. If the photon theory is correct, associated with this recoil
electron, a photon is scattered in the direction ϕ. If it should happen to eject a β-ray, the origin of this β-ray tells the direction in
which the photon was scattered. [A typical photograph of the
process was shown on the screen.] A measurement of the angle θ
at which the recoil electron on this plate is ejected and the angle ϕ
of the origin of the secondary β-particle shows close agreement
with the photon formula. This experiment is of especial significance, since it shows that for each recoil electron there is a scattered
photon, and that the energy and momentum of the system photon
plus electron are conserved in the scattering process.

"The evidence for the existence of directed quanta of radiation
afforded by this experiment is very direct. The experiment shows
that associated with each recoil electron there is scattered X-ray
energy enough to produce a secondary beta ray, and that this energy
proceeds in a direction determined at the moment of ejection of
the recoil electron. Unless the experiment is subject to improbably
large experimental errors, therefore, the scattered X-rays proceed
in the form of photons.

"Thus we see that as a study of the scattering of radiation is
extended into the very high frequencies of X-rays, the manner of
scattering changes. For the lower frequencies the phenomena could
be accounted for in terms of waves. For these higher frequencies
we can find no interpretation of the scattering except in terms of
the deflection of corpuscles or photons of radiation. Yet it is certain
that the two types of radiation, light and X-rays, are essentially the
same kind of thing. We are thus confronted with the dilemma of
having before us a convincing evidence that radiation consists of
waves, and at the same time that it consists of corpuscles.

"It would seem that this dilemma is being solved by the new
wave mechanics. De Broglie has assumed that associated with every
particle of matter in motion there is a wave whose wave length λ
is given by the relation

$$mv = h/\lambda$$

where mv is the momentum of the particle. A very similar assumption was made at about the same time by Duane to account for the

diffraction of X-ray photons. As applied to the motion of electrons, Schrödinger has shown the great power of this conception in studying atomic structure. It now seems, through the efforts of Heisenberg, Bohr, and others, that this conception of the relation between corpuscles and waves is capable of giving us a unified view of the diffraction and interference of light, and at the same time of its diffuse scattering and the photoelectric effect. . . ."

Compton's later work included researches on the diffraction of X rays by ruled gratings. In 1922 he had discovered that X rays could be totally reflected by polished surfaces if the glancing angle was very small (generally less than one degree), and had applied this discovery to the measurement of the refractive index of a substance for X rays. Shortly afterward (1923) he suggested that a ruled grating should produce diffraction of X rays if the glancing angle was less than the critical angle for total reflection, and in 1925 he succeeded in measuring X-ray wave lengths by this method, which, in spite of the smallness of the angles involved, has since been developed to give an accuracy of 1 part in 10,000.

About 1930 Compton turned his attention to the investigation of cosmic rays, particularly their variation in intensity with latitude and altitude; here too he did work of outstanding importance, the data he collected providing evidence that the rays do not originate in the solar system or even in the Milky Way, but in remote space far beyond.

CONSEQUENCES IN THEORY AND PRACTICE

The discovery made almost at the outset of his scientific career remains Compton's greatest single achievement, not only on account of its importance in the theory of X-ray scattering, but also because it lends additional support to Einstein's photon theory of light. The tracks observed by C. T. R. Wilson, when interpreted in the light of Compton's discovery, may be said to have provided the first direct experimental evidence in support of Einstein's theory.

1 9 2 7

CHARLES THOMSON REES WILSON

(1869–   )

"For his discovery of the vapor condensation method of rendering visible the paths of electrically charged particles." (The award for 1927 was shared with Arthur Holly Compton; see above, pp. 259-268.)

BIOGRAPHICAL SKETCH

CHARLES THOMSON REES WILSON WAS BORN ON FEBRUARY 14, 1869, at Glencorse, near Edinburgh, Scotland. On his father's death in 1873 the family moved to Manchester, where Wilson was educated, first at a private school, then at Owens College, which later became the Victoria University of Manchester. In October 1888 he entered Sidney Sussex College, Cambridge, with a scholarship, and made a special study of physics and chemistry, graduating in 1892.

At the beginning of 1895 he began the experimental study of clouds in the Cavendish Laboratory; at the end of that year he was appointed Clerk Maxwell Student and for the next three years devoted his whole time to research. He was then employed for a year by the Meteorological Council in research on atmospheric electricity. In 1900 he was elected a Fellow of Sidney Sussex College and appointed a university lecturer in physics; from then until 1918 he was in charge of the advanced practical physics teaching at the

Cavendish Laboratory, being also, from 1913, observer in meteorological physics at the Solar Physics Observatory. In 1918 he was
appointed reader in electrical meteorology and in 1925 Jacksonian
Professor of Natural Philosophy at the University of Cambridge.
He retired in 1934.

Wilson was elected a Fellow of the Royal Society of London in
1900 and was awarded the Hughes Medal in 1911 and the Royal
Medal in 1922. He was awarded the Hopkins Prize by the Cambridge Philosophical Society in 1920, the Gunning Prize by the
Royal Society of Edinburgh in 1921, and the Howard Potts Medal
of the Franklin Institute in 1925.

DESCRIPTION OF THE PRIZE-WINNING WORK

From his student days Wilson was interested in atmospheric
phenomena—in the formation of cloud and mist, and in atmospheric electricity. Out of this twofold interest arose the invention
for which he is famous.

Ordinary atmospheric air always contains a certain amount of
water vapor, the maximum amount which it is capable of containing under normal conditions decreasing with fall of temperature.
If the temperature of an enclosed saturated sample of air is lowered, for instance by causing the air to expand suddenly, the excess
water vapor condenses unless special precautions are taken to prevent the condensation, in which case the air becomes supersaturated.
The conditions necessary for condensation to take place were carefully studied by the Scottish physicist John Aitken, who in 1888
found that when compressed air is allowed to expand suddenly a
cloud is formed if the air contains dust particles, but not if it is
dust-free. The dust particles are needed as nuclei on which the water
vapor can condense; in their absence the air becomes supersaturated.
Wilson's earlier experiments were an extension of Aitken's. He
found that even in dust-free air a cloud did form if the expansion
exceeded a certain definite limit measured by the ratio of the initial
volume to the final volume. Wilson thought that in this case the
nuclei might be electrically charged atoms, that is, ions. This was

early in 1895, before X rays or radioactivity had been discovered. In the autumn of that year news of Röntgen's discovery reached Cambridge, and early in 1896 Wilson was able to test his idea by suddenly expanding saturated air while it was exposed to the action of the rays. A cloud was formed, even though the degree of expansion was less than the critical value needed for cloud formation in the absence of dust particles.

This was the beginning of a series of experiments on the subject which extended over many years. The cloud chamber which Wilson used at this time (1897) is shown in Fig. 32, in which P, the piston, is supported by the pressure of the air beneath it; when the valve V is opened by pulling back the rod R, the air below P rushes through the tube H into the large evacuated vessel to the right, the sudden fall of the piston P producing almost instantaneous expansion of the saturated air in the space D above it and in the expansion chamber connected with D. A pressure gauge G determines the amount of the expansion. The original form of expansion chamber had the disadvantage that eddy currents were produced by the sudden withdrawal of the air through the side tube leading from the expansion chamber. This drawback was overcome in an improved form of apparatus, devised in 1910, in which the top of the piston was made flat and formed the floor of the expansion chamber. The collapse of the floor now caused no eddy currents in the air of the chamber. In the spring of 1911 Wilson had the satisfaction of seeing for the first time the cloud track due to the passage of a charged particle— a track like a tiny vapor trail left in the wake of an airplane of less than atomic size, an electron or an alpha particle.

The following extracts * from Wilson's Nobel lecture describe the origin and development of the cloud chamber method.

"In September 1894 I spent a few weeks in the Observatory which then existed on the summit of Ben Nevis, the highest of the Scottish hills. The wonderful optical phenomena shown when the sun shone on the clouds surrounding the hill-top . . . made me wish to imitate them in the laboratory.

"At the beginning of 1895 I made some experiments for this

---

* Quoted by kind permission of Professor Wilson.

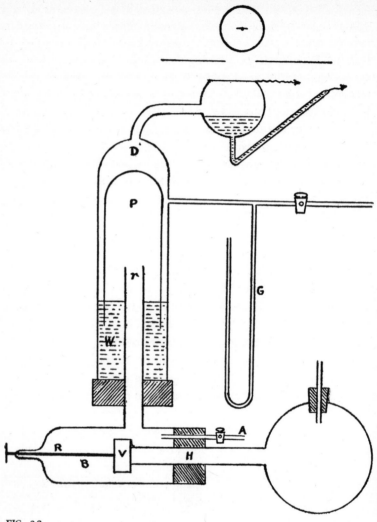

FIG. 32

C. T. R. Wilson's cloud chamber (1897).

purpose—making clouds by expansion of moist air after the manner of Coulier and Aitken. Almost immediately I came across something which promised to be of more interest than the optical
phenomena. . . . Moist air which had been freed from Aitken's
dust particles, so that no cloud was formed even when a consider-

able degree of supersaturation was produced by expansion, did appear to give a cloud if the expansion and consequent supersaturation exceeded a certain limit. A quantitative expansion apparatus was therefore made in which given samples of moist air could repeatedly be allowed to expand suddenly without danger of contamination, and in which the increase of volume to be made could be adjusted at will.

"It was found that there was a definite critical value (1.25) for the expansion ratio, corresponding to an approximately fourfold supersaturation. In moist air which had been freed from Aitken's nuclei by repeatedly forming a cloud and allowing the drops to settle, no drops were formed unless the expansion exceeded this limit, while if it were exceeded a shower of drops was seen to fall. . . .

. . . . .

"Further experiments with somewhat more elaborate apparatus which allowed of more sudden expansion showed that there was a second critical expansion corresponding to an approximately eight-fold supersaturation of the vapour. With expansions exceeding this limit dense clouds were formed in dust-free air, the number of drops in the cloud increasing with very great rapidity as the expansion was increased beyond it and giving rise on account of their small and uniform size to very beautiful colour phenomena. . . .

. . . . .

"While the obvious explanation of the dense clouds formed when the second supersaturation limit was exceeded was that here we had condensation occurring in the absence of any nuclei other than the molecules of the vapour or gas—those responsible for the rain-like condensation which occurred when the supersaturation lay between the two limits from the first excited my interest. The very fact that their number was so limited and yet that they were always being regenerated, together with the fact that the supersaturation required indicated a magnitude not greatly exceeding molecular dimensions, at once suggested that we had a means of making visible and counting certain individual molecules or atoms which were at the moment in some exceptional condition. Could they be electrically charged atoms or ions?

"In the autumn of 1895 came the news of Röntgen's great discovery. At the beginning of 1896 J. J. Thomson was investigating the conductivity of air exposed to the new rays—and I had the opportunity of using an X-ray tube . . . which had been made by Professor Thomson's assistant Mr. Everett in the Cavendish Laboratory. . . . I found at the first trial that while no drops were formed on expansion of the cloud chamber when exposed to X-rays if the expansion were less than 1.25, a fog which took many minutes to fall was produced when the expansion lay between the rainlike and cloud-like limits; X-rays thus produced in large numbers nuclei of the same kind as were always being produced in very small numbers in air within the cloud chamber.

.   .   .   .   .

"During the following two years [1896-1898] I investigated by means of the expansion apparatus the condensation nuclei produced in gases by X-rays, by the newly discovered uranium rays, by ultraviolet light, by point discharges and other agents.

"The purely ionizing agents all produced nuclei, identical as regards the minimum supersaturation required to cause water to condense upon them.

"The condensation nuclei produced by these ionizing agents were shown to be indeed themselves the ions by their behavior in an electric field. They could be completely removed by applying an electric field before expansion—so that no cloud was formed.

"Uncharged nuclei, not removable by a field, were also found to be produced in various ways and their properties were investigated.

.   .   .   .   .

"The following winter [1898-1899] was occupied in studying separately the phenomena of condensation on positive and negative ions. It was found that the measurement of the least expansion required to condense water in ionized air or other gas had all been concerned with the negative ion; to catch the positive ion the expansion ratio had to exceed a limit of about 1.31, corresponding to an approximately sixfold supersaturation instead of the fourfold super-saturation required by the negative ion.

"This [completed] a stage in my work, the behavior of ions as condensation nuclei. It was now possible to make visible the individual ions and to distinguish between positive and negative ions.

. . . . .

"Towards 1910 I began to make experiments with a view to increasing the usefulness of the condensation method.

"I had . . . in view the possibility of determining the ionic charge by a direct method, in which ions carrying a known charge were to be made visible by condensation, photographed and counted. The plan . . . was that of measuring an intermittent current from a negatively charged plate exposed to ultra-violet light within the cloud-chamber, thus obtaining a stream of ions divided into groups, and finding the number of ions per group by the condensation method.

". . . since my earlier experiments ideas on the corpuscular nature of the α- and β-rays had become much more definite, and I had in view the possibility that the track of an ionizing particle might be made visible and photographed by condensing water on the ions which it liberated. As I succeeded in this latter aim, and Millikan had by this time rendered the other project unnecessary, the determination of e by the method of direct counting of drops was never carried out.

"Much time was spent in making tests of the most suitable form of expansion apparatus and in finding an efficient means of instantaneous illumination of the cloud particles for the purpose of photographing them. In the spring of 1911 tests were still incomplete, but it occurred to me one day to try whether some indication of the tracks might not be made with the rough apparatus already constructed. The first test was made with X-rays . . . and in making an expansion of the proper magnitude for condensation on the ions while the air was exposed to the rays . . . the cloud-chamber filled with little wisps and threads of cloud—the tracks of the electrons ejected by the action of the rays. The radium-tipped

metal tongue of a spinthariscope * was then placed inside the
cloud chamber and . . . the clouds condensed along the tracks of
the α-particles was seen for the first time. The long thread-like
tracks of fast β-particles were also seen when a suitable source
was brought near the cloud chamber.

. . . . .

"The summer of 1911 was occupied in designing improved apparatus. The expansion apparatus [Fig. 32, p. 272] was constructed
in the workshop of the Cavendish Laboratory and is the one which
I have had in use up to the present time. . . .

"The essential conditions to be fulfilled if good pictures of the
tracks are to be obtained are mainly these. The expansion must be
effected without stirring up the gas; this condition is secured by
using a wide shallow cloud chamber of which the floor can be made
to drop suddenly and so produce the desired increase of volume.
The cloud chamber must be freed not only from 'dust' particles,
but from ions other than those produced by the ionizing particles
under observation; an electric field maintained between the roof
and floor of the cloud chamber serves this purpose.

"For the purpose of obtaining sharp pictures of the tracks the
order of operations has to be: firstly the production of the necessary
supersaturation by sudden expansion of the gas, secondly the passage of the ionizing particles through the supersaturated gas, and
finally the illumination of the cloud condensed on the ions along
the track.

"Perhaps the most important purpose that the photographs obtained at this time served was to confirm . . . conclusions which
had already been reached by less direct means and which in some
cases, but not in all, had come to be generally accepted."

CONSEQUENCES IN THEORY AND PRACTICE

Wilson's cloud chamber has proved of incalculable service in
the investigation of fundamental particles, so much so that Lord

---

* Instrument invented by Sir William Crookes to demonstrate the effect produced
by the radiation from a radium salt on a fluorescent screen.

Rutherford once referred to the invention as "the most original and wonderful in scientific history." We have already had one example of its use in J. J. Thomson's determination of the electronic charge e (p. 47) and another in the confirmation it afforded of Compton's theory. We shall meet it again in connection with the researches of Anderson (*q.v.* 1936) and of Blackett (*q.v.* 1948) on cosmic rays.

1 9 2 8

OWEN WILLANS RICHARDSON
(1879–   )

"For his work on the thermionic phenomenon and more especially for the discovery of the law named after him."

BIOGRAPHICAL SKETCH

OWEN WILLANS RICHARDSON WAS BORN ON APRIL 26, 1879, at Dewsbury, Yorkshire, England, where he attended school until 1897, when he entered Trinity College, Cambridge. After graduating in 1900 he did research work in the Cavendish Laboratory until 1906, having been elected a Fellow of Trinity College in 1902. In 1906 he came to the United States, serving as professor of physics at Princeton University until the end of 1913, when he returned to England to become Wheatstone Professor of Physics at King's College, University of London. In 1924 he was appointed Yarrow Research Professor of the Royal Society of London, and director of research in physics at King's College. He retired in 1944.

Richardson was elected a member of the American Philosophical Society in 1911 and a Fellow of the Royal Society of London in 1913. In 1920 he was awarded the Hughes Medal of the Royal Society and in 1930 the Royal Medal. He was president of the Physical Society of London from 1926 to 1928. He was knighted in 1939.

DESCRIPTION OF THE PRIZE-WINNING WORK

Richardson's researches covered a wide field—thermodynamics, photoelectricity, spectroscopy, X rays—but his name will always be associated with the emission of electricity from hot bodies, or *thermionics,* as he named the subject.

As long ago as 1603 Sir William Gilbert reported that an "excited electric" loses its "electric effluvium" when it is heated from an outside source. From the middle of the eighteenth century onward it was accepted that charged bodies lost their electricity when heated, but the subject did not receive serious attention until it was investigated by F. Guthrie in England in the 1870's. About 1880, Elster and Geitel in Germany began a systematic investigation in which they found that heated wires had a tendency to give off positive electricity at low temperatures, negative electricity at high temperatures. About the same time Thomas Edison in America showed that if an incandescent lamp is provided with an independent electrode which can be connected on the outside to either the positive or the negative end of the filament, a current flows when the electrode is connected to the positive terminal but not when it is connected to the negative. Sir Ambrose Fleming in 1890 explained this as due to the passage of electricity from the negative end of the filament across the vacuum to the positively charged electrode. In 1892 Branly, the inventor of the coherer mentioned in connection with Marconi's work, confirmed Elster and Geitel's results for metal wires, but found that the oxides of certain metals lost a negative charge at a red heat, but not a positive.

So far there was no satisfactory theory to guide future research. Then, in 1897, Sir J. J. Thomson discovered the electron and put forward his theory of the conduction of electricity in gases, according to which the carriers of the electricity were charged particles, or *ions,* moving under the influence of the applied electric field. It seemed, too, that there must be some definite connection between the electrical conductivity of an ionized gas and the loss of charge of a body when heated. In 1899 J. McClelland therefore investigated the conductivity of gases in the neighborhood of heated wires; his experiments showed that the electricity was carried away from the hot body by ions, but the process by which the ions originated in the first instance was still obscure. Later in the same year Thomson determined the ratio of charge to mass for the negative ions and found it to be very nearly the same as that found for the particles of the cathode rays (electrons). This was the stage matters had reached when, in 1900, Richardson, working in the Cavendish Laboratory, began his investigations into the phenomenon. For an account of these researches we turn to his Nobel lecture.*

". . . this subject . . . deals with the effect of heat on the interaction between electricity and matter. . . . Nearly 200 years ago it was known that air in the neighborhood of hot bodies conducted electricity. . . . Guthrie showed that a red-hot iron ball in air could retain a negative but not a positive charge. . . . Elster and Geitel examined the charge collected on an insulated plate placed near various hot wires in diverse gases at different pressures. The observed effects were very specific and varied, but there emerged a general tendency for the plate to acquire a positive charge at low temperatures and high pressures and a negative charge at high temperatures and low pressures. . . . J. J. Thomson showed that the discharge from an incandescent carbon filament in a vacuum tube was carried by negative electrons. . . . McClelland showed that the currents from a negatively charged platinum wire were influenced very little, if at all, by changes in the nature and pressure of the surrounding gas, if the pressure were fairly low. These facts seemed to me to be highly significant, and I resolved to investigate the phenomenon thoroughly.

"The view of these effects generally held . . . was that the electric discharges were carried by ions and electrons which were generated by the interaction of the neighbouring gas molecules with the hot body. It was an open question whether this action was merely thermal, a matter of kinetic energy, or was chemical or involved the intervention of radiation. The effects observed in the best vacua were attributed to the residual gas which could not be got rid of. This was, of course, easily possible. I felt, however,

---

* The following extracts are quoted by kind permission of Sir Owen Richardson.

that it was very likely that interacting gases had little to do with the main phenomenon, but that the negatively charged electrons and, possibly, the positively charged ions too were coming from the heated solid. This would be reasonable from the point of view of the theories of metallic conduction which had been put forward . . . by Thomson, Riecke and Drude. I decided . . . to get rid of the complications due to the presence of gases and to find out what, if anything, happened when gas effects were excluded.

". . . In those days the gas had all to be got away by hand pumps. As the heating of the tube walls and other parts of the apparatus by the hot wire generates gas from them which continues almost indefinitely this is a most tedious operation. . . . There was no ductile tungsten; the most refractory material readily available in a reasonably pure form was platinum. In 1901 I was able to show that each unit area of a platinum surface emitted a limited number of electrons. This number increased very rapidly with the temperature, so that the maximum current i at any absolute temperature T was governed by the law

$$i = A T^{1/2} e^{-w/(kT)} \quad \ldots \quad \ldots \quad \ldots \quad (1)$$

In this equation k is Boltzmann's constant *, and A and w are specific constants of the material. This equation was completely accounted for by the simple hypothesis that the freely moving electrons in the interior of the hot conductor escaped when they reached the surface provided that the part of their energy which depended on the component of the velocity normal to the surface was greater than the work function w.

"In 1903 I showed that the same conclusions could be drawn for sodium and more qualitatively for carbon. Further, that the differences of the work functions of different substances should be equal to their contact potential differences†, and the experimental values for platinum and sodium verified this. The results also verified the conclusion that the work functions for different elements should be of the same order of magnitude as $(1/2)\ (e^2/d)$,

---

* If the gas equation $pv = RT$ (p. 88) is written $pv = knT$, where n is the number of molecules present, then k is Boltzmann's constant; it has the value 1.381×10^{-16} erg per deg. C.

† The potential difference which exists between two different metals in contact (0.75 volts for copper and zinc); it varies with temperature.

where *e* is the electronic charge and *d* the radius of the atom, and also that it should vary roughly as the inverse cube root of the atomic volume. In the same year Wehnelt found that similar phenomena were exhibited by a large number of metallic oxides. The alkaline earths in particular had an exceptionally low work function and were in consequence very efficient emitters of electrons.

. . . . .

"The central idea which lies behind . . . equation (1) is that of an electron gas evaporating from the hot source. If this idea is correct, the thermionic currents should be able to flow against a small *opposing* electromotive force because the kinetic energy of the heat motion of the electron gas molecules, in other words the electrons, will carry some of them through it. Furthermore, we could at that time find out a great deal more about what the electrons in an electron gas were doing than we could about the molecules of an ordinary gas. Owing to the fact that they are electrically charged their motion can be controlled by an external electric field. By measuring the electronic current which flows against various directly opposing fields it is possible to ascertain the proportion of the emitted electrons which have a value of the component of their velocity perpendicular to the emitting surface between any assigned limits. . . .

. . . . .

"There were two other matters which required urgent investigation before the theory of electron emission could be regarded as securely founded. . . . If the electrons are really coming out of the hot body by virtue of their heat energy being able to overcome the work function *w*, the hot body should be cooled by this process. It is like the cooling of water by evaporation. I published a calculation of the magnitude of this effect in 1903, but the first experimental investigation was made by Wehnelt and Jentzsch in 1909. They observed a cooling effect, but the magnitude did not agree with the theory. In 1913 H. L. Cooke and I devised an improved experimental method of attacking this question, re-determined this cooling effect, and showed that it agreed with the value of the work function deduced from the variation of the thermionic currents with the temperature. Our conclusions have since been confirmed by . . . Davisson and Germer. . . .

"The other matter . . . is the converse of this. If a stream of electrons flows into a conductor from outside, there should be a development of heat which does not depend either on the temperature of these electrons or on the magnitude of the small potential differences used to drive them. H. L. Cooke and I devised and put into operation an apparatus for detecting and measuring this effect in 1910-1911. The results showed a satisfactory agreement with the value of the work function obtained by the other two methods.

"Despite the steadily accumulating mass of evidence to the contrary . . . the view had been fairly commonly held up to about 1913 that thermionic emission was not a physical phenomenon but a secondary effect of some chemical reaction between the hot body and the surrounding gas. The advent of ductile tungsten enabled me, in 1913, to get very big currents under better vacuum conditions than had hitherto been possible and to show that the mass of the electrons emitted exceeded the mass of the chemicals which could possibly be consumed. . . ."

Another problem in which Richardson became particularly interested was that of the emission of electricity as a result of chemical action. The history of this problem goes back to the last quarter of the eighteenth century. In 1781 Volta, in company with Antoine Lavoisier and Pierre Laplace, found that negative electrification was produced in the combustion of coal, in the effervescence of iron filings in dilute sulphuric acid, and even in the mere evaporation of water. They stood the vessels in which the experiments were carried out on an insulated metal plate connected by a wire to a condensing electroscope, an instrument invented shortly before by Volta: the electroscope acquired a negative charge. Volta gave a purely physical explanation of the phenomenon, supposing that, just as a substance in the vapour state has a greater capacity for the "calorific fluid" than in the solid or liquid state, so it also has a greater capacity for the "electric fluid"; that the vapour consequently withdraws electric fluid from the original substance, which is therefore, on the one-fluid theory, left negatively electrified. On the other hand, Claude Pouillet, who in 1827 found that the evaporation of water produced electrification only when a salt or some other body was present in solution, thought that chemical action played an essential part. Later, Carlo Matteucci (1800-1868) found that air which had passed over phosphorus acquired the power of discharging electrified bodies. It was not, however, until the closing years of the century that the subject received any sort of systematic investigation. Then, with the technique developed in the study of the ionization of gases, it was found that the gases liberated by chemical action, as well as those liberated in electrolysis, almost always contained positive ions. The conductivity of phosphorized air was found to be due to the presence in the air of ions of considerable size; that the ionization was due to chemical action was supported by the fact that no ions were produced when a chemically inactive gas was passed over the phosphorus.

It was natural that Richardson, whose fundamental work on the emission of electricity from hot bodies was done between 1900 and 1903, should next turn his attention to these other cases of ion-emission and should investigate particularly to what extent temperature changes influenced the phenomena. The results of the research were published in 1905 and showed that in the reaction between platinum and phosphorus vapour, which takes place energetically at 600°C, the platinum emits positive ions; that the rate of emission is increased if the platinum has previously been left cold in contact with phosphorus vapor.

Other cases of ion-emission were observed about this time by various investigators, but the emitted ions were always of at least atomic size and, except in a few cases of doubtful chemical origin, were positive. By 1909 no clear case of *electron*-emission purely as a result of chemical action had been established, but in that year Haber (q.v. *Chemistry,* 1918) and Just found that drops of the liquid alloy of sodium and potassium lost negative electricity when they reacted chemically with certain gases and vapours at low pressure, and they showed that the carriers of the electricity were electrons. This was as far as investigation had gone when Richardson, a year or so after his return to England, began a thorough study of the phenomenon at King's College, London. By painstaking experiments spread over a number of years—they were first described to the Royal Society in a paper read in the autumn of 1920—Richardson not only confirmed the emission of electrons in the cases examined by Haber and Just, but succeeded, where these investigators had failed, in deriving reliable quantitative information concerning the phenomenon, especially as regards the energy of the emitted electrons.

When Richardson took up his appointment at Princeton in 1906 the electron theory was still young, but even so J. J. Thomson had already suggested in 1904 that the atom might consist of electrons (*corpuscles*) revolving, not, as suggested in 1911 by Rutherford, about a positively charged nucleus, but in a sphere of uniform positive electrification (see p. 48). The first application of the electron theory to magnetism was made by Paul Langevin in a classical paper published in France the following year. Langevin's theory rendered more precise the generally accepted theory of magnetism which had been developed in the early 1850s by Wilhelm Weber, who followed up a suggestion made by Ampère shortly after the discovery of the magnetic effect of an electric current by Oersted in 1821. According to Weber's theory the molecules of a magnetic substance such as iron behave as minute magnets as a result of "molecular electric currents" circulating round them. Langevin replaced Weber's "molecular currents" by electrons describing closed orbits within the molecule. While Weber's theory accounted qualitatively for the phenomena of magnetism, Langevin's made quantitative deductions possible, since the mass and charge of the electron were known to a reasonable degree of accuracy.

(*) It was such a deduction that Richardson made in 1907—a deduction of particular interest, since its later experimental confirmation afforded strong independent evidence in support of the orbiting-electron theory of the atom on which it was based. He showed that, on the theory that the magnetic properties of bodies arise from the motions of the constituent electrons of their atoms, a freely suspended magnetic body such as a thin rod of iron, should, on being magnetised, experience a momentary twist purely as a result of the act of magnetisation; and he calculated the magnitude of this gyromagnetic effect in terms of the mass and charge of the electron.

(*) The following account is based on notes and references very kindly given me by Sir Owen Richardson.

The experimental detection of the effect was beset with difficulties: for one thing, it was essential that no external magnetic forces, such as that due to the earth's magnetic field, should act on the body, since the turning effect produced by an external field when the body was magnetised would mask the very much smaller effect being sought. When Richardson returned to England in 1914 the predicted effect had still not been detected experimentally. However, the search was not abandoned, for before leaving Princeton Richardson made arrangements for the experiments to be continued. Finally, in July 1917, John Q. Stewart was able to announce, in a paper published in the *Physical Review* for 1918, the successful outcome of these later experiments—but the magnitude of the effect was only half that predicted by Richardson.

In the meantime, shortly before Stewart began his final attack on the problem in the spring of 1915, Einstein and W. J. de Haas, unknown to Stewart, had succeeded by a less direct method in detecting and measuring this gyromagnetic effect, their value agreeing with that predicted by Richardson. The rather surprising result was that what had become known as the "Richardson Effect" now became known as the "Einstein-de Haas Effect." Richardson's calculations were based on the old mechanics; calculations based on the new quantum mechanics do actually give the value found experimentally by Stewart and also by S. J. Barnett, who, in 1914, had shown that a rotating cylinder of iron became magnetised, the converse of the Richardson effect.

CONSEQUENCES IN THEORY AND PRACTICE

Apart from the purely theoretical importance of Richardson's researches, his discoveries in connection with the emission of electricity by hot bodies have proved of the greatest importance technically: the thermionic valve, invented by Sir Ambrose Fleming, and so widely used in broadcasting today; the modern X-ray tube, in which the "cathode rays" are electrons evaporated from an electrically-heated tungsten filament; the cathode-ray oscillograph, the essential component of radar instruments and television sets—these are but a few examples of the many applications of thermionics.

1 9 2 9

PRINCE LOUIS-VICTOR DE BROGLIE
(1892–   )

"For his discovery of the wave nature of the electron."

BIOGRAPHICAL SKETCH

PRINCE LOUIS-VICTOR DE BROGLIE WAS BORN ON AUGUST 15, 1892, at Dieppe, France. He studied at the Lycée Janson de Sailly, Paris, and at the Sorbonne, where he obtained his L-ès-L in history in 1910. He then turned his attention to the physical sciences and in 1913 obtained his L-ès-Sc. He served in the army throughout the First World War, being attached to the wireless telegraphy section, in particular the wireless station at the Eiffel Tower.

After the war he returned to his scientific studies, specializing in theoretical physics, though at the same time taking considerable interest in experimental researches on X rays being carried on by his brother Maurice. In 1924 he obtained his D-ès-Sc for a thesis dealing with the quantum theory; this was the starting point for his later development of wave mechanics. In 1928 he was appointed professor of theoretical physics at the newly founded Henri Poincaré Institute at the Sorbonne. Since 1932 he has been professor at the Faculté des Sciences at the Sorbonne.

De Broglie has been a Member of the French Academy of Sciences since 1933, and Permanent Secretary since 1942. He was elected a Member of the French Academy in 1944.

DESCRIPTION OF THE PRIZE-WINNING WORK

Newton's corpuscular theory of light gave way at the beginning of the nineteenth century to the theory that light consists of transverse vibrations in a luminiferous ether. Toward the end of the century the discovery was made that ultraviolet light, falling on a metal plate, caused electrons to be ejected from the plate, and in 1902 Lenard, investigating this photoelectric effect, found that the energy of the electrons emitted was quite independent of the intensity of the incident light (p. 183). This result was very puzzling from the point of view of the wave theory. Einstein (q.v. 1921) gave the accepted explanation in 1905, but only by assuming that the incident light gave up its energy to the electrons in packets, each equal to $h\nu$, where h is Planck's constant and ν the frequency of the incident light. This in effect gave to light particle-like properties. Other phenomena, such as the Compton effect, discovered in 1923, could be readily explained on Einstein's semicorpuscular theory, but not on the wave theory; and the latter still had to be invoked to explain diffraction and interference. The two apparently irreconcilable theories thus existed side by side, light appearing to possess sometimes wave properties, sometimes particle properties, according to the phenomena under consideration.

Whatever difficulties had arisen in connection with the nature of light, that of matter was accepted, until well into the twentieth century, as presenting no problem apart from the nature of the ultimate particles of which it was supposed to consist. The electron and the proton were the building stones of which all matter was composed; atoms consisted of electrons revolving in planetary orbits about a nucleus made up of protons and electrons, the orbits and motions of the electrons being determined by certain quantum conditions. Though this theory proved remarkably successful in interpreting the results of observation, especially the spectra of the elements, by the early 1920's it was found to be in many respects inadequate.

Then, about 1923, de Broglie attacked the problem of the fundamental nature of matter from an entirely new angle. Just as Einstein had ascribed particle-like properties to light, so now de Broglie ascribed wavelike properties to particles of matter. He assumed that a particle, for instance an electron, has associated with it a system of "matter waves," and succeeded in representing the motion of the material particle as a combination of waves having slightly different velocities of propagation; at regular intervals along the line of propagation the waves would combine to form a wave-crest, the crest disappearing at one point to reappear an instant later at the next. The velocity of the crest—the so-called "group velocity"—is entirely different from the velocities of the various waves which combine to form the crest. De Broglie identified this group velocity with the velocity of the material particle; the distance between successive crests is the wave length of the "matter waves" and is known as the de Broglie wave length. Just as a wave is characterized by its wave length, so a moving particle is characterized by its momentum, i.e., mass $\times$ velocity (mv). De Broglie found that the wave length λ of the matter wave and the momentum mv of the associated particle were connected by the relation

$$\lambda = \frac{h}{mv}$$

where h is Planck's constant. For a slow electron moving at 100 cm. per sec., the de Broglie wave length is about 0.07 cm.; for an alpha particle emitted by radium it is about 7×10^{-13} cm., the order of magnitude of the diameter of an atomic nucleus.

The following extract, translated from the French of de Broglie's Nobel lecture*, gives an account of the considerations which led him to put forward his theory. It will probably be found helpful to read the extract from Schrödinger's Nobel lecture (p. 316) first.

"When in 1920 I resumed my studies . . . what attracted me . . . to theoretical physics was . . . the mystery in which the structure of matter and of radiation was becoming more and more enveloped as the strange concept of the quantum, introduced by

---

* By kind permission of Prince Louis de Broglie.

Planck in 1900 in his researches into black-body radiation, daily penetrated further into the whole of physics.

. . . . .

"For a long time physicists had been wondering whether light did not consist of minute corpuscles in rapid motion. This idea . . . was revived by Newton in the eighteenth century. After the discovery of the phenomenon of interference by Thomas Young and the wonderful work of Augustin Fresnel, the hypothesis of a corpuscular structure of light was entirely given up and the wave theory universally adopted. . . . But atomic theories, though expelled from optics, began to gain great success not only in chemistry . . . but also in the physics of matter, where they made it possible to explain a large number of the properties of solid, liquid, and gaseous bodies. In particular, they led to the construction of the wonderful kinetic theory of gases, which . . . has enabled a clear meaning to be given to the abstract concepts of thermodynamics. Experiments have also supplied decisive proofs in favor of an atomic constitution of electricity; thanks to Sir J. J. Thomson, the notion of a corpuscle of electricity made its appearance, and you all know to what advantage H. A. Lorentz put it in his theory of electrons.

"Thirty years ago, then, physics was divided into two camps: . . . the physics of matter, based on the concepts of particles and atoms which were supposed to obey the laws of classical Newtonian mechanics; [and] the physics of radiation, based on the idea of wave propagation in a hypothetical continuous medium, the luminous and electromagnetic ether. But these two systems of physics could not remain detached from each other: they had to be united by the formulation of a theory of exchanges of energy between matter and radiation. . . . In the attempt to bring the two systems of physics together, conclusions were in fact reached which were neither correct nor even admissible when applied to the energy equilibrium between matter and radiation in a thermally isolated enclosure. . . . Planck . . . instead of assuming, as was assumed in the classical wave theory, that a light source emits its radiation in a continuous manner, assumed that . . . it emits its radiation in equal and finite quantities—in quanta. The energy of each quantum had, moreover, a value proportional to the frequency ν of the radiation, being equal to $h\nu$, where h is a universal constant which has since become known as Planck's constant.

"The success of Planck's ideas has been accompanied by serious consequences. If light is emitted in quanta, must it not, once emitted, possess a corpuscular structure? The existence of quanta of radiation takes us back then to the corpuscular theory of light. On the other hand, it can be shown, as in fact Jeans and H. Poincaré did show, that if the motion of the material particles in a source of light took place according to the laws of classical mechanics, then the correct law of black-body radiation, Planck's law, could not be obtained. It must therefore be assumed that the old dynamics, even when modified by Einstein's relativity theory, cannot apply to motion on a very small scale.

"The existence of a corpuscular structure of light and other forms of radiation has been confirmed by the discovery of the photoelectric effect. If a beam of light or X rays is allowed to fall on a piece of matter, the latter ejects high-speed electrons. The kinetic energy of these electrons increases linearly with the frequency of the incident radiation and is independent of its intensity. This can be simply explained if we assume that the radiation consists of quanta $h\nu$ capable of giving up their whole energy to an electron belonging to the body irradiated. We are thus brought back to the theory of light quanta put forward by Einstein in 1905, which is, in short, a return to Newton's corpuscular theory supplemented by the proportionality relation between the energy of the corpuscles and the frequency. A number of arguments in support of his view were given by Einstein, and in 1922 the discovery by A. H. Compton of the scattering phenomenon of X rays . . . confirmed it. Yet it was still necessary to adopt the wave theory in order to explain interference and diffraction phenomena, and how to reconcile the wave theory with the existence of light corpuscles was by no means clear.

"As I have said, Planck's work had thrown doubts on the validity of classical mechanics when applied to very small scale phenomena. Picture a material point describing a small closed orbit—an orbit returning on itself. According to classical mechanics, an infinite number of such motions are possible, depending on the initial conditions, and the possible values of the kinetic energy form a continuous sequence. Planck, on the other hand, was led to assume that only certain preferential motions, *quantized* motions, are possible or at least stable, so that the energy is able to assume only values which form a discontinuous sequence. This idea appeared very strange at first, but its value had to be recognized, since it was this that had led Planck to the correct law of black-body radiation, and because it later proved its fruitfulness in many other fields. Finally, it was on this idea of the quantization of motion that Bohr based his famous theory of the atom. . . .

"The necessity for assuming two contradictory theories of light, the wave and the corpuscular; the impossibility of understanding why, among the infinite number of motions which, according to classical ideas, an electron ought to be able to possess, only certain ones were possible—such were the puzzles which confronted physicists at the time that I resumed my studies in theoretical physics.

"When I began to think about these difficulties, two things struck me particularly. On the one hand, the theory of light quanta could not be considered satisfactory, for it defined the energy of a light-corpuscle by the relation $W = h\nu$, in which the frequency ν occurs. Now a purely corpuscular theory does not contain any element permitting a frequency to be defined. If only for this reason, it is necessary in the case of light to introduce simultaneously the idea of a corpuscle and the idea of periodicity. On the other hand, the determination of the stable motions of the electron in the atom brings in whole numbers, and so far the only phenomena in physics where whole numbers come in are the phenomena of interference and of proper oscillations. This gave me the idea that electrons, too, could not be represented as simple corpuscles, but that to them also must be attributed a periodicity.

"Thus I arrived at the following general idea, which has guided my researches: for matter, just as much as for radiation, in particular light, we must introduce at one and the same time the corpuscle concept and the wave concept. In other words, in both cases we must assume the existence of corpuscles accompanied by waves. But corpuscles and waves cannot be independent, since,

according to Bohr, they are complementary to each other; consequently it must be possible to establish a certain parallelism between the motion of a corpuscle and the propagation of the wave
which is associated with it. The first thing to be done, then, was
to establish this correspondence."

[In the following paragraphs de Broglie tells how he worked
out this problem.]

"To do this, I began by considering the simplest case, that of an isolated
corpuscle, one removed from all external influence. With such a corpuscle we wish to associate a wave. Let us consider first a system of
reference with respect to which the corpuscle is motionless; this is the
"proper" system of the corpuscle in the sense of the relativity theory.
In this system the wave will be stationary, since the corpuscle is motionless; its phase will be the same at every point; it will be represented by
an expression of the form

$$\sin 2\pi\nu_0(t_0 - \tau_0)$$

where t_0 is the proper time of the corpuscle, and τ_0 is a constant.

"According to the principle of inertia, in every Galilean system the
corpuscle will have a uniform rectilinear motion. Let us consider such a
Galilean system and let the velocity of the particle in this system be
$v = \beta c$; there will be no loss of generality if we take the direction of
motion as the axis of x. The time t in this new system is, by the Lorentz
transformation, connected with the time t_0 by the relation

$$t_0 = \frac{t - \dfrac{\beta x}{c}}{\sqrt{1 - \beta^2}}$$

Consequently the phase of the wave will be given by

$$\sin 2\pi \frac{\nu_0}{\sqrt{1 - \beta^2}}\left(t - \frac{\beta x}{c} - \tau_0 \right)$$

and the wave will therefore have a frequency ν given by

$$\nu = \frac{\nu_0}{\sqrt{1 - \beta^2}}$$

and will be propagated in the direction of the x-axis with a phase
velocity V given by

$$V = \frac{c}{\beta} = \frac{c^2}{v}$$

By eliminating β between these two equations, the following relation defining the refractive index (n) in vacuo for the waves in question is easily obtained:

$$n = \sqrt{1 - (\nu_0^2/\nu^2)}$$

To this 'law of dispersion' there corresponds a 'group velocity' . . . with which the resultant amplitude of a group of waves of very nearly the same frequency is propagated. Lord Rayleigh has shown that this velocity U satisfies the equation

$$\frac{1}{U} = \frac{\partial(n\nu)}{\partial\nu}$$

in which U is found to be equal to v, that is to say, the group velocity of the waves is equal to the velocity of the corpuscle in this system [the system defined by the coordinates (x,y,z,t)]. This relation is of very great importance for the development of the theory.

"The corpuscle is thus defined in the system (x,y,z,t) by the frequency ν and the phase velocity V of its associated wave. To establish the parallelism of which we have spoken, we must look for a connection between these quantities and the mechanical quantities, energy and momentum. As the proportionality between energy and frequency is one of the most characteristic relations of the quantum theory and as, moreover, the frequency and the energy change in the same way when the Galilean reference system is changed, it is natural to put

$$\text{energy} = h \times \text{frequency}$$

or

$$W = h\nu$$

where h is Planck's constant. This relation must be valid in all Galilean systems, and in the proper system of the corpuscle, where the energy of the corpuscle reduces, according to Einstein, to its internal energy m_0c^2 (m_0 being the proper mass), we have

$$h\nu_0 = m_0c^2$$

This relation defines the frequency ν_0 as a function of the proper mass m_0, or conversely.

"The momentum p is equal to

$$\frac{m_0v}{\sqrt{1 - \beta^2}}$$

and we have

$$p = \frac{m_0v}{\sqrt{1 - \beta^2}} = \frac{Wv}{c^2} = \frac{h\nu}{V} = \frac{h}{\lambda}$$

The quantity λ is the distance between two consecutive crests of the wave, i.e., it is the wave length. Then

$$\lambda = \frac{h}{p}$$

This is the fundamental relation in the theory.

. . . . .

"The general formulas which establish the parallelism between waves and corpuscles can be applied to light-corpuscles if we assume that the proper mass m_0 is in this case infinitely small. If, in fact, for a given value of the energy W we make m_0 tend to zero, we find that v and V both tend to c and in the limit we obtain the two fundamental formulas on which Einstein established his theory of light-quanta:

$$W = h\nu$$

$$p = \frac{h\nu}{c}$$

"Such were the main ideas I developed in my first researches. They showed clearly that it was possible to establish a correspondence between waves and particles, such as the correspondence between the laws of mechanics and the laws of geometrical optics. But in the wave theory, geometrical optics . . . has its limits of validity and in particular, where the phenomena of interference and diffraction come in, it is altogether inadequate. This leads us to think that the old mechanics, too, is only an approximation in comparison with a wider mechanics of a wave nature. . . . This new mechanics has since been developed, thanks particularly to the fine work of Schrödinger."

CONSEQUENCES IN THEORY AND PRACTICE

De Broglie's work laid the foundations on which Schrödinger, Dirac, and others constructed the new system of wave mechanics which has proved so successful in dealing with problems of atomic physics. The theory of the wave nature of material particles received striking confirmation through the experiments of Davisson and Germer in New York and G. P. Thomson in Aberdeen, work for which Davisson and Thomson shared the Nobel Prize in Physics for 1937.

1 9 3 0

CHANDRASEKHARA VENKATA RAMAN
(1888–   )

*"For his work on the scattering of light and for
the discovery of the effect named after him."*

BIOGRAPHICAL SKETCH

CHANDRASEKHARA VENKATA RAMAN WAS BORN ON NOVEMBER
7, 1888, at Trichinopoly, southern India, his father being a teacher
in the S. P. G. College there. When Raman was four years old his
father was appointed a lecturer in physics in Vizagapatam; here
the next ten years of Raman's life were spent. In January 1902 he
entered the Presidency College at Madras, where he took his B.A.
degree in 1904, winning first place and the Gold Medal in physics;
he obtained his M.A., with the highest distinctions, in January
1907. In February of the same year he sat for the competitive examination for the Indian Finance Department and again secured
first place. In June 1907 he became assistant accountant general at
Calcutta.

The next ten years of his life were spent as an officer in the
Finance Department; he found time, however, to carry out experi-
mental research in the laboratory of the Indian Association for the
Cultivation of Science. His success attracted attention and when the
Palit Chair of Physics was endowed at Calcutta University, Raman
was invited to fill it. He held this post from 1917 until 1933, when

he became director of the Indian Institute of Science at Bangalore
(S. India). Since 1948 he has been director of the newly-founded
Raman Research Institute, Bangalore.

In 1919 Raman was appointed honorary secretary of the Indian
Association for the Cultivation of Science. In 1926 he founded,
and has since edited, the *Indian Journal of Physics*. He received an
Honorary D.Sc. from Calcutta University in 1922 and the Ph.D.
from Freiburg University in 1929. He was elected a Fellow of the
Royal Society of London in 1924; in 1928 he was awarded the
Matteucci Medal of the Italian Academy of Sciences. He was
knighted in 1929.

DESCRIPTION OF THE PRIZE-WINNING WORK

When light enters a darkened room through a hole in the
shutters, the light shows up, when viewed from the side, as a clearly
defined beam. This is because of the scattering of the incident light
by microscopic particles of dust in the air. The scattered light contains the same wave lengths as the incident light but not in the same
proportions, the short waves (blue light) being scattered more
than the long waves (red light). This was first demonstrated by
John Tyndall at the Royal Institution, London, in 1868. Tyndall
passed a beam of light from an arc lamp through a tube containing
air mixed with a small quantity of amyl nitrite vapor. Under the
action of the light, as Tyndall supposed, the amyl nitrite was precipitated as minute particles, so that a very fine cloud formed in
the tube. At first this cloud was of a delicate blue color; then, as
the particles increased in size, it became deep blue; finally, as the
particles became still larger, it assumed a whitish tinge. At first the
particles were so small that only the very short (blue) waves were
being scattered; with increase in the size of the particles, longer
and longer waves were scattered until all the constituents of white
light were present in the scattered light. This scattering of light
by minute particles was later investigated theoretically by Lord
Rayleigh (*q.v.* 1904), who followed Tyndall in ascribing the blue-
ness of the sky to the scattering of the short wave lengths to one
side; Rayleigh also explained the redness of the sky when the sun

is low in the heavens as being due to the scattering of all but the longest (red) wave lengths by the particles of the lower atmosphere, so that only the red light reached the eye of the observer. Rayleigh ascribed the scattering to molecules or groups of molecules in the atmosphere.

In 1925 H. A. Kramers and Heisenberg (*q.v.* 1932) predicted that when the incident light consisted of a number of monochromatic radiations, the scattered light should contain other wave lengths besides those present in the incident light; so far, however, there was no experimental evidence to support the prediction. At the same time Raman and his collaborators at the University of Calcutta were investigating molecular scattering experimentally, and in 1928 they found that when the intense light from a mercury-arc lamp was scattered by the molecules of a suitable liquid, the spectrum of the scattered light showed, in addition to the original lines, other, much weaker, lines that were not present in the spectrum of the incident light. In the following extracts * from his Nobel lecture Raman tells how he was led to take up the study of molecular scattering and how he came to make his discovery.

"1. *The Colour of the Sea.* . . . A voyage to Europe in the summer of 1921 gave me the first opportunity of observing the wonderful blue opalescence of the Mediterranean Sea. It seemed not unlikely that the phenomenon owed its origin to the scattering of sunlight by the molecules of the water. To test this explanation, it appeared desirable to ascertain the laws governing the diffusion of light in liquids, and experiments with this object were started immediately on my return to Calcutta in September, 1921. It soon became evident, however, that the subject possessed a significance extending far beyond the special purpose for which the work was undertaken, and that it offered unlimited scope for research. . . . the study of light-scattering . . . [became] the main theme of our activities at Calcutta from that time onwards.

"2. *The Theory of Fluctuations.* From the work of the first few months, it became clear that the molecular scattering of light was a very general phenomenon which could be studied not only in gases and vapours but also in liquids and in crystalline and

---

* Quoted by kind permission of Sir C. V. Raman.

amorphous solids, and that it was primarily an effect arising from molecular dis-array in the medium and consequent local fluctuations in its optical density. Except in amorphous solids, such molecular dis-array could presumably be ascribed to thermal agitation, and the experimental results appeared to support this view. The fact that molecules are optically anisotropic and can orientate freely in liquids was found to give rise to an additional type of scattering. This could be distinguished from the scattering due to fluctuations in density by reason of its being practically unpolarized, whereas the latter was completely polarized in the transverse direction.

· · · · ·

"4. *A New Phenomenon.* The investigations referred to above were in the main guided by the classical electromagnetic theory of light, the application of which to the problems of light-scattering is chiefly associated with the names of Rayleigh and Einstein. Nevertheless, the possibility that the corpuscular nature of light might come into evidence in scattering was not overlooked and was . . . [discussed in an essay] published at least a year before the well-known discoveries of Compton on X-ray scattering. While our experiments in the main appeared to support the electromagnetic theory of light, evidence came to hand at a very early stage of the investigations of the existence of a phenomenon which seemed to stand outside the classical scheme of thought. The scattering of light in transparent fluids is extremely feeble, much weaker in fact than the Tyndall effect usually observed in turbid media. It was experimentally discovered that associated with the Rayleigh-Einstein type of molecular scattering was another and still feebler type of secondary radiation, the intensity of which was of the order of magnitude of a few hundredths of the classical scattering and differed from it in not having the same wave-length as the primary or incident radiation. The first observation of this phenomenon was made at Calcutta in April 1923 by Ramanathan who was led to it in attempting to explain why in certain liquids (water, ether, methyl and ethyl alcohols) the depolarisation of scattered light varied with the wave-length of the incident radiation. Ramanathan found that after exhaustive chemical purification and repeated slow distillation of the liquid in vacuum, the new radiation persisted undiminished in intensity, showing that it was a characteristic property of the substance studied and not due to any fluorescent impurity. Krishnan observed a similar effect in many other liquids in 1924, and a somewhat more conspicuous phenomenon was observed by me in ice and optical glasses.

"5. *The Optical Analogue of the Compton Effect.* The origin of this puzzling phenomenon naturally interested us, and in the summer of 1925 Venkateswaran attempted to investigate it by photographing the spectrum of the scattered light from liquids, using sunlight filtered through colour screens, but was unable to report any decisive results. . . . This problem was taken up again by Krishnan towards the end of 1927. While his work was in progress, the first indication of the true nature of the phenomenon came to hand from a different quarter. One of the problems interesting us at this time was the behaviour in light-scattering of highly viscous organic liquids which were capable of passing over into the glassy state. Venkateswaran undertook to study this question, and reported . . . that the colour of sunlight scattered in a highly-purified sample of glycerine was a brilliant green instead of the usual blue. The phenomenon appeared to be similar to that discovered by Ramanathan in water and the alcohols, but of much greater intensity, and, therefore, more easily studied. . . . Tests were made with a series of filters transmitting narrow regions of the solar spectrum and placed in the path of the incident beam, which showed that in every case the colour of the scattered light was different from that of the incident light, and was displaced from it towards the red. The radiations were also strongly polarized. These facts indicated a clear analogy between the empirical characters of the phenomenon and the Compton effect. The work of Compton had made familiar the idea that the wave-length of radiation could be degraded in the process of scattering, and the observations with glycerine suggested to me that the phenomenon which had puzzled us ever since 1923 was in fact the optical analogue of the Compton effect. This idea naturally stimulated further investigation with other substances.

"The chief difficulty . . . in the study of the new phenomenon was its extreme feebleness in general. This was overcome by using a 7-inch refracting telescope in combination with a short-focus lens to condense sunlight into a pencil of very great intensity. . . .

. . . . .

"Thanks to the vastly more powerful illumination . . . the spectroscopic examination of the effect . . . now came within the reach of direct visual study. With a Zeiss cobalt-glass filter placed in the path of the incident beam, and one or other of a series of organic liquids as the scattering substance, a band in the blue-green region was observed by me in the spectrum of the scattered light, separated by a dark interval from the indigo-violet region transmitted by the filter. *Both* of these regions in the spectrum became sharper when the region of transmission was narrowed by the insertion of an additional filter in the incident beam. This suggested the employment, instead of sunlight, of the highly monochromatic radiations given by a mercury arc in combination with a condenser of large aperture and a cobalt-glass filter. With these arrangements, the spectrum of the scattered light from a variety of liquids and solids was visually examined, and the startling observation was made that the spectrum generally included a number of sharp lines or bands on a diffuse background which were not present in the light of the mercury arc.

"The quartz mercury lamp was so powerful and convenient a source of monochromatic illumination that, at least in the case of liquids and solids, photographing the spectrum of scattered light was found to present no extraordinary difficulties. The earliest pictures of the phenomenon were in fact taken with a portable quartz spectrograph of the smallest size made by the firm of Hilger. With a somewhat larger instrument of the same type, Krishnan obtained very satisfactory spectrograms with liquids and with crystals on which measurements of the desired precision could be made, and on which the presence of lines displaced towards the violet was first definitely established. . . .

"In interpreting the observed phenomena, the analogy with the Compton effect was adopted as the guiding principle. The work of Compton had gained general acceptance for the idea that the scattering of radiation is a unitary process in which the conservation principles hold good. Accepting this idea it follows at once that, if the scattering particle gains any energy during the encounter with the quantum, the latter is deprived of energy to the same extent, and accordingly appears after scattering as a radiation of diminished frequency. From thermodynamic principles it follows that the reverse process should also be possible. Adopting these ideas, the actual observations could be interpreted, and the agreement of the observed displacements with the infra-red frequencies of the molecules made it clear that the new method opened up an illimitable field of experimental research in the study of the structure of matter."

According to the Bohr theory an atom emits radiation when an electron jumps from one stationary orbit to another of lower energy; similarly, absorption of radiation is accompanied by a jump on the part of an electron from one orbit to another of higher energy. To each of the possible transitions there corresponds a definite line in the spectrum of the substance, the frequency of the emitted line being equal to the difference in the energy possessed by the electron in the two orbits divided by Planck's constant (p. 199). Incoming radiation can be absorbed by the atom only if its light-quantum, $h\nu$, where ν is the frequency, is identical with the energy difference between two orbits, i.e., is equal to a light quantum the atom is capable of emitting.

The Raman effect is in conflict with this theory as it stands, since light of one frequency is absorbed by the scattering atoms, whereas light of several different frequencies is emitted. According to what we have said above, when a light-quantum $h\nu$ falls on an atom, the atom can absorb the quantum only if this is equal to the energy difference between two electronic orbits, and the atom can emit only this same quantum of energy $h\nu$ when the electron returns to its original lower-energy orbit. Yet in the Raman effect, where a quantum $h\nu$ was absorbed, a quantum $h\nu_1$, say, is emitted. The explanation was given by Raman himself. It is this: when light of frequency ν emitted by the radiating substance falls on the atoms or molecules of the scattering substance, the light-quantum $h\nu$ corresponding to this frequency will be absorbed and a light-quantum $h\nu_1$ emitted if the *difference* between ν and ν_1 is equal to one of the frequencies which the atom or molecule of the substance is capable of emitting; radiation of frequency ν_1 will also be emitted if the *sum* of ν and ν_1 is a possible frequency for the scattering atom or molecule to emit.

CONSEQUENCES IN THEORY AND PRACTICE

The Raman effect has proved of the greatest importance in the study of molecular structure. Owing to the relatively low frequencies of rotation and vibration of a molecule, the spectra due to these motions often lie in the far infrared, outside the visible spectrum; but the Raman spectrum of the light scattered by the molecule lies in the visible region, in the neighborhood of the spectral line due to the incident light. From spectroscopic examination of the Raman spectrum deductions can then be drawn as to the structure of the molecule. For example, the molecule of nitrous oxide, the "laughing gas" used by dentists as an anesthetic, has the formula N_2O—two nitrogen atoms combined with one oxygen atom. Evidence from various sources, including X-ray measurements, shows that the three atoms are arranged in the form of a short rod, thus •—•—•. The question then arises: Is the arrangement symmetrical (N-O-N) or asymmetrical (N-N-O)? Now the Raman spectrum for a symmetrical molecule differs from that for an asymmetrical molecule, and in the case of nitrous oxide decides in favor of N-N-O. The structure of more complicated molecules can be elucidated in the same way.

1 9 3 1

No award

1 9 3 2

WERNER KARL HEISENBERG

(1901–   )

"For the creation of quantum mechanics, the application of which has led, among other things, to the discovery of the allotropic forms of hydrogen."

BIOGRAPHICAL SKETCH

WERNER KARL HEISENBERG WAS BORN ON DECEMBER 5, 1901, at Duisburg, near Düsseldorf, Germany, where his father, later a university professor, was at that time *privatdozent*. Heisenberg attended school in Munich, and in 1920 entered Munich University, where he studied theoretical physics under Arnold Sommerfeld. He obtained his doctor's degree in 1923 and then became assistant to Max Born at Göttingen, being appointed a lecturer there the following year. From 1924 to 1925 he studied under Bohr (*q.v.* 1922) at Copenhagen, where he became a lecturer in 1926. In 1927, however, he returned to Germany as professor of theoretical physics at the University of Leipzig. From 1942 to 1945 he was director of the Max Planck Institute at Berlin and professor at the university. He is now director of the Max Planck Institute for Physics at Göttingen.

DESCRIPTION OF THE PRIZE-WINNING WORK

By 1925 Heisenberg must have been particularly well versed in quantum theory and its applications to the problems of atomic physics. He had studied under Sommerfeld and been assistant to Born, both of whom had made major contributions to the subject. Not only that, but he had spent a year at Copenhagen with Bohr, the originator of the then generally accepted theory of the atom. This theory, in spite of its remarkable successes in the case of the hydrogen atom, had so far proved wanting when attempts were made to apply it to more complicated atoms, and by the early 1920's it had become clear that some drastic change in the method of approach to the problem of atomic structure was required. Then in 1924 de Broglie (*q.v.* 1929) put forward his novel theory of matter waves, on which Schrödinger and Dirac (*q.v.* 1933) built their wave mechanics. About the same time Heisenberg was attacking the problem from an entirely different angle. In the Bohr-Sommerfeld theory the atom was pictured as consisting of one or more electrons revolving round a nucleus; de Broglie replaced the particle electron by a matter wave.

In Heisenberg's view the Bohr theory failed because it was based on things which were not directly observable, such as electrons moving in orbits. He held that any theory of the atom must be based on such physical quantities as are directly open to observation, such *observables* being in the first instance the frequencies and intensities of the spectral lines emitted by atoms and molecules. In the system of atomic mechanics which he built up these directly observable quantities took the place of the hypothetical electron orbits in the older theory, pictorial representations of the atom being dispensed with altogether. Just as Einstein found the tool he needed in the mathematical analysis developed by Levi-Civita, so Heisenberg found his in matrix algebra; hence his system of quantum mechanics is generally known as *matrix mechanics,* to distinguish it from wave mechanics.

Heisenberg's theory not only gave the same results as Bohr's theory where the latter agreed with observation, but it also accounted for a number of observational facts not covered by the older theory. It dealt with *systems* rather than individuals, and so could be applied to molecules as well as to atoms. In 1925 Uhlenbeck and Goudsmit had explained certain features in atomic spectra by assuming that the electron possessed spin properties; now, in 1927, Heisenberg applied the new mechanics—by this time

Schrödinger had shown that matrix mechanics and wave mechanics were in fact equivalent—to explain alternations of strong and weak lines in the spectra emitted by diatomic molecules such as hydrogen. He showed that two forms of hydrogen molecule should exist, one (*ortho*hydrogen) in which the spins of the two separate hydrogen atom nuclei (protons) were in the same direction, the other (*para*hydrogen) in which they were in opposite directions; orthohydrogen is the ordinary form and Heisenberg showed that it should be three times more abundant than parahydrogen. Experimental evidence for the existence of these two forms of hydrogen molecule was found later (1929). Orthohydrogen and parahydrogen are the allotropic forms of hydrogen referred to in the citation for the Nobel Prize.

One extremely important deduction which Heisenberg made (1927) was that of the *uncertainty principle,* according to which there are limits to the accuracy with which certain atomic occurrences can be known. These limits are not imposed entirely by the imperfections of our senses and measuring instruments, but are inherent in the very nature of atomic phenomena. Thus, even if it were possible to observe the motion of an electron in its orbit, it would be quite impossible to determine simultaneously the position and the momentum (mass $\times$ velocity) of the particle with a degree of accuracy greater than that given by the uncertainty relation (p. 310), since the means used to enable the observation to be made—radiation of extremely short wave length—must necessarily affect the motion being determined. This principle introduces an element of uncertainty into all determinations on the atomic scale. In the following passage, translated from the German of his Nobel lecture*, Heisenberg discusses some of its implications.

". . . In classical physics, a problem was considered solved when a certain process had been established as occurring objectively in space and time, and when it had been shown to obey the general laws of classical physics as formulated by differential equations. It was quite immaterial in what way the knowledge of that process had been acquired and by what observations the process had been established experimentally. Likewise it was completely in-

* By kind permission of Professor Heisenberg.

different for classical theory, by what observations the predictions of the theory were to be verified. In quantum theory, however, we face a completely different situation. The formalism * of quantum mechanics cannot be translated into a visualizable picture of processes occurring in space and time. This very fact shows that quantum mechanics does not deal at all with the objective description of space-time events. The formalism of quantum mechanics is, rather, to be used so that, from the complex of experimental data concerning an atomic system, a conclusion is drawn as to the probability of the outcome of another experiment (provided that the system undergoes no perturbations other than those necessary for the two experiments).

"From the experimental determination of the system, be it as complete as possible, only the probability for a certain result of the second experiment is known; after completion of the second experiment, however, a definite result is known. This fact shows that every observation must lead to a discontinuous change in the formalism describing the atomic process, and therefore also result in a discontinuous change in the physical process itself. Whereas in classical theory the kind of observation is immaterial to the course of the process, in quantum theory the perturbation necessarily connected with any observation of the atomic processes plays a decisive part. Since, moreover, the result of an observation in general leads only to assertions as to the probability of definite results of later observations, the part of that perturbation which is in principle uncontrollable must, as Bohr has pointed out, be decisive for the consistent formulation of quantum mechanics. This difference between classical physics and atomic physics is quite understandable: for heavy bodies, such as the planets revolving round the sun, the pressure of the sunlight reflected on their surface and necessary for their observation does not play any part. For the smallest particles of matter, however, any observation involves a decisive interference with their physical behavior, on account of the smallness of their masses.

"Moreover, the perturbation due to the act of observation of the system is essential for fixing the limits within which a visualizable

---

* It has become customary in the literature of modern physics to use the word "formalism" to denote the mathematical structure of a physical theory.

description of atomic processes is possible. Suppose there were experiments which made possible a precise determination of all the data of an atomic system required for the calculation of the classical motion, e.g., experiments which would yield accurate values for position and velocity of every electron in the system at a definite time. The results of these experiments could not at all be used in the formalism; such a procedure would rather contradict the formalism directly. Here again it is the essentially uncontrollable part of the perturbation of the system due to the observation itself which prevents a precise determination of the data required to fix the classical behavior and so makes possible the application of quantum mechanics. A closer examination of the formalism shows that there exists a relation between the accuracy with which the position of a particle can be fixed and the accuracy with which, simultaneously, its momentum can be known: the product of the probable errors in position and momentum measurements is always at least as great as Planck's constant divided by 4π. More generally, this relationship is expressed by

$$\Delta p \cdot \Delta q \geqslant \frac{h}{4\pi}$$

where p and q are canonically conjugate variables. These uncertainty relations for the results of the measurements of classical quantities constitute the necessary condition for the possibility of expressing the result of a measurement within the formalism of quantum theory. Bohr has shown, by a series of examples, how the perturbation necessarily connected with every observation does in fact ensure that the limits imposed by the uncertainty relations cannot be exceeded. The fact that a part of this perturbation remains in principle unknown is, according to Bohr, ultimately due to an uncertainty which is introduced by the concept of measurement itself. The experimental determination of any process in space and time always presupposes a fixed frame to which all measurements are referred (say the coordinate system in which the observer is at rest). By the assumption that this frame is 'fixed' we renounce from the outset any knowledge of its momentum; for the very meaning of 'fixed' is that transfers of momentum do not produce any noticeable effect on the frame. The uncertainty necessary in principle at this stage spreads then via the measuring apparatus to the atomic process.

"In this situation it might be suggested that all uncertainties could be eliminated by combining object, measuring apparatus, and observer into one quantum-mechanical system. It is therefore important to emphasize that the act of measurement is necessarily visualizable, since, ultimately, physics is always concerned with the description by natural laws of processes happening in space and time. Thus the behavior of the observer as well as his measuring apparatus must be discussed according to the laws of classical physics, since otherwise we should not be dealing with a physical problem at all. Inside the measuring apparatus therefore, as Bohr has emphasized, every event is considered to be determined in the classical sense. This is also the necessary condition for the possibility of drawing, from the results of a measurement, an unambiguous conclusion as to what has taken place. Classical physics objectifies the results of observations by presupposing processes in space and time governed by natural laws. This scheme is therefore carried into quantum theory up to the point where it meets its fundamental limitation imposed by the nonvisualizable feature of atomic processes, symbolized by Planck's constant. A visualizable description of atomic processes is possible within certain limits of accuracy—but within those limits the laws of classical physics always hold. Moreover, by reason of the limits defined by the uncertainty relations, the visualizable representation of an atom is not determined uniquely. The visualizable description may be equally well based on either the corpuscular or the wave picture.

"The laws of quantum mechanics are in principle of a statistical nature. If all measurable quantities of an atomic system are determined by an experiment, the result of a future observation of the system cannot, in general, be predicted accurately. There are, however, at any later time certain observations whose results can be predicted accurately. As to other observations, only the probability of a certain outcome of an experiment can be stated. The degree of certainty which is still inherent in the laws of quantum mechanics leads to the conservation laws for energy and momentum still being strictly valid. They may be tested to any desired degree of accuracy, and they then hold to the degree of accuracy to which

they have been tested. The statistical character of quantum mechanical laws expresses itself, however, in the fact that an exact
investigation of the energy transfers excludes the simultaneous
tracing of the process in space and time."

CONSEQUENCES IN THEORY AND PRACTICE

In the hands of Heisenberg, Schrödinger, de Broglie, Pauli,
Born, Dirac, and others, the new quantum mechanics has pro-
foundly influenced the development of atomic and nuclear physics.
It is the indispensable tool of all who are engaged in theoretical
research in this field.

1 9 3 3

ERWIN SCHRÖDINGER
(1887–   )

PAUL ADRIEN MAURICE DIRAC
(1902–   )

"For the discovery of new and fruitful forms of atomic theory."

BIOGRAPHICAL SKETCH

SCHRÖDINGER

ERWIN SCHRÖDINGER WAS BORN ON AUGUST 12, 1887, IN Vienna. He was taught at home until he was eleven, then at the *Gymnasium*. From 1906 to 1910 he studied at the University of Vienna; here he was greatly influenced by Professor Fritz Hasenöhrl, professor of theoretical physics. In 1911 Schrödinger became an assistant in the Physics Department. During the First World War, in which his friend Hasenöhrl was killed, he served as an artillery officer on the southwest front.

In 1920 he went to Jena as assistant to Max Wien, who needed someone with a knowledge of the new theories. After one semester at Jena, Schrödinger spent a semester at Stuttgart as professor extraordinary, followed by another at Breslau as full professor. For the next six years he was professor at Zurich. In 1928 he succeeded Max Planck (*q.v.* 1918) as professor of theoretical physics at Berlin. Since 1940 he has been professor at the Dublin Institute for Advanced Studies.

Both the National University of Ireland and the University of Dublin conferred Honorary D.Sc. degrees on Schrödinger in 1940; the Royal Society of London elected him a Foreign Member in 1949.

DESCRIPTION OF THE PRIZE-WINNING WORK

SCHRÖDINGER

The highly mathematical nature of the researches of Schrödinger and Dirac makes their work unsuitable for discussion in any detail here; all that can be done is to attempt to give some general idea of their "new and fruitful forms of atomic theory."

The Bohr hydrogen atom, with its single electron, a material point, revolving about a heavy nucleus in any one of a number of possible stationary orbits, can easily be visualized. In only two respects does the Bohr atom fail to comply with Newtonian mechanics: in the assumptions that the electron (a) is restricted to certain discrete orbits, and (b) does not radiate as long as it remains in any given orbit, radiation being emitted or absorbed only when the electron makes a jump from one orbit to another. Moreover, the frequency of the radiation is neither that of the initial nor that of the final orbital frequency. How an electron describing one orbit can suddenly appear in another the theory makes no attempt to explain, any more than it explains the quantum conditions which govern the motion of the electron, for instance that only certain discrete values of the angular momentum are possible. In a sense the Bohr atom is a pictorial embodiment of a mass of data derived mainly from the study of spectra. It is a remarkable thing that by making suitable adjustments in the picture, for instance by introducing elliptical orbits and by imposing quantum conditions on the ratio of the major to the minor axis, it has proved possible to cover so much additional data.

How much of physical reality underlies the picture is quite another matter. In many respects the Bohr atom seems too intricate to be really convincing *as a picture of reality,* however excellent it may be as a novel kind of graph. Our ideas of what goes on in the subatomic world must be entirely based on deductions from observed results, and these ideas naturally tend to present themselves under the guise of familiar, often rather naive, pictures. It needed a venturous de Broglie (*q.v.* 1929) to break away from the familiar picture and put forward an idea utterly at variance with all our previous notions of the nature of matter—"matter waves"; and it needed a Schrödinger to work out the full consequences of the theory.

In order that a wave may be set up it is necessary that *something* should go through a series of periodic changes; the something is not necessarily a material object such as a vibrating point in a stretched string; it may be the pressure at a point in a column of air or the intensity at a point in an electric field. In addition, the disturbance must be passed on to neighboring points in the medium in question: the string, the air, or the ether. In de Broglie's theory of matter waves the question naturally arises, What is it that oscillates? The question cannot be answered, nor is an answer really necessary, as was shown by Schrödinger, who became interested in de Broglie's matter waves as soon as he came to know of them, about 1925. Schrödinger simply denoted the oscillating quantity by the Greek letter ψ and then proceeded to construct a differential equation representing the wave motion set up by the oscillations of ψ, just as differential equations exist for the displacement of a point in a vibrating string, the pressure in a vibrating column of air, or the intensity in an oscillating field. De Broglie's relation connecting the wave length of the matter wave and the momentum of the associated particle (p. 289) played an essential part in the derivation of Schrödinger's equation.

The wave theory of matter was applied with striking success to the problem of atomic structure, initially by de Broglie, more rigorously by Schrödinger. Whereas in the Bohr theory details of the theory had to be repeatedly adjusted to fit the facts, in the de Broglie-Schrödinger theory the facts emerge from the theory.

Some idea of the way in which the Bohr electron is replaced by the de Broglie matter wave may be gained by picturing an endless wave circulating round the nucleus, a wave whose wave length is an exact submultiple of the length of the orbit.* Such a standing wave corresponds to what in Bohr's theory had been called a stationary state of the atom, and had been regarded as the only "allowed" kind of state. In the wave theory this distinction disappears because waves can be superposed. There is no need to assume jump-like transitions, yet the discrete emission and absorption frequencies are quantitatively accounted for, and that in a very natural way. While in Bohr's theory they had nothing to do with the orbital frequencies, in the wave theory each of them is the *difference* of the frequencies of two standing waves. It is natural to think that a light-wave, whose frequency is equal to this difference, is emitted or absorbed whilst the amplitudes of the two standing waves change gradually, one increasing at the expense of the other. This consideration also leads to a correct estimate of the intensities of the spectral lines, in particular when the "natural" lines are split into many components under the action of an external electric field (the action of a magnetic field could not be correctly accounted for before Dirac's discovery of his wave equation, which included the magnetic properties of the electron).

In the following extracts, translated from the German of his Nobel lecture†, Schrödinger shows how the conventional *rays* of light used in geometrical optics are adequate for dealing with large-scale optical phenomena (reflection, refraction), but have to be replaced by *waves* of light when we are dealing with small-scale phenomena (diffraction, interference); in the same way, the old mechanics has had to be replaced by the new (wave) mechanics when minute mechanical systems are in question.

"When a ray of light passes through an optical instrument, such as a telescope or a photographic objective, it suffers a change of direction at each refracting or reflecting surface. The path of the ray can be constructed if the two simple laws governing the change of direction are known: the law of refraction . . . and the law of reflection. . . .

.   .   .   .   .

---

* Professor Schrödinger very kindly rewrote the rest of this paragraph.
† By kind permission of Professor Schrödinger.

"Fermat summarized the whole course of the ray of light from a much more general point of view. Light traverses different media with different velocities, and the path of the ray is such that the light seems set on reaching its destination *as quickly as possible.* . . . The slightest deviation from the path actually taken would mean a delay. This is Fermat's famous *principle of least time.* . . . The earth's atmosphere provides an example. The deeper a ray coming from outside penetrates into the atmosphere, the slower it travels as the air increases in density. Even though the changes in the velocity of propagation are only extremely small, Fermat's principle still requires that . . . the ray of light should curve toward the earth, so that it remains somewhat longer in the upper 'faster' layers and comes more quickly to its destination than by the shorter direct path. I expect you have all noticed that the sun, when it is low on the horizon, appears flattened instead of round . . . This is a result of the bending of the rays.

"On the wave theory of light, rays of light have only a fictitious meaning. They are not physical paths of any sort of light particles, but only a mathematical aid, the so-called orthogonal trajectories of the wave surfaces, imaginary guide lines, as it were, showing at each point the direction, at right angles to the wave surface, in which the latter is advancing. . . . It is surprising that so general a principle as Fermat's should be expressed in terms of these mathematical lines and not in terms of wave surfaces, and one might for this reason be inclined to regard the principle merely as a mathematical curiosity. But . . . it is only from the standpoint of the wave theory that Fermat's principle is really understandable. . . . For from the standpoint of the wave theory the so-called *bending* of the light rays is much more readily understandable as a *swinging round* of the wave surface, such as must result if adjacent parts of the wave surface advance at different speeds. . . .

· · · · ·

"Thus Fermat's principle plainly appears as the *quintessence* of the wave theory. It was therefore a really remarkable thing when Hamilton happened to make the discovery that the actual motion of point masses in a field of force—for example, that of a planet in its path round the sun or of a stone thrown in the earth's gravitational field—is also governed by an exactly similar general principle. . . . Hamilton's principle does not, it is true, assert exactly this, that the point mass chooses the quickest path, but still something *so* similar—the analogy with the principle of shortest time is *so* close—that it was puzzling. It appeared as if Nature had put into operation one and the same law twice over, but in entirely different ways: once with light by means of a fairly understandable wave motion, a second time with point masses, in which case it is by no means understandable unless some sort of wave motion is ascribed to them also. At first that seemed out of the question, since the 'point masses' on which the laws of mechanics had actually been experimentally confirmed were at that time only large visible bodies, some *very* large, such as the planets, for which anything like a wave motion did not seem to come into question.

"The smallest ultimate building stones of matter, which we today in a much truer sense call 'point masses,' were at that time something still purely hypothetical. Only in connection with the discovery of radioactivity did a constant refinement in methods of measurement lead to the possibility of studying the properties of these corpuscles or particles in detail; today we can photograph and measure the paths of such particles very exactly by the ingenious method devised by C. T. R. Wilson. As far as measurements go, they confirmed that the same mechanical laws are valid for the particles as for large bodies such as the planets. For the rest, it turned out that . . . the atom itself is a very complicated system. We began to form mental pictures of the atom as composed of particles, pictures which presented a certain likeness to the planetary system. It was natural that at first attempts were made to apply the same laws of motion that had been so marvelously confirmed for larger bodies. That is to say, Hamiltonian mechanics, which, as I have just said, culminated in Hamilton's principle, was applied also to the processes occurring within the atom. That Hamilton's principle bears a very close analogy to Fermat's optical principle had in the meantime been almost forgotten.

". . . [Fermat's] principle cannot in itself do away with the need for detailed study of the wave processes. The so-called diffraction and interference of light can only be understood as a result of such detailed study, since they depend not only on the point finally reached by the wave, but also upon whether at a given instant a crest or a trough of the wave arrives there. With the older, cruder, experimental methods these phenomena escaped observation. As soon, however, as they were noticed and had been correctly explained on the wave theory, it was easy to devise experiments which brought out the wave nature of light both in its finer details and in its broad general character.

"Let me illustrate this by two examples, taking first an optical instrument such as the telescope or microscope. The aim with these instruments is to produce a sharp image, that is, that all the rays coming from a point object should be brought together again in a point, the so-called point image. At first it was thought that the only difficulties in the way were those of geometrical optics, which in any case are great enough. It later became evident that even with the best-constructed instruments the extent to which the rays could be brought together fell considerably short of what was to be expected if each ray really exactly followed Fermat's principle, independently of its nearest neighbors. Light coming from a point object and received by an instrument is not brought together again in a point behind the instrument, but is spread over a small circular area, a so-called diffraction pattern. . . . The cause of . . . diffraction is this, that the whole spherical wave leaving the point object cannot be received by the instrument. The edges of the lenses and the possible diaphragms cut out only a portion of the wave surface and . . . the injured edges of the wound prevent the strict coming together at a point and produce an indistinct and fuzzy image. The fuzziness is most intimately connected with the *wave length* of the light and is therefore, for theoretical reasons, completely unavoidable. . . . it governs and limits the efficiency of the modern microscope, in which all other defects of the image have been completely overcome. If the object is comparable in size with the wave length of the light, we obtain images that bear little likeness, or none at all, to the original.

"A second, still simpler, example is provided by the shadow of an opaque object thrown on a screen by a point source of light. To construct the shape of the shadow we have to follow the course of each ray of light and see whether the opaque object prevents it from reaching the screen or not. The *edge* of the shadow is formed by those rays of light which just graze the edges of the body in passing. Now it is found from experience that the edge of the shadow is not really sharp, even with a point source of light and when the object throwing the shadow has a sharply defined boundary. The explanation is the same as in the previous case. The wave front is, so to say, cut in two by the body (Fig. 5) [Fig. 33], and the marks of the injury result in a lack of sharpness in the edges of the shadow; this would be unintelligible if the individual rays of light

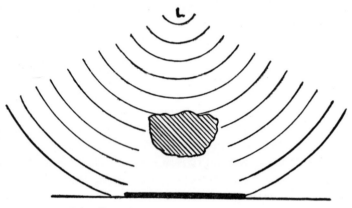

FIG. 33   *Schrödinger's Fig. 5*
[A wave front broken by an obstacle in its path.]

were independent realities advancing independently of one another and without interfering with one another.

"The phenomenon—it, too, is known as diffraction—is not in general very marked with larger bodies. But if the body throwing the shadow has at least one of its dimensions very small, then the diffraction manifests itself first in this, that in general no true shadow is produced; secondly—and this is much more striking—the small body becomes as it were self-luminous and radiates light in all directions, though chiefly in directions making small angles with the incident light. . . . the so-called 'dust motes' in the path of a beam of light entering a dark room; . . . or the loose hair on the head of a person standing against the sun . . . gleam wonderfully in the diffracted light. The visibility of smoke and cloud is due to the same cause. It does not really arise from the body itself, but from the immediate surroundings, where a considerable disturbance occurs in the incident wave front. It is interesting and, for what follows, important to note that, however small the disturbing body may be, the region of the disturbance always extends in every direction a distance of at least a wave length or maybe a few wave lengths. Here too, then, we have a close connection between diffraction phenomena and wave length. This is perhaps most clearly illustrated by reference to another wave process, namely sound. On account of the much greater wave lengths, here measured in centimeters and meters, the formation of shadows with sound becomes negligible, and diffraction plays a great and, in practice, important part: we can *hear* a person calling behind a high wall or round the corner of a solid house very well, even though we cannot see him.

"Let us now turn from optics back to mechanics and try to bring out the analogy fully. The *old* mechanics corresponds to the mental operations in optics with isolated rays of light, acting independently of one another; the *new* mechanics corresponds to the wave theory of light. What we gain from the change-over from the old to the new point of view is this, that we now include diffraction phenomena, or, better, something which is strictly analogous to the diffraction phenomena of light and which must in general, as in the case of light, be very small-scale phenomena, as otherwise the old conception of mechanics could not have proved completely satisfactory for so long. It is not difficult, however, to imagine that under certain circumstances the neglected phenomenon may become very marked and can take entire control of the mechanical situation, thus setting a riddle insoluble on the old conception; that this happens, moreover, when *the whole mechanical system in its extension is comparable with the wave length of the 'matter waves,'* which for mechanical events play the same part as the light waves in optics.

"It is for this reason that in those minute systems, the atoms, the old conception has to be given up; though for large-scale mechanical processes it still remains very closely correct, it is no longer valid for the small-scale interchanges occurring in domains of the order of magnitude of a wave length or less.

"We see that the starting point for the whole thing is this, that the diameter of the atom and the wave length of the hypothetical matter wave are of approximately the same order of magnitude. Here the question will no doubt occur to you: Is it to be regarded as pure chance that it is just at this point that we are brought up, in our analysis of the structure of matter, against the order of magnitude of the wave length, or is it to some extent understandable? Also, How do we know that this is so, since matter waves are something entirely new, which the theory demands but which are not known anywhere else? Or again, Was it perhaps simply necessary to make these *assumptions*?

"Now, the agreement between the orders of magnitude is no mere accident, but follows from the theory, without any need for special assumptions. Furthermore, there is the following remarkable circumstance. The researches of Rutherford and Chadwick on the scattering of alpha rays have, it may be truly said, provided experimental confirmation that the nucleus of the atom is very small compared with the atom itself. In what follows the nucleus may therefore be considered as a point center of attraction. Instead of the *electron* we now introduce hypothetical waves, whose wave length is, however, left an open question, since nothing is known about it. There is thus in our calculations a letter, say *a*, denoting a number as yet undetermined. We are used to this sort of thing in our calculations, and it does not prevent us from calculating that the nucleus of the atom must produce a kind of diffraction of these matter waves, just as a tiny dust particle does with light waves. And just as in the case of the dust particle, the spreading out of the field of disturbance surrounding the nucleus is closely related to the wave-length and is of the same order of magnitude. These we have had, however, to leave open.

"Now comes the most important step: *we identify the field of disturbance, the diffraction ring, with the atom; we say that the atom is in reality nothing more than the diffraction phenomenon of an electron wave caught, so to say, by the nucleus of the atom.* It is then no longer chance that the size of the atom and the wave length are of the same order of magnitude, but is self-evident. Numerically, however, we know neither the one nor the other; for in our calculations there is still always the *one* undetermined constant we have called *a*. To determine *a* there are two possibilities, each dependent upon the other. We can first so choose *a* that events depending upon processes within the atom come out quantitatively correct—above all, the emitted spectral lines, which are subject to very exact measurement. Secondly, we can choose *a* so that the diffraction ring has the size of the atom, which we know from other sources. These two determinations of *a*—the second is, of course, very much less definite, since 'size of the atom' is not a definite concept—*are in complete agreement with each other.* Finally we note that *a* has the physical dimensions, not of a length, but of *action,* that is, energy $\times$ time. It is but a step to put it equal to the numerical value of Planck's universal quantum of action, which is very accurately known from the laws of heat radiation. *We find ourselves back at the first, more exact, determination,* and the agreement is very close indeed.

"Thus in this theory the number of new assumptions needed is as small as it could ever be. The theory contains a single arbitrary constant, to which we find we have to assign a well-known numerical value from the old quantum theory, first, in order to make the diffraction ring agree in magnitude with the size of the atom, and secondly, to give the correct numerical values to the phenomena depending on events within the atom, such as the light emitted by it, or the ionization work."

At the time that Schrödinger published his first paper on wave mechanics (1926) the subject was being investigated in England by Dirac, then a research student at Cambridge.

BIOGRAPHICAL SKETCH

DIRAC

PAUL ADRIEN MAURICE DIRAC was born on August 8, 1902, at Bristol. He was educated at the Merchant Venturers' Secondary School, Bristol, and at Bristol University, where he studied electrical engineering, obtaining his B.Sc. degree in 1921. He spent a further two years at Bristol studying mathematics, then went to St. John's College, Cambridge, as a research student in mathematics. He obtained his Ph.D. degree at Cambridge in 1926 and the following year was elected a Fellow of St. John's College. Since

1932 he has been Lucasian Professor of Mathematics at Cambridge.

Since 1926 Dirac has traveled extensively and has studied at various foreign universities, including Copenhagen, Göttingen, Leiden, Wisconsin, Michigan, and Princeton.

Dirac was elected a Fellow of the Royal Society of London in 1930 and was awarded the Royal Medal in 1939. In 1938 he received the James Scott Prize of the Royal Society of Edinburgh. In 1952 he was awarded the Max Planck Medal by the German Physical Society.

DESCRIPTION OF THE PRIZE-WINNING WORK

DIRAC

* In contrast to de Broglie's pioneer work, Schrödinger had worked out his wave mechanics only in the non-relativistic limit, when—speaking in terms of point-mechanics—the velocity is small compared with that of light. He was aware, and indeed stated explicitly, that a relativistic treatment brings out finer details (the fine structure of the hydrogen lines), but gives them wrong. It also raises fundamental difficulties, which he was unable to overcome. In this Dirac succeeded in 1928 by giving the wave theory a fascinating new turn. Though it needed a genius to find it, the idea once discovered is plain and natural and free of special assumptions. It turned out that this new wave equation of Dirac's automatically accounted for the so-called spin properties, which Uhlenbeck and Goudsmit had ascribed to the electron as early as 1925 in order to account for the doublet nature of the terms of the alkali spectra. But theirs was a special hypothesis; they had assumed the electron to be a body of finite size possessing spin—and therefore a magnetic moment, since a rotating charged body behaves like a magnet. Dirac also obtained the correct fine structure of the hydrogen lines, which the de Broglie-Schrödinger theory had failed to account for. At the same time he deduced that an electron could exist in a state of nega-

---

* Professor Schrödinger very kindly rewrote all but the last three sentences of this paragraph.

tive energy—a result which at first sight seemed far from satisfactory. Dirac, however, very ingeniously interpreted the result as pointing to the existence of a *positive* counterpart of the negative electron—a prediction which was verified later when Anderson (*q.v.* 1936) in 1932 discovered the positron in cosmic radiation. As this is the part of his work with which Dirac dealt in his Nobel lecture, we may turn for that to his own account of the considerations which led him to this conclusion.*

"Matter has been found by experimental physicists to be made up of small particles of various kinds, the particles of each kind being all exactly alike. Some of these kinds have definitely been shown to be composite, that is, to be composed of other particles of a simpler nature. But there are other kinds which have not been shown to be composite and which one expects will never be shown to be composite, so that one considers them as elementary and fundamental.

"From general philosophical grounds one would at first sight like to have as few kinds of elementary particles as possible, say only one kind, or at most two, and to have all matter built up of these elementary kinds. It appears from the experimental results, though, that there must be more than this. In fact the number of kinds of elementary particles has shown a rather alarming tendency to increase during recent years.

"The situation is perhaps not so bad, though, because on closer investigation it appears that the distinction between elementary and composite particles cannot be made rigorous. To get an interpretation of some modern experimental results one must suppose that particles can be created and annihilated. Thus if a particle is observed to come out from another particle, one can no longer be sure that the latter is composite. The former may have been created. The distinction between elementary particles and composite particles now becomes a matter of convenience. This reason alone is sufficient to compel one to give up the attractive philosophical idea that all matter is made up of one kind, or perhaps two kinds, of bricks.

---

* The following extracts are quoted by kind permission of Professor Dirac.

"I should like here to discuss the simpler kinds of particles and to consider *what can be inferred about them from purely theoretical arguments*. The simpler kinds of particles are:

(i) the photons or light-quanta, of which light is composed.

(ii) the electrons and the recently discovered positrons, which appear to be a sort of mirror image of the electrons, differing from them only in the sign of their electric charge.

(iii) the heavier particles, protons and neutrons.

"Of these, I shall deal almost entirely with the electrons and the positrons . . . because in their case the theory has been developed further. . . .

.   .   .   .   .

"The question that we must first consider is how theory can give any information at all about the properties of elementary particles. There exists at the present time a general quantum mechanics which can be used to describe the motion of any kind of particle, no matter what its properties are. This general quantum mechanics, however, is valid only when the particles have small velocities, and fails for velocities comparable with the velocity of light, when effects of relativity come in. There exists no relativistic quantum mechanics (that is, one valid for large velocities) which can be applied to particles with arbitrary properties. Thus when one subjects quantum mechanics to relativistic requirements, one imposes restrictions on the properties of the particle. In this way one can deduce information about the particles from purely theoretical considerations, based on general physical principles.

"This procedure is successful in the case of electrons and positrons. It is to be hoped that in the future some such procedure will be found for the case of the other particles. I should like here to outline the method for electrons and positrons, showing how one can deduce the spin properties of the electron and then how one can infer the existence of positrons with similar spin properties and with the possibility of being annihilated in collisions with electrons.

"We begin with the equation connecting the kinetic energy W

and the momentum p_r ($r = 1, 2, 3$) of a particle in relativistic classical mechanics:

$$\frac{W^2}{c^2} - p_r{}^2 - m^2 c^2 = 0 \quad . \; . \; . \; . \; . \; . \; . \; (1)$$

. . . . .

". . . If one looks at equation (1), one sees that it allows the kinetic energy W to be either a positive quantity greater than mc^2 or a negative quantity less than $-mc^2$.

. . . . .

"Now in practice the kinetic energy of a particle is always positive. We thus see that our equations * allow of two kinds of motion for an electron, only one of which corresponds to what we are familiar with. The other corresponds to electrons with a very peculiar motion such that the faster they move, the less energy they have, and one must put energy into them to bring them to rest.

"One would thus be inclined to introduce, as a new assumption of the theory, that only one of the two kinds of motion occurs in practice. But this gives rise to a difficulty, since we find from the theory that if we disturb the electron, we may cause a transition from a positive-energy state of motion to a negative-energy one, so that, even if we suppose all the electrons in the world to be started off in positive-energy states, after a time some of them would be in negative-energy states.

"Thus in allowing negative-energy states, the theory gives something which appears not to correspond to anything known experimentally, but which we cannot simply reject by a new assumption. We must find some meaning for these states.

"An examination of the behaviour of these states in an electromagnetic field shows that they correspond to the motion of an electron with a positive charge instead of the usual negative one— what the experimenters now call a positron. One might, therefore, be inclined to assume that electrons in negative-energy states are just positrons, but this will not do, because the observed positrons certainly do not have negative energies. We can, however, establish

---

* Additional equations appear in the complete lecture.

a connection between electrons in negative-energy states and positrons, in a rather more indirect way.

"We make use of the exclusion principle of Pauli, according to
which there can be only one electron in any state of motion. We
now make the assumptions that in the world as we know it, nearly
all the states of negative energy for the electrons are occupied, with
just one electron in each state, and that a uniform filling of all the
negative-energy states is completely unobservable to us. Further,
*any unoccupied negative-energy state, being a departure from uni-
formity, is observable and is just a positron.*

"An unoccupied negative-energy state, or *hole,* as we may call it
for brevity, will have a positive energy, since it is a place where
there is a shortage of negative energy. A hole is, in fact, just like
an ordinary particle, and its identification with the positron seems
the most reasonable way of getting over the difficulty of the appearance of negative energies in our equations. On this view the positron is just a mirror-image of the electron, having exactly the same
mass and opposite charge. This has already been roughly confirmed
by experiment. The positron should also have similar spin properties to the electron, but this has not yet been confirmed by experiment.

"From our theoretical picture, we should expect an ordinary
electron, with positive energy, to be able to drop into a hole and
fill up this hole, the energy being liberated in the form of electromagnetic radiation. This would mean a process in which an electron
and a positron annihilate one another. The converse process, namely
the creation of an electron and a positron from electromagnetic
radiation, should also be able to take place. Such processes appear
to have been found experimentally, and are at present being more
closely investigated by experimenters."

CONSEQUENCES IN THEORY AND
PRACTICE

The wave mechanics constructed by Schrödinger, Dirac, and
others on the foundations laid by de Broglie has proved brilliantly
successful and has played a great part in the later development of
the theory of minute systems. Much the same thing has already been

said (p. 312) of the matrix mechanics put forward in 1925 by Heisenberg (*q.v.* 1932), but Schrödinger showed in 1926 that the two systems are in fact equivalent and lead to the same results. Wave mechanics and matrix mechanics—both forms of quantum mechanics—are two different methods of attacking theoretical problems in particle physics; which is to be preferred depends in part on the nature of the problem; in this respect they may be compared with pure geometry and analytical geometry.

1 9 3 4

No award

1 9 3 5

JAMES CHADWICK
(1891–   )

"For the discovery of the neutron."

BIOGRAPHICAL SKETCH

JAMES CHADWICK WAS BORN ON OCTOBER 20, 1891, AT MAN-
chester, England. He was educated at Manchester Secondary School
and at Manchester University, where he entered the Honours School
of Physics in 1908. After graduating in 1911 he did research work
in the physical laboratory until 1913, working under Rutherford on
problems in radioactivity. In 1913 he was awarded an 1851 Exhibition Scholarship and went to study under Professor H. Geiger in
the Physikalisch-Technische Reichsanstalt at Charlottenburg. He
was in Germany at the outbreak of the First World War and was in-
terned in the civilian prisoner-of-war camp at Ruhleben.

In 1919 he was awarded a studentship at Gonville and Caius
College, Cambridge, where he did research work on various problems in nuclear physics, being elected a Fellow of his college in
1921 and appointed assistant director of research at the Cavendish
Laboratory in 1923. In 1935 he was appointed professor of physics
at the University of Liverpool. During the Second World War he
worked at the Santa Fe experimental station in New Mexico. Since
1948 he has been Master of Gonville and Caius College, Cambridge.

Chadwick was elected a Fellow of the Royal Society of London
in 1927 and was awarded the Hughes Medal in 1932, the Copley
Medal in 1950. He was knighted in 1945.

DESCRIPTION OF THE PRIZE-WINNING
WORK

In the disintegration of radioactive substances two particles, in addition to γ rays, are emitted: alpha particles and beta particles. The alpha particle was at first identified with the helium atom carrying two charges equal in magnitude to that on the electron but opposite in sign, that is, to a helium atom which had lost two electrons—in the early years of the century the number of electrons in an atom was thought to be approximately equal to the atomic weight, four in the case of helium. When, later, the helium atom was assigned two planetary electrons revolving in orbits about a heavy positively charged nucleus, the alpha particle became simply the helium nucleus with a charge $+2e$, the charge on the electron being $-e$. The beta particles were early identified with high-speed electrons.

The simplest of all nuclei is that of the hydrogen atom, with a charge $+e$ and a mass practically equal to that of the hydrogen atom itself, since the mass of the electron is very small compared with that of the nucleus. According to the modern view the hydrogen nucleus is itself a fundamental particle, the proton, and the hydrogen atom consists of a nucleus composed of one proton with a single planetary electron revolving round it. Now the helium atom has a mass very nearly four times as great as that of the hydrogen atom, the chemical atomic weight of helium being 4.003. Since therefore practically all the mass of the atom is concentrated in the nucleus, the helium nucleus must, it appeared, consist of four protons. But as the charge on the helium nucleus, or alpha particle, is $+2e$, not $+4e$, it was supposed that the helium nucleus contained two electrons in addition to the four protons, so as to leave the nucleus with a net positive charge $+2e$. The same sort of argument applied to all the other elements, the number of protons in the nucleus being the nearest whole number to the chemical atomic weight, with a sufficient number of electrons in the nucleus to make the net positive charge on it equal in magnitude to the number of planetary electrons, and thus render the whole atom electrically neutral.

On this conception of the atom the *mass number, A,* of the element or its isotopes gave the number of protons in the nucleus, and the *atomic number, Z,* gave the net positive charge on the nucleus and, of course, the number of planetary electrons. The number of electrons in the nucleus would then be $A - Z$. In modern nuclear physics the mass number and atomic number are usually shown alongside the chemical symbol of the element. Thus the helium nucleus is represented by $_2^4He$ or by $_2He^4$; lithium, the third element in the periodic table, has two isotopes, one of mass number 6, the other of mass number 7; their nuclei are denoted by $_3^6Li$ and $_3^7Li$, respectively. On the theory that the nucleus contained electrons, these symbols indicated that the nucleus of the first isotope of lithium contained 6 protons and 3 electrons, that of the second 7 protons and 4 electrons, the number of planetary electrons in the atom being 3 in both cases. This was the generally accepted theory up to the time of Chadwick's discovery of the neutron. We shall return to the question of the composition of the nucleus after quoting * some extracts from Chadwick's Nobel lecture.

"The first suggestion of a neutral particle with the properties of the neutron we now know was made by Rutherford in 1920. He thought that a proton and an electron might unite in a much more intimate way than they do in the hydrogen atom, and so form a particle of no net charge and with a mass nearly the same as that of the hydrogen atom. His view was that with such a particle as the first step in the formation of atomic nuclei from the two elementary units in the structure of matter, the proton and the electron, it would be much easier to picture how heavy complex nuclei can be gradually built up from the simpler ones. He pointed out that this neutral particle would have peculiar and interesting properties. . . .

"No experimental evidence for the existence of neutral particles could be obtained for years. Some experiments were made in the Cavendish Laboratory in 1921 by Glasson and by Roberts, hoping to detect the formation of such particles when an electric discharge was passed through hydrogen. Their results were negative.

"The possibility that neutral particles might exist was, nevertheless, not lost sight of. I myself made several attempts to detect them

---

* By kind permission of Sir James Chadwick.

—in discharge tubes actuated in different ways, in the disintegration of radioactive substances, and in artificial disintegrations produced by α-particles. . . .

"Later, Bothe and Becker showed that γ-radiations were excited in some light elements when bombarded by α-particles. Mr. H. C. Webster, in the Cavendish Laboratory, had also been making similar experiments, and he proceeded to examine closely the production of these radiations. The radiation emitted by beryllium showed some rather peculiar features, which were very difficult to explain. I suggested therefore that the radiation might consist of neutral particles and that a test of this hypothesis might be made by passing the radiation into an expansion chamber. Several photographs were taken; some β-particle tracks—presumably recoil electrons—were observed, but nothing unexpected.

". . . Mme. and M. Joliot-Curie, who were also investigating the properties of this beryllium radiation . . . passed the radiation through a very thin window into an ionization vessel containing air. When paraffin wax or any other matter containing hydrogen was placed in front of the window the ionization in the vessel increased. They showed that this increase was due to the ejection from the wax of protons, moving with very high velocities.

"This behaviour of the beryllium radiation was very difficult to explain if it were a quantum radiation. I therefore began immediately the study of this new effect using different methods—the counter, the expansion chamber, and the high pressure ionization chamber.

"It appeared at once that the beryllium radiation could eject particles not only from paraffin wax but also from other light substances, such as lithium, beryllium, boron, etc., though in these cases the particles had a range of only a few millimetres in air. The experiments showed that the particles are recoil atoms of the element through which the radiation passes, set in motion by the impact of the radiation.

"The occurrence of these recoil atoms can be shown most strikingly by means of the expansion chamber. These experiments were carried out by Dr. Feather and Mr. Dee.

". . . Two photographs taken by Feather, using an expansion chamber filled with nitrogen, [show] two short dense tracks. Each is due to an atom of nitrogen which has been struck by the radiation. One track shows a short spur, due to collision with a nitrogen atom; the angle between the spurs is 90°, as it should be if the initial track is due to a nitrogen atom.

"The beryllium radiation thus behaved very differently from a quantum radiation. This property of setting in motion the atoms of matter in its path suggests that the radiation consists of particles.

[By measuring the maximum range of the protons ejected from paraffin wax and also the ranges of the recoil atoms produced in an expansion chamber filled with nitrogen, the mass of the hypothetical particles of the beryllium radiation can be deduced; it is found to be 0.9, the mass of the proton being 1.]

"We must conclude that the beryllium radiation does in fact consist of particles, and that these particles have a mass about the same as that of a proton. Now the experiments further showed that these particles can pass easily through thicknesses of matter, e.g., 10 or even 20 cm of lead. But a proton of the same velocity as this particle is stopped by a thickness of $\frac{1}{4}$ mm of lead. Since the penetrating power of particles of the same mass and speed depends only on the charge carried by the particle, it was clear that the particle of the beryllium radiation must have a very small charge compared with that of the proton. It was simplest to assume that it has no charge at all. All the properties of the beryllium radiation could be readily explained on this assumption, that the radiation consists of particles of mass 1 and charge 0, or neutrons.

"I have already mentioned Rutherford's suggestion that there might exist a neutral particle formed by the close combination of a proton and an electron, and it was at first natural to suppose that the neutron might be such a complex particle. On the other hand, a structure of this kind cannot be fitted into the scheme of the quantum mechanics, in which the hydrogen atom represents the only possible combination of a proton and an electron. . . . Similar arguments make it difficult to suppose that the proton is a combination of neutron and positive electron. It seems at present useless to discuss whether the neutron and proton are elementary particles or not; it may be that they are two different states of the fundamental heavy particle.

"In the present view of the β-transformations of radioactive bodies the hypothesis is made that a neutron in the nucleus may transform into a proton and a negative electron with the emission of the electron, or conversely a proton in the nucleus may transform into a neutron and a positive electron with the emission of the positron.

Thus
$$n \rightarrow p + e^-$$
$$p \rightarrow n + e^+$$

. . . . .

"As I have shown, observations of the momenta transferred in collisions of a neutron with atomic nuclei lead to a value of the mass of the neutron, but the measurements cannot be made with precision. To obtain an accurate estimate of the neutron mass we must use the energy relations in a disintegration process in which a neutron is liberated from an atomic nucleus. The best estimate at present is obtained from the disintegration of the deuteron * by the photoelectric effect of a γ-ray. . . . we then obtain a value for the mass of the neutron of 1.0085. The mass of the hydrogen atom is 1.0081. . . .

. . . . .

"The neutron in its passage through matter loses its energy in collisions with the atomic nuclei and not with the electrons. The experiments of Dee showed that the primary ionization along the track of a neutron in air could not be as much as 1 ion pair in 3 metres' path, while Massey has calculated that it may be as low as 1 ion pair in 10^5 km. This behaviour is very different from that of a charged particle, such as a proton, which dissipates its energy almost entirely in electron collisions. The collision of a neutron with an atomic nucleus, although much more frequent than with an electron, is also a rare event, for the forces between a neutron and a nucleus are very small except at distances of the order of 10^{-12} cm. In a close collision the neutron may be deflected from its path and the struck nucleus may acquire sufficient energy to produce ions. The recoiling nucleus can then be detected either in

---

* *Deuteron:* the nucleus of the hydrogen isotope of mass 2 (*deuterium*, D). Heavy hydrogen, D_2 heavy water, D_2O.

an ionization chamber or by its track in an expansion chamber. In some of these collisions, however, the neutron enters the nucleus and a disintegration is produced. Such disintegrations were first observed by Feather in his observations on the passage of neutrons through an expansion chamber filled with nitrogen.

.   .   .   .   .

"Fermi and his collaborators have also shown that the phenomenon of artificial radioactivity can be provoked in the great majority of all elements, even in those of large atomic number, by the bombardment of neutrons. They have also shown that neutrons of very small kinetic energy are peculiarly effective in many cases."

CONSEQUENCES IN THEORY AND PRACTICE

The earlier theory of the composition of the atomic nucleus was outlined above. This agreed well enough in a qualitative way with the known facts of nuclear disintegration, whether this was the spontaneous disintegration occurring in a radioactive substance or the "artificial" disintegration produced by bombardment with alpha particles. The protons were there to be ejected in pairs as alpha particles; so were the electrons to be ejected as beta particles. But with increasing knowledge of, for instance, the energy changes involved in these disintegrations, difficulties were encountered.

Chadwick's discovery of the neutron made it possible, in fact necessary, to revise the theory of the composition of the nucleus. The neutrons, like the alpha particles, were ejected from the nucleus. They too must therefore be constituents of the nucleus. Since the mass of the neutron is the same as that of the proton, it was a simple step to replace some of the protons by neutrons, the mass of the nucleus remaining unchanged; and by leaving only sufficient protons in the nucleus to balance the charge on the planetary electrons, it was no longer necessary to assume the presence of electrons in the nucleus. Of course, many other considerations had to be taken into account in arriving at this new theory of nuclear composition. While some difficulties were removed, fresh ones presented themselves. One of these was the emission of beta particles, since on the new theory the nucleus contained no electrons; another was the nature of the forces binding the nucleus together: on the older theory the negatively charged electrons in the nucleus served as a sort of "cement" between the positively charged protons.

The problem of the nucleus is still far from solved, but it is now generally accepted that the nucleus contains as many protons as there are planetary electrons in the atom, the balance of the atomic mass being made up by neutrons. The symbols ^6_3Li and ^7_3Li now mean that the nucleus of the first isotope of lithium contains 3 protons and $6 - 3 = 3$ neutrons, while that of the second also contains 3 protons, but $7 - 3 = 4$ neutrons. In fact, the only difference in the nuclei of the different isotopes of an element lies in the number of neutrons in the nucleus.

Important as was Chadwick's discovery from the theoretical point of view, it was even more important from the experimental point of view. Owing to their being uncharged, neutrons are not repelled by an atomic nucleus; they are therefore particularly effective in producing nuclear disintegrations. More will be said on this point later (see *Fermi, 1938*).

1 9 3 6

VICTOR FRANCIS HESS
(1883–)

"For the discovery of cosmic radiation."

CARL DAVID ANDERSON
(1905–)

"For the discovery of the positron."

BIOGRAPHICAL SKETCH

HESS

VICTOR FRANCIS HESS WAS BORN ON JUNE 24, 1883, AT SCHLOSS Waldstein, near Graz, in Styria, Austria. He was educated at the *Gymnasium* at Graz from 1893 to 1901, at Graz University from 1901 to 1905, and at the University of Vienna from 1905 to 1908. He obtained his doctor's degree from Graz University in 1906 *summa cum laude.*

From 1910 to 1920 he was assistant at the newly founded Institute for Radium Research of the Vienna Academy of Sciences, and also *privatdozent* at the University of Vienna. In 1920 he was appointed associate professor at Graz. During the years 1921 to 1923 Hess was on leave of absence in the United States, where he was director of the Research Laboratory of the U. S. Radium Corporation, and consulting physicist to the U. S. Department of the Interior (Bureau of Mines), Washington, D. C. He returned to the University of Graz in 1923, and in 1925 was appointed full professor of experimental physics there. In 1931 he went to Innsbruck, Austria, as professor of physics and head of the newly founded Institute for Radiation Research. Since 1938 he has been full professor of physics at Fordham University, New York.

Hess is a member of the American Physical Society and of the Academy of Sciences, Vienna. He holds an Honorary Sc.D. degree from Fordham University.*

DESCRIPTION OF THE PRIZE-WINNING WORK

HESS

Hess's researches dealt mainly with radioactivity and atmospheric electricity. His work on radioactivity included a study of the production of heat in radium (1912) and a determination of the number of alpha-particles emitted by a given quantity of radium (1918). His work on atmospheric electricity was largely concerned with the causes of the electrical conductivity of the atmosphere; it was his early interest in this matter that led to the discovery of cosmic radiation, for which he received the Nobel Prize.

The belief that air is to a very slight extent a conductor of electricity arose towards the end of the eighteenth century, when it was found that an insulated charged conductor lost its charge too rapidly for leakage along the support to be alone responsible. Several attempts to obtain conclusive evidence of the conductivity of air were made during the second half of the nineteenth century, but none proved decisive, though an experiment made by C. V. Boys in the late 1880s left little room for doubt. Boys found that the rate of collapse of the leaves of his electroscope was the same whether they were attached to a long thin quartz rod or to a short thick one; had there been any leakage along the rods, the rate of collapse in the latter case would have been much greater than in the former.

Towards the end of the century the subject was investigated in Germany by J. Elster and H. F. Geitel, who enclosed a carefully insu-

---

* Professor Hess very kindly read the original typescript of this biographical sketch and made a few amendments. Incidentally he makes it clear that the nearest equivalent to "professor *extraordinarius*" (e.g. at Graz) is "associate professor."

lated electroscope so completely that no air could enter or escape; the leaves still collapsed slowly.

In 1900 C. T. R. Wilson (*q.v.* 1927) made a special study of the conductivity of air enclosed in a sealed vessel. He overcame the uncertainty due to possible imperfect insulation by attaching the insulating support of the leaves of the electroscope to a metal rod maintained at the initial potential of the leaves. The only effect of imperfect insulation would be that electricity might leak *into* the leaves if the potential of the latter fell through loss of charge through the air. The fact that the leaves did slowly collapse fully established the slight conductivity of the enclosed air. Even more important, Wilson found that the air retained its conductivity after a considerable lapse of time.

It was of course by this time (1900) well known that gases were rendered conducting by the action of X rays or the radiation emitted by radioactive substances, a fact which J. J. Thomson explained (p. 42) as being due to the splitting up of the molecules into positively and negatively charged parts or *ions.* If, however, the gas is left to itself, the ions will, in the absence of an ionizing agent, rapidly recombine to form neutral molecules, and the gas cease to be conducting. It was natural, therefore, that the slight conductivity of ordinary atmospheric air should be put down to ionizing radiations emitted by traces of radioactive substances in the air or in the crust of the earth. This received support when in 1903 Rutherford found that the ionization in a closed vessel could be reduced by as much as 30 percent by surrounding the vessel with lead, but that increasing the thickness of the lead beyond 2 inches produced no further reduction. Of the three types of radiation emitted by a radioactive substance (p. 26) only the γ rays could penetrate this thickness of lead. It therefore appeared that the greater part of the ionization inside a closed vessel was due to these penetrating rays, though part might be due to traces of radioactive impurities in the walls of the containing vessel. During the next few years research on the whole tended to confirm this view. For example, it was found that the ionization in a closed vessel was much less over the sea and frozen lakes than over the land. On the other hand, more precise measurements of the amount of ionization led to doubts as to whether γ radiation could account fully for the observed effects.

One test which should provide useful information was to compare the ionization at a height of 300 meters or more with that at ground level, for it had been found that γ rays were almost completely absorbed by 300 meters of air. In 1910 Th. Wulf measured the ionization at the bottom and at the top of the Eiffel Tower, 300 meters high; he found that the ionization at the top was rather more than half that at the bottom and therefore considerably more than was to be expected if the ionization was caused by radiation from the ground. One possible explanation of the unexpectedly high value was that radioactive deposits from the atmosphere on the iron structure of the Eiffel Tower were responsible; another, that the absorption of γ rays in air was much less than had been estimated. The obvious thing to do, then, was to take an electroscope up in a balloon. This had in fact already been done in 1909, when the ionization at 1300 meters had been found to be only one-quarter that on the ground, but damage to the instrument made it desirable that the test should be repeated. In 1910 and 1911 A. Gockel in Switzerland made three balloon ascents, recording the ionization up to a height of 4500 meters; he found a definite decrease with altitude, but again considerably less than was to be expected if γ radiation from the ground were responsible. Unfortunately instrumental defects rendered Gockel's observations unreliable.

Hess's decision to investigate the problem arose in the spring of 1911 through reading an account of Wulf's Eiffel Tower experiments. Even at that time the results of the various experiments which had been made seemed to him to point to some unknown source of ionization. His first care was to make an accurate determination of the height at which γ rays from the ground could produce ionization. This investigation was carried out in Vienna, a large quantity of radium (1500 milligrams) being used as the source of γ rays. Hess found that the radiation is almost completely absorbed at a height of 500 meters above ground. His next care was the design and construction of apparatus which could be subjected to considerable changes of pressure and temperature without suffering damage. Equipped with these instruments—two or three were carried on each flight in order to eliminate instrumental errors—Hess made two balloon ascents in 1911, seven in 1912, and one in

1913, five being carried out at night. He found that the ionization soon ceased to fall off with height and began to increase rapidly, being at a height of several kilometers many times greater than at the earth's surface. He therefore came to the conclusion that an extremely penetrating radiation enters the earth's atmosphere from outside.

Hess's researches aroused widespread interest, though his conclusion did not receive general acceptance at the time. Research was interrupted by the First World War, but was resumed soon afterward on both sides of the Atlantic. Before long the existence of Hess's "penetrating radiation," to which Millikan (*q.v.* 1923) gave the name "cosmic rays" in 1925, was generally accepted. Naturally, two questions at once arose: Where does the radiation originate, and of what does it consist? In his Nobel lecture, published in German, Hess surveyed the progress that had been made up to 1936 in the search for answers to these questions.*

"I was able to show in 1912, through a series of balloon ascents, that the ionization in an hermetically sealed vessel diminished with height above the surface of the earth, due to the falling off of the effect of radioactive substances in the earth; but that above 1000 meters it increased noticeably and at a height of 5 kilometers reached a value several times that observed at the surface of the earth. From this I came to the conclusion that this ionization was due to a hitherto unknown radiation of extraordinarily high penetrating power which entered the earth's atmosphere from space and was still able to produce noticeable ionization in the air at the surface of the earth. . . . I tried to find the answer to the question of the origin of this radiation and to that end made a balloon ascent during an almost total eclipse of the sun which occurred on April 12, 1912, and carried out measurements at heights of between two and three kilometers. Since no lessening of the ionization during the eclipse could be detected, I concluded that in the main

* The following extracts are quoted by kind permission of Professor Hess, who at the same time informs me that a throat operation shortly before the Nobel Festival made it impossible for him to deliver the customary address. In 1940 he published a fuller account of the discovery of cosmic radiation in *Thought,* the Fordham University Quarterly. The account given above is based largely on this article, of which Professor Hess very kindly sent me a reprint.

the sun itself could not be the source of the cosmic rays, at least as long as one thought only of undeflected rays.

". . . The fluctuations in intensity of the radiation, at which I hinted as early as 1912, have been most thoroughly studied with better and better apparatus. The influence of a particular region of the heavens, which some observers thought they had found between 1923 and 1927, could not be confirmed by later observations.

"For the purpose of making a continuous record of the fluctuations in intensity of the cosmic radiation, I established, in the autumn of 1931, a small observatory on a mountain 2300 meters high, the Hafelekar near Innsbruck in Austria. A number of results have already been obtained, which I shall only mention briefly here. A small regular daily fluctuation in the intensity of the radiation with the time of day (maximum at midday) has been found; this was traced back to atmospheric influences, in particular to electric and magnetic effects in the highest layers of the atmosphere. Further, there are indications of a still smaller fluctuation during the night, which lend support to the hypothesis put forward by Professor A. H. Compton a year ago, according to which the cosmic rays arise outside and remote from our Milky Way system. Again, there is a simultaneous fluctuation from day to day in two pieces of apparatus (counting tubes as well as ionization chambers) set up 6 km. apart, one at a height of 600 meters, the other at a height of 2300 meters.

"How may we hope to solve the many problems still outstanding as to the origin and composition of the cosmic radiation? . . . the great need is that larger funds should be available. . . . The method so successfully used by Professor Regener of Stuttgart, who sent self-registering instruments to a height of over 25 km. by means of pilot balloons, needs to be further developed and improved. At the same time, useful results are to be expected from the method, already tried several times in America, by which observational data obtained on stratosphere flights are transmitted automatically by radiotelegraphy. Only through numerous measurements in the stratosphere will it be possible to find the . . . nature of cosmic rays before they give rise to the secondary radiation phenomena we know in the earth's atmosphere. Also, a study of the occurrence of the so-called 'showers' and 'Hoffmann bursts' * at various heights will throw new light on the effects of cosmic rays. Very important results are to be expected from a further investigation of the occurrence of these showers well below the surface of the earth, either in mines or by sinking registering apparatus in water several hundred feet deep.

". . . we must apply all the instruments at our disposal, if necessary simultaneously and side by side, a thing which so far has not been done, or only to a limited extent. Simultaneous recordings with ionization chambers and Wilson chambers, or with ionization chambers and counting tubes, are still lacking. Another method deserving of great attention is the photographic method, first successfully tried in the United States by Professor Wilkins of Rochester, N. Y., for observing the paths of the cosmic-ray particles; this, used in a strong magnetic field, makes possible the measurement of the energy of even the most penetrating particles, and is capable of still further development.

"The investigation of the possible effects of cosmic radiation on the living organism should also prove of great interest.

"The investigation of the paths of cosmic rays in strong magnetic fields by means of the Wilson chamber has led to the discovery of the positron, or positively charged electron, one of the building stones of matter hitherto unknown to us, by Professor Carl Anderson, who shares with me the Nobel Prize for 1936.

"It is expected that further investigation of the 'showers' and 'bursts' of cosmic rays may lead to the discovery of yet further elementary particles, such as the neutrino [see p. 377], whose existence has been postulated in recent years by some theoretical physicists."

BIOGRAPHICAL SKETCH

ANDERSON

CARL DAVID ANDERSON WAS BORN ON SEPTEMBER 3, 1905, IN New York, N. Y. He completed his education at the California

---

* The release of immense quantities of ions through the process of atomic disintegration.

Institute of Technology, Pasadena, where Millikan (*q.v.* 1923), whose work on cosmic rays has already been mentioned (p. 216), was director of the Norman Bridge Laboratory of Physics. Anderson was graduated in physics and engineering in 1927. From 1927 to 1928 he was Coffin Research Fellow, and from 1928 to 1930 Teaching Fellow in Physics, at the Institute. In 1930 he obtained his Ph.D. and became a Research Fellow on the physics staff. In 1933 he was appointed assistant professor of physics, from 1937 to 1939 was associate professor, and since 1939 has been professor.

In 1935 Anderson was awarded the Gold Medal of the American Institute of the City of New York, and in 1937 the Elliott Cresson Medal of the Franklin Institute; in 1937 he was also made an honorary doctor of science of Colgate University. He is a member of the National Academy of Sciences, the American Physical Society, and the American Philosophical Society.

DESCRIPTION OF THE PRIZE-WINNING WORK

ANDERSON

When, in 1927, Anderson began research work, the question to the fore in cosmic-ray research was that of the nature of the rays: Were they corpuscular or did they consist of very penetrating γ rays? If they consisted of charged particles they should be deflected by a magnetic field. The first attempts to detect any such deflection by means of a Wilson cloud chamber were unsuccessful—if the radiation was corpuscular, the energy of the particles was so high (it is now known to reach thousands of millions of electron-volts) that only a very strong magnetic field could produce a perceptible deflection. Millikan therefore set about organizing experiments on a large scale at Pasadena for the detailed study of cosmic radiation, Anderson being entrusted with the planning and direction of the research. When, in the summer of 1931, the installation was ready, the cosmic radiation was recorded photographically day and night every fifteen seconds. How, among the photographs of tracks obtained in this way, some were found which indicated particles hav-

ing the same mass as an electron but a positive charge, is told in the
following extract from Anderson's Nobel lecture.*

"After Skobelzyn in 1927 had first shown photographs of tracks
of cosmic-ray particles Professor R. A. Millikan and I in the spring
of 1930 planned a cloud-chamber apparatus suitable for cosmic-ray
studies, in particular to measure the energies of cosmic-ray particles
by means of their curvatures in a strong magnetic field. The chamber, of dimensions 17 x 17 x 3 cm, was arranged with its long
dimension vertical, and incorporated into a powerful electromagnet
capable of maintaining a uniform magnetic field up to 24,000 gauss
strength.

"In the summer of 1931 the first results were obtained with this
technique. The direct measurement of the energies of atomic particles was extended from about 15 million electron-volts, the highest
energy measured before that time, to 5 billion electron-volts. In the
spring of 1932 a preliminary paper on the energies of cosmic-ray
particles was published in which energies of 1 billion electron-volts
were reported. It was here shown that particles of positive charge
occurred about as abundantly as did those of negative charge, and
in many cases several positive and negative particles were found to
be projected simultaneously from a single centre. The presence of
positively charged particles and the occurrence of 'showers' of
several particles showed clearly that the absorption of cosmic rays
in material substances is due primarily to a nuclear phenomenon of
a new type.

"Measurements of the specific ionization of both the positive and
negative particles, by counting the number of droplets per unit
length along the tracks, showed the great majority of both the
positive and negative particles to possess unit electric charge. The
particles of negative charge were readily interpreted as electrons,
and those of positive charge were at first tentatively interpreted as
protons, at that time the only known particle of unit positive charge.

"If the particles of positive charge were to be ascribed to protons,
then those of low energy and sharp curvature in the magnetic field
(e.g. a curvature greater than that corresponding to an electron of
about 500 million electron-volts) should be expected to exhibit an

---

* Quoted by kind permission of Professor Anderson.

appreciably greater ionization than the negatively charged electrons. In general, however, the positive particles seemed to differ in specific ionization only inappreciably from the negatives. To avoid the assumption, which appeared very radical at that time, that the positive particles had electronic mass, serious consideration was given to the possibility that the particles which appeared to be positively charged and directed downward into the earth were in reality negatively charged electrons which through scattering had suffered a reversal of direction and were projected upward away from the earth. Although such a reversal of direction through scattering might be expected to occur occasionally, it seemed inadequate to account for the large number of particle-tracks which showed a specific ionization anomalously small if they were to be ascribed to protons.

"To differentiate with certainty between the particles of positive and negative charge it was necessary only to determine without ambiguity their direction of motion. To accomplish this purpose a plate of lead was inserted across a horizontal diameter of the chamber. The direction of motion of the particles could then be readily ascertained due to the lower energy and therefore the smaller radius of curvature of the particles in the magnetic field after they had traversed the plate and suffered a loss in energy.

"Results were then obtained which could logically be interpreted only in terms of particles of a positive charge and a mass of the same order of magnitude as that normally possessed by the free negative electron. In particular one photograph shows a particle of positive charge traversing a 6 mm plate of lead. If electronic mass is assigned to this particle its energy before it traverses the plate is 63 million electron-volts and after it emerges its energy is 23 million electron-volts. The possibility that this particle of positive charge could represent a proton is ruled out on the basis of range and curvature. A proton of the curvature shown after it emerges from the plate would have an energy of 200,000 electron-volts, and according to previously well established experimental data would have a range of only 5 mm, whereas the observed range was greater than 50 mm. The only possible conclusion seemed to be that this track, indeed, was the track of a positively charged electron. Examples similar to this and others in which two or more particles were found to be produced at one center gave additional evidence for the existence of particles of positive charge and mass small compared with that of the proton. These results formed the basis of the paper published in September 1932 announcing the existence of free positive electrons.

"Measurements by the droplet counting method of the magnitude of the specific ionization of the positive and negative electrons which occur with energies low enough to be appreciably curved in the magnetic field have shown that the mass and charge of the positive electron cannot differ by more than 20 percent and 10 percent, respectively, from the mass and charge of the negative electron.

"Blackett and Occhialini, using an apparatus similar to ours but with the added advantage that through the use of control by Geiger-Müller tube counters their apparatus was made to respond automatically to the passage of a cosmic-ray particle, in the spring of 1933 confirmed the existence of positive electrons, or positrons, and obtained many beautiful photographs of complex electron showers.

"That positrons could be produced by an agent other than cosmic rays was first shown by Chadwick, Blackett and Occhialini when they observed that positrons were produced by the radiation generated in the impact of alpha particles upon beryllium. The radiation produced in the beryllium is complex in character, consisting both of neutrons and gamma rays. In their experiment it was not possible to determine which of these rays was responsible for the production of positrons. Curie and Joliot by a similar experiment, in which they interposed blocks of lead and paraffin in the path of the rays from beryllium and measured the yield of positrons as a function of the thickness and material of the absorber, concluded that the positrons arose more likely as a result of the gamma rays than of the neutrons.

"Direct proof that the hard component of the gamma rays from Thorium C″ can give rise to positrons was first given by Neddermeyer and myself, and independently by Curie and Joliot, and by Meitner and Philipp, in the spring of 1933. . . .

"In addition to the methods already mentioned of producing positrons, i.e. by absorption of cosmic-ray photons and electrons, and by the absorption of sufficiently high-energy gamma rays from terrestrial sources, positrons have also been observed among the disintegration products of certain radioactive substances. The artificially produced radioactive elements first discovered by Curie and Joliot in 1934 are found to disintegrate either by the ejection of a positive or negative electron. Those elements whose atomic number is greater than that of the stable elements of the same mass number in general disintegrate by the ejection of a positron. . . .

"The present electron theory of Dirac provides a means of describing many of the phenomena governing the production and annihilation of positrons. Blackett and Occhialini first suggested that the appearance of pairs of positive and negative electrons could be understood in terms of this theory as the 'creation' of a positive-negative electron pair in the neighbourhood of an atomic nucleus. The energy corresponding to the proper mass of both of the particles, as well as to their kinetic energies, is, according to this view, supplied by the incident radiation. Since the energy corresponding to the proper mass of a pair of electrons is approximately one million electron-volts one should expect gamma rays of energy greater than this amount to produce positrons in their passage through matter, and further that the sum of the kinetic energies of the positive and negative electrons should be equal to the energy of the radiation producing them diminished by approximately one million electron-volts.

"Experiments by Neddermeyer and myself, and by Chadwick, Blackett and Occhialini, and others, have shown this relation to obtain in the production of positrons by Th C″ gamma rays, providing evidence for the correctness of this view of the origin of positive-negative electron pairs.

"The theory of Dirac requires further that a positron, when it finds itself in a very ordinary environment, as, for example, in passing through common substances, will, on the average, have only a very short life, of the order of one billionth of a second or less. The positrons and negative electrons will mutually annihilate one another in pairs, and in their stead will appear a pair of photons, each of approximately one-half million electron-volts energy. Although the life time of positrons has not been actually measured, it has been shown to be very short, and the radiation which results from their annihilation has been observed. The first to do this were Joliot and Thibaud. The annihilation radiation is of the proper intensity and the energy of its individual corpuscles is approximately the required amount of one-half million electron-volts, corresponding to the complete annihilation of the positron.

. . . . .

"Closely related to the process of the production of positive and negative electrons out of radiation, is the one which may be considered its inverse, namely, the production of radiation through nuclear impacts by a positive or negative electron in its passage through matter. Direct measurements on the energy loss of electrons, in the energy range up to about 400 million electron-volts, in their traversals through thin plates of lead, have shown that the loss in energy due to direct ionization by the electrons is but a small fraction of the total energy loss, and that the loss in energy over that due to ionization is in good accord with that to be expected theoretically through the production of radiation by nuclear impact. Furthermore, a small number of measurements at energies up to 1,000 million electron-volts has shown no significant deviation from the theoretical loss. These data on energy loss of high-energy electrons afford strong evidence that, at least in part, the origin of the cosmic-ray showers of photons and positive and negative electrons can be understood in terms of a chain of successive processes of photon production by radiative impacts with nuclei on the part of the high-energy positive and negative electrons, and the subsequent absorption of these photons in nuclear collisions resulting in the production of numerous positive-negative electron pairs which appear as the cosmic-ray showers. . . .

"Until quite recently it was not clear that the high-energy positive and negative electrons which have now been shown to exhibit high absorbability, behaved in a manner essentially different from the cosmic-ray particles of highly penetrating character. These highly penetrating particles, although not free positive and negative electrons, appear to consist of both positive and negative particles of unit electric charge, and will provide interesting material for future study."

The last sentence in Anderson's Nobel lecture refers to another type of particle discovered by him in cosmic radiation—the *meso-tron*, as he named it, though the name *meson* is now more general. At the time of his Nobel award Anderson still adopted a cautious attitude toward this new particle, though for some time past he had been coming across evidence which pointed to its existence as the penetrating component in the cosmic radiation. Anderson's own investigations showed that the particle, if it existed, must have a mass greater than that of the electron but less than that of the proton—hence the name*. He also found that it could carry either a positive or a negative charge. Between 1937 and 1941 several determinations of the mass were made, the values found differing considerably but all in the neighbourhood of 200 times the mass of an electron. In 1935 Yukawa (*q.v.* 1949) had predicted, as a result of a theoretical investigation into the forces holding the nucleus of an atom together, the existence of a particle having just this mass. It is now generally accepted that there is in fact quite a variety of particles—all known as mesons—with masses between that of the electron and that of the proton (see Powell, 1950), though doubts remain as to whether they are to be regarded as fundamental particles or not.

CONSEQUENCES IN THEORY AND PRACTICE

Hess, in establishing beyond question the existence of cosmic radiation, opened up a new field of research in modern physics, one which continues to engage the attention of some of our most distinguished physicists. At the same time his discovery set science some pretty problems. Anderson, in attempting to solve one of these, was led to the discovery of two hitherto undetected particles, the positron and the meson, both of which had been predicted on purely theoretical grounds. His work therefore not only served to add to our knowledge of the fundamental particles which go to build up the universe, but also lent strength to the theories through which these particles were predicted.

---

* Greek μέσος, *mesos*, middle, intermediate.

1 9 3 7

CLINTON JOSEPH DAVISSON
(1881–   )

GEORGE PAGET THOMSON
(1892–   )

*"For the experimental discovery of the interference
phenomenon in crystals irradiated by electrons."*

BIOGRAPHICAL SKETCH

DAVISSON

CLINTON JOSEPH DAVISSON WAS BORN ON OCTOBER 22, 1881,
at Bloomington, Illinois. He was graduated from high school there
in 1902, and entered the University of Chicago with a scholarship
in mathematics and physics. Here he came under the influence of
Professor R. A. Millikan (*q.v.* 1923), on whose recommendation
he was appointed assistant in physics at Purdue University in January, 1904. From June 1904 to August 1905 he was back at the
University of Chicago; then, again on the recommendation of Professor Millikan, he was appointed part-time instructor in physics
at Princeton University, where he remained until 1910, continuing
his own studies under Professor F. Magie, Professor E. P. Adams,
Professor (later Sir) James Jeans, and particularly under Professor
O. W. Richardson (*q.v.* 1928). In 1908 he received his B.S. degree
from the University of Chicago, where he had returned during the

summer sessions. He was awarded a fellowship in physics for the year 1910-1911, obtaining his Ph.D. at the end of that time for a thesis dealing with the thermal emission of positive ions, done under the supervision of Professor Richardson.

In September 1911 he was appointed an instructor in the Department of Physics at the Carnegie Institute of Technology, Pittsburgh, where he remained until 1917, visiting England in the summer of 1913 to work under J. J. Thomson in the Cavendish Laboratory, Cambridge. From 1917, during the First World War, he was on leave of absence from the Carnegie Institute to work in the Engineering Department of the Western Electric Company (later the Bell Telephone Laboratories) in New York; he remained on here after the war as a member of the technical staff, resigning an assistant professorship at the Carnegie Institute in order to do so. Since 1947 he has been visiting professor of physics, University of Virginia.

Davisson was awarded the Comstock Prize by the National Academy of Sciences in 1928, the Elliott Cresson Medal by the Franklin Institute in 1931, the Hughes Medal by the Royal Society of London in 1935, and the Alumni Medal of the University of Chicago in 1941. He has received honorary degrees (D.Sc.) from Purdue (1937), Princeton (1938), Lyon (1939), and Colby (1940). He is a member of many of the leading American scientific societies.

DESCRIPTION OF THE PRIZE-WINNING WORK

DAVISSON

While working in the Bell Telephone Laboratories in collaboration with L. H. Germer, Davisson made the discovery for which he received the Nobel Prize. They were investigating the reflection of electrons from ordinary metallic nickel, which consists of a very large number of minute crystals. During one of the experiments the vacuum tube containing the nickel target was shattered when a liquid-air bottle accidentally exploded; air rushing in on the hot target caused oxidation which was only removed after prolonged heating at high temperature. When the experiment was resumed it was found that the phenomenon they were investigating —the variation of electron density with direction—was completely changed. This change was ultimately traced to a re-crystallization of the nickel as a result of the heating to which it had been subjected: instead of a large number of very small crystals there were now only a few large ones.

Davisson and Germer therefore made a detailed study of the reflection of electrons from a single large crystal, and as a result were able to publish in 1927 an account of experiments which showed that a beam of electrons striking a crystal surface was diffracted by the regularly spaced atoms in the same way as X rays. Now diffraction is a characteristic of *waves:* X-rays are electromagnetic waves, but electrons are material particles. Here then was unexpected experimental confirmation of the wave theory of matter put forward by de Broglie (*q.v.* 1929) in 1924. Just as the Braggs (*q.v.* 1915) were able to determine the X-ray wave length from the distances between the layers of atoms in a crystal, so Davisson and Germer were able to determine the wave lengths of the "electron waves" from the known spacing of the atoms in the nickel crystal; they obtained values in excellent agreement with those calculated from the de Broglie formula (p. 289).

It will be remembered that the Braggs, using an ionization chamber, measured the strength of the ionization current produced by the reflected X rays in different directions. Davisson and Germer in their experiments measured the strength of the electronic current in different directions by means of a sensitive galvanometer. Their apparatus is shown schematically in Fig. 34 (p. 361). In the "electron gun," electrons emitted by a heated tungsten ribbon were accelerated to any desired velocity by an electric field. A narrow beam, formed by passing the electrons through collimating apertures, fell normally (i.e., at right angles) on the crystal surface, the particular surface chosen being one known to crystallographers as a (111) face—read "one-one-one" face—because the plane of the surface makes intercepts on the crystallographic axes which are in the ratio 1:1:1 (in the case of a cubic crystal such as nickel the crystallographic axes are parallel to the three edges meeting at a corner). A collector, connected to the galvanometer, could be rotated in a fixed plane about the point of impact of the electron beam; the crystal itself could be rotated about an axis in line with the incident beam.

The result of varying the angle θ between the incident and reflected beams is shown in Fig. 35 (p. 361), where each dot represents a galvanometer reading, the length of the line joining O to the dot being proportional to the electronic current, and the angle between it and the vertical line equal to that between the incident and reflected beams. For a particular setting (azimuth) of the crystal it was found that an incident beam of electrons accelerated by a 54-volt field gave rise to a reflected beam which increased rapidly in intensity as θ approached 50°, reached a maximum at 50°, and then fell off equally rapidly, forming the "spur" shown in the figure. If the collector was kept in the 50° position and the voltage —and therefore the speed of the incident electrons—was gradually increased or decreased, the spur became less and less pronounced, practically disappearing at 40 volts and also at 68 volts. With 181-volt electrons a second spur occurred for the same azimuth at 55°. Altogether more than twenty of these strong beams were found for different voltages and azimuths.

The occurrence of these strong beams in certain directions is readily explained on the assumption that *waves* are incident on the crystal; for, as was explained in connection with the Bragg experiments, the crystal acts as a three-dimensional diffraction grating, the diffracted waves being in phase in certain directions and so reinforcing one another to produce a strong effect. The wave length (λ) of these waves is given by the relation

$$n\lambda = d \cdot \sin \theta \; *$$

where d is the appropriate crystal spacing for the particular azimuth used, θ is the angle between the incident and reflected beams, and n has the values 1, 2, 3, etc. For the azimuth which gives the spur at 50° the value of d is 2.15×10^{-8} cm., so that $\lambda = 1.65 \times 10^{-8}$ cm. Treating the spur found for the same azimuth at 55° as

---

* This formula differs from the Bragg formula (p. 131) by the factor 2. In the scattering of X rays it is the successive *layers* of atoms in the crystal that count, the path difference being 2d · sin θ, where θ is the glancing angle. In electron diffraction it is the *surface* atoms that count, the path difference being in this case d · sin θ, where θ is the angle between the (normal) incident beam and the reflected beam.

a second-order spectrum ($n = 2$), we obtain $\lambda = 0.88 \times 10^{-8}$ cm., reasonably close to half the value for 50 deg. In de Broglie's formula ($\lambda = h/p$), p, the momentum (mass $\times$ velocity), can be expressed in terms of the accelerating potential and the constants e and m (electronic charge and mass, respectively)*. Calculation then gives, for the $50°$ spur (potential 54 volts), $\lambda = 1.67 \times 10^{-8}$ cm. and for the $55°$ spur (potential 181 volts), $\lambda = 0.91 \times 10^{-8}$ cm., in excellent agreement with the experimental values. The agreement was equally good in the case of the other spurs found.

A beam of electrons (material particles), falling on a suitable diffraction grating (the crystal with its regularly arranged atoms), behaves therefore exactly as if it consisted of a train of waves. Of course, the spectrum is spread out all round the crystal; all that can be done with the collector is to search out the directions in which the electrons are concentrated in strong beams and compare the relative intensity of the beams.

We now give some extracts from Davisson's Nobel lecture.†

". . . the idea that light for certain purposes must be regarded as corpuscular . . . , after receiving its quietus at the hands of Thomas Young in 1800, returned to plague a complacent world of physics in 1899. In this year Max Planck put forward his conception that the energy of light is in some way quantized, a conception which, if accepted, supplied, as he showed, a means of explaining completely the distribution of energy in the spectrum of black-body radiation. The quantization was such that transfers of energy between radiation and matter occurred abruptly in amounts proportional to the radiation frequency. The factor of proportionality between these quantities is the ever-recurring Planck constant h. Thus was reborn the idea that light is in some sense corpuscular.

· · · · ·

"In an extended examination carried on chiefly by Richardson and K. T. Compton, Hughes, and Millikan, it was brought out that

---

* $p = \sqrt{\dfrac{2meV}{300}}$, where V is the potential in volts and e is in e.s.u. (p. 48).

† By kind permission of Professor Davisson.

light imparts energy to individual electrons in amounts proportional to its frequency and finally that the factor of proportionality between energy and frequency is just that previously deduced by Planck from the black-body spectrum. The idea . . . had come from Einstein, who out-plancked Planck in not only accepting quantization, but in conceiving of light quanta as actual small packets or particles of energy transferable to single electrons in toto.

"The case for a corpuscular aspect of light, now exceedingly strong, became overwhelmingly so when in 1922 A. H. Compton showed that in certain circumstances light quanta—photons, as they were now called—have elastic collisions with electrons in accordance with the simple laws of particle dynamics. What appeared, and what still appears to many of us as a contradiction in terms, had been proved true beyond the least possible doubt—light was at once a flight of particles and a propagation of waves; for light persisted, unreasonably, to exhibit the phenomenon of interference.

· · · · ·

"In 1913 Niels Bohr gave us his strange conception of 'stationary' orbits in which electrons rotated endlessly without radiating, of electrons disappearing from one orbit and reappearing, after brief but unexplained absences, in another. It was a weird picture—in it were portrayed with remarkable fidelity the most salient of the orderly features which spectroscopic data were then known to possess; there was the Balmer series! and there the Rydberg constant!—correct to the last significant digit! . . . It is important to note that . . . Bohr made judicious use of the constant which Planck had extracted from the black-body spectrum, the constant h.

· · · · ·

". . . The feeling grew that, deeply as Bohr had dived, he had not, so to speak, touched bottom. What was wanted . . . was a new approach, a new theory of the atom which would embrace necessarily all the virtues of the Bohr theory and go beyond it—a theory which would contain some vaguely sensed unifying principle which . . . the Bohr theory lacked.

"Such an underlying principle had been sought for almost from the first. By 1924 one or two ideas of promise had been put forward and were being assiduously developed. Then appeared the brilliant idea which was destined to grow into . . . quantum mechanics. Louis de Broglie put forward in his doctor's thesis the idea that . . . matter like light possesses both the properties of waves and the properties of particles. The various 'restrictions' of the Bohr theory were viewed as conditions for the formation of standing electron wave patterns within the atom.

"Reasoning by analogy from the situation in optics and aided by the clue that Planck's constant is a necessary ingredient of the Bohr theory, de Broglie assumed that this constant would connect also the particle and wave aspects of electrons, if the latter really existed. De Broglie assumed that, as with light, the correlation of the particle and wave properties of matter would be expressed by the relations

$$\text{Energy of particle:} \qquad E = h\nu$$
(ν = frequency, waves per unit time)
$$\text{Momentum of particle:} \qquad p = h\sigma$$
(σ = wave number, waves per unit distance).

The latter may be written in the more familiar form $\lambda = h/p$, where λ represents the wavelength.

"Perhaps no idea in physics has received so rapid or so intensive development as this one. De Broglie himself was in the van of this development but the chief contributions were made by the older and more experienced Schrödinger.

"In these early days . . . attention was focussed on electron waves in atoms. The wave mechanics had sprung from the atom, so to speak, and it was natural that the first applications should be to the atom. No thought was given at this time, it appears, to electrons in free flight. It was implicit in the theory that beams of electrons like beams of light would exhibit the properties of waves, that scattered by an appropriate grating they would exhibit diffraction, yet none of the chief theorists mentioned this interesting corollary. The first to draw attention to it was Elsasser, who pointed out in 1925 that a demonstration of diffraction would establish the physical existence of electron waves. The setting of the stage for the discovery of electron diffraction was now complete.

"It would be pleasant to tell you that no sooner had Elsasser's suggestion appeared than the experiments were begun in New York which resulted in a demonstration of electron diffraction. . . . The work actually began in 1919 with the accidental discovery that the energy spectrum of the secondary electron emission has, as its upper limit, the energy of the primary electrons, even for primaries accelerated through hundreds of volts; that there is, in fact, an elastic scattering of electrons in metals.

"Out of this grew an investigation of the distribution-in-angle of these elastically scattered electrons. And then chance again intervened; it was discovered, purely by accident, that the intensity of elastic scattering varies with the orientations of the scattering crystals. Out of this grew, quite naturally, an investigation of elastic scattering by a single crystal of predetermined orientation. The initiation of this phase of the work occurred in 1925, the year following the publication of de Broglie's thesis, the year preceding the first great development in the wave mechanics. Thus the New York experiment was not, at its inception, a test of the wave theory. Only in the summer of 1926, after I had discussed the investigation in England with Richardson, Born, Franck and others, did it take on this character.

"The search for diffraction beams was begun in the autumn of 1926, but not until early in the following year were any found— first one and then twenty others in rapid succession. Nineteen of these could be used to check the relationships between wavelength and momentum, and in every case the correctness of the de Broglie formula $\lambda = h/p$ was verified to within the limit of accuracy of the measurements.

"I will recall briefly the scheme of the experiment. A beam of electrons of predetermined speed was directed against a (111) face of a crystal of nickel, as indicated schematically in Fig. 1 [Fig. 34]. A collector designed to accept only elastically scattered electrons and their near neighbours could be moved on an arc about the crystal. The crystal itself could be revolved about the axis of the incident beam. It was thus possible to measure the intensity of elastic scattering in any direction in front of the crystal face with

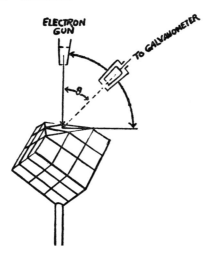

FIG. 34   *Davisson's Fig. 1*

Schematic diagram showing disposition of primary beam, nickel crystal, and collector.

the exception of those directions lying within 10 or 15 degrees of the primary beam.

The curve * reproduced in Fig. 2 [Fig. 35] shows the distribu-

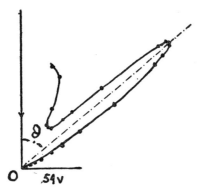

FIG. 35   *Davisson's Fig. 2*

Polar diagram showing intensity of elastic scattering. (The figure is explained on pp. 355-356; the lettering and broken line do not occur in the original.)

---

* *Curves* in the original—only one is reproduced here.

tion-in-angle of intensity for a particular azimuth of the crystal.
. . . For a particular wavelength a diffraction beam shines out. . . .

"The de Broglie relation was tested by computing wavelengths
from the angles of the diffraction beams and the known constant
of the crystal, and comparing these with corresponding wavelengths
computed from the formula

$$\lambda = h/p$$

where p, the momentum of the electrons, was obtained from the
potential used to accelerate the beam and the known value of e/m
for electrons.

· · · · ·

". . . Stern and Esterman in 1929 showed that atomic hydrogen also is diffracted in accordance with the de Broglie-Schrödinger
theory."

While Davisson and Germer were carrying out their researches
in New York, Professor G. P. Thomson of Aberdeen University,
unaware of their work, was also investigating the diffraction of
electrons: his results also were published in 1927, very shortly after
the announcement of the American discovery.

BIOGRAPHICAL SKETCH

THOMSON

GEORGE PAGET THOMSON was born on May 3, 1892, at Cambridge, England, the only son of Sir J. J. Thomson (*q.v.* 1906). He
was educated at Perse School, Cambridge, and at Trinity College,
Cambridge, where he took First Class Honours in the Mathematical
and Natural Sciences Tripos in 1913. He was then appointed a Fellow and lecturer of Corpus Christi College, Cambridge, but on the
outbreak of the First World War was commissioned in the Queen's
Regiment and served in France from 1914 to 1915. In 1915 he
was attached to the Royal Flying Corps for experimental work on
aerodynamical problems. In 1918 he came to the United States as
a member of the British War Mission.

At the end of the war he returned to Corpus Christi College and carried out various researches in the Cavendish Laboratory. In 1922 he was appointed professor of natural philosophy in the University of Aberdeen, and it was here that he did the work on the diffraction of electrons in crystals for which he received the Nobel award. In 1929 he came to the United States again for a few months to give the Baker lectures at Cornell University; he continued his researches there and lectured at the Franklin Institute. In 1930 he was appointed professor of physics at the Imperial College of Science and Technology, University of London, a post which he still holds.

During the Second World War Thomson was chairman of the (British) Commission on Atomic Energy (1940-1941), scientific liaison officer at Ottawa (1941-1942), deputy chairman of the (British) Radio Board (1942-1943), scientific adviser to the Air Ministry (1943-1944). From 1946 to 1947 he was scientific adviser to the British Delegation on Atomic Energy to the United Nations Commission.

Thomson was elected a Fellow of the Royal Society of London in 1929; he was awarded the Hughes Medal in 1939 and the Royal Medal in 1949. Numerous British and foreign universities and societies have conferred honorary degrees or membership on him. He was knighted in 1943.

DESCRIPTION OF THE PRIZE-WINNING WORK

THOMSON

Thomson's experiments differed in almost every detail from those of Davisson and Germer: he used the fast electrons of the cathode rays instead of the comparatively slow ones emitted by a hot filament; the electrons were passed through a metallic foil instead of being reflected from the surface layers of a single crystal; the resulting distribution of the diffracted electrons was recorded photographically instead of being observed electrically. Thomson's experiments therefore correspond to von Laue's, in which X rays were passed through a crystal, whereas Davisson and Germer's correspond to those of the Braggs, in which X rays were reflected from the surface of a crystal. Just as Davisson and Germer, like the Braggs, found strong peaks—"spectra"—in certain directions, so Thomson obtained photographs bearing a remarkable resemblance to von Laue's, both sets showing a dark central spot, formed by the undiffracted beam, surrounded by concentric rings of dark spots formed by the diffracted beams. At least, this was the case in Thomson's photographs when the metallic film was in its natural crystalline state; but when the film had been treated by rolling or beating so that the crystals assumed a random distribution, the diffraction pattern took the form of unbroken concentric rings, exactly like those obtained when X rays are passed through a similarly treated film or through a metallic powder. Moreover, the wave lengths of the electronic waves could be calculated from the diameters of the rings, the dimensions of the apparatus, and the known lattice spacing of the crystals; the results were in complete agreement with the values calculated from the de Broglie formula.

We now give Thomson's Nobel lecture almost *in toto.**

"Although Faraday does not seem to have realised it, his work on electrolysis, by showing the unitary character of the charges on atoms in solution, was the first step [in the history of the electron]. Clerk Maxwell in 1873 used the phrase 'a molecule of electricity' and v. Helmholtz in 1881, speaking of Faraday's work, said 'If we accept the hypothesis that elementary substances are composed of atoms, we cannot well avoid concluding that electricity also is divided into elementary portions which behave like atoms of electricity.' The hypothetical atom received a name . . . when [G.] Johnstone Stoney of Dublin christened it 'electron,' but so far the only property implied was an electric charge.

"The last years of the nineteenth century saw the electron take a leading place amongst the conceptions of physics. It acquired not only mass but universality, it was not only electricity but an essential part of all matter. If among the many names associated with this advance I mention that of J. J. Thomson I hope you will forgive a natural pride. It is to the great work of Bohr that we owe the demonstration of the connection between electrons and Planck's quantum which gave the electron a dynamics of its

---

* By kind permission of Sir G. P. Thomson.

own. A few years later Goudsmit and Uhlenbeck, following on an earlier suggestion by A. H. Compton, showed that it was necessary to suppose that the electron had spin. Yet even with the properties of charge, mass, spin and a special mechanics to help it, the electron was unable to carry the burden of explaining the large and detailed mass of experimental data which had accumulated. L. de Broglie . . . produced . . . the conception that any particle, and in particular an electron, was associated with a system of waves. It is with these waves, formulated more precisely by Schrödinger and modified by Dirac to cover the idea of spin, that the rest of my lecture will deal.

. . . . .

"A narrow beam of cathode rays was transmitted through a thin film of . . . metal [whose] thickness was of the order of 10^{-6} cm. The scattered beam was received on a photographic plate normal to the beam, and when developed the plate showed a pattern of rings, recalling optical halos and the Debye-Scherrer rings well known in the corresponding experiment with X-rays. An interference phenomenon is at once suggested. This would occur if each atom of the film scattered in phase a wavelet from an advancing wave associated with the electrons forming the cathode rays. Since the atoms in each small crystal of the metal are regularly spaced, the phases of the wavelets scattered in any fixed direction will have a definite relationship to one another. In some directions they will agree in phase and build up a strong scattered wave, in others they will destroy one another by interference. The strong waves are analogous to the beams of light diffracted by an optical grating. . . . the arrangement of the atoms . . . for the metals had been determined previously by the use of X-rays. According to de Broglie's theory the wave length associated with an electron is $h/(mv)$, which for the electrons used (cathode rays of 20* to 60,000 volts energy) comes out from 8×10^{-9} to 5×10^{-9} cm. . . . the patterns on the photographic plates agreed quantitatively in all cases with the distribution of strong scattered waves calculated by the method I have indicated. The agreement is good to the accuracy of the experiments, which was about 1%. There is no adjustable constant, and the patterns reproduce not merely the general fea-

* 20,000. Misprint in Nobel Report.

tures of the X-ray patterns but the details due to special arrangements of the crystals in the films which were known to occur from previous investigation by X-rays. Later work has amply confirmed this conclusion, and many thousands of photographs have been taken in my own and other laboratories without any disagreement with the theory being found. The accuracy has increased with the improvement of the apparatus, perhaps the most accurate work being that of v. Friesen of Uppsala who has used the method in a precision determination of e in which he reaches an accuracy of 1 in 1,000.

". . . there are two modifications of the experiments which should be mentioned. In the one, the electrons after passing through the film are subject to a uniform magnetic field which deflects them. It is found that the electrons whose impact on the plate forms the ring pattern are deflected equally with those which have passed through holes in the film. Thus the pattern is due to electrons which have preserved unchanged the property of being deflected by a magnet. This distinguishes the effect from anything produced by X-rays and shows that it is a true property of electrons. The other point is a practical one. To avoid the need for preparing the very thin films which are needed to transmit the electrons an apparatus has been devised to work by reflection, the electrons striking the diffracting surface at a small glancing angle. It appears that in many cases the patterns so obtained are really due to electrons transmitted through small projections on the surface. In other cases, for example when the cleavage surface of a crystal is used, true reflection occurs from the Bragg planes.

"The theory of de Broglie in the form given to it by Schrödinger is now known as wave mechanics and is the basis of atomic physics. It has been applied to a great variety of phenomena with success, but owing largely to mathematical difficulties there are not many cases in which an accurate comparison is possible between theory and experiment. The diffraction of fast electrons by crystals is by far the severest numerical test which has been made, and it is therefore important to see just what conclusions the excellent agreement between theory and these experiments permits us to draw.

"The calculations so far are identical with those in the corresponding case of the diffraction of X-rays. The only assumption made in determining the directions of the diffracted beams is that we have to deal with a train of waves of considerable depth and with a plane wave front extending over a considerable number of atoms. The minimum extension of the wave system sideways and frontways can be found from the sharpness of the lines. Taking v. Friesen's figures, it is at least 225 waves from back to front over a front of more than 200 A* each way.

"But the real trouble comes when we consider the physical meaning of the waves. In fact, . . . the electrons blacken the photographic plate at those places where the waves would be strong. Following Bohr, Born, and Schrödinger, we can express this by saying that the intensity of the waves at any place measures the *probability* of an electron manifesting itself there. This view is strengthened by measurements of the relative intensities of the rings, which agree well with calculations by Mott based on Schrödinger's equation. Such a view . . . is at variance with all ordinary ideas. Why should a particle appear only in certain places associated with a set of waves? Why should waves produce effects only through the medium of particles? For it must be emphasised that in these experiments each electron only sensitises the photographic plate in one minute region, but in that region it has the same powers of penetration and photographic action as if it had never been diffracted. We cannot suppose that the energy is distributed throughout the waves as in a sound or water wave; the wave is only effective in the one place where the electron appears. . . . Yet the motion of the electron, unlike that of a Newtonian particle, is influenced by what happens over the whole front of the wave, as is shown by the effect of the size of the crystals on the sharpness of the patterns. The difference in point of view is fundamental, and we have to face a break with ordinary mechanical ideas. Particles have not a unique track, the energy in these waves is not continuously distributed, probability not determinism governs nature.

. . . . .

". . . electron diffraction . . . has important practical applications to the study of surface effects. . . . X-ray diffraction has

---

* *Angstrom*, 10^{-8} cm. (very nearly).

made it possible to determine the arrangement of the atoms in a great variety of solids and even liquids. X-rays are very penetrating, and any structure peculiar to the surface of a body will be likely to be overlooked, for its effect is swamped in that of the much greater mass of underlying material. Electrons only affect layers a few atoms, or at most tens of atoms, in thickness and so are eminently suited for the purpose. The position of the beams diffracted from a surface enables us, at least in many cases, to determine the arrangement of the atoms in the surface. Among the many cases which have already been studied I . . . refer to one, the state of the surface of polished metals. Many years ago Sir George Beilby suggested that this resembled a supercooled liquid which had flowed under the stress of polishing. A series of experiments by electron diffraction carried out at the Imperial College in London has confirmed this conclusion. The most recent work due to Dr. Cochrane has shown that though this amorphous layer is stable at ordinary temperature as long as it remains fixed to the mass of the metal, it is unstable when removed, and recrystallises after a few hours. Work by Professor Finch on these lines has led to valuable conclusions as to the wear on the surfaces of cylinders and pistons in petrol engines."

CONSEQUENCES IN THEORY AND PRACTICE

The theoretical importance of the work of Davisson and Thomson lies in the fact that it established beyond reasonable doubt the existence of the matter waves postulated by de Broglie—at least as far as electrons are concerned; we shall see later that Stern (*q.v.* 1943) demonstrated that atoms and molecules, too, exhibit wave properties. The important practical applications of electron diffraction were mentioned by Thomson in his Nobel lecture.

1 9 3 8

ENRICO FERMI
(1901–   )

"For the discovery of new radioactive elements produced by neutron irradiation, and for the discovery of nuclear reactions brought about by slow electrons."

BIOGRAPHICAL SKETCH

ENRICO FERMI WAS BORN ON SEPTEMBER 29, 1901, IN ROME. After receiving a high-school education there, he went in 1918 to the University of Pisa, where he obtained his doctor's degree in physics in 1922. He then studied for some months under Professor Max Born at Göttingen, and at Leiden. On his return to Italy in 1924 he was appointed lecturer in mathematical physics and mechanics at the University of Florence. In 1927 he became professor of theoretical physics in the University of Rome, where he remained until 1938. He came to the United States in 1939 to take up an appointment as professor of physics at Columbia University. Since 1946 he has been professor of physics at the University of Chicago.

Fermi was awarded the Franklin Medal by the Franklin Institute in 1947. He holds honorary doctorates of several universities, including Yale, Columbia, Washington, Utrecht, and Heidelberg. He is a member of a number of Italian and other learned societies and academies, including the American Physical Society and the American Philosophical Society.

DESCRIPTION OF THE PRIZE-WINNING
WORK

In 1932 Chadwick (*q.v.* 1935) discovered the neutron, an un-charged particle equal in mass to the proton, the nucleus of the hydrogen atom. Not only did this discovery lead to important changes in the theory of nuclear composition, but it also provided the nuclear research physicist with a far more effective projectile for producing nuclear transformations than either the alpha particle or the proton, both of which are slowed up in their passage through matter as a result of the electrostatic repulsion between their own positive charges and those of atomic nuclei, and may lose their energy without having struck a nucleus. Lawrence (*q.v.* 1939) showed in 1933 that fast deuterons, "heavy hydrogen" nuclei composed of one proton and one neutron, are very effective in producing nuclear transformations, but they too, like all nuclei, carry positive charges and are therefore slowed up in their passage through matter. Again, the repulsion between two positive charges increases with the magnitude of either charge, so that the heavier the atom the greater the repulsion experienced by a positively charged particle. Such particles are therefore effective as bombarding particles only against nuclei of small or moderate mass. It is here that the neutron plays so important a part; for, being uncharged, it is able to penetrate the nucleus of an atom with ease, and is brought to rest only by actual collision (the range of a neutron in lead may be as much as 20 cm. whereas that of the alpha particle is only $\frac{1}{4}$ mm.). Neutrons are therefore especially effective as projectiles in attacks on atomic nuclei.

What happens when a nucleus is struck by a neutron can be observed in a Wilson cloud chamber; for though the neutron itself, being uncharged, does not produce tracks, the charged particles ejected by it from the nucleus do. Two tracks, sometimes more, are seen originating from a common point, one of the tracks being due to the recoiling nucleus, the others to the ejected particles. There is considerable variety in the reactions which occur when a nucleus is struck, and since 1933 the study of these reactions has grown to be a new branch of science, *nuclear chemistry,* in which the reactions are represented by equations similar to those used in ordinary chemistry. Thus the effect of bombarding the beryllium nucleus with an alpha particle is represented by the equation

$$_4^9\text{Be} + _2^4\text{He} \rightarrow _6^{12}\text{C} + _0^1 n$$

$_4^9\text{Be}$ denoting a beryllium nucleus of mass number 9 and charge $+4e$, where e is the magnitude of the electronic charge; $_2^4\text{He}$ an alpha particle, i.e., a helium nucleus, mass number 4, charge $+2e$; $_6^{12}\text{C}$ a carbon nucleus, mass number 12, charge $+6e$; $_0^1 n$ a neutron, mass number 1, charge zero. Examples of the possible effects of the bombardment of the nitrogen nucleus with neutrons are:

$$_7^{14}\text{N} + _0^1 n \rightarrow _5^{11}\text{B} + _2^4\text{He}$$

the products being a boron nucleus and an alpha particle;

$$_7^{14}\text{N} + _0^1 n \rightarrow _3^7\text{Li} + 2\,_2^4\text{He}$$

where the products are a lithium nucleus and *two* alpha particles; and

$$_7^{14}\text{N} + _0^1 n \rightarrow {}^{14}\text{C} + _1^1\text{H}$$

the products being an isotope of carbon, of mass number 14, and a proton, or hydrogen nucleus, mass number 1, charge $+e$. In these reactions the neutron is "captured" by the nucleus; the totals of the mass numbers and of the nuclear charges must then be the same on both sides of the equation.

The nuclei produced in the above reactions are stable. In 1933 Curie and Joliot produced *unstable* nuclei by bombardment of aluminum with alpha particles from polonium; neutrons were emitted and an isotope of phosphorus formed, the reaction being given by the equation

$$_{13}^{27}\text{Al} + _2^4\text{He} \rightarrow _{15}^{30}\text{P} + _0^1 n$$

The isotope of phosphorus $_{15}^{30}\text{P}$ (*radio-phosphorus*) is one which does not occur naturally; it is unstable and radioactive, the criterion for radioactivity being the emission of particles *after* the source of the bombarding particles has been removed, the "activity" falling to half-value in a definite and characteristic period of time. In this case positrons are emitted, the activity falling to half-value in 2.55

sec.; the radio-phosphorus "decays" into a stable, naturally occurring isotope of silicon ($^{30}_{14}$Si). The transformation is expressed
by the equation

$$^{30}_{15}P \rightarrow {}^{30}_{14}Si + e^+$$

where e^+ denotes a positron. Similar reactions were found to occur
with boron and beryllium, positrons again being emitted.

Toward the end of 1933 Fermi began his important researches
on artificial, or induced, radioactivity, using neutrons instead of
alpha particles as bombarding particles. As neutron source he used
beryllium powder in a bulb containing radon, or radium emanation, a radioactive gas given off by radium. The alpha particles
emitted by the radon bombarded the beryllium nuclei, causing
them to disintegrate with emission of neutrons, which were then
used to bombard the element under test. Some six months after
the commencement of these experiments Fermi and his collaborators made the extremely important discovery that the effectiveness
of the neutrons in producing activation was increased as much as a
hundredfold if they were first slowed down by passing them
through a substance rich in hydrogen, such as paraffin or water.
Collision between a neutron and an atomic nucleus generally results in the capture of the neutron or in the disruption of the nucleus; but the hydrogen nucleus, which consists of a single proton,
cannot be disrupted and only very rarely captures the neutron to
form a heavy hydrogen nucleus (deuteron). The result of a collision between a neutron and a hydrogen nucleus is therefore simply
to slow down the neutron.

The following extracts describing Fermi's work on neutron bombardment are taken * from his Nobel lecture, which he delivered
in English.

"[Rutherford] showed . . . that when the nucleus of a light
element is struck by a fast α-particle, some disintegration process
of the struck nucleus occurs, as a consequence of which the α-par-
ticle remains captured inside the nucleus and a different particle, in
many cases a proton, is emitted in its place. What remains at the
end of the process is a nucleus different from the original one;

---

* By kind permission of Professor Fermi.

different in general both in electric charge and in atomic weight.

"The nucleus that remains as disintegration product coincides sometimes with one of the stable nuclei, known from the isotopic analysis; very often, however, this is not the case. The product nucleus is then different from all 'natural' nuclei, the reason being that the product nucleus is not stable. It disintegrates further, with a mean life characteristic of the nucleus, by emission of an electron (positive or negative), until it finally reaches a stable form. The emission of electrons that follows with a lag in time the first practically instantaneous disintegration is the so-called artificial radioactivity, and was discovered by Joliot and Irène Curie at the end of the year 1933.

"These authors obtained the first cases of artificial radioactivity by bombarding boron, magnesium and aluminium with α-particles from a polonium source. They produced thus three radioactive isotopes of nitrogen, silicon and phosphorus, and succeeded also in separating chemically the activity from the bulk of the unmodified atoms of the bombarded substance.

"*The Neutron Bombardment.* Immediately after these discoveries it appeared evident that α-particles very likely did not represent the only type of bombarding projectiles for producing artificial radioactivity. I decided therefore to investigate from this point of view the effects of the bombardment with neutrons.

"Compared with α-particles, the neutrons have the obvious drawback that the available neutron sources emit only a comparatively small number of neutrons. . . . This drawback is, however, compensated by the fact that neutrons, having no electric charge, can reach the nuclei of all atoms without having to overcome the potential barrier due to the Coulomb field that surrounds the nucleus. Furthermore, since neutrons practically do not interact with electrons, their range is very long, and the probability of a nuclear collision is correspondingly larger than in the case of the α-particle or the proton bombardment. As a matter of fact, neutrons were already known to be an efficient agent for producing some nuclear disintegrations.

"As a source of neutrons in these researches I used a small glass bulb containing beryllium powder and radon. With amounts of radon up to 800 millicuries such a source emits about 2×10^7

neutrons per second. This number is of course very small compared
with the yield of neutrons that can be obtained from cyclotrons or
from high voltage tubes. The small dimensions, the perfect steadi-
ness and the utmost simplicity are, however, sometimes very useful
features of the radon + beryllium sources.

"*Nuclear Reactions Produced by Neutrons.*   Since the first experiments I could prove that the majority of the elements tested
became active under the effect of the neutron bombardment. In
some cases the decay of the activity with time corresponded to a
single mean life; in others to the superposition of more than one
exponential decay curve.

"A systematic investigation of the behaviour of the elements
throughout the periodic table was carried out by myself, with the
help of several collaborators, namely, Amaldi, D'Agostino, Ponte-
corvo, Rasetti and Segrè. In most cases we performed also a chemical analysis, in order to identify the chemical element that was the
carrier of the activity. For short living substances such an analysis
must be performed very quickly, in a time of the order of one
minute.

"The results of this first survey of the radioactivities produced
by neutrons can be summarized as follows: Out of 63 elements investigated, 37 showed an easily detectable activity; the percentage
of the activable elements did not show any marked dependence
on the atomic weight of the element. Chemical analysis and other
considerations, mainly based on the distribution of the isotopes,
permitted further to identify the following three types of nuclear
reactions giving rise to artificial radioactivity:

$$(1) \qquad {}^{M}_{Z}A + {}^{1}_{0}n = {}^{M-3}_{Z-2}A + {}^{4}_{2}\mathrm{He}$$
$$(2) \qquad {}^{M}_{Z}A + {}^{1}_{0}n = {}^{M}_{Z-1}A + {}^{1}_{1}\mathrm{H}$$
$$(3) \qquad {}^{M}_{Z}A + {}^{1}_{0}n = {}^{M+1}_{Z}A$$

where ${}^{M}_{Z}A$ is the symbol for an element with atomic number Z and
mass number M; ${}^{1}_{0}n$ is the symbol of the neutron.

"The reactions of the types (1) and (2) occur chiefly among the
light elements, while those of the type (3) are found very often
also for heavy elements. In many cases the three processes are found
at the same time in a single element. For instance, neutron bombardment of aluminium that has a single isotope ${}^{27}\mathrm{Al}$, gives rise to

three radioactive products: ^{24}Na, with a half period of 15 hours by process (1); ^{27}Mg, with a period of 10 minutes by process (2); and ^{28}Al with a period of 2.3 minutes by process (3).

. . . . .

"*The Slow Neutrons.* The intensity of the activation as a function of the distance from the neutron source shows in some cases anomalies apparently dependent on the objects that surround the source. A careful investigation of these effects led to the unexpected result that surrounding both source and body to be activated with masses of paraffin increases in some cases the intensity of activation by a very large factor (up to 100). A similar effect is produced by water, and in general by substances containing a large concentration of hydrogen. Substances not containing hydrogen show sometimes similar features, though extremely less pronounced.

"The interpretation of these results was as follows. The neutron and the proton having approximately the same mass, any elastic impact of a fast neutron against a proton initially at rest gives rise to a partition of the available kinetic energy between neutron and proton; it can be shown that a neutron having an initial energy of 10^6 volts*, after about 20 impacts against hydrogen atoms has its energy already reduced to a value close to that corresponding to thermal agitation. It follows that, when neutrons of high energy are shot by a source inside a large mass of paraffin or water, they very rapidly lose most of their energy and are transformed into 'slow neutrons'. Both theory and experiment show that certain types of neutron reactions, and especially those of type (3), occur with a much larger cross-section for slow neutrons than for fast neutrons, thus accounting for the larger intensities of activation observed when irradiation is performed inside a large mass of paraffin or water.

"It should be remarked furthermore that the mean free path for the elastic collisions of neutrons against hydrogen atoms in paraffin decreases rather pronouncedly with the energy. When, therefore, after three or four impacts the energy of the neutron is already considerably reduced, its probability of diffusing outside of the paraffin, before the process of slowing down is completed, becomes very small."

---

* Strictly, *electron-volts* (see p. 379, note).

By means of slow neutrons Fermi and his collaborators succeeded in producing radioactive isotopes of most of the elements, including the very heavy ones. In 1934, by bombarding uranium, the heaviest element then known, with neutrons, they obtained what appeared to be an isotope of a new element of still higher atomic number. The most widely occurring isotope of uranium has atomic number 92 and mass number 238, so that its nucleus is composed of 92 positively charged protons and 146 neutrons, its symbol therefore being $^{238}_{92}U$. The substance is radioactive, emitting alpha particles— emission of beta particles (negative electrons) would leave the nuclei with a higher positive charge, 93, but no element of atomic number 93 was then known. When Fermi bombarded uranium 238 with neutrons, he found that γ rays were emitted and that beta-particle emission was in fact set up and continued for some time. He interpreted this as due to the formation by neutron capture of a new element of mass number 239 (the original 146 neutrons + the captured neutron) and nuclear charge 93 (due to the emission of a beta particle).

The process is now known to take place in two stages, first the capture of the neutron and emission of the γ ray to form the uranium isotope $^{239}_{92}U$, as expressed by the equation

$$^{238}_{92}U + {}^{1}_{0}n \rightarrow {}^{239}_{92}U + \gamma$$

secondly, $^{239}_{92}U$ decays with emission of beta particles into the new element, later named *neptunium* ($^{239}_{93}Np$), according to the equation

$$^{239}_{92}U \rightarrow {}^{239}_{93}Np + \beta^-$$

where β^- denotes a negative beta particle. Neptunium is itself radioactive, decaying, again with emission of beta particles, into another new element, later named *plutonium* ($^{239}_{94}Pu$), of atomic number 94 and mass number 239, thus:

$$^{239}_{93}Np \rightarrow {}^{239}_{94}Pu + \beta^-$$

At the time, however, the mechanism of the process was by no means clear, and further investigations by Fermi and others produced a number of conflicting results; although Fermi's general observations were confirmed, the isotopic products showed considerable variety.

In 1938 Hahn (winner of the 1944 Nobel Prize in Chemistry) and Strassmann made a thorough investigation into the chemical nature of these new radioactive substances, in the course of which they found that uranium, when bombarded with neutrons, in part broke up into a number of isotopes of moderate atomic weight, including an isotope of barium. Thus was discovered *nuclear fission,* which was to make possible the atomic bomb of 1945. It was Fermi who, after his arrival in the United States, solved one of the main problems in connection with the controlled release of atomic energy, and in 1942 constructed the first atomic pile—the Fermi pile—for the purpose of producing plutonium.

On the theoretical side, Fermi investigated the problem of beta-ray emission in a radioactive change. It has already been mentioned (p. 337) that the proton-neutron theory of the nucleus left the emission of these beta particles unexplained. Fermi in 1934 put forward the theory, now the most generally accepted, that the proton and neutron are different states of a single fundamental particle, the *nucleon,* and that a positron is emitted when a proton turns into a neutron, a negative electron when a neutron turns into a proton. For reasons to do with the conservation of energy Fermi also assumed the existence of a hypothetical particle postulated shortly before by Pauli (*q.v.* 1945)—the *neutrino,* an uncharged particle of very small mass, no greater than that of the electron. According to Fermi's theory the emission of a positive or negative electron is always accompanied by that of a neutrino. No direct evidence for the existence of this particle has so far come to light, but indirect evidence is accumulating.

CONSEQUENCES IN THEORY AND PRACTICE

Fermi's work on induced radioactivity was of immense importance. It led to an intensive study of radioactive isotopes and the nuclear reactions by which they are produced. At the present time radioactive isotopes of all the elements including plutonium are known, with the single exception of hydrogen. The importance of Fermi's work on the controlled release of atomic energy does not need stressing.

1 9 3 9

ERNEST ORLANDO LAWRENCE
(1901–   )

*"For the discovery and development of the cyclo-
tron, and for the results obtained by its aid,
especially with regard to artificially radioactive
elements."*

BIOGRAPHICAL SKETCH

ERNEST ORLANDO LAWRENCE WAS BORN ON AUGUST 8, 1901,
in Canton, S. D. He attended the public schools of Canton and
Pierre, S. D. and did his undergraduate work first at St. Olaf College, Northfield, Minn., and then at the University of South Dakota,
where he studied physics, receiving his A.B. degree in 1922. He
then did postgraduate work at the University of Minnesota, obtaining his M.A. degree in 1923; here he came under the influence of
Dr. W. F. G. Swann, an authority on cosmic rays. After a period of
postgraduate work at the University of Chicago, Lawrence went to
Yale University, where Dr. Swann had been transferred; here
Lawrence took his Ph.D. degree in 1925, remaining on first as a
National Research Fellow, then as assistant professor. In 1928,
when Dr. Swann left Yale to become director of the Bartol Research Foundation, Lawrence, already recognized as one of the most
brilliant young physicists in the country, was appointed associate
professor of physics at the University of California, becoming professor of physics in 1930. In 1936 he also became director of the
Radiation laboratory. It was here at California that the work was
done which gained him the Nobel Prize.

Lawrence has been awarded the Elliott Cresson Medal by the Franklin Institute, the Research Corporation Prize, the Hughes Medal of the Royal Society of London, and the Comstock Prize of the National Academy of Sciences. He was elected a member of the National Academy of Sciences in 1934.

DESCRIPTION OF THE PRIZE-WINNING WORK

Between 1924 and the receipt of the Nobel Prize, Lawrence published no fewer than fifty-six papers, alone or in collaboration with his students and associates. His doctor's thesis of 1925 dealt with photoelectricity, a subject which continued to occupy his attention both at Yale and California. In 1926, while a National Research Fellow at Yale, he carried out an important research on the ionization potential of the mercury atom; this was the most precise determination of an ionization potential so far made.

The voltage required to remove an electron from an atom and so produce a positively charged ion is small, of the order of ten volts. Before the discovery of the neutron (*q.v.* 1935), to disrupt the nucleus of an atom and so produce a different atom required bombardment by high-energy particles—particles of a million or more electron-volts * energy. Though this energy is in itself minute, a million electron-volts being equal to about 1½ millionths of an erg (one foot-pound equals about seven million ergs), yet to impart a million *e*-volts energy to an electron still requires a potential difference of a million volts. Lawrence's great achievement lay in devising a method of obtaining particles of such high energies *without* the use of correspondingly high potential differences, and it was for this and his subsequent investigations that he received the Nobel Prize.

Lawrence happened to see a paper by a German physicist, R. Wideroe, who had succeeded in producing particles with an energy corresponding to a 50,000-volt potential drop while actually using only a 25,000-volt potential drop. Wideroe's arrangement did not lend itself to adaptation for obtaining high orders of

---

* An electron-volt is the energy acquired by an electron in falling through a potential difference of one volt.

energy, but Lawrence saw how it could be modified. The outcome
was the *cyclotron,* constructed by Lawrence and one of his students
in January 1930 and first publicly announced at the meeting of the
National Academy of Sciences in Berkeley in September of the
same year.

The principle of the cyclotron is this: a particle is made to cross
and recross repeatedly an electric field whose direction is reversed
between successive entries of the particle, which thus receives successive impulses in the direction of its motion. This was achieved
as follows. A flat horizontal circular metal drum was divided into
halves by a vertical plane. These *dees,* as they are called, were
placed, with a small gap between them, between the poles of a
powerful electromagnet sufficiently large to ensure a uniform
vertical magnetic field. If there is a potential difference between
the dees, a charged particle in the space between them will be
accelerated; it then enters one of the dees, where it is shielded from
the electric field, but its path is bent into a semicircle by the magnetic field, so that the particle again enters the space between the
dees. At this moment the direction of the electric field is reversed,
so that the particle is again accelerated. It then enters the second
dee, where its path is again bent by the magnetic field into a semicircle, but of slightly larger radius owing to the increased velocity
of the particle. The particle then re-enters the electric field, now in
the same direction as originally, and is further accelerated. This
process is repeated over and over again until the particle reaches
the outer edge of the dee, when it is withdrawn through a port-
hole, having attained an energy corresponding to a fall of potential
equal to the potential difference between the two dees multiplied
by the number of times it has crossed the gap.

The time taken by the particle to describe each semicircular path
is always the same, since it depends only on the mass and charge
of the particle and the strength of the magnetic field; it is independent of the radius of the path and the velocity of the particle; the
faster the particle is moving, the bigger the radius of the semicircle, but the time is always the same. The separate arrivals at the
gap are therefore separated by equal intervals of time and so can be
timed to take place at the moment the direction of the electric field
is reversed. The successive reversals of the electric field are effected

by connecting the dees to a source of alternating potential difference whose frequency is adjusted so that the arrivals of the particle at the gap coincide with the reversals in direction of the electric field. The particles in question are gas molecules which have been ionized by electrons emitted by a heated tungsten wire.

Because of the outbreak of the Second World War, the Nobel Prize presentation ceremonies at Stockholm were not held in 1939 and Lawrence did not deliver the usual Nobel lecture. We have therefore taken the following extracts from the account of his work which he published, jointly with M. Stanley Livingstone, in the *Physical Review,* Vol. 40 (1932), p. 19.

PRODUCTION OF HIGH-SPEED LIGHT IONS WITHOUT THE USE OF HIGH VOLTAGES

"The classical experiments of Rutherford and his associates and Pose on artificial disintegration, and of Bothe and Becker on excitation of nuclear radiation, substantiate the view that the nucleus is susceptible to the same general methods of investigation that have been so successful in revealing the extra-nuclear properties of the atom. Especially do the results of their work point to the great fruitfulness of studies of nuclear transitions excited artificially in the laboratory. The development of methods of nuclear excitation on an extensive scale is thus a problem of great interest; its solution is probably the key to a new world of phenomena, the world of the nucleus.

"But it is as difficult as it is interesting, for the nucleus resists such experimental attacks with a formidable wall of high binding energies. Nuclear energy levels are widely separated and, in consequence, processes of nuclear excitation involve enormous amounts of energy—millions of volt-electrons.

"It is therefore of interest to inquire as to the most promising modes of nuclear excitation. Two general methods present themselves: excitation by absorption of radiation (gamma radiation) and excitation by intimate nuclear collisions of high speed particles.

"Of the first it may be said that recent experimental studies of the absorption of gamma radiation in matter show, for the heavier elements, variations with atomic number that indicate a quite appreciable nuclear effect. This suggests that nuclear excitation by absorption of radiation is perhaps a not infrequent process, and therefore that the development of an intense artificial source of gamma radiation of various wave-lengths would be of considerable value for nuclear studies. In our laboratory, as elsewhere, this is being attempted.

"But the collision method appears to be even more promising, in consequence of the researches of Rutherford and others cited above. Their pioneer investigations must always be regarded as really great experimental achievements, for they established definite and important information about nuclear processes of great rarity excited by exceedingly weak beams of bombarding particles—alpha-particles from radioactive sources. Moreover, and this is the point to be emphasized here, their work has shown strikingly the great fruitfulness of the kinetic collision method and the importance of the development of intense artificial sources of alpha-particles. Of course it cannot be inferred from their experiments that alpha-particles are the most effective nuclear projectiles: the question naturally arises whether lighter or heavier particles of given kinetic energy would be more effective in bringing about nuclear transitions.

· · · · ·

"Though at present the relative efficacy of protons and alpha-particles cannot be established with much certainty, it does seem safe to conclude at least that the most efficacious nuclear projectiles will prove to be swiftly moving ions, probably of low atomic number. In consequence it is important to develop methods of accelerating ions to speeds much greater than have heretofore been produced in the laboratory.

"The importance of this is generally recognized and several laboratories are developing techniques of the production and the application to vacuum tubes of high voltages for the generation of high speed electrons and ions. . . .

· · · · ·

"These methods involving the direct utilization of high voltages are subject to certain practical limitations. The experimental difficulties go up rapidly with increasing voltage; there are the difficulties of corona and insulation and also there is the problem of design of suitable high voltage vacuum tubes.

"Because of these difficulties we have thought it desirable to develop methods for the acceleration of charged particles that do not require the use of high voltages. Our objective is twofold: first, to make the production of particles having kinetic energies of the order of magnitude of one million volt-electrons a matter that can be carried through with quite modest laboratory equipment and with an experimental convenience that, it is hoped, will lead to a widespread attack on this highly important domain of physical phenomena; and second, to make practicable the production of particles having kinetic energies in excess of those producible by direct high voltage methods—perhaps in the range of 10,000,000 volt-electrons and above.

"A method for the multiple acceleration of ions to high speeds, primarily designed for heavy ions, has recently been described in this journal*. The present paper is a report of the development of a method for the multiple acceleration of light ions. Particular attention has been given to the acceleration of protons because of their apparent unique utility in nuclear studies. In the present work relatively large currents of 1,220,000 volt-protons have been generated and there is foreshadowed in the not distant future the production of 10,000,000 volt-protons.

"*The Experimental Method.* In the method for the multiple acceleration of ions to high speeds, recently described, the ions travel through a series of metal tubes in synchronism with an applied oscillating electric potential. It is so arranged that as an ion travels from the interior of one tube to the interior of the next there is always an accelerating field, and the final velocity of the ion on emergence from the system corresponds approximately to a voltage as many times greater than the applied voltage between adjacent tubes as there are tubes. The method is most conveniently used for the acceleration of heavy ions; for light ions travel faster and hence require longer systems of tubes for any given frequency of applied oscillations.

---

* D. H. Sloan and E. O. Lawrence, *Physical Review,* Vol. 38 (1931), p. 2021.

"The present experimental method makes use of the same principle of repeated acceleration of the ions by a similar sort of resonance with an oscillating electric field, but has overcome the
difficulty of the cumbersomely long accelerating system by causing,
with the aid of a magnetic field, the ions to circulate back and forth
from the interior of one electrode to the interior of another.

"This may be seen most readily by an outline of the experimental arrangement (Fig. 1) [Fig. 36]. Two electrodes A, B in the

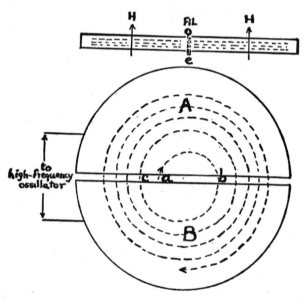

FIG. 36   *Lawrence's Fig. 1*

Diagram of experimental method for multiple acceleration of ions.

form of semi-circular hollow plates are mounted in a vacuum tube
in coplanar fashion with their diametral edges adjacent. By placing the system between the poles of a magnet, a magnetic field is
introduced that is normal to the plane of the plates. High frequency
electric oscillations are applied to the plates so that there results an
oscillating electric field in the diametral region between them.

"With this arrangement it is evident that, if at one moment there
is an ion in the region between the electrodes, and electrode A is
negative with respect to electrode B, then the ion will be accelerated

to the interior of the former. Within the electrode the ion traverses a circular path because of the magnetic field, and ultimately emerges again between the electrodes; this is indicated in the diagram by the arc *a .. b*. If the time consumed by the ion in making the semi-circular path is equal to the half period of the electric oscillations, the electric field will have reversed and the ion will receive a second acceleration, passing into the interior of electrode *B* with a higher velocity. Again it travels on a semi-circular path (*b .. c*), but this time the radius of curvature is greater because of the greater veloc-ity. For all velocities (neglecting variation of mass with velocity) the radius of the path is proportional to the velocity, so that the time required for traversal of a semi-circular path is independent of the ion's velocity. Therefore, if the ion travels its first half circle in a half cycle of the oscillations, it will do likewise on all succeed-ing paths. Hence it will circulate around on ever widening semi-circles from the interior of one electrode to the interior of the other, gaining an increment of energy on each crossing of the diametral region that corresponds to the momentary potential difference be-tween the electrodes. Thus, if, as was done in the present experi-ments, high frequency oscillations having peak values of 4000 volts are applied to the electrodes, and protons are caused to spiral around in this way 150 times, they will receive 300 increments of energy, acquiring thereby a speed corresponding to 1,200,000 volts.

·   ·   ·   ·   ·

"An ideal source of ions is one that delivers to the diametral region between the electrodes large quantities of ions with low components of velocity normal to the plane of the accelerators. This requirement has most conveniently been met in the present experiments merely by having a filament placed above the diametral region from which a stream of electrons passes down along the magnetic lines of force, generating ions of gases in the tube. The ions so formed are pulled out sideways by the oscillating electric field. The electrons are not drawn out because of their very small radii of curvature in the magnetic field. Thus, the beam of electrons is collimated and the ions are formed with negligible initial veloci-ties right in the region where they are wanted. The oscillating elec-tric field immediately draws them out and takes them on their spiral paths to the periphery. This arrangement is diagrammatically shown in the upper part of Fig. 1 [Fig. 36]."

Lawrence's first cyclotron measured only four inches in diameter, but even with this he was able to obtain a beam of hydrogen ions whose energy corresponded to that produced by 80,000 volts. In 1932, with an 11-inch cyclotron, he produced a beam of $1\frac{1}{4}$-million-volt hydrogen ions; with this he was able to disintegrate lithium. In the same year H. C. Urey (winner of the 1934 Nobel Prize in Chemistry), at Columbia University, discovered heavy hydrogen, and this, when used in the cyclotron, provided a beam of heavy-hydrogen nuclei, or deuterons, which proved most effective in producing nuclear disintegrations. By 1939 a cyclotron had been constructed which weighed 220 tons, the vacuum chamber being 60 inches in diameter; a five-foot beam of heavy-hydrogen nuclei issued into the air from the vacuum chamber, the energy of the particles being some sixteen million e-volts. A modified form of the original cyclotron, the synchro-cyclotron, is now in operation at the Radiation Laboratory, Berkeley; the electromagnet weighs nearly 4000 tons, with 300 tons of copper windings; it gives a deuteron beam of 200 million e-volts energy.

In 1932 Chadwick (*q.v.* 1935), in the Cavendish Laboratory, discovered the neutron, an uncharged particle with a mass equal to that of the hydrogen atom; the following year Lawrence bombarded beryllium with deuterons and obtained a copious emission of neutrons from the disintegration of the beryllium nuclei.

Later work carried out by Lawrence dealt with the production of new radioactive isotopes by bombardment with deuterons, in particular with the production of a radioactive form of sodium which, used as a tracer element, plays an important part in the study of biological processes. In the years just preceding the award of the Nobel Prize he was investigating the biological and physiological effects of neutrons.

CONSEQUENCES IN THEORY AND PRACTICE

Through his invention of the cyclotron Lawrence gave to science its most effective means of producing vast numbers of high-speed heavy particles—alpha particles, protons, deuterons—particles which play an all-important part in the study of nuclear reactions. For the production of radioactive isotopes the cyclotron is exceeded in efficiency only by the uranium pile.

1 9 4 0

No award

1 9 4 1

No award

1 9 4 2

No award

1 9 4 3

OTTO STERN
(1888–   )

"For his contributions to the development of the molecular ray method and for his discovery of the magnetic moment of the proton."

BIOGRAPHICAL SKETCH

OTTO STERN WAS BORN ON FEBRUARY 17, 1888, AT SORAU IN Brandenburg, Prussia. In 1892 his parents moved to Breslau, where Stern later attended high school. In 1906 he entered Breslau University, where he studied physical chemistry, obtaining his doctor's degree in 1912. For the next two years he worked with Einstein, first at Prague, then at the Federal Technical High School, Zurich, where he was *privatdozent*. From 1915 to 1921 he was *privatdozent* in theoretical physics at the University of Frankfort on the Main. In 1921 he was appointed associate professor of theoretical physics in the University of Rostock and two years later professor of physical chemistry and director of the laboratory in the University of Hamburg. Compelled to leave Germany in 1933, he came to the United States, where he was research professor of physics at the Carnegie Institute of Technology, Pittsburgh, from 1933 to 1945.

DESCRIPTION OF THE PRIZE-WINNING WORK

According to the kinetic theory of gases the molecules of a gas are in a state of violent agitation, darting about in the space occupied by the gas (or vapor) with a mean velocity depending on the temperature. Each molecule travels in a straight line until it collides with another molecule or with the walls of the containing vessel. Should there be a small hole in the wall of the vessel, every now and then a molecule traveling directly toward this hole will escape into the open air, there to be buffeted about by the molecules of the air. If, however, the hole leads into a high vacuum, the escaping molecules will meet few other molecules to deflect them from their straight-line paths and slow them up, so that, if the enclosure is at a sufficiently high temperature, a stream of fast molecules will issue from it and travel the length of the vacuum tube. These were the "molecular rays" used by Stern in his experiments; they are usually called molecular rays (or beams), though often they are really "atomic rays," as, for instance, in the case of vaporized silver, where the molecule consists of a single atom.

Stern's experiments, begun at Frankfort about 1920, were continued at Rostock in collaboration with Walter Gerlach, and brought to perfection at Hamburg. The gas or vaporized substance escaped through a narrow slit in the wall of an electrically heated "oven" into the vacuum chamber, where it was narrowed down by another slit before striking the opposite wall and there condensing. The arrangement is shown schematically in Fig. 37 (p. 393). How these earlier experiments demonstrated the correctness of the fundamental assumptions of the kinetic theory is told in the extracts from Stern's Nobel lecture given below; there, too, will be found an account of the experiments in which the method used by Fizeau to measure the velocity of light (see p. 53) was applied to determine the velocity distribution of the molecules.

Stern's most important researches, both then and later, dealt, however, with the effect of an applied magnetic field on the motion of the molecules or atoms, and the application of this effect to the measurement of the magnetic moment of an atom. An atom, being an electrically charged system in rotation, behaves like a minute magnet, that is, it possesses a magnetic moment. For simplicity, picture each atom as a minute bar magnet; then the magnetic moment is the strength of either pole multiplied by the distance between the poles. Such a magnet, on entering a *uniform* magnetic field, will tend to assume a position with its magnetic axis, the line joining the two poles, parallel to the field, but the direction of its forward motion will not be affected. If, however, the field is not uniform, i.e., is *inhomogeneous,* so that its strength varies from point to point, then one pole of the elementary magnet will find itself in a stronger part of the field than the other, and there will be a resultant force on the magnet as a whole tending to change the direction of the forward motion.

In the case of atoms, matters are not quite so simple. Even in the simplest of all atoms, the hydrogen atom, there are three separate motions to be taken into account, each of which gives rise to magnetic effects: the motion of the electron in its orbit, the spin of the electron, and the spin of the nucleus—the nucleus has been assigned spin properties in order to acount for what is known as the *hyperfine* structure of certain spectral lines. All these contribute to the total magnetic moment of the atom. Not only this, but associated with each motion is a purely mechanical *angular momentum*—it is the possession of angular momentum that makes a flywheel in motion difficult to bring to rest. The mechanical angular momentum of the atom opposes the change which the applied magnetic field, whether uniform or not, tends to produce in the direction of the magnetic axis of the atom. As a result the magnetic axis, instead of setting itself parallel to the direction of the field, describes a cone about this direction—it is said to execute a *Larmor precession* about the direction of the field, Sir Joseph Larmor having specially investigated this matter.

Atoms entering the magnetic field will have their magnetic axes inclined to the direction of the field at all possible angles. According to the *classical* theory the resulting Larmor precession can also make any angle θ with the direction of the field, so that, since the degree to which the atom is deflected from its original path by the inhomogeneous field depends on θ, the atom can strike the registering screen at any point within certain limits. If, as in Stern's experiments, the molecular beam is ribbon-shaped, the straight line produced in the absence of the magnetic field should, on the classical theory, simply be broadened out when the field is applied. On the *quantum* theory, however, only certain discrete values of θ are possible—only two in the case of silver, the alkali metals, and hydrogen—so that the original line, instead of being broadened

out, should be split into a number of *separate* lines, one corresponding to each of the possible values of θ. For the experiment to succeed, the magnetic field must, on account of the minute size of the
atomic magnets, change very rapidly from point to point. This
Stern and Gerlach secured by having one pole piece of the magnet
in the form of a knife-edge, the other grooved, the ribbon-shaped
beam of silver atoms passing broadside-on very close to the knife-
edge. The result obtained was that predicted by the quantum theory.
From the separation of the two lines produced it was possible to
calculate the magnetic moment of the atom, the value obtained
being in close agreement with that given by the theory.

Later, in 1933, Stern refined his apparatus to such an extent that
he was able to measure the magnetic moments of atomic nuclei, in
particular that of the nucleus of the hydrogen atom, the proton.

The following extracts * from Stern's Nobel lecture, which he
delivered in English, include a brief account of the experiments,
carried out at Hamburg, which demonstrated that atoms and molecules, like electrons, can be diffracted by a crystal and thus possess
wave properties.

"In the following lecture I shall try to analyze the method of
molecular rays. My aim is to bring out its distinctive features, the
points where it is different from other methods used in physics,
for what kind of problems it is especially suited and why. . . . I
consider the directness and simplicity as the distinguishing properties of the molecular ray method. For this reason it is particularly
well suited for shedding light on fundamental problems. I hope to
make this clear by discussing the actual experiments.

"Let us first consider the group of experiments which prove directly the fundamental assumptions of the kinetic theory. The
existence of molecular rays in itself, the possibility of producing
molecular rays, is a direct proof of one fundamental assumption
. . . [namely] that in gases the molecules move in straight lines
until they collide with other molecules or the walls of the containing vessel. The usual arrangement for producing molecular rays is
as follows (Fig. 1) [Fig. 37]: We have a vessel filled with gas or
vapor, the oven. This vessel is closed except for a narrow slit, the

---

* Quoted by kind permission of Professor Stern.

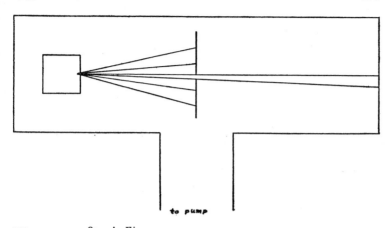

FIG. 37   *Stern's Fig. 1*
[Schematic diagram of Stern's apparatus for producing molecular rays.]

oven slit. Through this slit the molecules escape into the surrounding larger vessel which is continually evacuated so that the escaping
molecules don't suffer any collisions. Now we have another narrow
slit, the collimating slit, opposite and parallel to the oven slit. If the
molecules really move in straight lines then the collimating slit
should cut out a narrow beam whose cross section by simple geometry can be calculated from the dimensions of the slits and their
distance. That it is actually the case was proven first by Dunoyer in
1911. He used sodium vapor and condensed the beam molecules
hitting the wall by cooling it with liquid air. The sodium deposit
formed on the wall had exactly the shape calculated under the
assumption that the molecules move in straight lines like rays of
light. Therefore we call such a beam a molecular ray or molecular
beam.
    "The next step was the direct measurement of the velocity of the
molecules. The kinetic theory gives quite definite numerical values
for this velocity, depending on the temperature and the molecular
weight. For example, for silver atoms of 1000° the average velocity
is about 600 m/sec. (Silver molecules are monatomic). We measured the velocity in different ways. One way . . . was sending the
molecular ray through a system of rotating tooth wheels, the method
used by Fizeau to measure the velocity of light. We had two tooth

wheels sitting on the same axis at a distance of several centimeters. When the wheels were at rest the molecular beam went through two corresponding gaps of the first and the second wheel. When the wheels rotated a molecule going through a gap in the first wheel could not go through the corresponding gap in the second wheel. The gap had moved during the time in which the molecule travelled from the first wheel to the second. However, under a certain condition the molecule could go through the next gap of the second wheel, the condition being that the travelling time for the molecule is just the time for the wheel to turn the distance between two neighbouring gaps. By determining this time, that means the number of rotations per second for which the beam goes through both tooth wheels, we measure the velocity of the molecules. We found agreement with the theory with regard to the numerical values and to the velocity distribution according to Maxwell's law.

"This method has the advantage of producing a beam of molecules with nearly uniform velocity. However, it is not very accurate.

"As the last one in this group of experiments I want to report on experiments carried out in Pittsburgh by Drs. Estermann, Simpson and myself. . . . In these experiments we used the free fall of molecules to measure their velocities.

"In vacuo all bodies, large and small, fall equal distances in equal times, $s = \frac{1}{2}gt^2$ (t time, s distance of fall, g acceleration of gravity). We used a beam of cesium atoms about 2 meters long. Since the average velocity of the atoms is about 200 m/sec., the travel time is about 1/100 sec. During this time a body falls not quite a millimetre. So our cesium atoms did not travel exactly on the straight horizontal line through oven and collimating slit, but arrived a little lower depending on their velocity. The fast ones fell less, the slow ones more. So by measuring the intensity (the number of cesium atoms arriving per second) at the end of the beam perpendicular to it as a function of the distance from the straight line, we get directly the distribution of velocities. . . . The agreement with Maxwell's law is very good. I might mention that we measured the intensity not by condensation but by the so-called Taylor-Langmuir method worked out by Taylor in our Hamburg laboratory in 1928. It is based on Langmuir's discovery that every alkali atom striking the surface of a hot tungsten wire (eventually oxygen-coated) goes away as an ion. By measuring the ion current outgoing from the wire we measured directly the number of atoms striking the wire.

.   .   .   .   .

"The classical theory is a grandiose conception. The same fundamental laws govern the movements of the stars, the fall of this piece of chalk, and the fall of molecules. But it turned out that the extrapolation to the molecules did not hold in some respects. The theory had to be changed in order to describe the laws governing the movements of the molecules and even more of the electrons. And it was at this point that the molecular ray method proved its value. Here the experiment . . . gave a decisive answer in cases where the theory was uncertain and even gave contradictory answers.

"The best example is the experiment which Gerlach and I performed in 1922. It was known from spectroscopic experiments (Zeeman effect) that the atoms of hydrogen, the alkali metals, silver, and so on, were small magnets. Let us consider the case of the hydrogen atom as the simplest one even if our experiments were performed with silver atoms. There is no essential difference, and the results were checked with hydrogen atoms a few years later. . . .

"The essential point is that the classical theory and the quantum theory predict quite differently the behavior of the atomic magnets in a magnetic field. The classical theory predicts that the atomic magnets assume all possible directions with respect to the direction of the magnetic field. On the other hand, the quantum theory predicts that we shall find only two directions parallel and antiparallel to the field. (New theory, the old one gave also the direction perpendicular to the field).

"Our molecular ray experiment gave a definite answer. We sent a beam of silver atoms through a very inhomogeneous magnetic field. In such a field the magnets are deflected because the field strength on the place of one pole of the magnet is a little different from the field strength acting on the other pole. So in the balance a force is acting on the atom and it is deflected. A simple calculation shows that from the classical theory . . . we should find a broadening of the beam with the maximum intensity on the place of the beam without field. However, from the quantum theory . . . we should find there no intensity at all and deflected molecules on both sides. The beam should split up in two beams corresponding to the two orientations of the magnet. The experiment decided in favor of the quantum theory.

·   ·   ·   ·   ·

"In his famous theory which became the basis of the modern quantum theory, de Broglie stated that moving particles should also show properties of waves. The wave length of these waves is given by the equation

$$\lambda = \frac{h}{mv}$$

(h Planck's constant, m mass, v velocity of particle). The experimental proof was first given in 1927 by Davisson and Germer and by Thomson for electrons. Some years later we succeeded in performing similar experiments with molecular rays of helium atoms and hydrogen molecules using the cleavage surface of a lithium fluoride crystal as diffraction grating. We could check the diffraction in every detail. The most convincing experiment is perhaps the one where we sent a beam of helium gas through the two rotating tooth wheels which I mentioned at the beginning, thus determining the velocity v in a primitive, purely mechanical manner. The helium beam then impinged on the lithium fluoride crystal, and by measuring the angle between the diffracted and the direct beam we determined the wave length, since we know the lattice constant of the lithium fluoride. We found agreement with de Broglie's formula within the accuracy of our experiments (about 2%). There is no doubt that these experiments could be carried out also by using a ruled grating instead of the crystal. In fact we found hints of a diffracted beam with a ruled grating in 1928, and with the improved technique of today the experiment would not be too difficult.

"With respect to the differences between the experiments with electrons and molecular rays, one can say that the molecular ray experiments go farther. Also the mass of the moving particle is varied (helium atom, hydrogen molecule). But the main point is again that we work in such a direct primitive manner with neutral particles.

"These experiments demonstrate clearly and directly the fundamental fact of the dual nature of rays of matter."

CONSEQUENCES IN THEORY AND PRACTICE

Stern laid the foundations of the molecular-beam method of studying the magnetic properties of atoms and of atomic nuclei. By the use of this method he himself not only confirmed, in a particularly direct experimental manner, the existence of the magnetic moment of the atom, but also measured its magnitude. His quantitative results afforded additional confirmation of the fundamental correctness of the quantum theory. His discovery of the diffraction of atomic and molecular beams added further support to de Broglie's wave theory of matter.

1 9 4 4

ISIDOR ISAAC RABI
(1898–   )

"For his application of the resonance method to the measurement of the magnetic properties of atomic nuclei."

BIOGRAPHICAL SKETCH

Isidor Isaac Rabi was born on July 29, 1898, at Rymanow, Austria. He was brought to the United States in infancy and received his early education in New York City. In 1916 he entered Cornell University, with a New York State Scholarship and Cornell Tuition Scholarship; he obtained his B.Chem. degree in 1919. For the next three years he was engaged on nonscientific work. After a further year in the graduate school of Cornell University, specializing in physics, he went to Columbia University, where he obtained his Ph.D in 1927. During this period (1924-1927) he was employed as a tutor in physics at the College of the City of New York. From 1927 to 1929 he studied in Europe with the aid of a Barnard Fellowship of Columbia University and an International Education Board Fellowship. He spent two months with Sommerfeld in Munich, two months with Bohr in Copenhagen, a year with Pauli (*q.v.* 1945) and Stern (*q.v.* 1943) in Hamburg, two months with Heisenberg (*q.v.* 1932) in Leipzig, six months with Pauli in Zurich.

In 1929 he returned to Columbia University as a lecturer in physics, being appointed assistant professor in 1930, associate professor in 1935, and professor in 1937, a post which he still holds.

Since 1940 he has been a staff member and associate director of the Radiation Laboratory, Massachusetts Institute of Technology, and since 1947 a member of the Atomic Energy Commission.

Rabi was awarded the Elliott Cresson Medal by the Franklin Institute in 1942 and a U. S. Medal for Merit in 1948. He is a member of the American Physical Society, the American Philosophical Society, the National Academy of Sciences, and the American Academy of Arts and Sciences.

DESCRIPTION OF THE PRIZE-WINNING WORK

As already stated, while he was in Europe (1927-1929) Rabi spent a year at the University of Hamburg, where Stern was applying his molecular-beam method to the measurement of atomic magnetic moments. When, some years after his return to the United States, Rabi turned his attention to the same problem, the method he evolved was largely based on Stern's. Like Stern, he used molecular beams deflected from their original straight-line course by an inhomogeneous magnetic field. Instead, however, of determining the magnetic moment from the separation of the lines produced by the deflected beams, Rabi used a second inhomogeneous field, opposite in direction to the first, to bring the beam back to the point it would have struck in the absence of the fields.

The paths of two typical molecules are shown by the solid curves in Fig. 38 (p. 404), where A and B are the electromagnets producing the inhomogeneous fields; the small gyroscopes show the magnetic moment *vector* (μ)—the line representing the magnetic moment in magnitude and direction, the latter being that of the magnetic axis—precessing about the direction of the magnetic field H. If, after the molecule has passed through the slit S, anything occurs to cause a change in the angle between the magnetic axis and the direction of the field and so to increase or decrease the component of the magnetic moment in the direction of the field, such change occurring, of course, in "quantum jumps," then in the field due to the B magnet the molecule will follow a path similar to those indicated by the dotted lines in Fig. 38 and will therefore fail to arrive at the detector.

The ingenuity of Rabi's method lay in the introduction between the two inhomogeneous fields of a strong homogeneous field with an *oscillating* field at right angles to it. The homogeneous field, if it is sufficiently strong (a few thousand gauss), *decouples* the nuclear spins from each other, so that the molecules may be regarded as free nuclei. We may therefore forget that we are dealing with molecules and consider only what happens to the nuclei. The nucleus of an atom, like the atom as a whole, acts like a tiny magnet, that is, it possesses a magnetic moment—that the nucleus must be spinning and therefore possess a magnetic moment was suggested by Pauli (*q.v.* 1945) in 1924 to account for the *hyperfine* structure of certain spectral lines. In the homogeneous magnetic field the magnetic axis of the nucleus will execute a Larmor precession (see p. 391) about the direction of the field. The Larmor frequency ν in the homogeneous field H_0 is given by

$$\nu = \frac{\mu H_0}{hi} \qquad \text{or} \qquad \frac{\nu}{H_0} = \frac{\mu}{hi} \quad \ldots \ldots \text{(A)}$$

where μ is the nuclear magnetic moment, h is Planck's constant, and i is the spin quantum number, which, in the case of the nucleus, also represents the angular momentum. The equation shows that the Larmor frequency ν varies with the strength of the magnetic field. Suppose now that the frequency f of the oscillating magnetic field is equal, or very nearly equal, to ν; then the magnetic axis, and also the angular momentum (vector) will precess in time with the oscillations of the electric current producing the magnetic field—hence the name "molecular beam *resonance* method." The result will be that the magnetic axis sweeps out a cone of ever widening angle, or of diminishing angle if f and ν are in opposite directions. The nucleus will therefore assume a different quantum state as a result of its passage through the oscillating field, and will now have no chance of arriving at the detector.

In carrying out the experiment the frequency of the oscillating field was kept constant and H_0 was varied until the detector registered a minimum effect. Thus, for the $^7_3$Li nucleus, with an oscillating frequency of 5.585 megacycles per sec., the minimum beam intensity, which was about sixty percent of the undeflected beam intensity, occurred when H_0 was about 3380 gauss (Fig. 41, p.

407); this was therefore the Larmor frequency on entering the oscillating field of those nuclei which failed to arrive at the detector. Since, when resonance occurs, $\nu = f$, the frequency of the oscillating field, Equation (A) may be written

$$\frac{f}{H_0} = \frac{\mu}{hi}$$

so that

$$\mu = \frac{f}{H_0} \cdot hi$$

electromagnetic units. A unit of more convenient size in which to express nuclear magnetic moments is the *nuclear magneton*, so defined that it is equal to $\frac{eh}{4\pi Mc}$ e.m.u., where M is the mass of the proton (hydrogen nucleus) and $\frac{e}{c}$ (in which c is the velocity of light) is the electronic charge in electromagnetic units, e being the charge in electrostatic units. Expressed in terms of nuclear magnetons,

$$\mu = \frac{f}{H_0} \cdot i \times \frac{4\pi Mc}{e} \quad \cdots \cdots \cdots \cdots \text{(B)}$$

or, on substituting the appropriate values for π, M, c, and e,

$$\mu = \frac{f}{H_0} \cdot i \times (1.3122 \times 10^{-3})$$

The values of f/H_0 were calculated from the experimental results and are listed in the last column of Table 1 (p. 409); i, the nuclear spin quantum number, is known for the particular nucleus from other sources, being 3/2 for the $_3^7$Li nucleus. Thus for the case represented by Fig. 41 (the $_3^7$Li nucleus)

$$\mu = \frac{5.585 \times 10^6}{3380} \times \frac{3}{2} \times (1.3122 \times 10^{-3})$$

$$= 1650 \times \frac{3}{2} \times (1.3122 \times 10^{-3})$$

$$= 3.25$$

nuclear magnetons, the value given in Rabi's Table II (p. 410).

Owing to the war Rabi did not give the customary Nobel lecture.

Our extracts are therefore taken from the paper in *Physical Review*, Vol. 55 (1939), p. 526, in which he and his collaborators described their method.

THE MOLECULAR BEAM RESONANCE METHOD FOR MEASURING NUCLEAR MAGNETIC MOMENTS

"The magnetic moment of the atomic nucleus is one of the few of its important properties which concern both phases of the nuclear problem, the nature of the nuclear forces and the appropriate nuclear model. . . .

. . . . .

"In two letters to this journal [*Physical Review*], we reported briefly on a new precision method of measuring nuclear moment, and on some results. In this paper we shall give a more detailed account of the method, apparatus and results.

"*Method.*   The principle on which the method is based applies not only to nuclear magnetic moments but rather to any system which possesses angular momentum and a magnetic moment. We consider a system with angular momentum, J, in units of $\frac{h}{2\pi}$, and magnetic moment μ. In an external magnetic field H_0 the angular momentum will precess with the Larmor frequency, ν, (in revolutions per sec.) given by

$$\nu = \frac{\mu H_0}{Jh} \quad \cdots \cdots \cdots \cdots \quad (1)$$

Our method consists in the measurement of ν in a known field H_0. The measurement of ν is the essential step in this method, since H_0 may be measured by conventional procedures. . . .

"The process by which the precession frequency ν is measured has a rather close analog in classical mechanics. To the system described in the previous paragraph, we apply an additional magnetic field H_1, which is much smaller than H_0 and perpendicular to it in direction. If we consider the initial condition such that H_1 is perpendicular to both the angular momentum and H_0, the additional precession caused by H_1 will be such as to increase or decrease the angle between the angular momentum, J, and H_0, depending on the relative directions. If H_1 rotates with frequency ν this effect is cumulative and the change in angle between H_0 and J can be made very large. It is apparent that if the frequency of revolution, f, of H_1 about H_0 is markedly different from ν, the net effect will be small. Furthermore, if the sense of rotation of H_1 is opposite to that of the precession, the effect will also be small. The smaller the ratio H_1/H_0 the sharper this effect will be in its dependence on the exact agreement between the frequency of precession, ν, and the frequency f.

"Any method which enables one to detect this change in orientation of the angular momentum with respect to H_0 can therefore utilize this process to measure the precession frequency and therefore the magnetic moment. . . .

"In practice it is frequently more convenient to use an oscillating field H_1 rather than a rotating field. Although the situation is not quite as clear as for the rotating field, it is reasonable to expect that the effects will be similar if the oscillating field is sufficiently small. A simple calculation shows that no change in the magnitude of the projection of J on H_0 will occur unless the frequency of oscillation is close to the frequency of precession. . . .

"Although the reorientations of the system under the combined influence of H_0 and H_1 may be detected in a number of ways, the most delicate and precise is that of molecular beams.

"The arrangement used in our experiment is shown schematically in Fig. 1 [Fig. 38]. A stream of molecules coming from the source, O, in a high vacuum apparatus is defined by a collimating slit, S, and detected by some suitable device at D. The magnets, A and B, produce inhomogeneous magnetic fields, the gradients of which, $\dfrac{dH}{dz}$, are indicated by arrows. When these magnets are turned on, molecules having magnetic moment will be deflected in the direction of the gradient if the projection of the moment, μ_z, along the field is positive, and in the opposite direction if μ_z is negative. A molecule starting from O along the direction OS will be deflected in the z direction by the inhomogeneous A field and will not pass through the collimating slit unless its projected moment is very small or it is

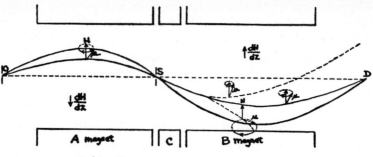

FIG. 38   *Rabi's Fig. 1*

Paths of molecules. The two solid curves indicate the paths of two molecules having different moments and velocities and whose moments are not changed during passage through the apparatus. This is indicated by the small gyroscopes drawn on one of these paths, in which the projection of the magnetic moment along the field remains fixed. The two dotted curves in the region of the *B* magnet indicate the paths of two molecules the projection of whose nuclear magnetic moments along the field has been changed in the region of the *C* magnet. This is indicated by means of the two gyroscopes drawn on the dotted curves, for one of which the projection of the magnetic moment along the field has been increased, and for the other of which the projection has been decreased.

moving with very high speed. In general, for a molecule having any moment, μ_z, and any energy, $\frac{1}{2}mv^2$, it is possible to find an initial direction for the velocity of the molecule at the source such that the molecule will pass through the collimating slit. This is indicated by the solid lines in the diagram. . . . The deflection in the *B* field will be in a direction opposite to that in the *A* field. . . . Thus if a molecule of any velocity has the same μ_z in both deflecting fields it will be brought back to the detector by the B field. A simple consideration shows that when the fields *A* and *B* are properly adjusted the number of molecules which reaches the detector is the same whether the magnets *A* and *B* are on or off. The molecular velocity distribution is also the same.

"Magnet *C* produces the homogeneous field H_0. In addition, there is a device, not pictured in Fig. 1 [Fig. 38], which produces an oscillating field perpendicular to H_0. If the reorientation which we have described takes place in this region the conditions for deflecting the molecules back to *D* by means of the *B* magnet no longer obtain. The molecule will follow one dotted line or the other depending on whether μ_z has become more positive or has changed sign. In fact, if any change in orientation occurs, the molecule will miss the detector and cause a diminution in its reading. We thus have a means of knowing when the reorientation effect occurs.

"Since most of the systems in which one is interested have small angular momenta $\left(< \dfrac{10h}{2\pi} \right)$ the classical considerations given above have to be reconsidered from the point of view of quantum mechanics. The reorientation process is more accurately described as one in which the system, originally in some state with magnetic quantum number, m, makes a transition to another magnetic level, m'. . . .

. . . . .

"The orders of magnitude involved can be seen from a simple example: consider a system with spin $\frac{1}{2}$ and a moment of 1 nuclear magneton in a field of 1000 gauss. . . . The resonance frequency is

$$\frac{\mu H}{hi} = \frac{(0.5 \times 10^{-23})(10^3)}{(6.55 \times 10^{-27})(\frac{1}{2})}$$

$$\simeq 1.5 \times 10^6$$

cycles per sec., which fortunately is in a very convenient range of radiofrequencies. . . .

. . . . .

"*The Apparatus.* The apparatus (Fig. 2) [Fig. 39] is contained in a long brass-walled tube divided into three distinct chambers, each with its own high vacuum pump. The source chamber contains the oven which is mounted on tungsten pegs. . . . The interchamber contains no essential parts of the apparatus, but provides adequate vacuum isolation of the receiving chamber from the gassing of the heated oven, by means of a narrow slit on each end of the chamber. . . . The receiving chamber contains most of the essential parts of the apparatus: the two deflecting magnets, A and B, the magnet, C, which produces the constant field, the radiofrequency oscillating field, R, the collimating slit, S, and the 1-mil tungsten filament detector, D.

. . . . .

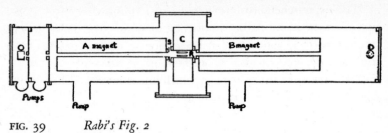

FIG. 39   *Rabi's Fig. 2*
Schematic diagram of apparatus.

"The oscillating field, R, consists of two $\frac{1}{8}''$ copper tubes, 4 cm long, carrying current in opposite directions. These tubes are flattened to permit their insertion between the pole faces of the C magnet when a space of about 1 mm between the tubes is left for the passage of the beam. The plane defined by the centers of these tubes is horizontal and is adjusted to be closely the same as the planes of symmetry of the A and B magnets. . . .

"The magnetic field, H_1, produced by a current in the tubes is about 2 gauss/amp. and is approximately vertical and therefore at right angles to the field H_0 produced by the C magnet. The high frequency currents in the tubes are obtained by coupling a loop in series with them to the tank coil of a conventional Hartley oscillator. . . .

"*Procedure.* A preliminary line-up of magnets, slits, and detector is made by optical means while the apparatus is assembled. . . .

. . . . .

"A sample of the molecular compound, the magnetic moments of whose constituent nuclei are to be determined, is placed in an oven. The oven is completely closed except for a slit about 0.03 mm wide. It is heated by means of spiral tungsten heaters passed through the oven block and electrically insulated from it by means of quartz tubing. When the temperature of the oven is sufficiently high so that the sample has a vapor pressure of the order of 1 mm of Hg a beam may be observed at the detector and a more precise line-up may be initiated.

. . . . .

"The experimental criterion which determines the exact position of the beam is that the weakening of a molecular beam at the
detector by the A and B fields taken separately must be equal. This
may easily be accomplished by a lateral displacement of the beam,
since for any such displacement the gradient increases in one of the
fields and decreases in the other. When this criterion is satisfied
the intensity of the refocused beam with a current of about 300
amp. in the windings of each of the two inhomogeneous fields is
about 95 percent of the beam observed in the absence of the fields.

⋅ ⋅ ⋅ ⋅ ⋅

". . . Observations are made of the beam intensity as a function
of the magnetic field, H_0, when the frequency is held fixed. Curves
relating the beam intensity to the field H_0, taken for $_3Li^7$, $_3Li^6$ and
$_9F^{19}$ are shown in Figs. 3, 4 and 5 [Figs. 40 and 41].*

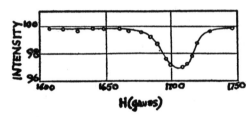

FIG. 40   *Rabi's Fig. 3*
Resonance curve of the Li^6 nucleus observed in LiCl.

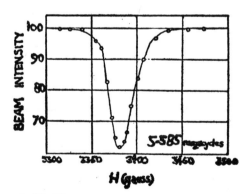

FIG. 41   *Rabi's Fig. 4*
Resonance curve of the Li^7 nucleus observed in LiCl.

* Figures 3 and 4 only are reproduced here.

"*Magnetic and Frequency Measurements.* Since the value of the magnetic moment of any nucleus is calculated from an observed magnetic field and an observed frequency it is essential that these quantities be known to a high degree of precision. The frequency of the oscillating magnetic field is determined to better than 0.03 percent by measuring the frequency of the oscillator with a General Radio Type 620A heterodyne frequency meter. It was found that the frequency of the oscillator varied by no more than 0.01 percent during the time required to obtain data on one resonance curve (about 15 minutes).

. . . . .

"*Results.* The first nuclei to be studied by this method were $_3$Li^6, $_3$Li^7 and $_9$F^{19} in the LiCl, LiF, NaF and Li$_2$ molecules. The resonance minima which are obtained are shown in Figs. 3, 4 and 5 [Figs. 40 and 41]. For each nucleus the f/H values corresponding to the resonance minima are constant to a very high degree for wide variations of frequency. This shows that we are dealing with a change of nuclear orientation and not with some molecular transition, since such a transition would not possess a frequency proportional to H. A representative sample of the results is shown in Table I. . . .

"The nuclear g * is obtained from the observed f/H values by use of the formula

$$g = \frac{4\pi}{e/(Mc)} \cdot \frac{f}{H} = 1.3122 \times 10^{-3} \cdot \frac{f}{H}$$

which follows immediately from Eq. (1) if the magnetic moment μ is measured in units of $\dfrac{eh}{4\pi Mc}$, the nuclear magneton, and $f = \nu$. . . . The nuclear spins of Li^6 and Li^7 are known from atomic beam measurements, and that of F^{19} from band spectra. The nuclear moments are obtained directly by multiplying g by i. The nuclear g's, the spins and the magnetic moments are listed in Table II. . . . The identification of the resonance minimum with

---

* The magnetic moment μ of the nucleus is connected with i, the nuclear angular momentum (or spin) by the relation $\mu = gi$ (nuclear magnetons), where g, known as the gyromagnetic factor or g-factor, is a quantity depending on the nuclear quantum numbers. Substitution in $\mu = gi$ of Rabi's expression for g given below leads to Equation (B) (p. 401).

a particular nucleus is made by using the same element in more than one molecule. For example, two of the resonance minima, observed for each of the molecules LiCl, LiF and Li$_2$ have f/H values which are the same in all three cases. These must be attributed to the nuclei of the two isotopes of lithium. . . .

"The accuracy of the nuclear moment values depends solely on a knowledge of the magnetic field, H, at which the Larmor frequency associated with the nuclear magnetic moment is equal to the frequency of the oscillating field. . . ."

TABLE I*

Nucleus	Molecule	f megacycles per sec.	H gauss	f/H
Li^6	LiCl	2.127	3405	624.6
		2.127	3400	625.6
		2.155	3455	623.8
		2.155	3446	625.3
	Li$_2$	1.714	2742	625.0
		1.714	2744	624.7
	LiF	2.193	3506	625.5
		2.193	3501	626.5
Li^7	LiCl	5.611	3399	1651
		5.610	3400	1650
		6.587	3992	1650
		2.113	1278	1654
		5.552	3383	1651
	LiF	5.621	3401	1653
		6.580	3981	1653
		3.517	2133	1649
	Li$_2$	3.056	1862	1651
		3.084	1879	1652
		3.129	1907	1651

* The results for the two isotopes of lithium only are reproduced here. Rabi's tables included similar results for the fluorine nucleus.

TABLE II

Nucleus	g	Spin	Moment
$_3\text{Li}^6$	0.820	1	0.820
$_3\text{Li}^7$	2.167	$\dfrac{3}{2}$	3.250

CONSEQUENCES IN THEORY AND PRACTICE

Rabi's molecular beam resonance method is a masterpiece of refined technique. Important as were Stern's experiments from a qualitative point of view, they did not lend themselves to actual measurement of atomic and nuclear magnetic moments with more than a moderate degree of accuracy. Rabi, however, succeeded in measuring these quantities with a degree of precision that hardly seemed possible. As the president of the Physics Section of the Nobel Committee said in a broadcast on the occasion of the award: Rabi literally established radio relations with the most subtle particles of matter, with the world of the electron and of the atomic nucleus.

1 9 4 5

WOLFGANG PAULI
(1900–   )

*"For the discovery of the exclusion principle, also
called the Pauli Principle."*

BIOGRAPHICAL SKETCH

WOLFGANG PAULI WAS BORN ON APRIL 25, 1900, IN VIENNA.
After receiving his schooling in Vienna, he studied under Sommerfeld at the University of Munich, obtaining his doctor's degree
in 1921. He then spent a year as assistant to Max Born at Göttingen,
followed by a year as assistant to Bohr at Copenhagen. In 1923
he became a lecturer at the University of Hamburg, where he remained until 1928, when he was appointed professor of theoretical
physics at the Federal Technical High School, Zurich, a post which
he still holds. From 1935 to 1936 he was visiting professor of
theoretical physics at the Institute for Advanced Study, Princeton
University, an appointment which he has also held since 1940. He
was visiting professor at the University of Michigan in the sum-
mers of 1931 and 1941, and at Purdue University in 1942. In
1946 he became a naturalized United States citizen.

Pauli is a member of the Swiss Physical Society, the American
Physical Society, and the American Association for the Advancement of Science.

DESCRIPTION OF THE PRIZE-WINNING
WORK

Since Pauli, like Heisenberg (*q.v.* 1932), studied under both
Sommerfeld and Born, and also, like Heisenberg, had the ad-

vantage of personal contact with Bohr (*q.v.* 1922), it was perhaps inevitable that he too should turn his attention to problems of atomic structure. But whereas Heisenberg discarded the accepted theory of the atom and made a fresh start, Pauli based his work on the Bohr-Sommerfeld theory.

According to the theory put forward by Bohr in 1913, the hydrogen atom consists of a single electron revolving about the nucleus in any one of a number of possible circular orbits. Each of these orbits was defined by a whole number, 1 for the orbit nearest the nucleus, 2 for the next, and so on. The difference in the energy possessed by the electron in two adjacent orbits is equal to $h\nu$, where h is Planck's constant and ν the frequency of the radiation emitted by the electron in jumping from the orbit of higher energy to that of lower energy (the one nearer the nucleus). The numbers defining the orbits are known as quantum numbers, a single quantum number (n) being all that is needed to define an orbit on this simple theory of the atom. Sommerfeld in 1916 extended Bohr's theory to include elliptical orbits, the nucleus being at one focus of the ellipse.

It can be proved that, if the relativistic change of mass with speed (p. 196) is neglected, the mean energy of an electron is the same for all elliptical orbits which have their major axes equal, and is the same as the energy of an electron describing a circular orbit whose diameter is equal to the major axis of the ellipse, a circle being in fact an ellipse whose major and minor axes are equal. Owing, however, to the very high speed of the electron, the relativistic change of mass with speed has to be taken into account, and since, moreover, the speed, and therefore the mass, increases as the electron approaches the nucleus in its elliptical path, the mean energy of an electron describing an elliptical orbit is not *quite* the same as when it is describing the corresponding circular orbit; also the difference is greater when the path is a flat ellipse (ratio of major to minor axis large) than when it is nearly a circle.

Corresponding to each of the original Bohr circular orbits (quantum number $n = 1, 2, 3 \ldots$), which give the coarse structure of the spectrum, there are therefore now a certain number of elliptical orbits and this gives a fine structure to the spectrum, each component of the structure corresponding to the jump of an electron from, say, one of the $n = 3$ orbits to one or another of the several $n = 2$ orbits. The fact that *lines* are emitted means that the difference in energy between the two orbits can have certain values only. This is secured by introducing a second quantum number (k), which expresses the ratio of the minor to the major axis of the ellipse. The number k can have any integral values from 1 to n; it cannot have the value 0, for then the ellipse would be a straight line passing through the nucleus; when $k = n$, the major and minor axes are equal and the ellipse has become a circle. Of the two quantum numbers introduced so far, n is called the *principal* or *total* quantum number, k the *azimuthal* quantum number.

In addition to these two quantum numbers a third is required to allow for the splitting of the spectral lines in a magnetic field (Zeeman effect). An electron describing an orbit behaves like an electric current and so produces a magnetic field whose direction is at right angles to the plane of the orbit. When an external magnetic field is applied, this tends to bring the field due to the orbiting electron into line with itself. On the other hand, the electron, because of its rotational inertia, resists this tendency to disturb its original motion. The result is a compromise which causes a swaying motion of the plane of the orbit, such that a line at right angles to the plane of the orbit, through the center, describes a cone about the direction of the external magnetic field. The third quantum number, the *magnetic* quantum number (m) is introduced to restrict the angle of this cone to certain discrete values; m may have any integral value between $-(k-1)$ and $+(k-1)$ [*], including 0, the negative values denoting that the two magnetic fields, the external field and that due to the orbiting electron, are in opposite directions. In the absence of an external magnetic field these energy-levels coalesce and are then said to be *degenerate*. If all the levels are non-degenerate, calculation shows that there are n^2 possible orbits.

This quantum theory of the atom accounts very satisfactorily for the spectral lines emitted by hydrogen, in which the single electron in each atom can occupy any one of the possible orbits. With many

[*] Generally l is used in place of $(k-1)$, so that m has the values $-l, -l+1,$ $-l+2, \ldots -1, 0, +1 \ldots \ldots +l-2, +l-1, +l$; i.e., $(2l+1)$ values in all.

electron atoms another problem arises: the distribution of the several electrons about the nucleus of the atom—are they, for instance, spread out at relatively wide intervals round the nucleus, like the planets round the sun, or do they crowd together in groups at a comparatively small number of distances from the nucleus?

Among the many things which have to be taken into account in arriving at a theory of the space distribution of the electrons in the different atoms is the periodic table of the chemists. In the modern form of this table the elements are arranged in the order of their atomic numbers—this, except in a few cases, is the order of the atomic weights—in eight *groups* (vertical columns), each group after element 19 (potassium) being divided into two subgroups. The elements in the same group, or subgroup, possess markedly similar chemical properties; in particular they have the same *valency,* or power of combining with other elements. Thus Group Ia contains hydrogen and the alkali metals, all of valency 1; Group VIIIb contains helium and the other inert gases, all of valency 0, i.e., they do not form compounds. The first *period* (horizontal row) contains hydrogen and helium only; the second begins with lithium (3) and ends with neon (10); the third begins with sodium (11) and ends with argon (18); the next two periods contain 18 elements each, with three elements in subgroup VIIIa; the sixth period contains 32 elements, including fifteen "rare earths" (57 to 71).

It has long been held that valency depends in some way on certain outer or "valency" electrons in the atom, the full complement of these electrons being eight. Thus sodium, valency 1, has one valency electron, calcium has two, argon (inert) the full complement of eight; phosphorus, valency 3 or 5, has five valency electrons, valency 3 arising from the possibility of completing the three vacant spaces, just as fluorine, with seven valency electrons, needs only one more to bring the number up to the full complement of eight, and therefore has valency 1. Now each element in the periodic table differs from the one immediately preceding it in having one more unit of charge on the nucleus of its atom (atomic number equals number of units of charge) and one more orbiting electron. The first element, hydrogen, has one electron, its valency being also 1; the second, helium, has two electrons, its valency being 0. The next element, lithium, has three electrons and its valency, like that of hydrogen, is 1. Adding electrons one at a time we come to neon with ten electrons and valency 0; next, to sodium, with eleven electrons and valency 1. In the fourth and fifth periods the addition of eighteen electrons is required to produce "inertness"; in the sixth, thirty-two. These facts alone suggested some kind of arrangement of the electrons in closed shells round the nucleus.

A definite closed-shell theory was put forward in 1917 by W. Kossel (son of A. Kossel, winner of the 1910 Nobel Prize in Medicine) in order to explain the emission of X-ray spectra. According to Kossel the electrons are arranged in shells round the nucleus; if for some reason an electron has been ejected from the innermost shell, then an electron from one of the outer shells can fall into the vacant place, a K line (see Barkla, p. 145) being emitted in the process; similarly an L line is emitted when an electron falls into a vacant space in the second shell, and so on. Kossel called these shells the K, L, M . . . shells, the names by which they are still known. In 1924 E. C. Stoner, to account for certain features of the periodic table, suggested the existence of subshells. Why the shells should become closed when they contained a certain number of electrons, in particular why the innermost or K shell should become closed in the helium atom with only two electrons, remained an unsolved problem.

Two outstanding points in connection with spectra were left unexplained by the Bohr-Sommerfeld theory of the atom: the doublet nature of the series of the alkali spectra and what is known as the *anomalous Zeeman effect*. Optical spectra, as distinct from X-ray spectra, are produced by the outermost, or valency, electrons, whereas X-ray spectra are due to the innermost electrons. The alkali metals have only *one* valency, or optical, electron, yet the spectra contain *double* lines like the yellow sodium line, which can be seen with an ordinary spectrometer to consist of two lines close together. In the anomalous Zeeman effect a spectral line is split up in a *weak* magnetic field, not into the normal Zeeman triplet, but into more components. As the strength of the magnetic field is increased these components are found to approach the normal triplet by grouping themselves into three closely spaced sets—this is known as the Paschen-Back effect after its discoverers. A. Landé made a detailed analysis of the anomalous Zeeman effect and attempted to account for it and the doublet nature of the alkali spectra by allowing the magnetic quantum numbers m to have half-integral values.

Pauli's investigations into both these problems played a great part in leading him to the formulation of his "principle." Instead, however, of modifying the recognized magnetic quantum number, he preferred to introduce what amounted to a fourth quantum number which could have one of two values only—the "two-valuedness not describable classically" to which he refers in his Nobel lecture. Later (1925) the Dutch physicists Uhlenbeck and Goudsmit put forward their hypothesis of electron spin, and Pauli's fourth quantum number became the *spin* quantum number (s) with the two possible values $+\frac{1}{2}$ or $-\frac{1}{2}$. A spinning electron, like a spinning top, possesses rotational angular momentum; it also behaves as a small magnet, since it is electrically charged. The electron spin therefore modifies the orbital angular momentum, with which the azimuthal quantum number k is connected, giving rise to two new levels corresponding to $k + \frac{1}{2}$ and $k - \frac{1}{2}$ and thus accounting for the doublet nature of the alkali spectra. Also the magnetic effect of the spin, superimposed on the magnetic effect of the orbital motion, gives rise to the anomalous Zeeman effect. Pauli himself, however, in introducing his fourth quantum number, assigned it no specific properties other than that of "two-valuedness," though for it to give rise to a splitting of the m levels something of the nature of a magnetic quantum number was implicit in it.

The exclusion principle is usually stated: no two electrons in the same atom can have all four quantum numbers equal. Pauli expressed the same thing somewhat differently: "An entirely non-degenerate energy level is already 'closed' if it is occupied by a single electron"; by this he meant that an energy-level (orbit) which requires all four quantum numbers for its specification cannot contain more than one electron.

We now turn to Pauli's Nobel lecture, which he delivered in English.*

---

* The following extracts are quoted by kind permission of Professor Pauli.

"The history of the discovery of the exclusion principle . . .
goes back to my student days. . . . [It] was at the University of
Munich that I was introduced by Sommerfeld to the structure of
the atom—somewhat strange from the point of view of classical
physics. I was not spared the shock which every physicist, accus-
tomed to the classical way of thinking, experienced when he came
to know of Bohr's 'Basic postulate of quantum theory.' . . . At
that time there were two approaches to the difficult problems connected with the quantum of action. One was an effort to bring
abstract order to the new ideas by looking for a key to translate
classical mechanics and electrodynamics into quantum language
which would form a logical generalization of these. This was the
direction which was taken by Bohr's Correspondence Principle.*
Sommerfeld, however, preferred . . . a direct interpretation . . .
of the laws of spectra in terms of integral numbers. . . . Both
methods . . . influenced me. The series of whole numbers 2, 8,
18, 32 . . . giving the lengths of the periods in the natural system of chemical elements, was zealously discussed in Munich, including the remark of the Swedish physicist Rydberg, that these
numbers are of the simple form $2n^2$, if n takes on all integer values.
Sommerfeld tried especially to connect the number 8 and the number of corners of a cube.

"A new phase of my scientific life began when I met Niels Bohr
personally for the first time. This was in 1922, when he gave a
series of guest lectures at Göttingen, in which he reported on his
theoretical investigations on the periodic system of elements. . . .
[The] essential progress made by Bohr's considerations at that time
was in explaining, by means of the spherically symmetric atomic
model, the formation of the intermediate shells of the atom and
the general properties of the rare earths. The question as to why
all electrons for an atom in its ground state were not bound in the
innermost shell, had already been emphasized by Bohr as a fundamental problem in his earlier works. In his Göttingen lectures he
treated particularly the closing of this innermost K shell in the
helium atom and its essential connection with the two non-com-
bining spectra of helium, the ortho- and para-helium spectra. How-

---

* Bohr (*q.v.* 1922) postulated that any system of *atomic* mechanics must reduce
to *classical* mechanics when applied to the motions of the atom as a whole.

ever, no convincing explanation for this phenomenon could be given on the basis of classical mechanics. It made a strong impression on me that Bohr at that time and in later discussions was looking for a *general* explanation which should hold for the closing of *every* electron shell and in which the number 2 was considered to be as essential as 8 in contrast to Sommerfeld's approach.

"Following Bohr's invitation, I went to Copenhagen in the autumn of 1922, where I made a serious effort to explain the so-called 'anomalous Zeeman effect', . . . a type of splitting of the spectral lines in a magnetic field which is different from the normal triplet. On the one hand, the anomalous type of splitting exhibited beautiful and simple laws and Landé had already succeeded to find the simpler splitting of the spectroscopic terms from the observed splitting of the lines. The most fundamental of his results thereby was the use of half-integers as magnetic quantum numbers for the doublet-spectra of the alkali metals. On the other hand, the anomalous splitting was hardly understandable from the standpoint of the mechanical model of the atom, since very general assumptions concerning the electron, using classical theory as well as quantum theory, always led to the same triplet. . . . We know now that at that time one was confronted with two logically different difficulties simultaneously. One was the absence of a general key to translate a given mechanical model into quantum theory which one tried in vain by using classical mechanics to describe the stationary quantum states themselves. The second difficulty was our ignorance concerning the proper classical model itself which could be suited to derive at all an anomalous splitting of spectral lines emitted by an atom in an external magnetic field. It is therefore not surprising that I could not find a satisfactory solution of the problem at that time. I succeeded, however, in generalizing Landé's term analysis for very strong magnetic fields, a case which, as a result of the magneto-optic transformation (Paschen-Back effect), is in many respects simpler. This early work was of decisive importance for the finding of the exclusion principle.

"Very soon after my return to the University of Hamburg, in 1923, I gave there my inaugural lecture as *privatdozent* on the periodic system of elements. The contents of this lecture appeared very unsatisfactory to me, since the problem of the closing of the elec-

tronic shells had been clarified no further. The only thing that was
clear was that a closer relation of this problem to the theory of
multiplet structure must exist. I therefore tried to examine again
critically the simplest case, the doublet structure of the alkali spectra. According to the point of view then orthodox . . . a non-
vanishing angular momentum of the atomic core was supposed to
be the cause of this doublet structure.

"In the autumn of 1924 I . . . proposed instead . . . the assumption of a new quantum theoretic property of the electron,
which I called a 'two-valuedness not describable classically.' At this
time a paper of the English physicist Stoner appeared which contained, besides improvements in the classification of electrons in
subgroups, the following essential remark:

> For a given value of the principal quantum number is the number of
> energy levels of a single electron in the alkali metal spectra in an external
> magnetic field the same as the number of electrons in the closed shell of
> the rare gases which corresponds to this principal quantum number.

On the basis of my earlier results on the classification of spectral terms in a strong magnetic field the general formulation of the
exclusion principle became clear to me. The fundamental idea can
be stated in the following way: The complicated numbers of electrons in closed subgroups are reduced to the simple number *one*
if the division of the groups by giving the values of the 4 quantum
numbers of an electron is carried so far that every degeneracy is
removed. An entirely non-degenerate energy level is already 'closed'
if it is occupied by a single electron; states in contradiction with
this postulate have to be excluded. The exposition of this general
formulation of the exclusion principle was made in Hamburg in
the spring of 1925, after I was able to verify some additional conclusions concerning the anomalous Zeeman effect of more complicated atoms during a visit to Tübingen with the help of the spectroscopic material assembled there.

"With the exception of experts on the classification of spectral
terms, the physicists found it difficult to understand the exclusion
principle, since no meaning in terms of a model was given to the
fourth degree of freedom of the electron. The gap was filled by
Uhlenbeck and Goudsmit's idea of electron spin, which made it

possible to understand the anomalous Zeeman effect simply by assuming that the spin quantum number of one electron is equal to $\frac{1}{2}$ and that the quotient of the magnetic moment by the mechanical angular momentum* has for the spin a value twice as large as for the ordinary orbit of the electron. Since that time, the exclusion principle has been closely connected with the idea of spin. Although at first I strongly doubted the correctness of this idea because of its classical mechanical character, I was finally converted to it by Thomas's calculations on the magnitude of doublet splitting. On the other hand, my earlier doubts as well as the cautious expression 'classically non-describable two-valuedness' experienced a certain verification during later developments, since Bohr was able to show on the basis of wave mechanics that the electron spin cannot be measured by classically describable experiments (as, for instance, deflection of molecular beams in external electromagnetic fields) and must therefore be considered as an essentially quantum mechanical property of the electron."

CONSEQUENCES IN THEORY AND PRACTICE

Let us now see how the application of Pauli's exclusion principle determines the closing of the electronic shells. We begin with the hydrogen atom in its ground state, that is, with its single electron in the innermost ($n = 1$) orbit; for this electron $n = 1$, $k = 1$, $m = 0$ (p. 413). The helium atom has one more electron, for which also $n = 1$, $k = 1$, $m = 0$. By the exclusion principle these two electrons cannot have all *four* quantum numbers the same; their fourth quantum numbers must therefore be different, i.e., one must have $s = +\frac{1}{2}$, the other $s = -\frac{1}{2}$. No more electrons with $n = 1$ are possible, so this shell, the K shell, is now closed. A third electron, forming a lithium atom, must go into a new shell, the L shell. For this electron $n = 2$ and $k = 1$, with $m = 0$, or $n = 2$ and $k = 2$, with $m = -1$, 0, or $+1$; also for each value of m the fourth quantum number (s) has the value $+\frac{1}{2}$ or $-\frac{1}{2}$. Therefore this electron can choose any one of eight possibilities, and the remainder are open for the successive atoms formed by the addition

---

* *Moment* in the original.

of further electrons. The L shell, therefore, which is completed in neon, can contain eight electrons altogether.

With the next element, sodium, a new shell, the M shell is begun, for which $n = 3$. The possible values for k, m, and s are

$k = 1$, with $m = 0$ $s = +\frac{1}{2}$ or $-\frac{1}{2}$ (2 electrons)

$k = 2$, with $m = -1, 0$, or $+1$ $s = +\frac{1}{2}$ or $-\frac{1}{2}$ (6 electrons)

$k = 3$, with $m = -2, -1, 0, +1$, or $+2$ $s = +\frac{1}{2}$ or $-\frac{1}{2}$ (10 electrons)

There can therefore be up to 18 electrons in the M shell. Of these the two electrons for which $k = 1$ and the six electrons for which $k = 2$ together form a subshell closing with argon (18); the ten electrons for which $k = 3$ go into a second subshell which, however, does not close until it has taken up a further eight electrons, when it closes with krypton (36), the next inert gas after argon. The matter becomes somewhat more complicated with later shells and subshells, but the final result is completely satisfactory.

Pauli's exclusion principle, based originally on the old quantum theory, plays an equally important part in the new wave theory of the atom. It is in fact one of the great guiding principles which must always be taken into account in dealing with problems of atomic structure.

1 9 4 6

PERCY WILLIAMS BRIDGMAN
(1882–   )

"For the invention of apparatus for obtaining very high pressures, and for the discoveries which he made by means of this apparatus in the field of high pressure physics."

BIOGRAPHICAL SKETCH

PERCY WILLIAMS BRIDGMAN WAS BORN ON APRIL 21, 1882, IN Cambridge, Mass. He received his early education in the public schools of Newton, Mass., where his parents had moved. In 1900 he entered Harvard University, where he obtained his A.B. in 1904, his A.M. in 1905, and his Ph.D. in 1908 for a thesis dealing with the effects of high pressures, a subject on which he has continued to work up to the present time. Immediately on receiving his Ph.D. Bridgman was appointed Fellow for Research at Harvard, a position which he held until 1910, when he was made an instructor. In 1913 he became assistant professor and in 1919 professor. Since 1926 he has been Hollis Professor of Mathematics and Natural Philosophy at Harvard.

Bridgman has been awarded the Rumford Medal of the American Academy of Arts and Sciences, the Elliott Cresson Medal of the Franklin Institute, the Comstock Prize of the National Academy of Sciences, and the Roozeboom Medal of the Royal Academy of Sciences of the Netherlands. He is a member of the National Academy of Sciences, the American Physical Society, the American

Association for the Advancement of Science, the American Academy of Arts and Sciences, the Washington Academy of Sciences, and the American Philosophical Society; he is also a Corresponding Member of the Mexican National Academy of Sciences and an Honorary Fellow of the Physical Society of London. He was elected a Foreign Member of the Royal Society of London in 1949.

DESCRIPTION OF THE PRIZE-WINNING WORK

In 1861 Thomas Andrews (1813-1885), professor of chemistry at Belfast, discovered the critical phenomena in gases (see p. 91). During the next thirty years considerable work was done on the behavior of liquids and gases under pressure, chiefly by L. P. Cailletet, whose work on the liquefaction of gases has already been mentioned (p. 110), and E. H. Amagat. The latter, in the late 1880's, succeeded in attaining pressures of 3000 atmospheres* and investigated a number of the properties of gases and liquids at these pressures. Amagat's pressures were not exceeded until early in the twentieth century, when Bridgman began work on a subject which he has made peculiarly his own.

In 1905 Bridgman was studying the influence of high pressure on certain optical phenomena. The method of sealing the pressure chamber then in use was inadequate for the pressure applied and the apparatus broke down. While it was being repaired, Bridgman turned his attention to the problem of securing more efficient packing and worked out a method by which the packing automatically became tighter as the pressure was increased. This worked so well that the range of pressures was now limited only by the strength of the material of which the apparatus was constructed. Even in his earliest experiments he was able to reach pressures of 20,000 atmospheres. For higher pressures he made use of the principle that the resistance of a vessel subjected to internal pressure is increased if

---

* Note that

$$1 \text{ atmosphere} = 1 \text{ kg./sq.cm.} \quad \text{(very nearly)}$$
$$= 14\tfrac{1}{4} \text{ lb./sq.in.}$$
$$\left.\begin{array}{c} 1000 \text{ atmospheres} \\ or \\ 1000 \text{ kg./sq.cm.} \end{array}\right\} = 6.4 \text{ tons/sq.in.} \quad \text{(nearly)}$$

at the same time it is subjected to external pressure. Figure 43 (p. 426) shows the general arrangement adopted. The internal-pressure vessel has an external conical surface which fits closely into a conical opening in a heavy surrounding collar. The liquid, represented by the shaded portion, is enclosed between two pistons in a cylindrical cavity in the internal-pressure vessel. As the pressure on the liquid is increased the conical vessel is forced more tightly into the collar. The pistons were made of tungsten carbide, "carboloy." With this apparatus Bridgman reached pressures of 50,000 atmospheres. For pressures above this, the pressure vessel itself was made of carboloy and was entirely enclosed in a liquid under a pressure of 30,000 atmospheres. Pressures of as much as 400,000 atmospheres and more could now be attained, though the volume of liquid used was necessarily very small indeed.

The mere attainment of higher and higher pressures was only one part of the task which Bridgman set himself. Means had to be devised for estimating the magnitude of the pressure; this demanded a detailed investigation into the behavior of substances under pressure so as to find transition points which could themselves be used as indications of the applied pressure in subsequent experiments. This again was merely incidental to Bridgman's main work, the investigation of the effect of high pressures on a variety of physical and chemical phenomena. One of these, the production of two hitherto unknown modifications of phosphorus, is mentioned in the extract from his Nobel lecture. Others dealt with the effect of high pressures on both ordinary water and heavy water, on electrical resistance, on thermoelectric phenomena, on the conduction of heat in gases, on the viscosity of fluids, and on the elastic properties of solid bodies. His book, *The Physics of High Pressure* (1931), has become the standard work on the subject.

On the theoretical side Bridgman has investigated the thermodynamics of the processes involved in high-pressure phenomena, in particular the thermodynamics of electrical phenomena in metals.

Bridgman is greatly interested in the more philosophical aspects of modern physics, his published works including *The Logic of Modern Physics* (1927) and *The Nature of Physical Theory* (1936). In this connection he has developed a philosophical approach to physical problems known as Operational Analysis.

The following extracts* from Bridgman's Nobel lecture describe how the technical difficulties were overcome and give some idea of the nature of the work carried out at high pressures.

". . . I shall [deal] first with technical matters of producing and measuring high pressure, and secondly with the physical phenomena which occur under high pressure.

"With regard to technique, several different ranges of pressure are to be recognized. The first step was to devise a method of packing which should be without leak, since leak had limited the range of previous experiments. A packing was devised, shown in Fig. 1 [Fig. 42], which automatically becomes tighter the higher the pres-

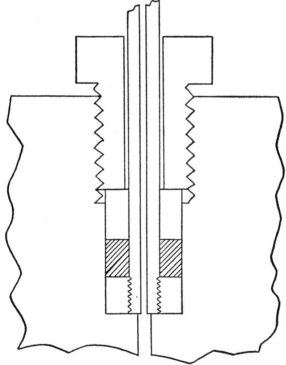

FIG. 42   *Bridgman's Fig. 1*

The general scheme of the packing by which pressure in the soft packing materials is automatically maintained a fixed percentage higher than in the liquid.

---

* Quoted by kind permission of Professor Bridgman.

sure, so that any pressure is accessible up to the strength of the containing vessels. If the vessels are made of one-piece construction, from the best heat-treated alloy steels, it is possible to reach pressures of 12,000 kg/cm² as a routine matter and on occasion for short intervals of time as high as 20,000. For many years my work was confined to this range, and in this range it proved feasible to measure nearly all the ordinary physical properties of substances. The next step was to give the pressure vessel external support which increases in magnitude at the same time the internal pressure increases. A simple method of doing this is to make the external surface of the pressure vessel conical in shape, and to push it into a heavy collar with a force which increases as the internal pressure increases, as illustrated in Fig. 2 [Fig. 43]). With apparatus of this kind it is possible to make routine experiments up to 30,000 kg/cm² with volumes of the order of 15 cm³, to get electrically insulated leads into the apparatus, and practically to repeat all the former work in the range to 12,000. I am still engaged in carrying out this program. An extension of the same technique on a smaller scale with capacities of the order of 0.5 cm³ can be made up to

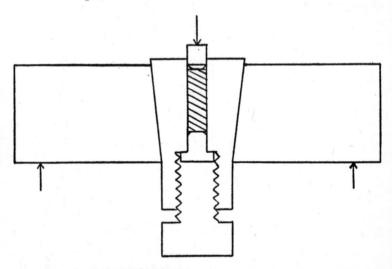

FIG. 43   *Bridgman's Fig. 2*

Illustrating the general principle of the method for giving external support to the pressure vessel in such a way that support increases automatically with the increase of internal pressure.

50,000 kg/cm². In this range all ordinary liquids freeze solid, electrically insulated leads cannot be got into the apparatus, and the
phenomena which can be studied are limited to various volume
effects, such as compressibilities and phase changes, including
fusions and polymorphic transitions.

"The external support of the vessel is only one of the factors
that make possible the extension of range from 12,000 to 50,000.
No steel piston will support as much as 50,000; carboloy, however,
. . . proves to have a compressive strength high enough for the
purpose.

"The next step in extension of range, from 50,000 to 100,000
kg/cm², demands still more effective support of the pressure vessel.
This is done by immersing the entire pressure vessel in a fluid
under pressures ranging up to 30,000 kg/cm². The pressure apparatus has to be made still smaller; the pistons are only 1.6 mm
in diameter, and the capacity is only a few cubic millimeters. The
pressure cylinder itself, as well as the pistons, is now made of
carboloy with an external jacket of shrunk-on steel to give it greater
strength. Even with this type of construction so great an extension
of range as from 50,000 to 100,000 would not have been possible
if it were not for a fortunate change in the properties of metals
under pressure. At pressures of 25,000 kg/cm² ordinary grades of
steel become capable of almost indefinite deformation without fracture, so greatly has their ductility been increased. Even carboloy
loses its normal brittleness and becomes capable of supporting
higher tensile stresses without fracture than steel.

"Up to the present, the compressibilities and polymorphic transitions of some 30 elements and simple compounds have been studied
in the range to 100,000.

"Much higher pressures than 100,000 can be reached in very
small regions by constructing the apparatus entirely of carboloy,
but up to the present no particularly important physical results have
been attained in this range.

"In addition to the problem of attaining the pressures, there is
the problem of measuring them and measuring the effects which
they produce. This demands in the first place the establishment of
various fixed points. In the range up to 30,000 a sufficient number
of such points has been established to permit measurement to an

accuracy of about 0.1 per cent. A transition of bismuth in the neigh-borhod of 25,000 gives one convenient such point. An essential part of the measuring technique is the utilization of the change of resistance of manganin under pressure, first suggested by Lisell at Uppsala. Above 30,000 the territory is not so well marked out; it is probable that the measurements to 100,000 have an accuracy of about 2 per cent.

"It is natural to think of volume compression as the simplest and most fundamental of all the effects of hydrostatic pressure. . . . It is not, however, the simplest to measure experimentally, because the measurements immediately obtained are relative to the contain-ing vessel, which is itself distorted. Elaborate procedures may be necessary to eliminate the effect of such distortion.

"The compression of gases is outside the range of this work; at pressures of 1,000 kg/cm^2 or more the densities of gases become of the same order of magnitude as those of their liquid phase, and there ceases to be any essential difference between gas and liquid. If the volume of any ordinary liquid is plotted as a function of pressure at constant temperature, a curve will be obtained which at low pressures has a high degree of curvature and a steep tangent, meaning a high compressibility, but as pressure increases the curva-ture rapidly becomes less and the curve flattens off. In Fig. 5 [Fig. 44] the volume of a typical liquid, ether, is shown as a function of pressure. For comparison, the curve of the most compressible solid, caesium, is also shown. Two different physical mechanisms are primarily responsible for the different behavior in the low and high pressure ranges. The low range of high compressibility is the range in which the chief effect of pressure is to push the molecules into closer contact, eliminating the free spaces between them. In this range individual substances may show large and characteristic in-dividual differences. In the higher range the molecules have been pushed into effective contact, and the compressibility now arises from the decrease of volume of the molecules themselves. . . .

· · · · ·

"We have so far been discussing transitions which are thermo-dynamically reversible: when the pressure is released the original

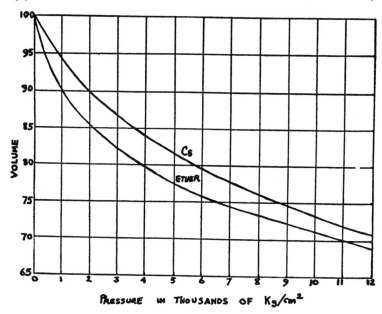

FIG. 44   *Bridgman's Fig. 5*
Volume as a function of pressure for a typical liquid, ether. The corresponding curve is also shown for caesium, the most compressible solid. The liquid is initially much more compressible than the solid, but at higher pressure is less compressible.

form is resumed. In addition . . . the existence of irreversible transitions is to be recognized, that is, of changes effected by pressure which remain permanent when they have once taken place. Two well-marked examples of this have been found. . . . If ordinary yellow phosphorus is exposed to pressures above 12,000 kg/cm² at temperatures above 200° C, it is permanently changed into a black solid much like graphite in appearance and like it a conductor of electricity, although yellow phosphorus is a good insulator. . . . Recently I have found that ordinary liquid carbon bisulfide may similarly be changed permanently into a black solid at temperatures in the neighborhood of 200° C and by pressures of the order of 40,000 kg/cm². This black substance is definitely not a mixture of sulfur and carbon, . . . but is apparently a unitary substance, truly a black solid form of carbon bisulfide. It has been suggested that the structure may be that of a single giant molecule like the known structure of silicon dioxide, which from the atomic point of view is very similar. . . . Until we have theoretical understanding of these two known permanent transitions, we can not help attaching a certain reasonableness to the assumption of the possible existence of other such substances. . . . In experiments in which I combined high shearing stresses with high hydrostatic pressure I have observed some cases of irreversible transitions to forms already known, and have also observed a large number of color changes, which are the indication of some sort of permanent change. It was not possible to establish whether new substances were formed under these conditions because the quantities of material involved were too small to permit satisfactory analysis."

CONSEQUENCES IN THEORY AND PRACTICE

Quite apart from the obvious importance of the technique developed for obtaining exceedingly high pressures, the experimental results obtained at these high pressures have proved of immense scientific value. New and unexpected phenomena have been discovered and fresh light has been thrown on phenomena already known but only imperfectly understood.

1 9 4 7

EDWARD VICTOR APPLETON
(1892–   )

*"For his work on the physical properties of the
high atmosphere, and especially for his discovery
of the so-called Appleton Layer."*

BIOGRAPHICAL SKETCH

EDWARD VICTOR APPLETON WAS BORN ON SEPTEMBER 6, 1892,
at Bradford, England. He was educated there and at St. John's College, Cambridge, where he was graduated with a B.A. in natural
science. From 1924 to 1936 he was Wheatstone Professor of Experimental Physics at King's College, University of London; from
1936 to 1939, Jacksonian Professor of Natural Philosophy in the
University of Cambridge; from 1939 to April, 1949, permanent
secretary to the Department of Scientific and Industrial Research.
In May, 1949, he was appointed principal and vice-chancellor of
the University of Edinburgh. Since 1934 he has been president of
the International Scientific Radio Union.

Sir Edward Appleton (he was knighted in 1941) is a Fellow of
the Royal Society of London, and a Foreign Member of the American Academy of Arts and Sciences, of the Norwegian and the
Swedish Academies of Sciences, and of the Belgian Society of Engineers and Industrialists. He has been awarded the Hughes Medal
of the Royal Society, the Faraday Medal of the Institution of Electrical Engineers, the U. S. Medal for Merit, and the Norwegian

Cross of Freedom. In 1950 he was awarded the Albert Medal by the Royal Society of Arts. He is an Officer of the Legion of Honor.

DESCRIPTION OF THE PRIZE-WINNING WORK

When Marconi succeeded in 1901 in establishing wireless communication across the Atlantic, the fact that the waves seemed to follow the contours of the earth led Heaviside in England and Kennelly in America to suggest the existence of an electrically conducting layer high up in the atmosphere which reflected the waves back to earth, and so prevented their becoming dissipated in space. No conclusive proof, however, of the existence of this so-called Heaviside-Kennelly Layer was found until the early 1920's. About that time, Appleton, whose interest in problems connected with radio signaling arose out of his work as a radio officer during the First World War, began those researches which were to lead to such far-reaching developments. The general course of his investigations and the results he obtained are admirably described in the following extracts from his Nobel lecture.*

". . . I wish to draw your attention to certain features of the electrical state of the higher reaches of the earth's atmosphere. . . .

"Now the most striking feature of the atmospheric air at high levels is that it is ionised, and for that reason the spherical shell surrounding the earth at the levels with which we are concerned is called the ionosphere. . . .

"There were originally two lines of evidence which suggested that the upper atmosphere might be electrically conducting. In the first place Balfour Stewart, in 1882, put forward the hypothesis that the small daily rhythmic changes of the earth's magnetic field were due to the magnetic influence of electric currents flowing at high levels. [He] pictured such currents as arising from electromotive forces generated by periodic movements of the electrically conducting layer across the earth's permanent magnetic field. The movements, he suggested, were largely tidal in character and therefore due to the gravitational influence of the sun and the moon.

---

* Quoted by kind permission of Sir Edward Appleton.

"The second indication . . . of a conducting layer in the upper atmosphere came from the study of the long-distance propagation of radio waves. The successful communication established by Marconi between England and Newfoundland in 1901 prompted many theoretical studies of the bending of electric waves round a spherical earth. These mathematical investigations . . . showed conclusively that Marconi's results could not be explained in terms of wave diffraction alone. Some factor . . . had evidently not been taken into account.

"Suggestions as to the nature of this factor were fortunately to hand, for, in 1902, Kennelly and Heaviside had independently pointed out that, if the upper atmosphere were an electrical conductor, its influence would be such as to guide the radio waves round the earth's curvature, energy being conserved between the two concentric conducting shells and so not lost in outer space.

"The Kennelly-Heaviside theory did not, however, gain universal acceptance, for direct evidence of the existence of the conducting layer was lacking. Opponents of the theory, for example, sought to explain Marconi's results in terms of the refractive bending of the waves due to the stratification of the air and water vapour in the lower atmosphere near ground level.

"During the 1914-18 war, when I served as a radio officer in the British Corps of Royal Engineers, I became interested in the problems of radio propagation and the fading of radio signals. As a result after the war, when I returned to Cambridge, I began to work on the subject, starting first to develop more accurate methods of radio signal measurement. The initiation of broadcasting in Britain in 1922 greatly assisted these experiments, for powerful continuous wave senders became generally available for the first time. Measurements of received signal intensity, made at Cambridge on waves emitted by the London B.B.C. sender, showed that, whereas the signal strength was sensibly constant during the day-time, slight fading was experienced at night. A possible explanation was that such fading was due to interference effects between waves which had travelled straight along the ground, from sender to receiver, and waves which had travelled by an overhead route by way of reflection in the upper atmosphere.

". . . in Fig. 1 [Fig. 45] . . . we see that radio waves can travel from the sender to the receiver by two paths—one direct and one indirect. Now if there is a whole number of wave-lengths in the path-difference betwen the ground and the atmospheric ray paths, there will be a maximum of radio signal intensity at the receiver; while if the path-difference is equal to an odd number of half-wavelengths a minimum of signal will be experienced. Let us suppose now that the wave-length of the radiation emitted by the sender is slowly and continuously altered. This will produce a suc-

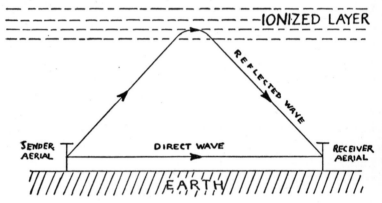

FIG. 45   *Appleton's Fig. 1*
[Radio waves reflected at ionized layer.]

cession of maxima and minima of signal intensity at the receiver, and, if the number of either is counted, and the initial and final wave-lengths of the change are known, the difference in length between the ground and atmospheric paths may be found. . . . When the path difference is known, the equivalent height of the reflecting layer can be found by simple triangulation.

"The first experiment of this type, using the variation of wave-length (or frequency), was carried out on December 11th, 1924. . . . The B.B.C. sender at Bournemouth was used and the receiving station was established at Oxford. This experiment immediately yielded evidence of a sequence of artificially produced maxima and minima of received signal intensity. The estimated height of reflection was found to be about 90 km above the ground.

"In another series of experiments, the angle of incidence of the reflected waves on the ground was measured. This was done by comparing the simultaneous signal variations on two receivers, one with a loop aerial and the other with a vertical antenna. These results also indicated the reception of downcoming waves from about the same level in the upper atmosphere. The two sets of observations therefore directly established the existence of the Kennelly-Heaviside Layer.

"In the winter of 1926-27, using experimental methods of the same type, I found that, before dawn, the ionisation in the Kennelly-Heaviside Layer (E Layer) had been sufficiently reduced by combination to permit of its penetration. Reflection, however, was found to take place at an upper layer which was richer in ionisation and which I termed the F Layer, the lower boundary of which was . . . 230 km above the earth.

". . . experiments of the kind I have described have been continued and extended. It was soon found that the technique could be so improved as to permit the study of radio reflection of radio waves incident normally on the reflecting layers. This greatly simplified the interpretation of the results. In addition to using the frequency-modulation method of measuring the distance of the reflecting stratum, . . . the elegant pulse modulation method of making the same type of measurement, which Breit and Tuve had invented in 1925, was also adopted and developed. This method has proved the most powerful tool in ionospheric research. In its application in England, cathode-ray oscillograph delineation of the ground pulse and the subsequent echo pulses was also employed. It was by using a technique of this kind that the phenomenon of magneto-ionic splitting of echoes was discovered by G. Builder and myself. This confirmed, in a direct manner, what J. A. Ratcliffe and I had previously suspected from our experiments on the circular polarisation of downcoming waves, that the ionosphere was a doubly-refracting medium due to the influence of the earth's magnetic field. The result indicated that free electrons, and not atomic or molecular ions, were the effective electrical particles in the ionosphere and paved the way for the development of the basic theory of a method of measuring electron densities in the ionosphere.

"The first systematic experiments on the determination of the variation of the electron densities in the ionosphere were carried out in a 24-hour run on January 11-12, 1931, the E Layer being selected for study. It was then found that the E Layer maximum electron density starts to increase round about sunrise, reaches a maximum at noon and then wanes as the sun sets. Through the night, the ionisation sinks to a low value, though there are often observed nocturnal sporadic increases of ionisation which may possibly be due to meteoric dust. Later, the same critical frequency method was applied in the study of the F Layer. In this way there was inaugurated the long-term study of the ionisation in the various layers which has continued to the present time, when over 50 stations, using the critical-frequency method, are operating in different parts of the world.

"Such continuous measurements of ionospheric densities, started in January 1931, in England, immediately showed a variation of noon ionisation in sympathy with sunspot activity, which, in turn, indicated that the ultra-violet light from the sun, which is responsible for the electron production, varied substantially through the sunspot cycle. It was found, for example, that the E Layer ionisation density was 50% greater in years of sunspot maximum than in years of sunspot minimum, indicating that the solar ultra-violet varied by as much as 125% between the same two epochs. No such variation is to be noted in the heat and light we receive at ground level from the sun throughout the sunspot cycle.

· · · · ·

"On the practical side of applications, ionospheric research has provided the basic ideas underlying the development of practical radiolocation of solid objects, for both the pulse-modulation and the frequency-modulation methods of measuring the distance of a reflecting surface by radio means have been used in the techniques of radar. Also, since we now have a fair understanding of the way in which the ionisation in the reflecting layers varies through the day, through the season and through the sunspot cycle, it is possible to forecast what I may call 'ionospheric weather' some time ahead. There has thus developed, on the practical side, the subject of 'ionospheric forecasting' by which it is possible to forecast, say, three months ahead, the most suitable wave-lengths for use at any time of the day, over any distance of transmission, in any part of the world. . . ."

CONSEQUENCES IN THEORY AND PRACTICE

Appleton's researches have opened up a new branch of physical science, radio physics, with applications extending far beyond radio telegraphy, with which they began. Out of them developed radar, which played so important a part during the Second World War, and which is now an indispensable aid to air navigation. The methods used for investigating the ionosphere have proved of immense importance in the study of certain problems in astronomy, geophysics, and meteorology.

1948

PATRICK MAYNARD STUART BLACKETT
(1897–   )

"For his improvement of the Wilson cloud-chamber method and for the resulting discoveries in the field of nuclear physics and cosmic rays."

BIOGRAPHICAL SKETCH

PATRICK MAYNARD STUART BLACKETT WAS BORN IN LONDON on November 18, 1897. In 1910 he entered Osborne Naval College to train as a regular officer in the Royal Navy. He served throughout the First World War at sea, taking part in the battles of Falkland Islands and Jutland. In 1919 he resigned from the navy with the rank of lieutenant, and entered Cambridge University, where he studied physics under Lord Rutherford, who had just succeeded J. J. Thomson as Cavendish Professor. Blackett took his B.A. degree in 1921 and then did research work until 1924. From 1924 to 1925 he worked at Göttingen with James Franck (*q.v.* 1925). In 1925 he resumed his research work at Cambridge, remaining there until 1933, when he was appointed professor of physics at Birkbeck College, University of London. In 1937 he succeeded Sir Lawrence Bragg (*q.v.* 1915) as professor of physics at Manchester University, an appointment which he still holds.

At the outbreak of war in 1939 Blackett joined the Instrument Section of the Royal Aircraft Establishment. In 1940 he became scientific adviser to General Pile, C-in-C, Anti-Aircraft Command, and in 1941 to Air Marshal Joubert at Coastal Command, where he built up a strong operational research group to study the anti-U-boat war. Later he became director of naval operational research at the Admiralty, continuing his study of the anti-U-boat war and other naval problems.

Blackett was elected a Fellow of the Royal Society of London in 1933 and in 1940 was awarded the Royal Medal by the Society. In 1946 he received the U. S. Medal for Merit in recognition of his services in connection with the U-boat campaign.

DESCRIPTION OF THE PRIZE-WINNING WORK

It was in 1911 that C. T. R. Wilson (*q.v.* 1927) began to develop his cloud-chamber method of rendering visible the tracks of ions, but it was not until the early 1920's that the immense value of the cloud chamber in research became apparent. The full realization of its value was largely due to the work of Blackett, who has played throughout a leading part in the development of the method. The extracts from the Nobel lecture quoted below tell how Blackett, through Rutherford, came to take up his researches on the impact of alpha particles on atomic nuclei, and how, by means of the cloud chamber, the first photographs of a nuclear disintegration were obtained in 1925. By accurate measurements on these photographs Blackett showed that the classical laws of the conservation of energy and momentum held for collisions with atomic nuclei, provided the relativistic energy-mass was taken into account.

In the autumn of 1931 Blackett turned his attention to the study of cosmic rays by means of the cloud chamber. With the simple form of cloud chamber devised by Wilson it was entirely a matter of chance whether or not a photograph happened to show a cosmic-ray track—most of the photographs did not, though it was on one of the comparatively few successful ones that Anderson (*q.v.* 1936) discovered the evidence which established the existence of the positron, or positive electron. Blackett, working in collaboration with Occhialini in the Cavendish Laboratory, devised a method

whereby the expansion of the cloud chamber and the taking of
the photograph occurred only when a cosmic ray happened to enter
the apparatus. This was achieved by arranging two Geiger counters,
one above, the other below, the expansion chamber. The Geiger
counter, in its earliest form, was devised by Hans Geiger, one of
Rutherford's students at Manchester, for the purpose of "counting"
alpha particles. A later modification is shown schematically in
Fig. 46, in which T is a brass tube forming the walls of an ionization chamber. Projecting into the tube, but insulated from it, is a

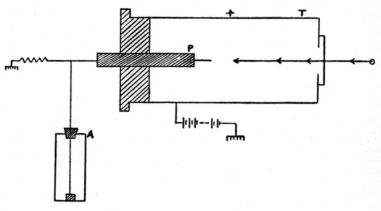

FIG. 46
Schematic diagram of a Geiger counter.

sharp pointed rod P. A potential difference is maintained between
P and T which is just below the value required for a discharge to
take place. Any increase in the electrical conductivity of the surrounding gas will, however, lead to a discharge. When an ionizing
particle, for example an alpha particle or a beta particle, enters the
chamber through the mica window, ionization occurs near the
point, followed immediately by a short discharge. The occurrence
of such a discharge can be detected by means of the string galvanometer A, a very sensitive instrument for measuring minute currents. In Blackett's arrangement the simultaneous discharge of the
two counters due to the passage of a cosmic ray through them both,
and therefore also through the closed chamber, was made to operate a mechanism which caused the expansion and also took the

photograph. In this way a cosmic ray "took its own photograph."

We may now turn to the account of his work given by Blackett in his Nobel lecture.*

"The experimental researches with which I have been occupied during the 24 years of my career as a physicist have been mainly concerned with the use of Wilson's cloud chamber for the purpose of learning more about the intimate processes of interaction of the sub-atomic particles. . . .

"In 1919 Sir Ernest Rutherford . . . found that the nuclei of certain light elements, of which nitrogen was a conspicuous example, could be disintegrated by the impact of fast alpha particles from radio-active sources, and in the process very fast protons were emitted. What actually happened during the collision between the alpha particle and the nitrogen nucleus could not, however, be determined by the scintillation method then in use. . . . Rutherford [looked] to the Wilson cloud method to reveal the finer details of this newly discovered process. The research worker chosen to carry out this work was a Japanese physicist Shimizu, then working at the Cavendish Laboratory. . . . Shimizu built a small cloud chamber and camera to take a large number of photographs of the tracks of alpha particles in nitrogen with the hope of finding some showing the rare disintegration processes. Unfortunately Shimizu had to return unexpectedly to Japan with the work hardly started. Rutherford's choice of someone to continue Shimizu's work fell on me. . . .

"Shimizu's cloud chamber was improved and made fully automatic, taking a photograph every 15 seconds—this rapid rate was only possible because of its small size, 6.0 cm diameter by 1.0 cm deep. The first task was clearly to study the forked tracks due to the normal collisions of alpha particles with nitrogen, hydrogen and helium atoms, so as to verify that the normal collisions were truly elastic—that is that no energy was lost in the process. . . .

"The study of these forked tracks was one of the first quantitative investigations of the dynamics of *single* collisions of sub-atomic particles.

---

* The following extracts are quoted by kind permission of Professor Blackett.

"Rutherford's original experiments . . . were not able to reveal what happened to the alpha particle after the collision. . . . The alpha particle might leave the nucleus again as a free particle, or it might be captured, so forming a heavier nucleus. In the former case, one would expect to find a forked track showing the track of the incident alpha particle, with three emergent tracks due to the alpha particle, the ejected proton, and the recoil nucleus. In the latter case one would find only two tracks, that of the proton and the recoil nucleus. The eight anomalous tracks all showed only two emergent particles, so proving that the assumed 'disintegration' of nitrogen by alpha particles was in reality an 'integration' process. Applying the principles of conservation of charge and mass, it was immediately deduced that the new nucleus formed must be a heavy isotope of oxygen, O_{17}^{8}, the nuclear reaction being

$$He_4^2 + N_{14}^7 \rightarrow H_1^1 + O_{17}^8$$

At the time of these experiments this isotope of oxygen was not known, but shortly afterwards it was discovered by the analysis of band spectra.

. . . . .

"These experiments gave for the first time detailed knowledge of what is now known to be a typical nuclear transformation process. Owing to the laborious nature of the task of photographing the collisions of natural alpha particles with nuclei, not very much subsequent work has been carried out with this method. But with the discovery in 1932 of the neutron by Chadwick and of the disintegration of nuclei by artificially accelerated particles by Cockcroft and Walton, very many nuclear transformations have been studied in many laboratories by the use of the cloud chamber. In recent years the use of special photographic emulsions to record the tracks of nuclear particles, first used successfully by Blau and Wambacher, and later most fertilely exploited particularly at Bristol by Powell, Occhialini and their co-workers, has made possible the study of many types of nuclear collision processes with much greater facility than can be achieved with the cloud chamber.

. . . . .

"In the autumn of 1931 in collaboration with G. P. S. Occhialini, I started to study the energetic particles found in cosmic rays by means of the cloud method. About 4 years previously Skobeltzyn in Leningrad had investigated the beta rays from radio-active sources using a cloud chamber in a magnetic field of 1,500 gauss. On some of the photographs he noticed a few tracks with very little curvature, indicating an energy over 20 MeV*; that is much higher than any known beta ray. He identified these tracks with the particles responsible for the 'Ultrastrahlung' or 'cosmic rays,' whose origin outside the earth's atmosphere had first been demonstrated . . . [by] Hess and which had subsequently been much studied . . . by Millikan . . . and others.

"Skobeltzyn noticed also that these energetic particles occasionally occurred in small groups of 2, 3, or 4 rays, apparently diverging from a point somewhere near the chamber.

"Skobeltzyn's work was followed up by Kunze in Kiel, and by Anderson in Pasadena. . . .

.   .   .   .   .

"The method used, that of making an expansion of a cloud chamber at a random time and taking the chance that one of the rare cosmic rays would cross the chamber during the short time of sensitivity—generally less than $\frac{1}{4}$ second—was much consuming of time and photographic film, since in a small chamber only some 2% to 5% of photographs showed cosmic ray tracks.

"Occhialini and I set about, therefore, the devising of a method of making cosmic rays take their own photographs, using the recently developed Geiger-Müller counters as detectors of the rays.

"Bothe and Rossi had shown that two Geiger counters placed near each other gave a considerable number of simultaneous discharges, called coincidences, which indicated in general the passage of a single cosmic ray through both counters. Rossi devised a neat valve circuit by which such coincidences could easily be recorded.

"Occhialini and I decided to place Geiger counters above and below a vertical cloud chamber, so that any ray passing through the two counters would also pass through the chamber. By a relay

---

* MeV, million electron-volts.

mechanism, the electric impulse from the coincident discharge of
the counter was made to actuate the expansion of the cloud chamber, which was made so rapid that the ions produced by the ray
had not time to diffuse much before the expansion was complete.
The chamber was placed in a water-cooled solenoid giving 3,000
gauss. Having made the apparatus ready, one waited for a cosmic
ray to arrive and take its own photograph. Instead of a small fraction of photographs showing a cosmic ray track, as when using the
method of random expansion, the counter-controlled chamber
yielded a cosmic ray track on 80% of the photographs. The first
photographs by this new method were made in the early summer of
1932.

"In the autumn of the same year, Anderson, working with a
normal chamber taking photographs at random, reported the finding of a track which he interpreted as showing the existence of a
new particle—the positive electron.

"The track described by Anderson traversed a lead plate in the
centre of the chamber and revealed the direction of motion of the
particle by the difference of curvature on the two sides. From
the direction of motion and the direction of the magnetic field, the
charge was proved positive. From the range and ionisation, the mass
could be proved to be much less than that of a proton. Anderson
thus identified it as a new particle, the positive electron or positron.

"During the late autumn of 1932, Occhialini and I, using our
new counter-controlled cloud method, accumulated some 700
photographs of cosmic rays, among which groups of associated rays
were so striking a feature as to constitute a new phenomenon and
to deserve a name. From their appearance they came to be known as
'showers' of cosmic ray particles. As many as 23 particles were
found on a single photograph, diverging from a region over the
chamber. Roughly half the rays were due to positively charged and
half to negatively charged particles. From their ionisation and
range, the masses of the positive particles were evidently not much
different from those of negative electrons. So not only was Anderson's discovery of the positive electron further confirmed by a wealth
of evidence, but it was proved that the newly discovered particles
occurred mainly in showers along with approximately an equal
number of negative electrons. This fact of the rough equality of

numbers of positive and negative electrons, and the certainty that the former do not exist as a normal constituent of matter on the earth, led us inevitably to conclude that the positive [and negative]* electrons were born together in collision processes initiated by high energy cosmic rays."

Later, working with Chadwick (*q.v.* 1935), Blackett found that these electron pairs were also produced when hard gamma rays were absorbed by heavy atoms such as lead. It has also been found that a positive electron can apparently "annihilate" a negative electron, an X ray or γ ray appearing in their stead. The energy relations are in agreement with Einstein's formula for the conversion of mass into energy. It seems, then, that electromagnetic radiation (X rays, γ rays) can be transformed into material particles (positive and negative electrons) and *vice versa.*

CONSEQUENCES IN THEORY AND PRACTICE

Blackett's counter-controlled chamber has proved of immense value in the investigation of cosmic rays. In the hands of Blackett and others it has provided a mass of data which may ultimately lead to a solution of the mystery of cosmic radiation.

---

* Omitted in the Nobel report.

1 9 4 9

HIDEKI YUKAWA
(1907–   )

"For having predicted, as a result of his theoretical work on nuclear forces, the existence of mesons."

BIOGRAPHICAL SKETCH

HIDEKI YUKAWA WAS BORN ON JANUARY 23, 1907, IN TOKYO, Japan. His father having been appointed professor of geology in the University of Kyoto, Yukawa was brought up in that city and later attended the university there. He was graduated in 1929 and then did research work in theoretical physics, especially on the theory of elementary particles. In 1932 he was appointed lecturer in physics at Kyoto University. From 1933 to 1936 he was lecturer at Osaka University; it was during this period, in 1935, that he published the paper in which he predicted the existence of the meson. From 1936 to 1939 he was assistant professor of physics at Osaka, where he obtained his D.Sc. in 1938. Since 1939 he has been professor of theoretical physics at the University of Kyoto. In 1948 he was invited to the Institute for Advanced Study at Princeton University as visiting professor, and since 1949 has been visiting professor at Columbia University.

Yukawa was awarded the Imperial Prize of the Japanese Academy in 1940 and the Order of Decoration of Japan in 1943. He is a member of the Japanese Academy, the Japanese Physical Society, and the Science Council of Japan; he is also a Foreign Associate of the (American) National Academy of Sciences and a member of

446

the American Physical Society. Yukawa is the first Japanese to receive a Nobel award.

DESCRIPTION OF THE PRIZE-WINNING WORK

According to a report in the *New York Times* (November 4, 1949) Yukawa turned to theoretical and mathematical physics as a result of an unhappy experience while glass-blowing in his student days. Perhaps atomic nuclei seemed more manageable than glass tubing, for it was to these that he gave his attention. As has already been pointed out (p. 332), on the older theory of the composition of the nucleus of an atom the nucleus was thought to consist of a certain number of protons and electrons. This was based on the fact that in radioactive changes alpha particles (helium nuclei, consisting of four protons and two electrons) and beta particles (fast electrons) are ejected from the nucleus of the atom. The proton-neutron theory, although removing other difficulties, did not account for the emission of beta particles nor for the fact that a large number of positively charged particles could apparently remain closely packed together in the nucleus without flying apart as a result of the electrostatic repulsion always found to exist between bodies, however small, carrying like electric charges.

Fermi (*q.v.* 1938) put forward the most generally accepted solution of the first problem in 1934. The second problem was the one tackled by Yukawa. In 1935 he postulated the existence of a new type of field of force, neither electromagnetic nor gravitational, but analogous to an electromagnetic field. He then deduced mathematically that there must be associated with this new type of field a particle having a mass approximately 200 times that of an electron, and a charge, either positive or negative, equal in magnitude to the electronic charge. The possibility of the existence of a particle with a mass somewhere between that of an electron and that of a proton was suggested about this time by Anderson (*q.v.* 1936) and Neddermeyer at the California Institute of Technology as a result of their researches on cosmic rays, but its existence was not definitely established until the summer of 1936. Between that date and the end of 1941 a number of determinations of the mass of the new particle were made, the values obtained ranging from 120 to 250 times that of the electron. Thus did Yukawa's bold theory receive experimental confirmation.

In the following extracts* from Yukawa's Nobel lecture, delivered in English, we have omitted the mathematical assumptions on which his meson theory was largely based.

"The meson theory started from the extension of the concept of the field of force so as to include the nuclear forces in addition to the gravitational and electromagnetic forces. The necessity of introduction of specific nuclear forces, which could not be reduced to electromagnetic interactions between charged particles, was realized soon after the discovery of the neutron, which was to be bound strongly to the protons and other neutrons in the atomic nucleus. As pointed out by Wigner, specific nuclear forces between two nucleons†, each of which can be either in the neutron state or the proton state, must have a very short range of the order of 10^{-13} cm, in order to account for the rapid increase of the binding energy from the deuteron to the alpha-particle. The binding energies of nuclei heavier than the alpha-particle do not increase as rapidly as if they were proportional to the square of the mass number A, i.e. the number of nucleons in each nucleus, but they are in fact approximately proportional to A. This indicates that nuclear forces are saturated for some reason. Heisenberg suggested that this could be accounted for, if we assumed a force between a neutron and a proton, for instance, due to the exchange of the electron or, more generally, due to the exchange of the electric charge, as in the case of the chemical bond between a hydrogen atom and a proton. Soon afterwards, Fermi developed a theory of beta-decay based on the hypothesis by Pauli, according to which a neutron, for instance, could decay into a proton, an electron, and a neutrino, which was supposed to be a very penetrating neutral particle with a very small mass. This gave rise, in turn, to the expectation that nuclear forces could be reduced to the exchange of a pair of an electron and a neutrino between two nucleons, just as electromagnetic forces were

---

* Quoted by kind permission of Professor Yukawa.
† The view is held that in the nucleus the proton and neutron are alternative states of a single fundamental particle, the *nucleon* (see also p. 377).

regarded as due to the exchange of photons between charged particles. It turned out, however, that the nuclear forces thus obtained were much too small, because the beta-decay was a very slow process compared with the supposed rapid exchange of the electric charge responsible for the actual nuclear forces. The idea of the meson field was introduced in 1935 in order to make up this gap. Original assumptions of the meson theory were as follows:

. . . . .

III. In order to obtain exchange forces, we must assume that these mesons have the electric charge $+e$ or $-e$, and that a positive (negative) meson is emitted (absorbed) when the nucleon jumps from the proton state to the neutron state, whereas a negative (positive) meson is emitted (absorbed) when the nucleon jumps from the neutron to the proton. Thus a neutron and a proton can interact with each other by exchanging mesons just as two charged particles interact by exchanging photons.

. . . . .

IV. In addition to charged mesons, there are neutral mesons with the mass either exactly or approximately equal to that of charged mesons. . . .

". . . The discovery of particles of intermediate mass in cosmic rays in 1937 was a great encouragement to further developments of meson theory. At that time, we came naturally to the conclusion that the mesons which constituted the main part of the hard component of cosmic rays at sea level were to be identified with the mesons which were responsible for nuclear forces. Indeed, cosmic ray mesons had the mass around 200 m_e [m_e, mass of an electron] as predicted and moreover, there was the definite evidence for the spontaneous decay, which was the consequence of the following assumption of the original meson theory:

V. Mesons interact also with light particles, i.e. electrons and neutrinos, just as they interact with nucleons. . . . Thus a positive (negative) meson can change spontaneously into a positive (negative) electron and a neutrino. . . .

. . . . .

"Already, in 1941, the identification of the cosmic ray meson with the meson, which was supposed to be responsible for nuclear forces, became doubtful. In fact, Tanikawa and Sakata proposed in 1942 a new hypothesis as follows: The mesons which constitute the hard component of cosmic rays at sea level are not directly connected with nuclear forces, but are produced by the decay of heavier mesons which interact strongly with nucleons.

"However, we had to wait for a few years before this two-meson hypothesis was confirmed, until 1947, when two very important facts were discovered. First, it was discovered by Italian physicists that the negative mesons in cosmic rays, which were captured by lighter atoms, did not disappear instantly, but very often decayed into electrons in a mean time interval of the order of 10^{-6} sec. This could be understood only if we supposed that ordinary mesons in cosmic rays interacted very weakly with nucleons. Soon afterwards, Powell and others discovered two types of mesons in cosmic rays, the heavier mesons decaying in a very short time into lighter mesons. Just before the latter discovery, the two-meson hypothesis was proposed by Marshak and Bethe independent of the Japanese physicists above mentioned. In 1948, mesons were created artificially in Berkeley and subsequent experiments confirmed the general picture of two-meson theory. The fundamental assumptions are now:

(i) The heavier mesons, i.e. π-mesons with mass about 280 m_e, interact strongly with nucleons and can decay into lighter mesons, i.e. μ-mesons and neutrinos with a life-time of the order of 10^{-8} sec. . . . They are responsible for at least a part of nuclear forces. . . .

(ii) The lighter mesons, i.e. μ-mesons, with the mass about 210 m_e, are the main constituent of the hard component of cosmic rays at sea level and can decay into electrons and neutrinos with the life-time 2×10^{-6} sec. . . . As they interact only weakly with nucleons, they have nothing to do with nuclear forces.

"Now, if we accept the view that π-mesons are the mesons that have been anticipated from the beginning, then we may expect the existence of neutral π-mesons in addition to charged π-mesons. . . . Very recently, it became clear that some of the experimental results obtained in Berkeley could be accounted for consistently by considering that, in addition to charged π-mesons, neutral π-mesons with the mass approximately equal to that of charged π-mesons were created by collisions of high energy protons with atomic nuclei and that each of these neutral mesons decayed into two mesons with the life-time of the order of 10^{-13} sec. or less."

CONSEQUENCES IN THEORY
AND PRACTICE

Yukawa's theoretical deduction of the existence of a particle, unknown at that time but later found in cosmic rays, ranks with Dirac's deduction of the existence of the positron as one of the most brilliant examples in recent years of the application of mathematical reasoning to a physical problem. The identification shortly afterwards of the predicted particle in cosmic rays at the same time lent support to his theory of nuclear forces, a theory which has proved of great service in interpreting observational results.

1 9 5 0

CECIL FRANK POWELL
(1903–   )

"For his development of the photographic method in the study of nuclear processes and for his discoveries concerning mesons."

BIOGRAPHICAL SKETCH

CECIL FRANK POWELL WAS BORN ON DECEMBER 5, 1903, AT Tonbridge, Kent. His father was one of a family of gunsmiths which had long practised the trade in the town; his mother, who was of Huguenot descent, was the daughter of a schoolmaster. Powell attended a local elementary school until the age of eleven, when he won a scholarship to Judd School, a secondary school founded by the City of London Skinners Company. From there he won a scholarship to Sidney Sussex College, Cambridge, where he graduated second in his year in physics. After graduation Powell worked for two years as a research student under C. T. R. Wilson (*q.v.* 1927) and Rutherford (*Chemistry,* 1908) in the Cavendish Laboratory. In 1928 he was appointed research assistant to Professor A. M. Tyndall, director of the newly opened H. H. Wills Physical Laboratory at the University of Bristol. Here, except for a period in 1935-36 when he went as seismologist with an expedition to investigate seismic and volcanic activity in Montserrat, West Indies, he has remained, filling in turn the posts of lecturer, reader, and finally, since 1948, that of Melville Wills Professor of Physics.

Powell was elected a Fellow of the Royal Society of London in

1949. The Physical Society of London awarded him its Vernon Boys Prize in 1947, and the Royal Society its Hughes Medal in 1949.

The research which Powell carried out in the Cavendish Laboratory was undertaken with a view to finding out whether better cloud track photographs could be obtained with a Wilson cloud chamber by working at temperatures other than that of the room. However, the results of the research were more far-reaching than this, for they enabled Powell to explain the abnormally high rate of discharge of steam through nozzles, and were found to have a bearing on the design and performance of the steam turbine.

At Bristol, during the four years following his appointment as research assistant, Powell carried out, with Professor Tyndall, an elaborate series of investigations into the mobilities of positive ions in gases, in particular the mobilities of the alkali ions sodium, potassium, etc. in the rare gases helium, neon, and argon. Their results, published in joint papers in 1929 and 1932, cleared up a number of uncertainties which had previously existed and threw light on the formation of complex ions.

DESCRIPTION OF THE PRIZE-WINNING WORK

Shortly before going on the expedition to Montserrat Powell was engaged on the construction of a generator for accelerating fast protons and deuterons. The generator was of a type designed by Cockcroft* and used by him in collaboration with Ernest Walton in pioneer work in which he disintegrated the lithium nucleus by means of proton bombardment at a time (1932) when the Lawrence cyclotron (p. 380) was still in the early stages of its development. Powell resumed work on the Cockcroft generator on his return to Bristol, his intention being to use the machine to produce neutrons with which to study the effects of the neutron bombardment of protons, the energy of the bombarding neutrons being determined from the tracks of the recoiling protons—it will be remembered that neutrons themselves produce far too little ionization for their paths to appear as tracks in the Wilson cloud chamber

---

* Now Sir John Cockcroft, Director of the Harwell Atomic Energy Research Establishment. He was awarded the Nobel Prize in Physics for 1951.

(see p. 271), the only evidence of the passage of a neutron being the tracks due to particles, e.g. protons, struck by the neutron. Originally Powell intended to use a Wilson cloud chamber in these investigations, but it happened that in 1938 he took part in some experiments on cosmic radiation, in which the tracks of the particles were directly recorded in photographic emulsions. This method was by no means new, having been used early in the century for demonstrating the radiation emitted by radioactive substances. The charged particle enters the emulsion, where it produces ionization, the ionized atoms of the silver salt (silver bromide) appearing as dark specks along the path of the particle. Since fast particles produce less ionization in a given length of path than slow ones, the average distance between the specks increases with the speed of the particles; for very fast particles such as those that occur in the cosmic rays, the method cannot be used except with special plates sufficiently sensitive for the particle to produce enough ionization to render its path visible. By the early 1930s sensitized plates were available which were able to record the passage of swift protons and could be used in the study of nuclear processes. By 1935 yet further improvements had been made in the plates and the method was being used with success in the study of cosmic rays. Owing, however, to uncertainty in calculating the energy of the particles from the length of the paths the method was not in favour for the laboratory study of nuclear processes. It was therefore rather in the nature of a "try-out" when, on the completion of the Cockcroft generator later in 1938, Powell and his collaborators decided to use the photographic emulsion method for recording the tracks of the recoil protons subjected to neutron bombardment. The success of their experiments quickly established the great advantages of the method; shortly afterwards it was used by Chadwick (*q.v.* 1935), working in collaboration with Powell, in an investigation into the scattering and disintegration produced by fast deuterons generated by the cyclotron at Liverpool, where Chadwick was at that time professor of physics.

The war interrupted work on the development of more effective emulsions, but during the years 1939-1945 Powell and his collaborators were busy improving the research technique and the apparatus for analyzing the particle tracks. Then, in 1946, an emulsion became available which was in every way superior to any previously produced. With the new plates and the improved technique and apparatus the photographic method took its place as at least as effective a means for the investigation of nuclear processes as the Wilson chamber, with the great advantage that, whereas the Wilson chamber is operative only during the instant of exposure, the photographic plate registers continuously.

Powell now made a fresh attack on the problem of cosmic radiation, being assisted by Occhialini (see p. 439), who had joined him in Bristol in 1945. At first the plates were exposed on mountains, at heights up to 17,000 feet above sea level; later they were sent up in free balloons to altitudes many thousands of feet above the surface of the earth. It was this high altitude work and the discoveries concerning mesons to which it led that Powell described in his Nobel Lecture, which we now reproduce in full.*

"Coming out of space and incident on the high atmosphere, there is a thin rain of charged particles known as the primary cosmic radiation. As a result of investigations extending over more than 30 years, we now know the nature of the incoming particles, and some, at least, of the most important physical processes which occur as a result of their passage through the atmosphere.

"Today the study of the cosmic radiation is, in essence, the study of nuclear physics of the extreme high-energy region. Although the number of incoming particles is very small in comparison with those which are produced by the great machines, most of them are much more energetic than any which we can yet generate artificially; and in nuclear collisions they produce effects which cannot be simulated in the laboratory. The study of the resulting transmutations is therefore complementary to that which can be made at lower energies with the aid of the cyclotrons and synchrotrons.

"For the investigation of the cosmic radiation, it is necessary to solve two principal technical problems:—first, to detect the radiation, to determine the masses, energy and transformation properties of the particles of which it is composed, and to study the nuclear transmutations which they produce. Second, to develop methods of making such observations throughout the atmosphere and at depths underground.

---

* By kind permission of Professor Powell.

"For the detection of the radiations, the same devices are available as in the general field of nuclear physics, and two main classes can be distinguished.

"In the first class are found the trigger mechanisms such as the Geiger counter and the scintillation counter. Such devices record the instants of passage of individual particles through the apparatus. Their most important advantages are (a) that they allow observations to be made of great statistical weight; and (b) that the relationship in time of the instants of passage of associated particles can be established. With modern instruments of this type, the time interval between the arrival of two charged particles can be measured even although this is as small as one or two hundredths of a microsecond*. These devices have made possible contributions of the greatest importance to our knowledge of the subject, and they have proved especially valuable when the nature of the physical processes being studied has been well understood.

"In the second class of detectors are the devices for making manifest the tracks of particles; namely, the Wilson expansion chamber and the photographic plate. These instruments have the particular advantage, amongst others, that they allow a direct and detailed insight into the physical processes which accompany the passage of charged particles through matter. On the other hand, it is arduous to employ them to obtain observations of great statistical weight. The two classes of instruments thus provide complementary information, and each has made a decisive contribution.

"The second principal technical problem to be solved is that of making experiments at great altitudes. Some information has been obtained by means of V.2 rockets which pass almost completely out of the earth's atmosphere, but their time of flight is restricted to only a few minutes. Alternatively, balloons can be made to ascend to great altitudes and to give level flights for many hours. The simplicity of the photographic method of recording the tracks of charged particles makes it very suitable as a detector in such experiments.

"Today the most suitable types of balloons for experiments on the cosmic radiation are those made of thin sheets of a plastic material,

---

* *Microsecond,* one millionth of a second.

'polyethylene.' Although rubber balloons can sometimes be made to ascend higher into the atmosphere, their performance is erratic. The rubber, whether natural or synthetic, appears to perish rapidly under the action of the solar radiation high above the clouds: it is therefore difficult, even when employing many rubber balloons in a single experiment, to secure the sustained level flight which is desirable. On the other hand, polyethylene is chemically inert, and the fabric of the balloon can remain for many hours at high altitudes without any serious effect on its mechanical strength.

"In Bristol, we construct balloons of polyethylene by methods similar in principle to those developed in the U.S.A. by the General Mills Corporation. We employ 'polyethylene' sheet $1\frac{1}{2}$ thousandths of an inch thick, the shaped pieces of which are 'heat-sealed' together to form an envelope which, when fully inflated, is nearly spherical in form. Unlike those of rubber, these balloons are open at the lower end; and just before launching, the envelope is very slack and contains only a small fraction of its total volume filled with hydrogen. As the balloon ascends, the pressure falls and the balloon inflates. Near maximum altitude its envelope becomes tensed and hydrogen escapes from the bottom aperture. Balloons of this type, 20 metres in diameter, give—with light loads of about 20 kgs—level flights at altitudes of the order of 95,000 feet. It is anticipated that a similar balloon 50 metres in diameter should reach about 120,000 feet.

"By observations at great altitudes we now know that the primary cosmic radiation is made up of atomic nuclei moving at speeds closely approaching that of light. It is possible to record the tracks of the incoming particles [see *Frontispiece*] and to determine their charge; and thence the relative abundance of the different chemical elements. Recent experiments prove that hydrogen and helium occur most frequently, and the distribution in mass of the heavier nuclei appears to be similar to that of the matter of the universe. Thus elements more massive than iron or nickel occur, if at all, very infrequently.

"The detailed study of the 'mass spectrum' of the incoming nuclei has an important bearing on the problem of the origin of the primary particles; but it is complicated by the fact that, because of their large charge, the particles rapidly lose energy in the atmosphere by making atomic and nuclear collisions. They therefore rarely penetrate to altitudes less than 70,000 feet. It is for this reason that exposures at high altitudes are of particular interest.

"A second reason for making experiments at extreme altitudes is that the primary nuclei commonly suffer fragmentation in making nuclear collisions. A primary nucleus of magnesium or aluminium, for example, may decompose into lighter nuclei such as lithium, α-particles and protons. The mass spectrum at a given depth is therefore different from that of the primary radiation, and such effects are appreciable at 90,000 feet, where the mass of overlying air is about 20 gm. per cm². They would be much reduced at 120,000 feet (6 gm. per cm²), an altitude which, we have seen, appears to be accessible with very large balloons.

"The primary protons and α-particles, because of their smaller charge, penetrate to much lower altitudes. In collisions they disintegrate the nuclei which they strike and, in the process, lead to the creation of new forms of matter, the π-mesons of mass 274 m_e* These particles are usually ejected with great speed and proceed downwards towards the earth.

"The π-mesons are now known to have an average lifetime of about 2×10^{-8} secs. This period is so short that, when moving in a gas—in which their velocity is reduced, by loss of energy through ionisation, at a relatively slow rate—they commonly decay in flight. In a solid material, however, they can be arrested before they have had time to decay. This was the most important of the factors which prevented the identification of the particles until after the development of the photographic method of recording the tracks.

"When brought to rest in a photographic emulsion, the positive π-particles decay with the emission of a μ-meson of mass $212m_e$. This particle commonly emerges with a constant velocity, so that its range varies only within the narrow limits due to straggling. It follows that in the transmutation of the π-meson, the μ-meson is accompanied by the emission of a single neutral particle. It has now been shown that this neutral particle is of small rest-mass and that it is not a photon. It is therefore reasonable to assume, tenta-

---

* m_e, mass of the electron.

tively, that it is a neutrino, the particle emitted in the process of nuclear β-decay.

"When a negative π-meson is arrested in a solid material, it is captured by an atom, interacts with a nucleus and disintegrates it. It follows that the particle has a strong interaction with nucleons, and in this respect its properties are similar to those predicted for the 'heavy quanta' of Yukawa.

"When the π-mesons are created in nuclear collisions occurring in the atmosphere, they commonly transform, whilst in flight, into μ-mesons and neutrinos. It is these μ-particles which form the 'hard' or 'penetrating' component of the cosmic radiation and they are responsible for most of the residual ionisation in air at sea-level. The μ-mesons are penetrating because, unlike the π-mesons, they are able to traverse the nuclei with which they collide without interacting with them, and some of them reach great depths underground.

"The production of mesons by protons and α-particles of great energy in nuclear encounters appears to be a result of interactions between nucleons. Accordingly, the heavy nuclei of the primary radiation—if of sufficient energy—also produce similar effects when they collide with other nuclei. Because of the large numbers of nucleons involved in such an encounter, the number of mesons produced may be very great.

"In addition to producing the charged π-mesons, the primary protons in making nuclear collisions also produce neutral π-particles. The neutral π-mesons are very short-lived and each transforms spontaneously into two quanta of radiation. Such a quantum, when it happens to pass near an atomic nucleus, can in turn transform into a pair of electrons, one positive and one negative; and the electrons can generate new photons in further collisions. A succession of such processes results in the production of the well-known cascades of electrons and photons which form the 'soft' or easily absorbed component of the cosmic radiation.

"Although much longer lived than the π-mesons, some of the μ-mesons also decay in flight to produce electrons and neutrinos. The electrons contribute to the soft component, whilst the neutrinos join the similar particles arising from the decay of the π-mesons to produce a flux of neutral radiation which has a very weak interaction with matter, and of which the fate is at present unknown.

"In addition to the π and μ-mesons, recent experiments at Manchester and Bristol and in other laboratories have shown that more massive types of mesons exist. Although they occur much less frequently than the π-mesons, the elucidation of their properties appears to be of great importance for the development of nuclear physics.

"We are only at the beginning of our penetration into what appears to be a rich field of discovery. Already, however, it seems certain that our present theoretical approach has been limited by lack of essential information; and that the world of the mesons is far more complex than has hitherto been visualized in the most brilliant theoretical speculations. The fast protons and α-particles generated by the cyclotrons are not sufficiently energetic to produce these more massive mesons, but this may become possible when the proton synchrotrons now under construction come into operation.

"Only about twenty-five years have passed since it was generally recognized that part of the residual conductivity of a gas at sea level is due to the arrival from out of space of a radiation of great penetrating power. In the 1928 edition of the 'Conduction of Electricity in Gases,' J. J. Thomson and G. P. Thomson, commenting on this conclusion, remark that 'It would be one of the romances of science if these obscure and prosaic minute leakages of electricity from well-insulated bodies should be the means by which the most fundamental problems in the evolution of the cosmos came to be investigated.'

"In the years which have passed, the study of what might, in the early days, have been regarded as a trivial phenomenon has, in fact, led us to the discovery of many new forms of matter and many new processes of fundamental physical importance. It has contributed to the development of a picture of the material universe as a system in a state of perpetual change and flux; a picture which stands in great contrast with that of our predecessors with their fixed and eternal atoms. At the present time a number of widely divergent hypotheses, none of which is generally accepted, have been advanced to account for the origin of the cosmic radiation. It will indeed be of great interest if the contemporary studies of the primary radiation lead us—as the Thomsons suggested, and as present tendencies seem to indicate—to the study of some of the most fundamental problems in the evolution of the cosmos."

CONSEQUENCES IN THEORY
AND PRACTICE

Powell's greatest contribution to cosmic ray research and to nuclear physics in general is undoubtedly his development of the photographic emulsion method of recording the tracks of particles. This, combined with the ancillary apparatus he has perfected for extracting precise quantitative information from the tracks, has already led him to fundamental discoveries concerning the particles occurring in cosmic radiation at high altitudes. Not only that, but he has opened up a new line of research which he and his collaborators at Bristol are zealously pursuing and from which yet further discoveries of outstanding importance may be expected.

No more fitting close for our account of the work of the Nobel Laureates in physics could be found than the last two paragraphs of Professor Powell's Address, work which has "led to the discovery of so many new forms of matter and so many new processes of fundamental physical importance," and which "has contributed to the development of a picture of the material universe as a system in a state of perpetual change and flux."

NAME INDEX

SUBJECT INDEX

(Words or figures in italics denote definitions or brief explanations.)

468